ARMY RELATIONS WITH CONGRESS

Thick Armor, Dull Sword, Slow Horse

Stephen K. Scroggs

PRAEGER

Westport, Connecticut
London

Library of Congress Cataloging-in-Publication Data

Scroggs, Stephen K., 1954–
    Army relations with Congress : thick armor, dull sword, slow horse
/ Stephen K. Scroggs.
        p.   cm.
    Includes bibliographical references and index.
    ISBN 0–275–96175–3 (alk. paper).—ISBN 0–275–96176–1 (pbk. :
alk. paper)
    1. Civil–military relations—United States.   2. United States.
Army—Political activity.   3. United States. Congress.   I. Title.
JK330.S27   2000
322'.5'0973—dc21   99–13258

British Library Cataloguing in Publication Data is available.

Library of Congress Catalog Card Number: 99–13258
ISBN: 0–275–96175–3
        0–275–96176–1 (pbk.)

First published in 2000

Praeger Publishers, 88 Post Road West, Westport, CT 06881
An imprint of Greenwood Publishing Group, Inc.
www.praeger.com

Printed in the United States of America

The paper used in this book complies with the
Permanent Paper Standard issued by the National
Information Standards Organization (Z39.48–1984).

10 9 8 7 6 5 4 3 2 1

Personally, this book is dedicated to my loving parents and to my wife, Patricia, and my daughter, Sarah Marie, who give my life purpose and joy.

Professionally, this book is dedicated to General Max Thurman, 1931–95, a combat arms officer whose example, experience, and presence are sorely missed in today's U.S. Army.

Contents

Preface

The only thing more difficult than getting an old idea out of the military mind is getting a new one in.

—B.H. Liddell Hart

A SHORT TALE OF THE ARMY AND CONGRESS: JUNE 1993

The Army was in trouble. Several weeks earlier it had been surprised by Chairman Earl Hutto's "mark up"[1] of the fiscal year 1994 House Defense Authorization Bill in the Readiness Subcommittee of the House Armed Services Committee. The Chairman's actions would place the Army Pre-position Afloat (APA) Program on hold.[2] In early 1993, the U.S. Marine Corps' top brass had failed to convince the senior leadership of the Pentagon that resources planned for this program would be more efficiently and effectively directed toward an enhancement of its maritime pre-positioned ship squadrons.

Having lost the battle in the Pentagon, supporters of the Marine Corps' view were working to turn the issue around in Congress. As an Army lieutenant colonel working on force structure and strategic issues in the Secretary of the Army's legislative liaison, I was handed the Army sealift issues to work on for two months before Chairman Hutto's mark. I coordinated a team of two colonels on the Army staff whom I escorted to countless meetings with targeted members of Congress and committee staff. Our team briefed Congress on the importance of the APA Program, with an emphasis on why this program was a critical foundation for Department of Defense (DOD) and Joint Chiefs of Staff (JCSs) Mobility Requirements Study (MRS) recommendations.[3] Our goal was to ensure that the relevant committees understood the positions of the Office of Secretary of Defense, the JCS, and the Army, and understood that the proposal by Hutto's congressional subcommittee would transform the MRS from a moderate-cost, medium-risk, strategic mobility plan to one that was moderate cost and high risk for getting heavy combat forces to a major regional contingency (MRC) within a specified time frame.

Often a subcommittee mark will be followed in a day or so by the full committee mark. The Army was fortunate, in this instance, to have almost a month's time between the subcommittee mark and the full committee mark. My team of colonels was able to gain access to most key members of the House Armed Services Committee and staff, but on the Senate Armed Services Committee, the best I could do was to arrange briefings for the Military Legislative Assistants (MLAs) of committee members, because we lacked the rank or relationships to gain access to the senators themselves.

My primary concern was to reverse the House Committee's Readiness Subcommittee mark on APA, but I also wanted to ensure that our message was understood by the Senate Armed Services Committee. From the MLAs' reactions, I felt we were making progress in getting our message out on the Senate side—until I dropped by to talk with a Senate Armed Services Committee Professional Staff Member (PSM) with whom I had developed a good working relationship.[4] The PSM cautiously indicated that the Marines, with their strong relationships with the Senate Armed Services Committee, were making this a priority issue. A committee vote against the Army program was a distinct possibility.

Racing back to the Pentagon, I sounded the alarm, arguing that unless we took unusually proactive steps with key Senate Armed Services Committee Members prior to their mark, we likely would end up with an anti–APA provision in that committee as well. My team of colonels would not suffice; I recommended that within the next several days our senior generals had to engage the Senate Committee on this issue. The Chief of Legislative Liaison (CLL) agreed, and we immediately generated a plan that recommended which three- or four-star generals should meet with which senators. Most of the generals we identified could not find time for a visit to the Hill on short notice, but some did place telephone calls. One senior Army general, however, did agree to meet with a senator we knew carried great weight with his colleagues on these types of issues. The busy calendars of the senator and general officer were reconciled, and a meeting was scheduled for the following day. The attendees at this meeting would be the senator, his MLA, the general, and myself.

Part of good LL activity is eliminating surprises for the key actors involved. I felt that there was an additional person who needed to know about this meeting, and because the Army was asking for the meeting with the senator, it was best that this person learn about the meeting from the Army and not from the senator's office. Therefore, I placed a call to the Senate Armed Services PSM who supported and worked directly with the senator on his committee business. He appreciated the call and informed me that he would arrange to attend the meeting. He also stated that in addition to his interest in the strategic mobility issue to be discussed, there was also a minor issue he would raise with the general officer that was of great interest to the senator.

The Army general who would meet with the senator was a distinguished and highly decorated combat arms general. Although he had more Pentagon experience than his Army peers, he also had significantly less Washington experience than his counterparts in the other services. On our drive across the Potomac, I could sense that the general was not looking forward to this meeting. During the initial niceties, the general's comments reflected both his discomfort and anxiety. He stated that he appreciated the senator seeing him and hoped it was not an inconvenience. For his part, however, the senator seemed genuinely glad to see the general.

The general then launched into an exegesis of the entire Army Strategic Mobility Program (of which the APA is but a part), rather than candidly and directly addressing the Army, Joint Staff, and Office of Secretary of Defense problem with the Marine Corps position. He was suddenly interrupted by the committee staffer who stated, "Please, excuse me General, pardon the interruption Senator, but I can't take it any longer. Senator, what you have taking place today by the U.S. Marine Corps is a 'drive-by shooting' with the APA Program clearly in its sights. If the Marines are successful in stalling or killing this program on the Hill, it will be to the detriment of DOD and national security interests."

It was short, concise, to the point, and what the senator expected to hear from a general officer. The senator: "General, why didn't *you* tell me that?" The general: "Sir, I'm not over here to *lobby* or bash a sister service, but. . . ." Before he could finish the sentence, the senator moved almost nose-to-nose with him and said, "But don't you understand, general, they do it to you!" An eerie silence followed the senator's comment. The rest of the meeting was anticlimactic, with the senator underscoring his support for APA and the committee staffer raising the smaller issue for the Army to consider.

On our return ride, I enthused about the outcome of the meeting. The general responded that yes, we got the vital support we were seeking on the APA issue, but he complained that now we would have to look into the minor issue raised by the PSM. Rather than seeing this issue as an opportunity to re-engage the senator by providing information or ideas that could strengthen our working and personal relationships with him and his staff, he viewed it as a burden that had not existed previously.

The Army's handling of this problem—from insufficient advance senior flag officer engagement with members on its priority programs, to its reactive approach to engagement of those members, to treating increased congressional interaction as a burden—helps to spotlight a series of Army congressional relations problems that are the topic of this book.

ARMY CULTURE IN CRISIS ON THE HILL

The Army's culture significantly influences the way its leaders view and approach the task of representing Army interests to Congress through lobbying of congressional members and their personal and committee staffs. As a complex public organization, the Army's lobbying effectiveness is largely explained by its culture, and Army culture is useful in understanding why Army behavior on the Hill is both distinctive and different from the lobbying behavior of the other services, all of which are also complex public agencies. This book will examine the impact of cultural factors on the ability of the Army to represent its institutional interests to Congress.

A cultural focus helps to explain agency-specific tendencies, certain basic assumptions, and values held by agency leaders, and illuminates some of the strengths and weaknesses in agency—Congress relations that are often not apparent to the leaders themselves. Various definitions of culture exist in the literature, but all in one way or another refer to patterned values, beliefs, or attitudes shared and passed to new members of that organization or group. Cultural patterns are viewed as "the routine, largely unexamined options deriving from widely shared assumptions, meanings and values of a group or people."[5] These widely shared assumptions or norms limit the options leaders and other members consciously or unconsciously consider in making decisions and addressing problems. Culture sets boundaries on permissible behavior; it labels and often stigmatizes activity that cannot or should not be done. This culture becomes a lens through which problems are seen and addressed by the leadership and collective group desiring to succeed within that organization.

Edgar H. Schein defines culture as a "pattern of shared basic assumptions that the group learned as it solved its problems of external adaption and internal integration, that has worked well enough to be considered valid and, therefore, to be taught to new members as the correct way to perceive, think, and feel in relation to those problems." His definition, with its emphasis on patterns of shared basic assumptions that color the way an organization views and approaches a problem (like working with Congress) is one that will be relied on in this study.[6]

These patterns of shared basic assumptions, or cultural dimensions, are held by members and leaders of an organization and can often predetermine the organization's behavior and decisions. These assumptions persist and influence behaviors that repeatedly lead people to make decisions that may have worked in the past. These assumptions are therefore infused into junior members explicitly in training or implicitly by the example of the leadership's (and peer) behavior.

These assumptions and cultural dimensions recede into the background of people's consciousness with repeated use but continue to influence organizational decisions and behaviors, even when the organization's environment changes. They become fixed and unquestioned, often characterized as "the way we do things here,'' even when these ways are no longer appropriate. They are often so basic, pervasive, and totally accepted as ''the truth'' that no one questions their validity.[7] While pervasive and enduring, culture is not fixed and can change over time.

There is extensive literature dating to the early 1980s on the importance of organizational culture and its ties to leadership in promoting needed change within organizations.[8] Carl Builder's excellent work, *The Masks of War*, innovatively explores and attempts to map comparatively the distinct ''personalities'' of the three armed services.[9] His cultural lens was elevated to a macro level, but he highlighted the enduring quality of a service personality that can often lead military service leaders to make decisions that appear to outsiders to make little sense. Schein addresses the critical link of leadership and culture that goes to the heart of this study:

Culture and leadership are two sides of the same coin in that leaders first create cultures when they create groups and organizations. Once cultures exist, they determine the criteria for leadership and thus determine who will or will not be a leader. *But if cultures become dysfunctional, it is the unique function of leadership to perceive the functional and dysfunctional elements of the existing culture and to manage cultural evolution and change in such a way that the group can survive [or be effective] in a changing environment* [emphasis added].

The bottom line for leaders is that if they do not become conscious of the cultures in which they are embedded, those cultures will manage them. Cultural understanding is desirable for all of us, but it is essential to leaders if they are to lead.[10]

With the interrelationship of culture and an organization's leadership and behavior in mind, the following key questions guided the research for this book:

1. What kind of lobbying activity is conducted by all federal agencies, despite the existence of statutory law prohibiting ''lobbying'' of Congress by public agencies?

2. How are some public agencies organized to carry out these legal lobbying activities?

3. Why do certain public agencies work better with and develop closer relationships with Congress than others?

4. Why do some agencies make more effective use of their agency resources and capabilities in improving and nurturing that relationship?

Despite their structural similarities, it is the cultural contexts in which the individual services pursue their respective organizational goals with Congress that differ in ways that significantly affect their relative success in achieving their goals. In this regard, the cultural context in which Army officials operate impedes their efforts to most effectively represent Army interests. Although the focus of this study is on the cultural underpinnings of Army relations with Congress, of necessity, both explicit and implicit comparisons with the cultures that affect the lobbying activities of other services are made by asking questions such as:

1. Why does the Army rely primarily on its lieutenant colonels and its one two-star general in its legislative liaison office, whereas the other services rely more often on three- and four-star generals throughout their service to carry their respective messages to Congress?
2. Why are Army generals more uncomfortable with lobbying activities generally and being perceived as "lobbyists" in particular?
3. Why are Army representatives more reluctant to offer professional advice to Congress that appears to make value judgments about other services vis-à-vis their own?

Army-patterned behavior on the Hill is relevant only in relation to the other services. Navy admirals in and out of Washington appear to be more engaged and focused on cultivating relationships, more willing to state views different from official DOD policy, and more effective in communicating with the congressional audience. The patterned tendency of the U.S. Marine Corps to direct valuable agency resources toward proactive, "wide net" outreach and education of congressional and other external audiences is significant with the example being set at its four-star flag officer level. Although smaller, with significantly fewer issues, the Marine Corps succeeds at embracing Congress as a team player rather than an adversary in defense policymaking. It views engagement with Congress as an opportunity, not a burden.

The Air Force would never consider placing a three-star general in a key Air Staff position as a first assignment in Washington, much less make that flag officer its Chief of Staff two years later. Its senior leadership is selected out of a competitive pool of its most promising field grade officers who have significant Washington experience. Their experience and understanding of Washington policymaking are most evident in their effective engagement within the Pentagon and the executive branch.

This study explains how the historical and evolutionary experiences of the Army and the professional development and experiences of its senior officer corps contribute to a culture that makes engagement and institutional self-promotion on the Hill more difficult for its senior flag officers. This cultural distancing from external audiences, to include Congress, is manifest in the Army. Also illuminated is why the other services' senior flag officers are more likely to view lobbying Congress as a critical professional responsibility directly linked to justifying and garnering the resources their service requires from constitutionally empowered civilian decision makers. Accordingly, these services establish career paths centered around developing competencies needed in their senior flag officers at these higher levels.

The major source of data for this book is more than 130 interviews conducted between January 1995 and January 1996, but the Army–Hill patterns identified then are, for all practical purposes, unchanged today. These interviews with congressional, legislative liaison (LL), and senior Army leaders involved in Army–Congress relations and knowledgeable about various aspects of LL between the services and Congress included 20 Members of Congress serving on the two defense authorization committees: the House National Security Committee (HNSC)[11] and the Senate Armed Services Committee (SASC); with PSMs, 10 on the House National Security Committee and 15 on the SASC; and 39 others, to include personal staff who work on defense issues, and MLAs, for Members of Congress on the HNSC and SASC. It was important to get a significant sampling of interviews from Members, PSMs, and MLAs because of the different degrees and levels of engagement they have with liaison officials from the several services.[12]

To identify and rank the relative importance of culture factors argued as characterizing Army behavior on Capitol Hill, over 30 key senior Army (active and retired) military and civilian leaders were interviewed, including five former Chiefs of Staff of the Army (CSA); several Vice Chiefs of Staff of the Army (VCSA), Theater Commander in Chiefs (CINCs), and 21 senior flag officers (three- and four-star generals). In addition, several senior civilian, politically appointed Army leaders were interviewed. Interviews were also conducted with 17 individuals who served in one of the four service LL offices and worked later for a private lobbying firm in Washington.[13] These interviews capture insights into the interservice differences in working in LL. They also are crucial in delineating the advantages and disadvantages LL officers possess in relation to private lobbyists working in Washington lobbying firms to influence Congress.

An insider case study is used to supplement the extensive interview data. It focuses on an example in which culture impeded Army effectiveness on the Hill: the legislative proposal that became law in 1994, requiring the Army to transfer 84 of its M1A1 tanks to the U.S. Marine Corps. Even though the Office of the Secretary of Defense and the Joint Staff supported the Army position, the Army lost an intense legislative battle to a more effective and sophisticated Marine Corps strategy.

In support of both the interviews and case study, this study also includes information and data from the congressional record, budget data analysis from defense appropriation records, and comparative data on the Washington experience of the senior military leadership of each of the four services.

In-depth study of this topic is important for several reasons. It can illuminate an important kind of lobbying activity conducted to some degree by all federal agencies, despite the fact that the law prohibits lobbying. Additionally, there has been little scholarly attention directed toward agency LL offices and how effectively their parent agencies or public organizations use them in conducting what may be termed "pseudo-lobbying." This research also will attempt to bridge the gap between private and public lobbying, focusing on the many parallels and the few, but still important, differences that legally exist for private lobbyists and agency LL officers as they represent their respective interests to Congress.

xvi   Preface

Finally, the study provides an empirical example of the problems, noted by James Madison, of factional self-interest in a free society.[14] With respect to the U.S. Armed Forces, the assumptions are that the playing field on which the several services engage Congress is level and each service is equally equipped to, and capable of, representing its interests to Congress. This book demonstrates that these assumptions may not be borne out, and this may have serious consequences for the nation's security interests in the post–Cold War world.

NOTES

1. After hearings, the Committee or subcommittee will "mark up" or make revisions or additions, some of which are significant, to a bill under consideration in the legislative process. Believed by many to be the heart of the legislative process, Members will often go line-by-line of a bill in Committee, literally "marking it up" and amending as they see fit. These revisions are voted on by Committee members. Rarely does a controversial bill come out of the Committee process without changes.

2. In early 1992, the Army was assigned the Pre-position Afloat mission in the JCS MRS, which, in response to lessons learned during the Gulf War, laid out a plan for significantly expanding U.S. defense sealift capabilities. Under the MRS, the Navy would convert or construct nine large, medium-speed, "roll-on, roll-off" ships the Army would use to pre-position a heavy brigade worth of equipment and theater opening supplies at sea. Chairman Hutto's Readiness Subcommittee provision would put the APA Program on hold to allow further study of the merits of redirecting those resources toward "enhancing" the U.S. Marine Corps Maritime Pre-positioning Force (EMPF).

3. The MRS had been mandated by Congress, and its recommendations had been strongly supported and approved by the administration and the JCS.

4. PSMs are Committee staff selected or hired by the subcommittee and Committee chairmen of the majority party as well as a reduced number selected by the more senior minority party Members. These Committee staff have responsibilities for personnel, strategic missile defense, procurement or acquisition, readiness, and so on. Usually, different PSMs will be responsible for research and development for the various services. These Committee staff work to develop expertise and institutional memory on set issue areas. Over time they accrue considerable influence because of the turnover of personnel (and priorities) in the Pentagon and the multitude of demands other than defense competing for Committee Members' time.

5. See Allan Kornberg, *Politics and Culture in Canada* (Ann Arbor, MI: Center for Political Studies, Institute for Social Research, 1988), 3. He comments on the unpublished work of Samuel Barnes, *Political Culture and Politics* (University of Michigan, 1986), preface.

6. Edgar H. Schein, *Organizational Culture and Leadership*, 2nd ed. (San Francisco: Jossey-Bass, 1992), 12.

7. See Jay M. Shafritz and J. Steven Ott, *Classics of Organizational Theory*, 3rd ed. (Pacific Grove, CA: Brooks-Cole, 1991), 482.

8. For the most scholarly and yet practical examples of this research, see Schein, *Organizational Culture and Leadership*; Don Hellriegel and John W. Slocum, Jr., *Organizational Behavior*, 6th ed. (New York: West Publishing, 1992); Paul Harris and R.T. Morgan, *Managing Cultural Differences* (Houston, TX: Gulf Publishing, 1987); Thomas

Peters and R.H. Waterman, *In Search of Excellence* (New York: Harper & Row, 1982); and Vijay Sathe, *Culture and Related Corporate Realities* (Homewood, IL: Irwin, 1985). With a focus on specifically public agencies, see James Q. Wilson, *Bureaucracy: What Government Agencies Do and Why They Do It* (New York: Basic Books, 1989), 90–110.

9. Carl H. Builder, *The Masks of War: American Military Strategy and Analysis* (Baltimore: Johns Hopkins University Press, 1989), 7–10. See also Arthur T. Hadley, *The Straw Giant: Triumph and Failure, America's Armed Forces* (New York: Random House, 1986), 67–73, for his description of the "differing psychological attitudes stamped on each officer" by military service culture.

10. Schein, *Organizational Culture and Leadership*, 15.

11. After the Republicans took over the House in the 104th Congress, the House Armed Services Committee's name was changed to the House National Security Committee.

12. Although the Defense Subcommittee of the House and Senate Appropriations Committees are as important as the two authorization committees in policy and budgetary issues for the military services, it was not feasible to conduct interviews of Members and staff on all four committees in the time available for this study. After working with the authorization committees for three years, I was able to use established credibility to gain access to and information from my interviewees that rarely, if ever, is available to many academic investigators. Additionally, key policy issues for the services are more closely examined and debated in the authorization committees, making this group the most appropriate one for ascertaining the effectiveness of how services represent their institutional interests. More important, the two appropriations subcommittees insist on not using the military services' LL offices for information or services, nor do they tolerate attempts of LL personnel to provide these resources. The executive uniformed personnel who work with the appropriators come out of the services' comptroller and budget offices. They work for a service's comptroller and not its CLA. Because this research uses LL operations as the forum of its examination of cultural impediments to Army representational effectiveness, it is logical to exclude the appropriators from the study.

13. This tally does not include the 10 active-duty Army LL officers interviewed for this study.

14. See *The Federalist Papers*, no. 10 (New York: New American Library, 1961), 77–84. Madison saw factions or interest groups as inherently bad because they were united "by some common impulse of passion, or of interest, adverse to the . . . permanent and aggregate interests of the [larger] community." He believed factions emerged from human nature and could not be naturally prevented nor should force be directed by the government to eliminate them and thereby sacrifice liberty. Therefore, ideally the "mischiefs of faction" are contained by pitting "ambition" against "ambition" of competing factions in a continual battle of countervailing selfish interests. Madison therefore favored a setting that allowed for the largest, most effective, and widest variety of factional competition to prevent any one narrow factional interest from gaining a position of dominance in our government and society. See also *The Federalist Papers*, no. 51.

Acknowledgments

This study would never have been possible without the enormous professional assistance, support, and opportunities provided by the Army leadership, the National Defense University, and the American Political Science Association's (APSA) Congressional Fellowship Program. Army leadership provided the time and thereby opportunity to conduct this study, cooperated in exploring this sensitive issue, and evinced interest in the results; and the National Defense University Press sponsored me as a Visiting Military Fellow within the Institute of National Strategic Studies, National Defense University. The logistical and administrative support provided by these institutions were critical to this comprehensive research undertaking. The APSA's Congressional Fellowship Program provided my first glimpse of how the various services represent interests on the Hill from a "staffer" vantage point, and helped me secure a position in Army Legislative Liaison (LL) Programs Division.

I am extremely grateful to the following individuals on Capitol Hill, in the Pentagon, and the private sector who provided me with their candid insights, which form the heart of this study and make it unique:[1]

General Officers and Senior Army Leadership: John Hamre, Jack Marsh, Norman Augustine, David Chu, General Bernard W. Rogers, General Edward C. Meyer, General John A. Wickham, Jr., General Carl E. Vuono, General Gordon Sullivan, General Max Thurman, General Robert Riscassi, General William Tuttle, General Jack Merritt, General Don Keith, General Jimmy Ross, General Leon E. Saloman, Lieutenant General Don Pihl, Lieutenant General Chuck Dominy, Lieutenant General Walt Ulmer, Lieutenant General Ted Stroup, Lieutenant General Jay Garner, Lieutenant General Dan Christman, Lieutenant General Hank Hatch, Lieutenant General William Odom, Lieutenant General Lawrence F. Skibbie, Major General Jerry Harrison, Major General Maury

Boyd, Major General John C. Thompson, Major General Bill Eicher, Brigadier General William A. West, Colonel Bill Foster, Colonel Ken Allard, Colonel Jack LeCuyer, Colonel Jon Dodson, Colonel Chuck Feldmayer, Colonel Tom Leney, and Colonel Tom Davis.

Legislative Liaison Officers/(Lobbyists): Gordon Merritt, James P. Crumley, Jim Rooney, Fred Moosally, Denny Sharon, Billy Cooper, Dave Matthews, Bob Lange, Win Shaw, Cork Colburn, John Schroeder, Roy Alcala, Dan Fleming, Mike O'Brien, Jess Franco, Jay McNulty, Mike Landrum, Lieutenant Colonel Kim Doughtery, Commander Sean P. Sullivan, Colonel John Sattler, Colonel John F. Kelly, Sam Brick, and Karl F. Schneider.

Congressional Audience Interviews:

Members of Congress, House National Security Committee: Rep. (former) H. Martin Lancaster (D-NC); Rep. Ike Skelton (D-MO); Rep. John Spratt (D-SC); Rep. John M. McHugh (R-NY); Rep. Herb Bateman (R-VA); Rep. Glen Browder (D-AL); Rep. Paul McHale (D-PA); Rep. Joel Hefley (R-CO); Rep. Chet Edwards (D-TX); Rep. Sonny Montgomery (D-MS); Rep. Jim Talent (R-MO); Rep. Walter Jones (R-NC); Rep. Floyd Spence (R-SC); Rep. Steve Buyer (R-IN); Rep. Owen Pickett (D-VA); Rep. Tillie Fowler (R-FL); Rep. Lane Evans (D-IL); and Rep. (now Senator) Jack Reed (D-RI).

Member of Congress, Senate Armed Services Committee: Senator Lauch Faircloth (R-NC).

Professional Staff Members, House National Security and Senate Armed Services Committees: Steve Ansley, John Chapla, Bill Andahazy, Robert Rangel, Jean Reed, Doug Necessary, Bob Brauer, Dr. Arch Barrett, Karen Heath, Kim Wincup, Brigadier Dick Reynard (Ret.), Arnold Punaro, Romie (Les) Brownlee, George Lauffer, Don Deline, Rick DeBobes, Charlie Abell, Creighton Greene, Patrick (P.T.) Henry, Joe Pallone, Steve Saulnier, Ken Johnson, Judy Ansley,

Military Legislative Assistants, House National Security Committee: Perry Floyd, Skip Fischer, Nancy Lifset, Ned Michalek, Mike Mclaughlin, Vickie Plunkett, Jeff Crank, Rob Warner, Christian Zur, Bill Fallon, Jim Lariviere, Wade Heck, Cary Brick, Lisa Morena, Hugh Brady, Tom O'Donnel, Bill Klein, Vickie Middleton, Al Oetkin, Bill Natter, John Webb, and Lindsey Neas.

Military Legislative Assistants, Senate Armed Services Committee: Sam Adcock, Richard Fieldhouse, Grayson Winterling, Tom Lankford, Joanne Quilette, John Lilley, Steve Wolfe, Rick Schwab, Matt Hay, Dale Gerry, Ann Sauer, Dave Davis, Lisa Tuite, Andy Johnson, and Geddings Roche.

I want to express special appreciation for the mentorship and friendship of Representative John Spratt (D-SC) and former Principal Deputy Assistant Secretary of the Army Arch Barrett, two widely respected masters of the legislative process.

In addition, there were many individuals, in and out of Washington, DC, who played a critical role in bringing this research to completion. I will always be indebted to Dr. Allan Kornberg of Duke University for his unswerving encouragement over the years and his invaluable focus, motivation, and leadership for this study. Without his mentorship, this study never would have been completed. I also want to acknowledge and thank Professors Peter Feaver, Albert Eldridge, and Joel Sokolsky of Duke University for their many insightful comments and recommendations regarding this research. Additionally, I relied heavily on the advice and assistance of many of my former colleagues in the Department of Social Sciences at the U.S. Military Academy at West Point and other talented officers on the Army and Joint Staff. I want to especially thank Earl W. Walker, George Edwards, Douglas MacGregor, Michael Brown, Bill Foster, Dan Kaufman, Robert Baratta, Mike Reopel, and Frank Finelli for their support and sage counsel on this endeavor.

I want to acknowledge the untiring efforts, constant support, and superb editorial skill of Mary Sommerville over the last three years. Special thanks go to Steve Curry for his timely encouragement to persevere with this study. I would also like to thank Charles Heller, Matt Christ, Cherie Previtt, David Schock, Frank Prindle, Steve Ansley, Linda Coleman, MG Jerry Harrison, and MG Maury Edmonds for their advice, assistance, and encouragement throughout this long process.

But most important, my most profound thanks go to my wife, Patricia, a foreign service officer who understands more than she ever desired about Army relations with Congress. She served multiple roles as supportive wife, reader of draft chapters, and diplomatic but persistent editor. Her counsel, love, and support sustained me throughout the process of writing this book about the Army I so dearly love.

NOTE

1. The individuals listed here were formally interviewed by the author for this study. In addition, this study cites comments and views of congressional and senior military individuals who are not on this list based on their request or on the fact that their comments were made in the presence of the author in the conduct of my earlier legislative liaison (LL) duties.

Chapter 1

Introduction:
Liaising versus Lobbying

This chapter explores and describes the kind of lobbying activity conducted by all federal agencies, despite the existence of statutory law prohibiting "lobbying" of Congress by public agencies. For the benefit of the military, and especially the Army audience, this representational lobbying activity will be referred to as "liaising" and will be differentiated from similar activities of private lobbyists in the nation's capital. While reviewing the formal statutory restrictions that many bureaucrats and senior flag officers believe largely limit public agency lobbying with Congress, this chapter will highlight the more important informal norms and constraints that Congress imposes that effectively control the scope of what is considered permissible liaising activity on the Hill. The chapter will also highlight the evolution of LL operations in general and briefly compare the organizational structures of the four services' LL operations.

THE "L" WORD: TO LOBBY OR LIAISE

The Army's cultural problems in representing its interests on Capitol Hill are compounded and reinforced by the confusing and complex "antilobbying" criminal laws and regulations that have been on the books for over 70 years.[1] Additionally, the taint of impropriety that has been associated historically with the terms "lobbying" and "lobbyists" persists today with many individuals inside and outside the Army.[2] As a consequence, senior Army leaders have difficulty adopting a perspective that views proactively engaging Congress on behalf of their service's interests as a legitimate and appropriate component of their professional responsibility.

The intimidating power and perceptual stigma of "lobbying" often limit the quality and quantity of senior Army flag officers' interactions with Congress and emanate from several factors. These include the extent of experience and understanding of Washington operations, the quantity and quality of established working relationships with the Hill, understanding of the Constitution and Congress's well-established role in defense matters, and ability and willingness to engage important Washington external audiences.

The Army's CLL starts his prepared speech to newly promoted brigadier generals by stating, "The Army does not lobby Congress."[3] If the Army does not lobby Congress, what term describes what LL offices and officials do? The problem with the term lies in its imprecision and the different meanings it conveys to different people. A Senate Special Committee reporting on its investigation into lobbying in 1957 commented on the confusion and misunderstanding of this term:

One man thinks of lobbying as the factual presentation of useful information to legislators. To another, it means sinister influence peddling by pressure groups with reckless disregard for the general welfare. Indeed some state statutes limit the definition of lobbying to attempts to exert *improper* influence.[4]

No one is sure where this imprecise term originated, but it likely evolved from a derogatory reference to individuals who waited in the lobby of the Capitol building to ambush passing legislators to advocate a particular position on pending legislation.[5] Jeffrey M. Berry, in his excellent work on interest groups, defines lobbying as "any *legal* means used to try to influence government."[6] Lester Milbrath defines lobbying as "the stimulation and transmission of a communication, by someone other than a citizen acting on his own behalf, directed to a governmental decisionmaker with the hope of influencing his decision."[7] Both are close to defining lobbying-type activities responsibly undertaken by public agencies; however, neither definition succeeds in differentiating these activities from private Washington lobbying efforts. Even private Washington lobbyists try to avoid this label because of the stigma associated with their profession.[8] Because of the stigma of applying the "L" word to LL activity, the term "liaise" rather than "lobby" is used in this book to discuss military service LL activity. Communicating directly to establish and maintain mutual understanding between an agency and Congress is liaising activity.

Private Washington lobbyists attempt to influence, urge, or press Members of Congress or congressional staffers on issues through a variety of means, on behalf of a third party. Additionally, the individual lobbyist and senior leadership in the company represented can benefit financially from influencing that Member or staffer. In contrast, LL officers and their senior leadership receive no personal monetary gain for their activities. They are engaged as public servants whose goals are institutional enhancement, bettering the condition of the Armed Forces personnel in the field, and contributing to defense and the general welfare of the nation by enhancing the ability of Congress to make informed decisions pertinent to the conduct of their oversight and legislative responsibilities in de-

fense matters. Open communication and mutual understanding of concerns require credible and trusted relationships that LL officers and senior service leaders
"liaise" to establish and maintain.

While the roles of agency liaisers and private lobbyists with Congress are
different, both are seen by the Hill generally as representatives of interests that
have a legitimate right and need to be expressed in the legislative process. The
congressional audience finds both essential in carrying out its constitutional responsibilities.

Whether referred to as agency lobbying or liaising, it is important to realize
that LL operations, an executive branch innovation, are restricted in their activities, formally and informally, by Congress. To the least experienced, the *formal*
laws prohibiting executive lobbying of Congress are the most restrictive when
viewed in a literal sense. However, the *informal* restraints imposed by Congress
do more to establish the limits of what is acceptable agency lobbying or "liaising" activity.

FORMAL LEGAL RESTRAINTS ON EXECUTIVE
LOBBYING

Formal restrictions on lobbying by public agencies are rooted in two sources:
criminal statutes and provisions in appropriation acts. The Anti-Lobbying Act,
enacted in 1919 in response to extensive use of telegrams by government agencies urging citizens to lobby Congress on appropriations, is a criminal statute
that prohibits the use of appropriated funds by public organizations to lobby
Congress. Violations of the law are punishable by one-year confinement and a
$500 fine or both, plus removal from federal employment.[9] The Anti-Lobbying
Act states that:

No part of the money appropriated by any enactment of Congress shall, in the absence
of express authorization by Congress, be used directly or indirectly to pay for any personal service, advertisement, telegram, telephone, letter, printed or written matter, or
other device, intended or designed to influence in any manner a Member of Congress,
to favor or oppose, by vote or otherwise, any legislation or appropriation by Congress,
whether before or after the introduction of any bill or resolution proposing such legislation or appropriation; but this shall not prevent officers or employees of the United
States or of its departments or agencies from communicating to Members of Congress
on the request of any Member or to Congress, through proper official channels, requests
for legislation or appropriations which they deem necessary for the efficient conduct of
the public business.[10]

Anti-lobbying anxieties of public agency leaders do not rest solely on the
prohibitions in the Anti-Lobbying Act. In each year's Defense Appropriations
Act there is a miscellaneous provision that prohibits the use of appropriated
funds "directly or indirectly, to influence congressional action on any legislation

or appropriation matters pending before Congress.''[11] This has been interpreted to prohibit the same activities as criminalized in the Anti-Lobbying Act. Additionally, the defense appropriators place a provision in their yearly Act that prohibits the use of appropriated funds for ''publicity or propaganda purposes not authorized by Congress.'' This provision is targeted at public relations activities as well as activities related to Congress.[12] Finally, there is the law in the U.S. Code that restricts the use of official mail to send ''any article or document unless: (1) a request therefore has been previously received by the department or establishment; or (2) its mailing is required by law.''[13]

If the Anti-Lobbying Act and these other formal anti-lobbying provisions are interpreted in a literal sense, one understands the uneasiness a public agency leader might have about representing his or her agency's institutional interests to Congress and ensuring that his/her actions are largely reactionary responses to requests for congressional information. However, to operate effectively in the nation's capital, one must understand the legal interpretations of these formal restrictions. ''Although the broad wording of 18 U.S.C. section 1913 and section 8014 of the Defense Appropriations Act would seem to prohibit virtually any effort by the executive branch to influence congressional action, the Department of Justice and the Comptroller General have consistently read the provisions quite narrowly.''[14]

These legitimate interpretations allow a certain type of lobbying and prohibit other types. Direct lobbying that entails direct contact with a legislator, staff, or other government official ''either in person or by various means of written or oral communication'' is largely permitted. Prohibitions for government officials center on ''indirect'' or ''grassroots'' lobbying where ''the lobbyist contacts third parties, either members of special interest groups or the general public, and urges them to contact their legislators to support or oppose something.''[15]

Because of this long-standing narrow interpretation, there has been no criminal prosecution since the Act was enacted in 1919. However, the Justice Department Criminal Division and its Public Integrity Section frequently receive referrals for evaluation on whether the Act was violated. No one has been fined or sent to jail, but there have been repercussions for government employees for activities called into question because of the Act. Therefore, over time the Criminal Division of the Justice Department has developed guidelines on what the Act and related provisions mean and has identified permissible activities.[16]

The General Accounting Office (GAO) serves an important role in evaluating particular situations or actions to determine if *possible* violations of the Anti-Lobbying Act or the appropriation provisions have taken place. The GAO does not decide whether a given action constitutes a violation; the Anti-Lobbying Act is a criminal statute; therefore responsibility for enforcement rests with the Department of Justice and the courts. However, the GAO will determine whether appropriated funds were used in a given instance and refer the matter to the Justice Department. Generally, the GAO does so if asked by a Member of Congress or where available information provides reasonable cause to suspect that a violation may have occurred. In evaluating these particular situations to determine possible violations of the Anti-Lobbying Act, the GAO applies the Justice Department's narrow interpretation of that statute, reducing the number of cases it refers.[17]

In summary, under the Anti-Lobbying Act, government employees are allowed to (1) communicate directly with Members of Congress and their staffs in support of administration or department positions; (2) communicate with the public through public speeches, appearances, and published writings, to support administration positions, including using such public forums to call on the public to contact Members of Congress in support of or opposition to legislation; (3) communicate privately with members of the public to inform them of administration positions and to promote those positions—but only to the extent that such communications do not contravene specified limitations; and (4) lobby Congress or the public to support administration positions on nominations, treaties, or any non-legislative, non-appropriations issue. The Act applies only to legislation or appropriations.[18] Under the Anti-Lobbying Act, government employees may not engage in substantial "grassroots" lobbying campaigns of telegrams, letters, and other private forms of communication expressly asking recipients to contact Members of Congress, in support of or opposition to legislation. Grassroots lobbying does not include communication with the public through public speeches, appearances, or writings.[19]

Despite the narrow and more permissive interpretations by the Justice Department of the Anti-Lobbying Act and other related legal provisions, *other interpretations* serve to broaden and thereby restrict some of these loopholes. For example, the Comptroller General has construed that the "grassroots" lobbying restriction is triggered by an explicit request by government employees asking for citizens to contact their representatives in support or in opposition to pending legislation. Given the Comptroller General's interpretation, and given the difficulty of predicting what may or may not be perceived as a grassroots campaign in a particular context, agencies generally err on the side of caution by refraining from including in their communications with private citizens any requests to contact Members in support or opposition to legislation.[20]

The Department of Justices's published opinions do not set out a detailed, independent analysis of "publicity or propaganda" riders contained in the Appropriation Acts of some agencies. However, the Comptroller General has suggested that, under such riders, government employees also *may not* (1) provide administrative support for the lobbying activities of private organizations, (2) prepare editorials or other communications that will be disseminated without an accurate disclosure of the government's role in their origin, and (3) appeal to members of the public to contact their elected representatives in support or opposition to proposals before Congress.[21]

Collectively, the GAO, the Department of Justice and its Office of Legal Council, the Comptroller General, and the Office of the Army Judge Advocate General have interpreted the Anti-Lobbying Act and related provisions to prohibit the use of appropriated funds to encourage, pressure, or suggest that private citizens, citizen groups, corporations, associations, or other organizations contact or solicit Congress on a legislative matter. However, the Anti-Lobbying Act and Appropriation Acts do not prohibit direct contacts between the Department of the Army and other services' officials and the Congress. Thus, Armed Forces officials in Washington may provide information to Members of Congress or solicit congressional support for legislation supported by the administration.

This dissection of the formal restrictions of the Anti-Lobbying Act and provisions reveals an intended ambivalence by Congress toward executive branch attempts to influence legislation. On the one hand, Congress sends a clear signal that it will never tolerate the executive branch using appropriated funds to lobby Congress as if it were a private interest group. LL officers and senior military flag officers interviewed for this study were all aware that criminal anti-lobbying statutes were on the books. They serve their purpose in making liaising executives act carefully in carrying out their respective roles. On the other hand, Congress does not want to be responsible for constructing roadblocks to information and assistance it needs to carry out its constitutional duties.

The law most effectively sends the signal to executive agencies to avoid grassroots-oriented lobbying activities and the collective guidelines recommend that agencies err on the side of safety and avoid working apparent loopholes in this area. By doing so, agencies and their leadership avoid the additional scrutiny, embarrassment, and reputational damage of having their agency operation investigated and referred for possible violations of the Act. Grassroots lobbying is for private lobbyists and even the perception of such activity is best avoided by all government personnel.

At the same time, congressional hearings on the subject have affirmed the importance of intentional loopholes to the prohibitive language in the law that authorize the executive to initiate direct communications with Congress through "proper official channels," and protect the "propriety of having executive officers respond to inquiries from individual members and committees," which undermines any broad or literal interpretation of the formal prohibition.[22] While many Members may not like being directly lobbied or liaised by public agencies, they understand that their need for information and assistance from these agencies is of a higher order.

It is significant that the narrow interpretation of the criminal statute has resulted in no criminal prosecutions since the Act's enactment in 1919.[23] A broader and more literal interpretation of the statutes and provisions likely would be determined unconstitutional by the courts. Additionally, it would work against the interests of both the executive and legislative branches by limiting direct contact between the two institutions. The executive branch would have a more difficult time in explaining its budget and programs. Members of Congress would be deprived of a wealth of timely information and associations that facilitate fulfilling their constitutional responsibilities. The legal restrictions on agency lobbying or liaising are narrowly interpreted by both branches because liaisers impart information critical to both. Congressional restrictions, both formal and informal, are concerned largely with ensuring that the favorable environment conducive to timely information exchange is not controlled by the executive branch.

These legal restrictions, created by Congress for its own purposes, only partially define the congressional limitations imposed on public agency liaising. Direct public agency liaising activities on the Hill in support of administration positions are legal and legitimate endeavors that are restricted primarily through *informal* rather than *formal* congressional mechanisms.

INFORMAL CONGRESSIONAL RESTRAINTS ON EXECUTIVE LOBBYING

Although less appreciated by many agency bureaucrats, the informal restrictions Congress imposes upon agency lobbying or liaising are more profound than the formal limitations discussed in the previous section. Violations of these informal limitations will likely prompt cries of "foul play" or "lobbying" by Members toward that agency, or result in a less permissive liaising environment afforded to that agency or LL officer by Members until agency behavior has been atoned. These informal but effective restraints on liaison officers and senior agency leaders are centered around closely guarded congressional norms and needs. They include restraints against: overly crude styles of agency liaising; attempts to limit or control congressional ties back to the agencies; and a clear extra-legal prohibition against liaising its appropriators.[24]

First, Members of Congress will not tolerate a heavy-handed or crude style of agency liaising. They may tolerate rough handling from their constituents and maybe to a lesser degree from White House LL personnel, but they will not tolerate it from agency or military service LL and senior flag officer personnel. Arm-twisting or implied threats to Members or their staff violate this informal limitation. Holtzman defines arm-twisting as implied threats "to deny a congressman certain requests or aid in connection with his personal legislation or appropriations for his district and state, or to deprive him and his constituency of existing programs or services."[25] The threats do not have to be overt; even implicit ones will tend to infuriate a Member's staff.

Crudeness in style can be manifested in having Members approached by agency personnel who are unskilled in liaising and who are uninformed on the issue on which they are approaching the Member. An individual unskilled in liaising is less likely to understand the background, interests, and pressures under which particular Members and staff operate. This can come across as condescending to the staffer or Member.[26] If liaising activity is conducted, a Member or staffer expects to have it conducted by someone knowledgeable on the subject as well as sensitive to the congressional environment. Allowing the contentiousness of an issue to "get personal" is rarely tolerated, whether the slight is directed at a Member or staff.[27]

Agency liaisers are never allowed to control or interfere with congressional ties to their agency. Efforts by LL or agency leaders to channel all agency communications with the Hill directly through a centralized office are met with unequivocal congressional opposition. Holtzman gives an interesting example of such an effort by the Assistant Secretary of State for Congressional Relations in 1962.[28] This official circulated a memorandum directing the establishment of a central file on all congressional contacts between State Department officers and their subordinates. More importantly, State Department personnel were given cards to complete and forward to his office that detailed any contact with a Member or staffer on the Hill. This memorandum was immediately canceled by the Assistant Secretary of State after he was bombarded with congressional outrage at this effort.[29]

Finally, an informal limitation on agency LL activity centers around their exclusion from liaising Members of the Appropriations Committees of the Congress.[30] Appropriators, especially on the House side, resist associations with an agency's LL personnel because of their long-standing relationships with another segment of the agency's bureaucracy: its budget and comptroller personnel. Richard Fenno's landmark work on the House Appropriations Committee noted that its Members and staff saw their Committee role as unique and most important in safeguarding the federal treasury.[31]

By choosing to work only with budget officers and stay clear of an agency's LL officers, they believe (1) they are dealing with officers with greater budgetary expertise who speak their language and can get them accurate information more quickly (2) budgetary personnel tend to be civil servants who have a longer and less political perspective, (3) comptroller personnel are less controlled and motivated by the interests of the political departmental secretary, unlike the LL personnel who are directly responsible to the service secretary, (4) they see department LL officers' policy focus as a potential obstruction to their channels of information back into the agency,[32] and (5) they are dealing with a set of officers whom they trust and believe will not mislead them.[33]

While LL officers may on occasion involve themselves in appropriations matters, the latter are primarily indirect and tangential. Agency LL personnel try to ensure that the comptroller personnel working with the appropriators are familiar with policy concerns and positions of the agency. A representative from this office will often attend key meetings with LL personnel where congressional concerns are being addressed. In general, LL officers will focus their energies on their legitimate audience—Members and staff serving on authorizing or other non-appropriating committees—hoping that these authorizing Members and staff will then assume their mission and represent these positions to the Appropriations Committees.

SIMILARITIES IN LOBBYING AND LIAISING

Using Lester Milbrath's broad definition of lobbying as a communication process, both LL officers and private lobbyists initiate communication (not as

Table 1-1
Commandments of "Good" Lobbying and Liaising

---

1. Tell the truth.
2. Never promise more than you can deliver.
3. Know how to listen so that you can accurately understand what you are hearing.
4. Staff is there to be worked with, not circumvented.
5. Spring no surprises.

---

individual citizens acting on their own personal behalf) with Members and staff, hoping to influence their decisions. Milbrath states that "one common thread running through the variety of definitions of lobbyist was that all lobbyists try to influence governmental decisions in some way."[34] Both LL and private lobbyists devote significant agency and group resources, respectively, to influencing congressional decisions. In Holtzman's study of LL operations in eight executive departments, to include Defense, he addressed similarities, noting that: "Both represent political superiors and larger systems; both are employed to shape a favorable climate in which their leaders may interact with legislative actors; both are concerned with the legislative process and with policy output; both utilize somewhat similar strategems and tactics."[35]

While the roles of LL officers and private lobbyists with Congress are different, both are seen by the Hill generally as representatives of interests that have a legitimate right and need to be expressed in the legislative process. The congressional audience finds both LL officers and lobbyists useful in carrying out their constitutional responsibilities. Both provide Members and staff with services that assist in taking care of constituents and in making policy that benefits the nation and the re-election prospects and overall stature of the legislators.

Congress expects both LL officers and lobbyists to "treat them with honesty and respect, and that they recognize the significance of the political situation in the legislators' constituencies and committees." Finally, both LL officers and lobbyists operate on the Hill knowing that Members can impose sanctions. These include a withdrawal of trust and confidence, eliminating valued access, voting against your interests, and publicly attacking or initiating investigations of your interests.[36]

There are similarities in the manner by which both liaisers and lobbyists approach the Hill. Bruce Wolpe's work outlines overarching commandments and important fundamentals of responsible and effective private lobbying.[37] All apply to agency liaisers, adjusting for their different roles and the congressional norms that limit those roles (see Tables 1-1 and 1-2).

Table 1-2
Fundamentals

---

1. Define the issues in any lobbying visit. Determine at the outset what you want.
2. Know the players.
3. Know the committees.
4. Know what the public policy rationale is on the issue.
5. Prepare materials.
6. Anticipate the opposition.
7. Be solicitous of your political allies.
8. Understand the process: the rules of procedure and the rules of compromise.
9. Enlist the support of your allies.
10. Observe basic courtesies.

DIFFERENCES IN LOBBYING AND LIAISING

Despite the many similarities, significant differences exist between liaising and lobbying.[38] The most fundamental is the objective of the influence: the private lobbyist works to maximize the economic benefits for stockholders, employees, and leadership of one or more private entities while the agency liaiser works to promote the interests of the nation and its citizens. This fundamental difference gives both entities a distinct set of advantages and disadvantages. In addition, each has distinct resources the other lacks that help influence legislators and legislation. These inherent advantages and disadvantages dictate how the liaiser and the lobbyist establish and utilize relationships with Congress.

Because private lobbyists are hired to maximize the economic benefits that congressional decisions can convey, these lobbyists claim they can normally command the attention of substantial and high-level resources within the commercial organization very quickly. Stockholders' interests, as well as thousands of jobs, depend on congressional decisions. While the stakes for the public agency are also high, the impact usually involves policy outcomes and has fewer direct ramifications on the agency's viability or the economic interests of its employees. For example, when Secretary of Defense Weinberger ordered and the Congress allowed the Army's DIVAD weapon system to die, no Army jobs were lost. The company with that contract went immediately from 23,000 to 16,000 employees.

For this reason, private lobbyists claim that when they have important issues riding on impending Hill action, they do not have to explain the importance of the CEO's presence and personal involvement. The CEO makes time to energetically pursue corporate interests. Also, private lobbyists note that top corporate industry leaders are generally accustomed to taking risks required to survive in the business world. Their willingness to accept a certain level of risk assists the Washington lobbyist by increasing the quantity and quality of options or components available to implement in a corporate legislative campaign plan. Many top military service leaders, on the other hand, may question why their involvement with Congress on certain issues is necessary and tend to be more cautious about the reactions of the Office of the Secretary of Defense (OSD) and the administration to their activities, thereby limiting the legislative strategy devised by LL personnel. Moreover, while it may be common in the business world to play hardball among competitors when a company's interests and bottom line are at stake, it is rare to see the senior military leadership of the services directly confront each other in public fora.

Another important resource that private lobbyists have that public liaisers lack is the ability to exert influence over congressional actors from several different directions and sources, including mobilizing resources in a Member's district to press for specific issues. Given the prohibitions on grassroots lobbying by public agencies discussed earlier, public liaisers cannot use this type of resource. Another key source of influence for the private lobbyist and his corporate client is campaign contributions, often through political action committees (PACs), which are important means of obtaining access and a hearing for a private lobbyist's views. Public liaisers, of course, cannot influence in this manner.

A final important advantage enjoyed by private lobbyists is the experienced personnel they can devote to building and maintaining relations with Congress. Unlike public sector liaisers, who are often ''amateurs'' doing a single assignment in an LL office with little training or experience, private sector lobbying firms generally have a significant number of lobbyists with many years of experience who have developed a sophisticated understanding of congressional rules, procedures, and norms; a wide network of contacts, and substantive expertise. Public agencies, with some exceptions, rarely place comparable emphasis on the skills, understanding, and relationships with Congress of their liaisers. In addition, because the economic impact of a specific congressional decision usually extends beyond one company, private lobbyists for different organizations often combine their expertise and resources to develop and implement a congressional strategy. As noted above, these joint lobbying efforts incorporate not only Washington-based strategy but also efforts to approach Members of Congress from their constituent base, using contractors and subcontractors. While military service liaisons may occasionally work together on specific issues, they usually operate separately, and prohibitions on grassroots lobbying make services wary of combining efforts that could be perceived as inappropriate collaboration with the lobbying activities of private lobbyists. However, it was repeatedly mentioned for this study that the Navy (USMC) and Air Force are far more sophisticated and comfortable than their departmental Army counterparts in knowing how to collaborate effectively with private lobbyists and contractors on weapons program legislative campaigns and allowing the private firms to conduct the grassroots lobbying.

On the other hand, while the private lobbyist benefits from the significant and high-level corporate resources associated with ''bottom-line'' commercial interests and fewer constraints on lobbying activity, the obvious pursuit of profit also has the downside of making congressional actors suspicious of the motives of private lobbyists and their clients. Public agency liaisers, on the other hand, are able to present their interests in altruistic, patriotic, and national security terms. This provides them a higher level of credibility and constant opportunities to establish and maintain relationships with a broad spectrum of congressional actors that would be difficult and take many years to replicate in the private sector. Senior military leaders are a particularly effective resource, given the esteem with which Congress holds them and their commitment to national security. Private lobbyists cannot easily replicate this instant credibility and access afforded senior military officers, which transcends party and initially even the personality and capabilities of the senior flag officer who appears on the Hill.

In addition, parochial commercial agendas of private lobbyists can make congressional Members and staff wary of the appearances of being seen as ''captured'' by special interest; however, these congressional actors are far more willing to actively and publicly engage with senior flag officers and public liaisers, who are seen as supporting public interests. One area in which this phenomenon is particularly pronounced is travel by Members and staff. The military service congressional liaisons regularly use invitations for Members or their staff to travel to military or military-related facilities as a means of educating them about service interests, capabilities, and problems, and about building personal ties away from the competing pressures of Washington. Members and staff are more cautious about accepting this type of travel or entertainment from private lobbyists; in addition, these lobbyists cannot produce the same quality of subject matter experience as a public agency with its unique resources. Another area where the perception of public agency liaisers as less parochial and, as legitimate representatives of the executive branch, becomes important is the fact that they are often invited to ''closed'' congressional events such as committee marks, especially on the House side, to which a private lobbyist would never be given access to on ethical grounds.

Moreover, in addition to the messengers being considered more credible, the information they provide to support their case, which is generally compiled using the resources of their public agency, is also viewed with less skepticism by those on Capitol Hill than data compiled by private companies. This is partly a function of the vast research capabilities of many public agencies and partly due to the perception that government researchers and analysts have less of a parochial agenda than their private sector counterparts.

A final but very important advantage enjoyed by public liaisers, and particularly military services, is that they are able to identify and give priority to requirements through the executive budget process. In this manner, the services themselves set the agenda and frame the debate. While private lobbyists can and do challenge these requirements and priorities, they are usually fighting a reactive battle and their "greed" motives are often questioned. Congressional actors open themselves up to charges of "pork barrel" spending when they fund programs beyond what the services have listed as necessary, and to the criticism of undermining national security by cutting programs deemed essential by the services.

In sum, private lobbyists benefit from an ability to quickly mobilize high-level support from their clients because of the bottom-line nature of their work; to utilize a broader range of tools, many of which are legally unavailable to public liaisers, to exert influence; and to benefit from personnel with many years of experience in working with Congress. Public liaisers, on the other hand, benefit from perceptions that they are working for public, rather than parochial, interests; the greater credibility assigned to senior military leaders and the information they present; and their ability to set the agendas through their budget requests.

LEGISLATIVE LIAISON AND POLITICAL APPOINTEES

Where do civilian political appointees fit into the liaising equation? Military service liaisers are members of the executive branch who work under the Secretary of Defense and directly for their politically appointed service secretary. This provides civilian control of the predominantly professional military LL officer operation. It is a check to keep policy decisions from being made by uniformed rather than politically accountable officials.

Service secretaries and other service political appointees also serve the essential role expected by Congress of addressing issues and concerns from a partisan and strictly political perspective. As stated earlier, senior military leaders and service LLs must be and appear to be bipartisan in taking their representational message and concerns to the Hill. When an issue surfaces that is partisan in nature, the uniformed military should step aside and alert the political appointees to the nature of the problem for resolution. Congress desires to have the professional military channel present and engaged as policy collaborators and advocates to provide information and professional judgments that enable them to make the best-informed decisions. However, Congress also wants to retain the partisan and strictly political channel open for "political collaboration" where these party or re-election interests can be pursued. Members of Congress want the senior uniformed leadership and the LLs sensitive to the political concerns and environment in Washington, but do not want these individuals as partisan or strictly political collaborators.

LL officers work for the service secretary but also must respond to the top senior military leadership. The military services that have the greatest synchrony, communication, and cooperation between their military service staff and civilian political "secretariat" staff are able to enhance LL effectiveness. Military services that have structural and cultural dysfunctions in working as a team are less effective on the Hill and often place LL officers in a difficult position. To be effective, the uniformed military should understand and appreciate the value of the service secretaries and other appointed civilians in informing and justifying service concerns to the Hill.

The most effective representational efforts for a service on the Hill take place when the service secretary understands, actively supports, and in many cases takes the lead in promoting many of the major initiatives and programs deemed critical by the senior military leadership on the Hill. Likewise, the senior military leadership works to ensure that the secretary is not surprised by military staff actions and is kept informed of planned campaigns on the Hill:

The service secretary can have a major impact, if he or she chooses to do so, on how effectively a service represents its interests on the Hill and to other external audiences. According to interviewees, the Navy, in particular, has had strong secretaries who were instrumental in opening the eyes of Navy admirals to the long-term institutional benefits of more effective engagement with Congress and the public. Beginning with Secretary James Forrestal, who later became the first Secretary of Defense, these secretaries made improving relations with the Hill a clear priority, put their best people in LL, and ensured that the promotion process, particularly to admiral, placed weight on experience in dealing with external (to the Navy) audiences.[39]

The service secretary working closely with the chief of that service can also make a great impact on the skills, talents, and experience found in a service's future senior flag officers by affecting the promotion process. The service secretary can give specific instructions to a promotion board stating that he wants x number of officers selected with the following background and experiences.

Based on interviews conducted with Members and staff, political appointees are expected to carry the administration's party line even when asked for their personal opinion by Members. While this provides opportunities that Congress recognizes and will try to use for partisan and strictly political reasons, it often diminishes the perceived value of their information and recommendations on what is best for the military services. As discussed in Chapter 4, the importance given to the views of senior uniformed military as credible message carriers in most cases outweighs their civilian political appointee counterparts with the Hill audience. The political appointees are more likely to know how to work an issue and assess its feasibility in a strictly political sense. The professional military is more likely to be viewed as able to discuss and explain a position in terms of it being the right thing to do from a national security perspective. A service that can combine these strengths on the same issues on the Hill can be an effective team.

LEGISLATIVE LIAISON OPERATIONS

While the scholarly literature on LL organizations is limited,[40] Abraham Holtzman's *Legislative Liaison: Executive Leadership in Congress* provides the most accurate and relevant analysis of cabinet-level and White House LLs in general and how they are similar and different from department to department.[41] Although he interviewed the DOD rather than individual military service LL officers, many of his observations hold true today for service LLs.[42]

LL officers' primary purpose is to serve as the administration's official conduit with the legislative branch, which entails everything from maintaining good relations and communication with Congress to promoting or opposing congressional action deemed important to the administration's positions on legislative proposals and programs. In these activities, LL officers and senior flag liaisers are primarily executive agents attempting to inform and influence a Member's position on legislation important to their executive superiors by helping the Member understand the administration's position. However, as we will see in the next chapter, Congress views the scope of LL and senior flag officers' liaising roles as not only articulating administration positions, but also providing information to questions, when asked.

THE EVOLUTION OF EXECUTIVE LEGISLATIVE LIAISON ORGANIZATIONS

The development of a specialized LL staff has its roots in the larger shift of legislative initiative from the Congress to the President, evident in the 1920s and in the fast growth of the federal bureaucracy in the Roosevelt administration. Holtzman lists three factors that influenced the growing shift of initiative in legislation from the Congress to the President:

- The development of a central legislative clearance and coordinating staff in the executive office of the President and its link with the new concept of a presidential legislative program.
- The tremendous expansion and complexity of legislation, which imposed a considerable burden upon the ability of Congress to cope with its primary responsibility.
- The promotional activities of the new governmental agencies, created initially by the Roosevelt administration and expanded as a result of the war and postwar crises.[43]

Holtzman identified evolutionary steps in how the executive system approached Congress in the environment of this cooperative shift in roles.[44] He viewed LL as a final developmental step in the reshaping of the executive system that resulted in a strengthening of the presidency relative to Congress and the executive political leadership in relation to the bureaucracy.[45]

The first step centered on the "establishment of budgetary controls at the departmental level, under the impact of the Budget and Accounting Act (of 1921) and in response to the guidance of the Budget Bureau in the Office of the President." Thus, the passage of the Budget and Accounting Act of 1921 formally shifted the initiative for developing the fiscal and legislative program of the federal government from the Congress to the Presidency.[46] Now that the President had the responsibility of proposing an integrated budget to Congress, this necessitated greater White House control over departmental budgets. Departmental secretaries were given additional staff to help evaluate bureau proposals.

The second step required "acceptance of the concept of legislative programming at the White House and the secretarial levels and the strengthening of the office of the general counsel or solicitor within the departments." The final step involved the development and acceptance of separate LLs with specialized staffs, most of which evolved from the offices of general counsel, at the departmental and White House levels.[47]

Besides departmental expenditure policies, the departmental secretaries were held increasingly accountable by the White House for advancing the administration's departmental programs in Congress.

Legislative programming at the White House gained momentum when the Bureau of the Budget was transferred from the Treasury Department to the Executive Office of the President in 1939. The Bureau was now to "assist the President by clearing and coordinating departmental advice on proposed legislation, and by making recommendations as to presidential action on legislative enactments in accordance with past practice."[48] Specialized White House staff now worked with counterparts in the departments to ensure departmental legislative proposals were consistent with administration program guidelines.[49]

There were serious concerns at this time by elite actors in both the executive and legislative branches that excessive power rested in the growing bureaucracy and around particularized interests of "bureau chiefs" rather than in political leaders who were responsible for running those departments.[50] A 1949 Hoover Commission highlighted that bureau chiefs of the departments and not the department secretaries were developing and promoting legislation with individual Members and committees. In addition, bureau chiefs often undermined the authority and effectiveness of departmental secretaries by their close working relationships with cooperating Members of Congress.[51]

Under White House pressure to control their legislative programs, departmental secretaries assigned these responsibilities to lawyers in their General Counsel office. Their legal expertise on legislative intent in brokering technical compromises and their frequent associations with members on drafting legislation made them an obvious choice. Since the lawyers were responsible for coordinating legislative programs, it made sense for these same individuals to conduct LL as well. These important offices were strengthened with larger and more specialized staff. Seven out of ten department LLs developed out of their General Counsel's or solicitor's office.[52]

The key hurdle to acceptance of LLs in the federal government was the high-profile, bipartisan recommendations of the Hoover Commission in 1949. The Commission's recommendations helped legitimize LLs by stressing that they were the responsible to the departmental secretaries and that their operations should be institutionalized. At that time, only the DOD had special LL staffs organized at the departmental level. Following the recommendations, the State Department established the Office of Assistant Secretary for Congressional Relations in 1949.[53] The formal establishment of special LL offices in the White House by Presidents Eisenhower and Kennedy further institutionalized and strengthened LLs in the departments.[54] By 1955, the DOD, State, and Health, Education and Welfare, Post Office, and Commerce Departments established LL offices in varying degrees of specialization. All 10 departments had specialized LLs by 1963, with only Post Office and Justice LL staff focusing on congressional relations less than full-time.[55]

Until the late 1940s the Department of War (Army/Air Force) and Department of the Navy (Navy/USMC) were cabinet-level departments. After the 1947 Defense Reorganization Act created a DOD with its own LL, it was decided (and required by Congress) to keep most of the Pentagon's LL assets at the military service (less partisan) level. Additionally, the LL congressional focus has deep roots in the military departments. The military service departments were unique in organizing staff at their highest levels to focus on congressional concerns decades before LL offices formally came into existence.

Holtzman's study draws three major conclusions that are relevant to this volume. First, he concludes that LLs are significant in strengthening the senior political executives in the departments and the White House in their relations with Congress. Leadership was institutionalized at both executive levels with LLs being a critical component in carrying information about the decisions of these executive leaders over to the Hill. Second, he concludes that LLs greatly strengthen the senior political executives in the departments and White House to better control the bureaucracy. A departmental LL operation makes it more difficult for non-elected bureaucrats, who lack political responsibility for programs, to operate with Congress independently. Finally, he concludes that, in general, Congress values its relations with the LLs and view their *roles* as legitimate and necessary.

While the executive branch is responsible for defining the roles and determining the significance attributed their LL personnel and their liaising roles in general, it is the Congress who has granted legitimacy to these roles and has defined what is and is not permissible liaising activities in carrying out these roles through the formal and informal restrictions on liaisers previously discussed. Morris Fiorina's critical commentary of Congress and the Washington establishment in 1977 highlighted how LL operations, an executive branch innovation, enable both branches to take mutual advantage of each other. "I wish to suggest how congressman have taken advantage of an executive innovation, an innovation probably intended to take advantage of them."

MILITARY SERVICE LEGISLATIVE LIAISON OPERATIONS

Many might logically assume that patterned differences in the way the various military services liaise Congress are largely a function of differences in their LL office structure and organization.[56] However, as Figures 1-1 through 1-4 depict, the military service LL offices are more similar than different in structure

Figure 1-1
Military Service Legislative Liaison Organization

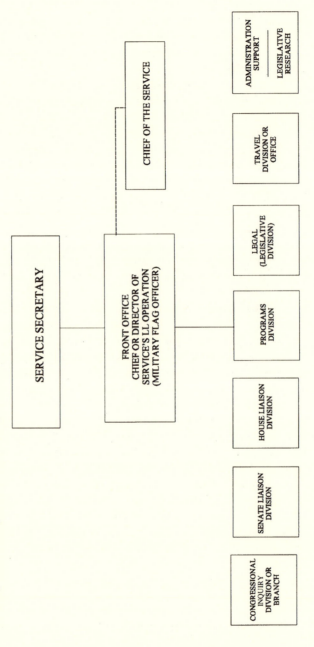

SERVICE SECRETARY

FRONT OFFICE
CHIEF OR DIRECTOR OF
SERVICE'S LL OPERATION
(MILITARY FLAG OFFICER)

CHIEF OF THE SERVICE

CONGRESSIONAL
INQUIRY
DIVISION OR
BRANCH

SENATE LIAISON
DIVISION

HOUSE LIAISON
DIVISION

PROGRAMS
DIVISION

LEGAL
(LEGISLATIVE
DIVISION)

TRAVEL
DIVISION OR
OFFICE

ADMINISTRATION
SUPPORT
——
LEGISLATIVE
RESEARCH

Figure 1-2
Army Legislative Liaison Organization

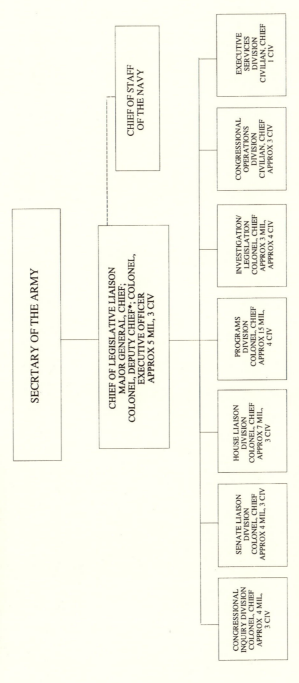

SECRTARY OF THE ARMY

CHIEF OF STAFF OF THE NAVY

CHIEF OF LEGISLATIVE LIAISON
MAJOR GENERAL, CHIEF;
COLONEL, DEPUTY CHIEF*; COLONEL,
EXECUTIVE OFFICER
APPROX 5 MIL, 3 CIV

CONGRESSIONAL INQUIRY DIVISION
COLONEL, CHIEF
APPROX 4 MIL, 3 CIV

SENATE LIAISON DIVISION
COLONEL, CHIEF
APPROX 4 MIL, 3 CIV

HOUSE LIAISON DIVISION
COLONEL, CHIEF
APPROX 7 MIL, 3 CIV

PROGRAMS DIVISION
COLONEL, CHIEF
APPROX 15 MIL, 4 CIV

INVESTIGATION/ LEGISLATION
COLONEL, CHIEF
APPROX 3 MIL, 4 CIV

CONGRESSIONAL OPERATIONS DIVISION
CIVILIAN, CHIEF
APPROX 3 CIV

EXECUTIVE SERVICES DIVISION
CIVILIAN, CHIEF
1 CIV

*This position was changed from a colonel to a civilian slot in 1996. The Army leadership, however, is considering upgrading this key position to brigadier general (similar to Air Force organizational structure) in 1999, to improve Army relations on the Hill and strengthen Army LL organization.

Figure 1-3
Air Force Legislative Liaison Organization

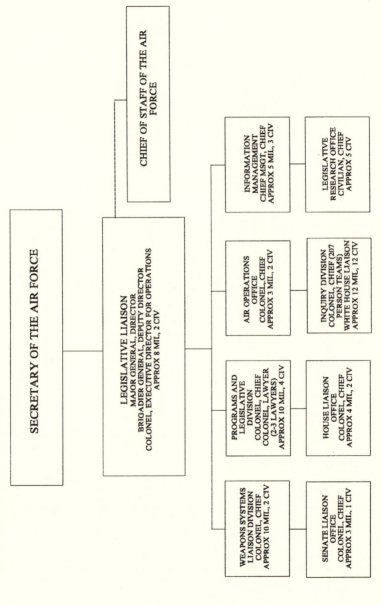

SECRETARY OF THE AIR FORCE

CHIEF OF STAFF OF THE AIR FORCE

LEGISLATIVE LIAISON
MAJOR GENERAL, DIRECTOR
BRIGADIER GENERAL, DEPUTY DIRECTOR
COLONEL, EXECUTIVE DIRECTOR FOR OPERATIONS
APPROX 8 MIL, 2 CIV

WEAPONS SYSTEMS
LIAISON DIVISION
COLONEL, CHIEF
APPROX 10 MIL, 2 CIV

PROGRAMS AND
LEGISLATIVE
DIVISION
COLONEL, CHIEF
COLONEL, LAWYER
(2-3 LAWYERS)
APPROX 10 MIL, 4 CIV

AIR OPERATIONS
OFFICE
COLONEL, CHIEF
APPROX 3 MIL, 2 CIV

INFORMATION
MANAGEMENT
CHIEF MSGT, CHIEF
APPROX 5 MIL, 3 CIV

SENATE LIAISON
OFFICE
COLONEL, CHIEF
APPROX 3 MIL, 1 CIV

HOUSE LIAISON
OFFICE
COLONEL, CHIEF
APPROX 4 MIL, 2 CIV

INQUIRY DIVISION
COLONEL, CHIEF (207
PERSON TEAMS)
WHITE HOUSE LIAISON
APPROX 12 MIL, 12 CIV

LEGISLATIVE
RESEARCH OFFICE
CIVILIAN, CHIEF
APPROX 5 CIV

Figure 1-4
Navy (U.S. Marine Corps) Legislative Liaison Organization

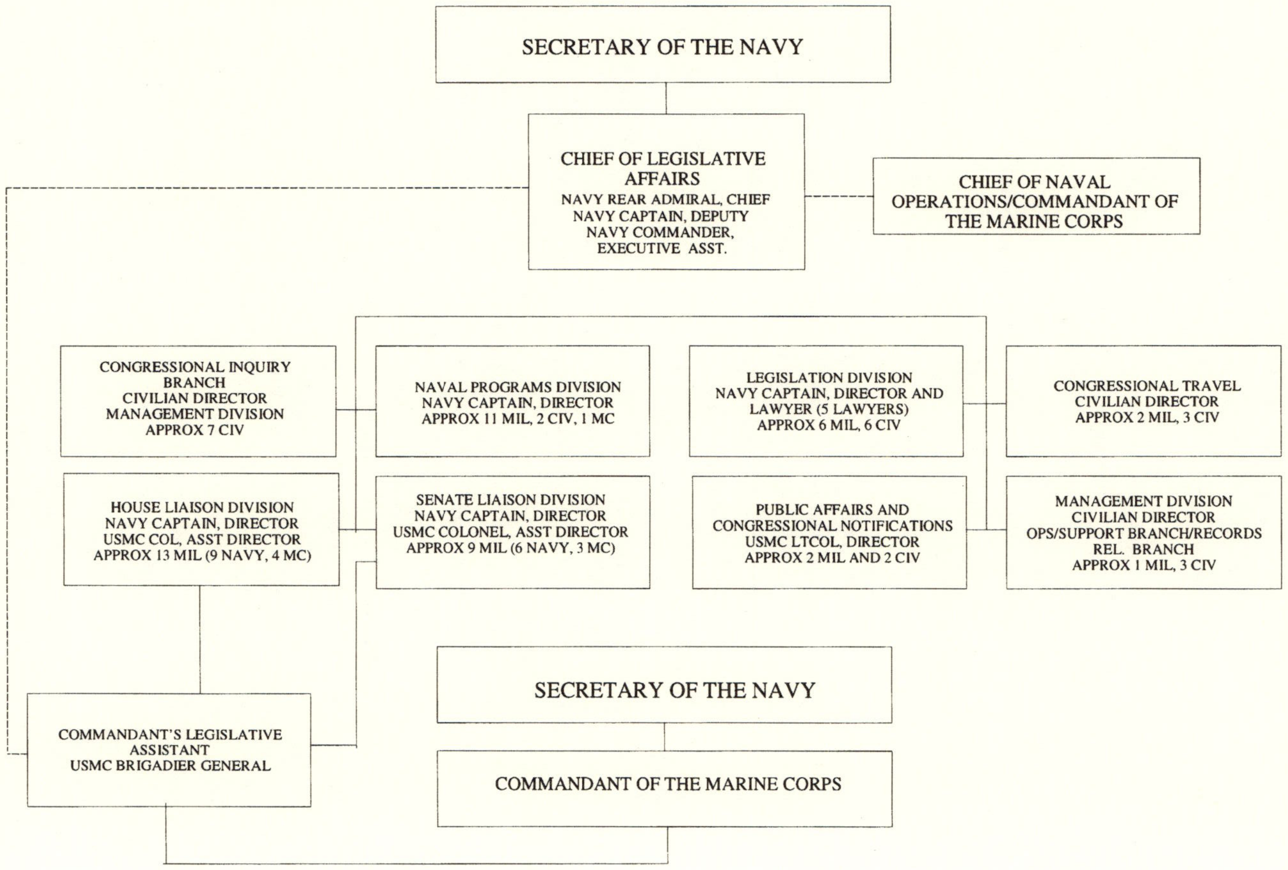

SECRETARY OF THE NAVY

CHIEF OF NAVAL OPERATIONS/COMMANDANT OF THE MARINE CORPS

CHIEF OF LEGISLATIVE AFFAIRS
NAVY REAR ADMIRAL, CHIEF
NAVY CAPTAIN, DEPUTY
NAVY COMMANDER, EXECUTIVE ASST.

CONGRESSIONAL TRAVEL
CIVILIAN DIRECTOR
APPROX 2 MIL, 3 CIV

MANAGEMENT DIVISION
CIVILIAN DIRECTOR
OPS/SUPPORT BRANCH/RECORDS
REL. BRANCH
APPROX 1 MIL, 3 CIV

LEGISLATION DIVISION
NAVY CAPTAIN, DIRECTOR AND
LAWYER (5 LAWYERS)
APPROX 6 MIL, 6 CIV

PUBLIC AFFAIRS AND
CONGRESSIONAL NOTIFICATIONS
USMC LTCOL, DIRECTOR
APPROX 2 MIL AND 2 CIV

NAVAL PROGRAMS DIVISION
NAVY CAPTAIN, DIRECTOR
APPROX 11 MIL, 2 CIV, 1 MC

SENATE LIAISON DIVISION
NAVY CAPTAIN, DIRECTOR
USMC COLONEL, ASST DIRECTOR
APPROX 9 MIL (6 NAVY, 3 MC)

SECRETARY OF THE NAVY

COMMANDANT OF THE MARINE CORPS

CONGRESSIONAL INQUIRY
BRANCH
CIVILIAN DIRECTOR
MANAGEMENT DIVISION
APPROX 7 CIV

HOUSE LIAISON DIVISION
NAVY CAPTAIN, DIRECTOR
USMC COL, ASST DIRECTOR
APPROX 13 MIL (9 NAVY, 4 MC)

COMMANDANT'S LEGISLATIVE
ASSISTANT
USMC BRIGADIER GENERAL

and organization. All service LL offices contain some form of these operational structures designed to carry out the following basic functions or responsibilities.

The Front Office: Located in the Pentagon, this is the office of the CLL, a flag officer, who is directly responsible to the service secretary and responds to the service chief when required on all matters concerning relations with Congress.

Congressional Inquiries: Located primarily in the Pentagon, this division focuses on providing timely information in response to constituent inquiries, written and/or verbal, from Members or staff.

Senate Liaison Division (SLD): Collocated in the Russell Senate Office building, SLD is a one-stop shop for any senator or Senate staff to ask questions or address concerns on a service-related matter.

House Liaison Division (HLD): Collocated in the Rayburn House Office building, HLD is a one-stop shop for any House Member or staff to ask questions or address concerns on a service-related matter.

Programs: This division, located in the Pentagon, is responsible for communicating information and service positions on all weapons systems and hardware programs, and on certain service policy matters.

Legal: LL lawyers coordinate, monitor, and report legislative and investigative actions of interest to that service.

Travel: This division has responsibility for assisting LL escort officers in obtaining military and civilian transportation support and in arranging schedules and other travel logistics to facilitate congressional travel to military facilities or other locations related to military activities.

Administration Support: This division or section performs administrative support for all LL operations.

A comparison of the schematic figures demonstrates the structural similarities of the Army, Air Force, and Navy LL organizations and their relationships to their service secretary and their service chief. However, some interesting differences in structures and functions exist as well.

In the LL front offices, it is apparent that the Air Force has the benefit of a flag officer in both its Chief and Deputy Chief positions. The Army had a similar arrangement, but decided to downgrade this position in the 1980s when the services were forced to reduce the number of their flag officer slots. There are many advantages to having a general officer in the Deputy position, according to current Air Force LL and retired Army LL personnel. First, it is a natural position to groom a future chief of LL. Second, having an additional general officer slot in LL institutionally increases the upward mobility for officers with special talents in this area and provides greater opportunities for future Army leaders to gain experience with the Hill.

The Navy Chief of Legislative Affairs is a one-star flag officer, unlike his two-star Army and Air Force counterparts.[57] However, he is assisted in many of his legislative efforts on the Hill by the one-star "Legislative Assistant to the Commandant" of the U.S. Marine Corps. This Marine Brigadier General is not a formal part of the Navy LL organization, but he works closely with Marine Corps (and Navy) personnel in the Navy LL organization to represent Marine and Navy interests with Congress. The Army is the only departmental service to have one flag officer whose primary focus is communicating service interests to Congress.

Differences in structure and function are also apparent in the inquiry divisions of the various LLs. The Army's LL inquiry division is not only the largest but is handled primarily by Army civilians. The Army inquiry division handles only written inquiries, oversees and manages the casework investigation, and writes the final responses to Members of Congress. The Air Force inquiry division is one-third the size but is similarly composed of correspondence teams assigned casework concerns of individuals for a state or regional area. However, junior Air Force officers, rather than civilians, handle the casework. The Navy's inquiry branch is much smaller, all civilian, and primarily serves to track rather than prepare congressional inquiries. Navy inquiries are sent to responsible Navy field-type units to prepare responses.

With the essence of the Army being its soldiers and force structure rather than weapon system platforms, it is not unexpected that it would have the largest inquiry branch, as personnel issues dominate congressional inquiries. While Army inquiry division always relied heavily on Army civilians, the most notable change over the last five years has been the Army decision to cut by over 50 percent officer involvement in Army LL casework, eliminating an important grooming ground for Army LL officers, according to retired and active Army LL interviewees.

The Air Force's Inquiry Division serves this ancillary grooming function, by having Air Force majors in charge of their inquiry "blue and silver"[58] teams composed of captains and majors working the actual cases. The Air Force sees this flow of young officers into Air Force LL as a positive institutional mechanism that provides a wide base of officers with an understanding of Congress, regardless of whether they ultimately serve in LL, that makes them more effective in their future operational and Washington assignments.

The Navy has the one LL office to operate a public affairs and congressional notifications branch, which may contribute to or be a reflection of the emphasis that the Navy's civilian leadership since World War II has placed on senior naval officers engaging with external audiences to ensure future Navy relevance. Thus, it is no surprise that the Navy is viewed by the Hill as the most effective service department in representing its interests to the Hill.

The Air Force is perceived by many interviewees to be the most astute of the various services in winning resource and policy battles within the Pentagon and OSD in particular.

It is interesting that only Air Force LL has a White House Liaison branch or structure in its formal LL organization. The chief of this branch visits the White House Military Office (WHMO) one or two times a month to develop effective liaison relationships with the rotating Chief of Staff or civilian.[59]

Hill interviewees perceived the Army as the most honest and straightforward of the services in representing its interests, but also the most wary of engaging with external audiences in representing those same interests. Therefore, it should come as no surprise that the Army is the only service LL to have a division of military lawyers with a focus on investigations, Investigations and Legislation (I&L), and that this office of Army LL lawyers is separate from the LL programs officers working Army "legislative" policy issues on the Hill. The institutional separation of the LL lawyers from the LL "programs" policy advocates promotes greater focus and saliency of the lawyer's interests in investigations and their cautionary role in keeping the Army leadership out of real or perceptual trouble on the Hill and within OSD.

Navy LL has a legislation division composed primarily of lawyers as well, but this same division serves as the Navy's policy team to the Hill on personnel, health, environmental, base realignment and closure (BRAC) and other Navy-wide policy issues. The Air Force, like the Navy, has combined its policy team with its lawyers in its "Programs and Legislation" division, but unlike the Navy, only two or three of its policy team LL officers are actually lawyers.

However, despite these minor differences, the structures are very similar and structural differences do not adequately explain different service effectiveness or behavior in representing their interests to Congress. For example, although all services have House and Senate Liaison Divisions located on Capitol Hill, they are operated very differently, a difference in approach that is a function of culture, not structure. Later chapters of this book will examine these cultural underpinnings of behavior.

NOTES

1. Two excellent sources of information addressing restrictions on lobbying by government officials can be found in "Principles of Federal Appropriations Law," GAO/OGC-91-5, vol. 1, 2nd ed. (Washington, DC: General Accounting Office, July 1991), and Attorney General, Office of Legal Counsel of the Department of Justice, *Antilobbying Act Guidelines*, April 18, 1995. These sources provide discussion of the interpretations of the criminal statutes and provisions in Appropriations Acts.

2. See Margaret Susan Thompson, *The Spider's Web—Congress and Lobbying in the Age of Grant* (Ithaca, NY: Cornell University Press, 1985), 56, where she cites typical negative definitions of lobbying from political dictionaries of the late nineteenth century. An example: "Lobby, The, is a term applied collectively to men that make a business of corruptly influencing legislators. The individuals are called lobbyists. Their objective is usually accomplished by means of money paid to Members, but any other means that is considered feasible is employed." Eberit Brown and Albert Strauss, *A Dictionary of American Politics* (New York: Barnes and Noble, 1968), 253. See also Lester W. Milbrath, *The Washington Lobbyists* (Chicago: Rand McNally, 1963), 6, for a documentation of studies that support the contention that "the public and press have a lively distrust of lobbying."

3. Major General Jerry C. Harrison, the Army's CLL 1992–1995, understood well the negative baggage that the audience he was addressing associated with the term.

However, political scientists, who understand the legitimacy of and positive functions of lobbying, see the Army and all other public agencies as engaged in a lobbying activity.

4. Congress, Senate, Special Committee to Investigate Political Activities, Lobbying and Campaign Contributions (McClellan Committee), *Final Report*, 85th Cong., 1st sess., May 31, 1957, 64–65, in Lester W. Milbrath, *The Washington Lobbyists* (Chicago: Rand McNally, 1963), 7.

5. Jeffrey Birnbaum, *The Lobbyists* (New York: Random House, 1992), 8–9, states that the term originated in Britain "to refer to journalists who stood in lobbies at the House of Commons, waiting to interview newsmakers. Its initial modern usage in America came in 1829. According to essayist H.L. Mencken, "privilege seekers in Albany were referred to as lobby-agents. Three years later, the term was abbreviated to 'lobbyist' and was heard frequently in Washington, mostly as an expression of disdain." Other accounts claim that the more widespread use of the term derived from privilege seekers waiting in the lobby of the Willard Hotel in Washington, DC, to influence soon-to-be-inaugurated President Grant.

6. Jeffrey M. Berry, *The Interest Group Society* (Boston: Little, Brown and Company, 1984), 6.

7. Milbrath, *The Washington Lobbyists*, 8.

8. Instead of lobbyists, they often refer to themselves as managers or directors of congressional relations, congressional consultants, legislative affairs specialists, or chief of Washington operations, to name just a few.

9. "Principles of Federal Appropriations Law," 4–157.

10. 18 U.S. Code, Section 1913. It was the grassroots lobbying practices of that era by bureau chiefs that gave rise to this criminal statute and is the basis for its interpretation today. The following remarks from Representative Good in the floor debate took place for the original legislation referenced in 58 Cong. Rec. 403 (1919) and quoted in GAO Report OGC-91–5: "The bill also contains a provision which . . . will prohibit a practice that has been indulged in so often, without regard to what administration is in power—the practice of a bureau chief or the head of a department writing letters throughout the country, sending telegrams throughout the country, for this organization, for this man, for that company to write his congressman, to wire his congressman, in behalf of this or that legislation. The gentleman from Kentucky . . . during the closing days of the last Congress was greatly worried because he had on his desk thousands upon thousands of telegrams that had been started right here in Washington by some official wiring out for people to wire Congressman Sherley. . . . Now, it was never the intention of Congress to appropriate money for this purpose, and section 1913 will absolutely put a stop to that sort of thing."

11. Section 8014 in the 1995 Defense Appropriations Act, Public Law 103–335. This same type of prohibitive provision is found in Appropriations Acts other than Defense.

12. Section 8001, 1995 Defense Appropriations Act, Public Law 103–335. This prohibition has appeared in Appropriations Acts in some form since 1951.

13. 39 U.S. Code, Section 3204 (a). Note that there is no requirement that the request for the article or document be previously received in writing.

14. U.S. Department of Justice, Office of Legal Counsel, "Constraints Imposed by 18 USC § 1913 on Lobbying Efforts," September 28, 1989; and "Anti-Lobbying Act Guidelines," memorandum, April 14, 1995, and supporting document, "Guidelines on 18 USC § 1913."

15. "Principles of Federal Appropriations Law," 4–156.

16. U.S. Department of Justice, Office of Legal Counsel, I.

17. "Principles of Federal Appropriations Law," 4–158.

18. Ibid., 2.

19. Ibid. "Although the 1989 Barr opinion does not define the meaning of "substantial" grass roots campaigns, the opinion notes that the 1919 legislative history cites an expenditure of $7,500—roughly equivalent to $50,000 in 1989—for a campaign of letter-writing urging recipients to contact Congress."

20. U.S. Department of Justice, Office of Legal Counsel, "Constraints," 2–3.

21. Ibid., 3.

22. Congress, House, Select Committee on Lobbying Activities, *Hearings on Legislative Activities of Executive Agencies*, 81st Cong., 2nd sess. (Washington, DC: U.S. Government Printing Office, 1950), part 10, 1–2 and 61, in Abraham Holtzman, *Legislative Liaison: Executive Leadership in Congress* (Chicago: Rand McNally, 1970), 44–46. Holtzman highlights that the Chairman of this select Committee interpreted the Anti-Lobbying Act law as recognizing "the necessity for the executive branch to be able to make its views known to Congress on all matters on which it had responsibilities, duties, and opinions. Executive agencies, "he affirmed," had a definite requirement to express their views to Congress, to request legislation, to draft bills, to make suggestions; they had the right to seek to 'influence, encourage, promote or retard legislation' *through proper channels*."

23. See note 81 in "Principles of Federal Appropriations Law," 4–158. For commentary favoring a broader interpretation, see Richard L. Engstrom and Thomas G. Walker, "Statutory Restraints on Administrative Lobbying—'Legal Fiction,' " 19 *Journal of Public Law* 89 (1970).

24. Holtzman, *Legislative Liaison*, 64–76. Holtzman's discussion of informal limitations imposed on executive lobbying is by far the best and appears, from my interviews and experience in working in Army LL, to be accurate 25 years after the publication of his work.

25. Ibid., 65.

26. An SASC (and former Army officer) PSM recounted an example of an Army general officer who was escorted by an Army LL lieutenant colonel to discuss a training mishap before SASC PSMs. All the Committee staff were former military or combat veterans who bit their lips and quietly listened as this general talked down to them about how realistic training can lead to these accidents as if they were novices to the military. The SASC PSM placed more of the blame on the LL officer for not preparing the general on his target audience. Violation of this informal limitation results, as in this example, in the agency official's message being ineffectual at best, and can often prompt a Committee reaction that is embarrassing or costly to the agency involved.

27. Military service LL officers have been quickly relieved of their LL duties when in frustration they allow an issue to get personal. This occurred once when a service LL officer foolishly faxed another service LL officer a heated message questioning the motives of that service in regard to an ongoing interservice issue. Not only was this a mistake in getting personal with another service's LL officer, but the officer in question included a senior PSM's name on the fax as well. Needless to say, the fax was soon in the hands of that PSM and the LL officer's actions were reported by the PSM directly to the Chief and Secretary of that service. The final message conveyed by the irate PSM was that this LL officer would never be allowed to do business with his side of the Committee. At that point, the officer's utility as an LL officer was damaged beyond repair.

28. Holtzman, *Legislative Liaison*, 68–70. He notes that the memorandum circulated by the Assistant Secretary of State for Congressional Relations and other information on the incident can be found in Congress, Senate, Committee on the Judiciary, Subcommittee to Investigate the Administration of the Internal Security Act, *Hearings on State Department Security*, 87th Cong., 2nd sess. (Washington, DC: U.S. Government Printing Office, March 15, 1962), 429–430.

29. It is important to note that the Assistant Secretary of the State justified his action in terms of his department providing better services to Congress and of better agency understanding of congressional concerns. These justifications were consistent with rather than contrary to congressional norms and needs. He in no way tried to justify the propriety of his office intervening between the communications of Congress and individuals in his department, though Members strongly believed this was a primary motivation behind the effort. In this sense they believed he was threatening a valuable norm that would obstruct their access to valuable and timely agency information.

30. Holtzman, *Legislative Liaison*, 70–76.

31. See Richard Fenno, *The Power of the Purse: Appropriations Politics in Congress* (Boston: Little, Brown & Company, 1966), 98–102.

32. Holtzman, *Legislative Liaison*, 73. He notes that Members and staff on the Appropriations Committee are aware that their contacts and associations into the agency's comptroller world must be protected in order to garner facts and information from them that they need. LL policy officers might obstruct the release of this data as detrimental to political efforts to garner more spending that currently is not on the books.

33. Ibid., 74. Congressional norms reflect the fact that Congress values traditions. Traditionally, authorizers and appropriators have always been handled by different people. Congress respects and prefers these established and traditional arrangements for dealing with the executive branch.

34. Milbrath, *Organizational Culture and Leadership*, 20–21.

35. Holtzman, *Legislative Liaison*, 289–290.

36. Ibid., 290.

37. Bruce C. Wolpe, *Lobbying Congress: How the System Works* (Washington, DC: Congressional Quarterly Press, 1990), 3–61.

38. This research is indebted to Mr. Win Shaw, lobbyist for Gulfstream Aerospace, Inc., former Army LL officer, for many of the insights presented in this section.

39. Michael T. Isenberg, *Shield of the Republic* (New York: St. Martin's Press, 1993), 438–440. Many former Navy LL officers interviewed gave Secretary of the Navy Lehman credit for strengthening Navy understanding and experience in working with the Hill. Lehman is credited with initiating the home-porting theme in his push for a 600-ship Navy. If you have a service secretary out in front on these important service issues, it frees the senior flag officers to follow up with the supporting requirements and professional advocacy.

40. For a more detailed discussion of the literature in this area, see Steven Scroggs, "Army Relations with Congress: The Impact of Culture and Organization" (Ph.D. diss., Duke University, 1996), 39–43.

41. Holtzman, *Legislative Liaison*, 2. Based on interviews with LL agents at the 10 cabinet departments and the White House, senior officials in the executive branch, and Members and staff on the Hill, his analysis comprehensively addressed all department LLs operating at the end of the Kennedy administration.

42. Until the late 1940s, the Department of War (Army/Air Force) and Department of the Navy (Navy/USMC) were cabinet-level departments. After the 1947 Defense Reorganization Act created a DOD with its own LL, it was decided (and required by Congress) to keep most of the Pentagon's LL assets at the military service level. Additionally, the LL congressional focus has deep roots in the military departments. The military service departments were unique in organizing staff at their highest levels to focus on congressional concerns, decades before LL offices formally came into existence. Holtzman references Neustadt's work with this point. Richard E. Neustadt, ''Presidential Clearance of Legislation'' (Ph.D. diss., Columbia University, 1950), 309. Finally, if military service budgets, their LLs, and other agency resources are compared with other cabinet-level departments, they often exceed or are comparable to these higher level departments. The differences that do exist come largely from the fact that military services have no political appointees in their LL operations; they are military and civilian (civil servant) personnel. Headed by a uniformed military flag officer, service LLs attempt to avoid any perception of partisanship.

43. Holtzman, *Legislative Liaison*, 6. Congress was also turning to the executive branch more frequently for help in meeting its primary responsibilities. Members found the legislative demands following the New Deal and the end of World War II increasing complex. Whether it was requests for drafting services, technical information, or constituent-oriented services. Members increasingly turned to the executive branch for assistance. In meeting this increased role of government, the departments began to use their inroads of information and services to Members and their limited staff to promote administration and departmental legislative proposals and programs. Richard Neustadt highlighted the ''increasing initiative in legislation on the part of the expanding promotional agencies'' in his 1950 work on the Bureau of the Budget. See Neustadt, ''Presidential Clearance of Legislation,'' 309.

44. Literature that examines this shift of initiative and growth of the bureaucracy includes Richard E. Neustadt; Paul H. Appleby, *Big Democracy* (New York: Knopf, 1945); Wilred E. Binkley, *The Man in the White House: His Powers and Duties*, rev. ed. (New York: Harper & Row, 1964), chaps. 7 and 8; Lawrence H. Chamberlain, *The President, Congress, and Legislation* (New York: Columbia University Press, 1946); Edwin C. Corwin, *The President, Office and Powers, 1787–1957* (New York: New York University Press, 1957), chap. 7; Clinton I. Rossiter, *The American Presidency*, 2nd ed. (New York: Harcourt, Brace & World, 1960); David B. Truman, *The Congressional Party: A Case Study* (New York: Wiley, 1959), 1–10, 317–319; Peter Woll, *American Bureaucracy* (New York: Norton, 1963).

45. Holtzman, *Legislative Liaison*, 5. This reshaping of the political leadership took place at the departmental and White House levels in relation to Congress.

46. A Bureau of the Budget was created in the same year to assist the president in proposing a fiscal year budget and legislative program.

47. Ibid., 9.

48. Ibid., 6. He quotes testimony by Roger W. Jones, Assistant Director for Legislative Reference, Bureau of the Budget, U.S. House of Representatives, Select Committee on Lobbying Activities, Hearings on Legislative Activities of Executive Agencies, 81st Cong., 2nd sess. (Washington, DC,: U.S. Government Printing Office, 1950), parts 10, 8. The shift of initiative from the Congress to the president continued with the passage of the Employment Act of 1946, allowing the Budget Bureau's legislative clearance role to expand into responsibility for the ''President's legislative program.'' Now the presi-

dent would deliver three major messages at the beginning of each session: the state-of-the-union message, the budget message, and an economic report.

49. Ibid., 7. Additionally, the Bureau of Budget required departments and agencies to submit "all drafts of legislation which they themselves originated, all reports they made on legislation as requested by the committees and by individual congressmen, and even, on very important matters, copies of formal statements of testimony, so that the bureau could determine their relationship to the President's program."

50. LL officers working directly for departmental secretaries have only been on the executive-legislative scene since the late 1940s.

51. Holtzman, *Legislative Liaison*, 2–3. He refers to the Commission on Organization of the Executive-Branch of the Government, Task Force Report on Departmental Management (Washington, DC: U.S. Government Printing Office, January 1949), parts 1–2, 1–35.

52. Ibid., 11.

53. G. Russell Pipe, "Congressional Liaison: The Executive Branch Consolidates its Relations with Congress," *Public Administration Review* 26 (March 1966), 15.

54. Holtzman, *Legislative Liaison*, 14–15.

55. Ibid., and 4.

56. Morris P. Fiorina, *Congress: Keystone of the Washington Establishment*, 2nd ed. (New Haven, CT: Yale University Press, 1989), 63–67. "In theory the establishment of liaison officers would help the executive branch to lead Congress, to coordinate the decentralized power centers in that body, to show parochial committee barons why they should not amend a presidential initiative umpteen ways to Sunday. In practice, however, liaison officers are a hot line into their respective departments."

57. According to interview comments from a retired Navy LL officers, the CLA position in the Navy used to be a two-star authorized slot that the Navy downgraded when flag officer endstrength was reduced in the late 1980s.

58. Blue and silver are the official Air Force colors that symbolize sky and aircraft, central to the relevancy of the institution.

59. The White House Military Office (WHMO) is composed of approximately 12 to 13 people with a four-star equivalent political appointee as its director and a military 0–6-grade (colonel/captain) military officer as its Chief of Staff. The WHMO is responsible for the 1,800 military personnel who provide communication, medical, transportation, and other logistical support necessary in White House operations and travel.

Chapter 2

Roles of Legislative Liaison and Military Service Liaisers

We [Congress] couldn't operate effectively without military service *advocacy* taking place that explains and justifies the administration's programs and budget for that fiscal year. Frankly, the antilobbying provisions as written are asinine. If taken literally, Congress would be the loser. We need the services' credible input.

—Member of Congress on the House Armed Services Committee

To understand how liaising in the LL offices of the military services is *effectively* conducted, the roles that LL and senior military liaisers serve in the executive-legislative arena need to be examined. The roles of LL personnel are products of the expectations and desires of the executive and legislative branches they attempt to serve and bridge. Holtzman identifies the executive branch as largely responsible for defining the roles and determining the significance attributed to its LL personnel and their roles.[1] Executive branch leaders can enhance or discount the importance of the liaising roles.

However, as discussed previously, Congress, which views these roles as legitimate, is largely responsible for establishing the "rules of the game" and defining the scope of what is permissible in carrying out these roles.[2] Congress finds it in its self-interest to approve and accept executive LL activity, regardless of its formal prohibitions against executive lobbying. Congress, however, also carefully guards its legislative prerogatives and has both formal and informal ways to control the climate of permissiveness given to the activities of LL and other liaising personnel. Congress in large part determines the latitude given to LL officers in carrying out these roles. This latitude is given on both an individual Member and corporate congressional basis.

Good LL officers must be sensitive to and work to keep both their executive superiors and legislative target audience informed and satisfied. Lost confidence with either client will either end the LL office conduit or marginalize its usefulness; this holds true whether it is the result of an action by an individual LL officer or an entire departmental LL operation. Once a conduit is severed or adversely impacted, it may take years to reestablish.

Good executive liaison activity for the military services involves excelling and having a reputation with both branches of government for excelling in seven interrelated roles, adapted from Holtzman's cabinet-level departmental study:

1. Advising the service secretary and senior military leadership on congressional matters and concerns.

2. Speaking for and representing the service secretary and senior service military leadership on issues to Congress.

3. Facilitating and coordinating the most effective service-congressional interaction.

4. Gathering intelligence on congressional matters and ensuring that timely information is communicated to the Hill.

5. Expediting constituent-oriented services to Congress.

6. Providing legislative-oriented services and working with the legislative ranking and minority leadership, committee members, and supporters as *policy or information collaborators* on issues deemed important by the service and/or administration.

7. Serving as a *policy advocate* on service and administration supported issues with Congress.[3]

Holtzman's role of ''administration partisans'' is not appropriate for military service LLs, and service LLs are effective by avoiding this partisan role.[4] Military liaisers must be sensitive to political dynamics in working with the various actors in the executive-legislative systems, but must work to avoid engaging in partisan activity. It is also significant that no political appointee works in the service LL officers and that each service LL is headed by a uniformed flag officer who wears his uniform on the Hill. Because most service LL officers are military, displays of partisanship are both inappropriate and counter to overall military culture that supports civilian, not party, control of the military.[5]

ADVISING THE SERVICE SECRETARY AND SENIOR MILITARY LEADERSHIP

Each of the military services has a flag officer who heads its LL operation. These flag officers are the principal staff assistants responsible to their respective service secretary for the department's relations and liaison with all Members, staff, and committees, except for the Appropriations Committees.[6]

While this role is especially applicable to the heads of each LL operation, it applies as well to more junior LL officers who perform this role on a more narrow set of issues or under particular circumstances where they are representing the head of LL at a meeting. The adviser role allows LL officers to give the secretary and the senior military leadership advice and counsel on what is taking place on the Hill and what should be done in response or in anticipation of congressional activities or events. LL officers can be instrumental in advising the senior leadership on how those in Congress will be likely to react to service proposals or actions. An astute LL officer can be invaluable in devising strategies for acquiring support for a service proposal or countering a threat to a specific service effort or program. The strategies usually involve whom to see, a timeline of departmental activity, who from the department should carry the message, and key aspects of the message that must be conveyed upfront. This role can keep the secretary and the senior leadership from inadvertently creating problems on the Hill and advised of ways to mitigate those that are unavoidable.

LL advice deals with both process and substantive aspects of a problem. These liaisers are not the subject matter experts, but over time become well-grounded in these issue areas. They must be able to understand the substance of an issue in the context of potential political problems that might surface on the Hill, and advise the senior military leadership accordingly.

REPRESENTING THE SERVICE SECRETARY AND SENIOR SERVICE MILITARY LEADERSHIP

A good LL officer, especially the head of the LL operation, must be seen by the Congress and others in the executive branch as speaking for the service secretary and the senior service military leadership on congressional concerns. This allows LL personnel to directly and quickly deal with many matters on the Hill for the secretary and the service. It allows matters to get resolved before they grow into larger problems and helps the secretary and senior leadership in their efforts to maintain good relations on the Hill. They serve as the first line of information for Members and staff.

An example of this important role is reflected in an account of an Army LL officer during a mark-up of a defense authorization bill before the full House Armed Services Committee (HASC). The LL officer was attending that day because a controversial subcommittee provision that his service, the JCS, and the administration had opposed was being considered. The LL officer, who had responsibility for this issue, felt confident that the votes were there to defeat the subcommittee chairman's provision.

Just as the committee chairman called for this particular subcommittee's mark-up to be addressed before the full committee, the subcommittee chairman entered the committee hearing room in the Rayburn Building waving a piece of paper and announcing that he had spoken by phone with Chairman of the Joint Chiefs of Staff General Powell and that they had agreed on compromise ''report language'' that he, as subcommittee chairman, was now willing to support in lieu of his earlier ''bill language'' provision. The hope that a contentious vote could be avoided and that the Chairman of the JCS, who had earlier expressed his opposition to the controversial subcommittee provision, was now on board, caused an immediate positive reaction by certain Members whom the LL officer classified as supporters.

The LL officer had heard of no such compromise language; he was wearing his beeper and had received no such alert. As this was taking place, one of three Members of Congress sitting together, all of whom were active supporters of the LL officer's campaign to defeat the controversial bill language; looked out in the room and motioned with his finger for the LL officer to come up to the dais. The LL officer joined the Members, one of whom asked bluntly, "Does the Army support this report language as written?"

The LL officer, who knew the Army, JCS, and DOD shared position on this issue, responded, "The Army definitely does not support this language and I'm surprised to hear that the Chairman of the JCS supports it." With that, two Members immediately sprang to their feet, exclaiming that "the Army does not support this compromise language." Chaos ensued as their voices competed with other Members who, upset that the subcommittee chairman was backing down from his earlier bill language provision, were railing against the compromise as well. Committee Chairman Dellums, realizing that he had lost control of the committee, called a prudent short recess. The LL officer telephoned his CLL and explained the situation and his actions. This flag officer was unaware of this compromise and agreed that in its present state it was insupportable. During the recess, the LL officer and supporting Members revised the language to clear up intent. The revised compromise language was supported by the subcommittee chair. It passed, and his former bill language provision was soundly defeated.

The situation in that mark-up session was atypical but provides a clear example of the role good LL officers are expected to play in speaking on behalf of the senior political and military leadership of their service. Possessing a reputation for credibility in speaking on that issue for the service secretary is a prerequisite. The senior service leadership was not in the mark-up session, nor was there time to contact them, but their position was communicated and affected the final outcome.

This spokesman role is important for the Hill as well. It provides the congressional audience with an official service "point of view" that many Members and staff find valuable and convenient. This official administration point of view may differ from the point of view of the senior military leadership or the individual LL officer's own assessment. However, the congressional audience is assured of knowing where the politically responsible executive branch stands on a particular issue without having to schedule a meeting or get through via phone call to these senior civilian leaders. It saves time for parties on both sides of the Potomac.

COORDINATING EFFECTIVE SERVICE–CONGRESSIONAL INTERACTION

Good LL officers spend much of their day coordinating and working to arrange events between executives in the Pentagon and Members and staff on the Hill, a role critical to providing support and direction to the service secretary's programs and to integrating the service's activities into a common departmental approach to Congress. Without an LL operation, a military service would have far more of its individual divisions, branches, and interests, both in and out of Washington, being represented in a freelance, contradicting, and uncoordinated fashion. While a degree of that will always exist because Congress encourages independent sources of reliable information and gets uneasy if LL operations appear to restrict their information flow into the executive branch, good LL operations attempt to convey "one voice" or "one message" to Congress.

In this role, LL officers attempt to "focus the intervention of their senior leaders in the Congress"—get the right senior civilian or military leaders to meet with particular Members or staff at the right time. LL officers understand that their senior leadership, especially their three- and four-star flag officers "constitute an extremely valuable resource around which strategy" should be designed.[7] While a Member of Congress or Committee staff at times asks to meet with a particular person, often they ask for "someone" to come discuss a particular problem. Based on the circumstances of the problem or issue, a good LL officer can gauge the situation and recommend who, at what level, should engage with this congressional audience at a particular time. The request for a meeting could serve as an opportunity to engage a senior civilian or flag officer in developing a relationship with the Member. If the senior official agrees to go the Hill, the LL officer and the subject matter expert from the military staff often will meet the day before to prepare the official or flag officer for the Hill event. If there is no time to prepare, certain situations may call for a senior official to go to the Hill for the sole purpose of listening to the Member's concerns, not providing answers but a commitment to look into the problem for the Member. A timely display of attention by senior officials often goes a long way in resolving problems with individuals on the Hill.

LL officers also coordinate many meetings on the Hill by preparing and escorting non-flag officer substantive experts to answer questions for Members, MLAs, and PSMs on the committees. At times the congressional audience would rather have a subject matter expert who can answer their array of questions than a more senior civilian or military official. The LL officer must play an active role in determining who and how many people should go to the Hill for a particular meeting and in preparing both sides for the upcoming event.

This coordination role also requires LL involvement in the preparation of information papers, reports, and hearing testimony to ensure that what is being stated by one part of the organization is known to another and that the final coordinated product makes sense from a congressional LL perspective. This requires LL officers in many program divisions to review staff actions as they are being developed and before they are sent to the senior service leadership for approval. Incorporating the LL perspective into a staff action early rather than late in the process saves the staff action officer time in the long run and improves the staff product sent to the military leadership and service secretariat in the approval process.

COLLECTING AND DISSEMINATING INFORMATION EFFECTIVELY

This is a critical role that good LL operations perform primarily for the executive and to a lesser degree for the legislative branches. For this study, intelligence is defined broadly as "information and news" that actors in the executive and legislative branches value in order to be effective in their respective spheres of influence. This role involves gathering, assessing, and communicating information and concerns of Members, staff, and committees which in turn enable LL officers to be effective in their aforementioned roles of adviser, coordinator, and spokesman.

Effective LL officers spend considerable time with their congressional audience gathering information on their thinking on general and specific issues; on their constituent concerns; on their likes, dislikes and idiosyncracies; on communications that seem to have broken down; and on rumors of expected activity. Without this Hill information, LL officers are ill equipped to advise the secretary and the senior military leadership about the risks associated with various service proposals. Gathering this information and sharing it with executive branch personnel prior to meetings, hearings, or before issues arise promote more effective preparation and engagement of those executive leaders with Congress and serve the purpose of satisfying the needs of both the members and the service, if possible. Finally, possessing Hill information serves the LL officer well in effectively and sensitively carrying out his spokesman role for the secretary with Congress.

However, more is required of the LL "intelligence" officers than just gathering information; that information must also be placed into context with other Hill information to assess its significance. This assessment capability, a mark of an effective LL officer, is necessary because of the value placed on the currency of information by many legislators and staff and a reticence on the part of many to share this information.

Therefore, a good LL officer must analyze every piece of information, recognizing that it is partial at best and, on the surface, does not necessarily reflect what really motivates the various actors on the Hill. The credibility of LL officers with their executive superiors depends upon a thoughtful and perceptive analysis of information to assess its significance and avoid stirring up wrong or unnecessary controversies in the Pentagon and on the Hill.

An Armed Services Committee staffer who had previous experience in a service LL operation stressed that many times issues are not what they appear on the Hill. It is important to ask the right questions and dig below surface observations and explanations.

Finally, good LL officers know that as information is gathered and assessed, they must ensure that the information flows and is communicated to the senior service leadership in a timely and appropriate manner. Most LL officers will forward and centralize this information with the flag officer who heads the service's LL operation. This flag officer, who normally has previous LL experience, will also have additional information coming in from other LL officers and Hill sources that can aid in both the assessment and communication process. This flag officer will make the decision in most cases about what information goes forward and to whom. Some service LL officers have direct lines of communication to their senior service leadership and only have to keep the head of their LL operation informed of their communications with higher echelons.[8] Much of the intelligence gathered by LL officers is not time-sensitive and is retained by LL officers for later use in preparing senior service leadership for meetings or hearings.

Ensuring that timely information is gathered, assessed, and communicated for use by executive officials is not the only part of LL officers' intelligence role. Information is a two-way street. Effective LL officers work to ensure that they are aware of actions and issues being worked in their service and the Pentagon in general. If an action is moving toward a decision that will have a significant impact on key Members or falls in the domain and interest area of key Committee staff, good LL officers use their contacts in the bureaucracy to learn of the action sooner rather than later. The LL officer then begins to assess the impact and ensures someone more senior in the executive branch is aware of the impact and considering a notification strategy. Someone must communicate service departmental decisions to Members and staff prior to them hearing about them from local media or constituent sources.

Good LL "intelligence" officers want to avoid surprises on the part of both clients. When impending decisions could negatively affect Members, LL officers often can steer key congressional audiences in discussions of the environment in which an issue is being considered and ensure that they understand the vulnerabilities of particular alternatives to begin preparing them for a final decision. However, before a decision has been made, it is imperative that thought and effort go into the notification process. Many times, a recommendation has been made at the service level, but a final decision is still pending approval at the DOD level. This is where service LL officers feel extraordinary pressures to communicate information that was sent higher. However, it is important that they resist this temptation. Credibility should never be risked on what individuals at higher levels may or may not do. There are times when OSD will decide to change parts or all of a recommended plan. Raising expectations, or worse, claiming that certain decisions will be made endangers credibility with a Member or staff.

An effective LL officer will ensure that the sensitivity of the Member's situation is made apparent to the senior leadership and that an adequate notification window of the decision is incorporated into the final decision timeline process for the Member to prepare his response. Members and staff need a jump on the media and their constituents in packaging bad news as well. Nothing burns bridges with Hill supporters like giving them inadequate notice of bad news. Once a service commits that sin, the relationship and trust developed over many years are immediately shattered.[9]

Advisory, spokesman, coordinator, and intelligence roles all feed together in making an effective LL officer. Weakness in one role automatically diminishes the effectiveness in carrying out the others.

Obtaining and disseminating information to contractors and other interested parties are also sometimes an LL function. Working with interest groups involves activities undertaken by only a small number of personnel in a service's LL operation, normally those working on specific weapon system programs or equipment programs on the Hill. The goal of the LL operation is to promote open communication and information exchange between the contractor and the military service.

The goal is to identify where a service's and private industry's priorities coincide or may be disparate, especially because of budgetary constraints. By doing so, corporate allies are less likely to lobby Congress to divert scarce resources from prioritized service programs that otherwise could become the bill payer for the corporation's weapon system request on the Hill.

EXPEDITING CONSTITUENT-ORIENTED INFORMATION AND SERVICES

Effective LL officers for each military service spend a significant amount of effort expediting services and responding in a timely manner to the requests for information and assistance for constituents that emanate from the Congress. Members of Congress, in fulfilling their representational and legislative roles, are constantly making inquiries, asking for information, and requesting favors that will allow them to assist and respond to their constituents, enhance their re-election prospects, and strengthen their effectiveness and stature among their peers. Service LL officers invest significant time and effort reacting daily to these mostly routine but occasionally highly visible and sensitive requests, in order to promote general "goodwill" between their military service and the legislators and staffers involved.

The military services, like all agencies, understand that to be effective on the Hill, programs are more easily justified and explained in a climate of good rather than poor relations. Close attention given Member officers and committees in expediting requested information and services does not guarantee support on future votes, but inattention and insensitivity to Members' constituency and legislative concerns are likely to elicit an attention-getting "antiservice" vote or series of votes until they are taken more seriously. All service LLs, therefore, attempt to expeditiously respond to and resolve problems, regardless of how minor and routine they may appear in a departmental sense, because they are important to Members and their constituents.

Information and services that meet Member constituent needs can be as simple as providing the congressional office with the name and rank of a particular person in a senior position in the military service to opening a "congressional" case and assigning a caseworker to head the investigation of a constituent's claim of wrongdoing or mistreatment. Some information and services can be answered for the Member or staff immediately in person or over the phone, others take months to complete to the satisfaction of the Member. As mentioned earlier, each LL office has a legal section, a section that does primarily casework, a section that focuses on providing information related to a service's programs, and other sections that address more basic Member inquiries and provide military travel assistance. All are designed to provide these services expeditiously and effectively.

LIAISING AS POLICY OR INFORMATION COLLABORATORS

Effective LL officers and operations understand and value the role of *policy* or *information collaborators* as one of their most important to master in improving relations and engaging Members on the Hill. While being one of the most constructive LL roles, it is also one of the most misunderstood, especially among certain military service audiences, because of powerful negative terms associated with and stigmatizing these activities. Many effective liaisers have been stymied by accusations that their collaborative engagements with Members and staff on the Hill might be seen as "lobbying," "political," and/or "partisan." However, policy and information collaboration is fundamental to effective liaising efforts on the Hill. It does not include *partisan* collaboration or entail any efforts to promote *grassroots* pressures on other Members. It is only *political* in the sense of a military senior flag officer understanding the unique congressional terrain in which he operates. Policy and information collaboration involves LL and senior flag liaisers informing, discussing, and shaping defense policy ideas and programs, early rather than late in the policymaking process, with Members of Congress who alone have the delineated constitutional authority to make and authorize defense policy. It selectively seeks congressional input and suggestions during the formative stages of service program planning and seeks to discover and hopefully resolve issue areas that, if ignored, would likely endanger congressional support for the service program.

This policy and information collaborator role is one LL programs officers, working in tandem with their service's senior leadership, must play with Congress in order to effectively influence policymaking critical to service interests. This role is performed effectively only by LL officers and senior military leaders who have earned the trust, credibility, and confidence with both their executive and legislative clients.

This early and continued policy and information collaboration takes place with chairmen and ranking Members, and key PSMs of committees or subcommittees of both parties, to provide them "legislative oriented resources" that better inform and assist them in making policy. Unlike the constituent-oriented services, these resources "are services and favors that enhance the congressman's role as legislator affecting policy and process within his own system, that cater to his status and his influence among his colleagues, and that, at the same time, benefit his district."[10] Holtzman's study of LL operations stressed that providing these legislative-oriented resources pays significantly greater dividends for an agency or department than the constituent-oriented services provided by LL officers in their "expediter of constituent-oriented information and services" role discussed earlier. Military liaisers interviewed find this to still be true 30 years later.

The positive aspects of collaboration—promoting open communications, close relationships, and opportunities to cooperatively affect the other branches' proposals—clearly are in the interest of both executive and legislative actors, but are understood, as we shall see in the next chapter, to varying degrees by the liaisers of the four military services. What's more, a great collaborative service-congressional relationship provides the opportunity for good LL officers to carry out their other essential liaising role: advocacy. Therefore, the ability of LL and senior leadership to effectively advocate and sell programs to Congress is related closely to their established ability to effectively collaborate and engage with Members and staff.

SERVING AS A "POLICY ADVOCATE"

In Holtzman's study of LL officers throughout the federal government, LL officers saw themselves as active advocates for their department in practically all cases. As advocates, these LL officers "explained the features and effects of bills to members of Congress and endeavored to sell them on the legislation."[11] Most effective LL officers will acknowledge that when opportunities present themselves they will attempt to justify, explain, and/or defend a service position or bill. Doing so is expected of them and often appreciated by the Hill as long as it is done with congressional norms and sensitivities in mind. This "advocacy role and expectation" raises a concern with a few LL officers and senior military leaders that "advocating" and trying to sell a position or piece of legislation puts them in a vulnerable position of violating the anti-lobbying provisions. As explained earlier, this is a misperception as long as grassroots lobbying is avoided and congressional norms on liaising are not violated.

The definition of advocate is "one who defends, vindicates, or espouses any cause by argument; a pleader."[12] The expectation of the service secretaries is that each service's LL officers represent and defend the administration's position on a particular issue to Congress. They expect LLs to state the service's position and gauge the level of information needed by a particular Member or staff. The Congress likewise expects the service's LL personnel to attempt to sell, to convince them of, or to justify service positions. They see this role as both proper and necessary for the government to function properly. Holtzman's congressional respondees reflected the view that the advocacy role for LL officers was necessary and legitimate because they provide legislators with a necessary point of view. Interviews with Members for this book showed the same sentiments: "We couldn't operate effectively without military service advocacy taking place that explains and justifies the administration's programs and budget for that fiscal year. Frankly, the anti-lobbying provisions as written are asinine. If taken literally, Congress would be the loser. We need the services' credible input."[13]

An SASC MLA stressed that "a service better initiate contact on anything they believe will be of interest to a Member on the SASC. If they know of something brewing in the House or within another service that is contrary to the administration's position that they believe the SASC needs to know, they should be over advocating the concern and position. The importance of their advocacy can not wait on us asking them about the issue."[14]

All Members and staff did stress the importance of the fact that when senior service leaders and their LLs initiate contact, providing information and advocating positions and programs on the Hill, these positions should be supported and not opposed by the administration, the Secretary of Defense, and their service secretary. Earlier we discussed the Marine Corps' opposition to the Secretary of Defense's and Secretary of the Navy's position that the V-22 program should be killed. What are the "rules of the game" when agency LLs and their senior uniformed leadership differ from the administration on issues? How should LLs and other liaisers be used in these situations? What is considered appropriate and inappropriate behavior on the Hill?

CAUGHT BETWEEN TWO ROCKS

LL officers and their senior military leadership often find themselves caught between two competing and powerful forces: the administration in the form of service secretary and Secretary of Defense positions on the one hand, and Members of Congress who, often for partisan, constituent, institutional, or policy reasons, disagree with those administration positions. This can place LL and especially senior military officers in the difficult predicament of being asked by Members and staff for their professional and personal opinion on issues where disagreement exists with the administration position. This situation is made more complex when the top senior military leadership of a service wages an intense bureaucratic battle on an issue within the Pentagon and loses.

In these situations, both branches have a constitutional basis for placing what amounts to contradictory demands on senior military leaders. As professional members of the executive branch, senior civilian political leaders expect the military to make their case in the Pentagon, but once a decision has been made by the administration, they are expected to support that decision and do nothing formally or informally to undermine that Pentagon position on the Hill. They cite, from the Constitution Article II, Sections 2 and 3, the President's Commander-in-Chief power, the authority that the President "shall commission all the officers of the United States," shall appoint all flag officers for advancement and "shall from time to time give to the Congress information of the state of the union, and recommend to their consideration such measures as *he shall judge necessary and expedient*" [emphasis added] as a basis for this expectation.

Director of Legislative Reference Service Sam Brick, in the DOD Office of General Counsel, emphasized the latter power and stated that the Constitution:

was specific in providing the President, not the Secretary of Defense or a senior military flag officer, as the person who can determine the way his administration provides information on legislation to Congress. Flag officers and service LLs are members of the administration. They represent the service secretary and the administration.[15]

Office of Management and Budget (OMB) Circular A-19 is predicated on this constitutional presidential prerogative and is sent to all military departments and agencies each year to keep them from communicating information that is or may be contrary to administration positions.[16] In regard to agency recommendations for legislation that OMB has reviewed, it states: "In the case of proposed legislation, the originating agency shall not submit to Congress any proposal that OMB has advised is in conflict with the program of the President or has asked the agency to reconsider as a result of the coordination process. In such cases, OMB will inform the agency of the reasons for its actions."[17] In regard to proposed legislation that OMB has not cleared, "Agencies shall not submit to Congress proposed legislation that has not been coordinated and cleared within the executive branch in accordance with this circular."[18]

The outlined prohibitions and constraints in the Circular are partial in nature, referring largely to written material and information; the regulation does not prohibit agency actors from talking about proposed legislation, even during hearings, as long as they are precise in accurately articulating the administration's position on their recommendation or analysis and characterizing other positions verbally and clearly as personal opinion. It also does not address informal conversations and meetings involving advocacy and personal professional judgments given to Congress by senior military officers.[19]

However, the power of the President to appoint flag officers and nominate individuals for key positions creates a strong incentive for promoting rather than questioning administration positions. Doing something that could be interpreted as undermining administration positions could make other "team player" flag officers uncomfortable and slow the upward mobility of an aspiring chief or commandant.

Finally, officers are commissioned by the President of the United States. In that commission, to "discharge the duties of [his or her] office by doing . . . all manner of things . . . during the pleasure of the President" or until the officer resigns the commission. While "all manner of things" could be no more vague, it may be inferred by some that the "during the pleasure of the President" clause compels senior flag officers to espouse only positions supported by the administration. While that may apply in prohibiting flag officers, other than the top chiefs, from making public pronouncements that are at odds with administration positions, it does not necessarily preclude these same officers from providing these pronouncements or assessments privately when asked by Members of Congress.

Members of Congress, on the other hand, go beyond extolling their power of the purse in authorizing and funding programs and focus on the enumerated powers in defense matters specified by the Founding Fathers in the Constitution Article I, Section 8. They make clear that their powers to declare war, support and maintain the Army and Navy, "to make rules for the Government and Regulation of the land and naval forces" require them to have access to the best possible information for making their constitutionally based legislative decisions. Members of Congress are aware that the oath military officers take pledges to support, defend, and "bear true faith and allegiance" to the Constitution of the United States, a Constitution that clearly gives Congress responsibility and powers in these vital defense matters.[20]

Finally, military officers are appointed to flag ranks by the President only with the advice and consent of the U.S. Senate. To be confirmed by the Senate, senior military leaders must assure the SASC, often both in writing and verbally, that if asked, they will provide Members their honest personal professional judgment on an issue, regardless of party, and regardless of the administration position. The SASC also holds confirmation hearings on key senior flag rank nominations where it is standard procedure to ask this question regarding candor.

Congressmen from both parties made similar points in regard to senior military officers describing or defending (advocating) positions different from the administration. The theme was that senior flag officers have a professional and moral responsibility to voice these positions as long as they do so responsibly and according to the established congressional "rules of the game" in this area. Members view this kind of advocacy as critical to their ability to gain insightful information that leads to more informed congressional decision making on defense issues. And such informed decisionmaking is essential if Congress is to fulfill its Article I, Section 8 constitutional responsibilities:

When it comes to defense related issues, our constitutional form of government requires Members of Congress to be privy to military service concerns, priorities, and interests. The administration does not have the constitutional responsibility to "raise and support

Armies,'' ''to provide and maintain a Navy,'' ''to make rules for the government and regulation of the land and naval force''—and there are others—it's not the executive branch but Congress who is obligated to the American people to fulfill those duties. How are we to carry out these constitutional responsibilities if we are fed only the administration's position? The administration's position is only a recommendation or request that they have to justify to us. How can we as Members on this Committee evaluate their justification if we are deprived of the candid professional recommendations and viewpoints of the senior military leadership?[21]

However, many Members complained in interviews about the difficulty of getting the best possible information, not just the administration line, from senior military leaders:

My complaint is that it is so difficult to find out the true needs of the military. The civilian executive leadership of the military stifles that input. The President appoints the Chairman; Joint Chiefs of Staff and the Chiefs of each service to include the Commandant of the Marine Corps. They have to ''carry the water for the man.'' It puts Congress in the position of having to dig to find out the real priorities of the military services by going under the table.[22]

A Republican on the HNSC:

The blind worship of the chain of command makes it nearly impossible to get the best information for congressional decisionmaking. I have tremendous respect for the military 4-stars, but sitting in front of us they refuse to give us the best possible information to base our decision on. Instead they feed us the administration's party line. I've really gotten frustrated at times and have accused them of selling out. There ought to be a way of getting beyond that chain of command. Members of both parties would respect generals and admirals who come before us in hearings and when asked their views would candidly acknowledge: ''I know the Secretary of Defense's position and I'm prepared and willing to carry it out, however this is what I would do if I was free to do it.'' That's the kind of best information I'm talking about. Why have hearings if all you are going to hear is the OSD [Office of Secretary of Defense] position. That is the reason attendance at the hearings keeps going down and why Members don't bother to stay longer beyond getting their own questions placed on the record.[23]

However, regardless of party, all Members described patterned ways, rules of the game that exist and are used to elicit candid assessments from flag officers. This primarily focuses on the obligation of senior military officers to provide ''personal opinions'' if asked. A Democrat with a reputation for working closely with a particular service and promoting that service's interests with legislative proposals that run counter to OSD positions reiterated this expectation:

Unless I, as a Member, ask for the senior military officer's personal opinion, the individual should give the administration's position. If I sense his lack of enthusiasm and ask for his personal opinion, he is bound by ethics and is morally obligated to answer candidly and honestly. The officer should not be over-freelancing—he should reflect Secretary of Defense policy. However, if a Member asks for their personal opinion it should be given.[24]

Several Republican Members on the HNSC stressed the utility of the "personal opinion" question and the value of the "hypothetical situation" to make the necessary point for the record. An HNSC subcommittee chairman stated:

In my opinion, senior military flag officers have been less forthright over the last few years and more prone to give us the party line in congressional hearings. However, I recognize the difficulty for our professional military leadership at the top levels to undermine positions taken by the Secretary of the Defense and the administration. Granted, they have the option to resign that would allow them to speak out, but for obvious reasons that is an option few take. I can't expect the Chairman, Joint Chiefs of Staff to assert positions publicly contrary to the President's policies. That is just a disadvantage under which Congress must labor. However, the situation doesn't get grotesque, unless the Congress fails to utilize its options in discerning how the military really feels about an issue.

Privately, a senior four-star might ask you to refrain from asking for his "personal opinion" on an issue in a hearing with his civilian principal sitting at his side. It all depends on the situation, issue, and personalities involved. Another four-star on the same issue might not have a concern with a personal opinion question. You try to work with these folks because in most cases you respect and like them.

Another approach for getting information on the record is to pose questions in the hypothetical. By positing particular assumptions, the more realistic the better, you can frame questions that allow senior military to address concerns and more closely identify risks that are being accepted in the administration's current plans. "Let us assume that you have a Major Regional Contingency similar to the Gulf War that has broken out in the Middle East, and a month later, North Korea invades South Korea. Does our force structure allow us to . . ."

Then of course I find great value in "back door conversation" that takes place with those senior military flag officers with whom I have developed personal relationships. The quality of that conversation is based on the human dynamics and personalities of the individuals involved. A Member gets more valuable and personal advice from his strong, more personal relationships. I must trust him and he must trust me. I would never use the information he provides in any way that would embarrass him. But armed with that information and understanding, I can work to make good things happen on this side of the river.[25]

Another senior Republican on the HNSC explained his technique for drawing out service priorities from the top senior military leaders that were not recognized in the administration's budget request:

I need to know what their [military services] needs are. I need to find out service priorities that were turned down by OSD. [Office of Secretary of Defense]. Administration political appointees are not going to be forthcoming with that kind of information. If I ask one of the Chiefs about the need for a particular program not requested in the President's budget, he'll respond "yes, there is a need if we had enough dollars, but we don't have those dollars available" [in the President's budget]. By asking the question this way, I put the Chief in an awkward position of implicitly questioning parts of the administration's budget request. I have to remind myself that the President either picked this Chief or this Chief wants to make it through for his entire 4-year tour of duty. While there are exceptions, many four-star flag officers got to the very top by "going along" rather than "rocking the boat."

A better approach for discovering service priorities the administration turned down is to ask the question in a way that enables the top flag officers to respond and still support the President's budget request. I ask "what if we had $2B in additional funding for your service in this fiscal year, what would you spend it on?" Suddenly you see their eyes light up as these cautious 4-stars are freed of their administration shackles. Not only will you get an itemized list of service priorities, but you will get a justification for these priorities. As a Member of Congress on this Committee, I can then determine how these justifications compare with others in the administration's budget request.[26]

According to another Member, LL officers often play a role in preparing the groundwork for such questions to be asked:

As they should, senior flag officers of the services arrive over here explaining and justifying an administration position. I usually know how these flag officers feel about the issue ahead of our meeting because of the close relationship that exists between their LL at the lieutenant colonel and colonel level and my staff. [A particular service] LL will give my MLA the straight scoop at this lower level. My MLA also has contacts outside of LL with service staff working certain programs in the Pentagon. So generally, it's no surprise. The skids have been greased. Then when the senior flag officers enter and state the administration's position on the issue, it is apparent from their demeanor that they are less than thrilled with it. That is when I ask for their personal opinion on the issue. The flag officers for this service are then especially candid, or at least they are with me, because they trust me and know I'm a supporter of theirs.

He went on to stress the importance of congressional sensitivity to the professional plight senior military find themselves in Washington and to the unacknowledged information they provide to Congress:

However, on those opinions or views that diverge from administration positions, I understand as a Member that you have to protect these people. You can't just use that information and attribute it to that senior flag officer or you expose them to political attack by administration proponents in the Building [Pentagon]. What's the value of information that can't be acknowledged? Plenty! First, their personal and professional assessment of an issue may be what changes an individual Member's position on that issue. Second, if the Member agrees with the assessment, the Member may choose to offer suggestions on strategy and how to devise ways that acknowledgeable information could be acquired. For example, a Member might ask the senior military flag officer if they would feel comfortable with questions asked in a hearing setting, worded in a particular way, that could get certain information on the record. Finally, and most importantly, that personal and private assessment may inspire and motivate a Member of

Congress to talk up an issue with other Members. It's hard to beat Member-to-Member lobbying![27]

Congress does have an additional resource to leverage in its quest for the best and most timely information from the executive branch. Relationships with and information garnered from flag officers, military personnel, and civilian bureaucrats located outside of Washington are vital in helping Members carry out their constitutional responsibilities. A Member with Navy and some Army facilities in his district commented that ''I have extensive contact with Navy and Army people at the local level. I pick up a lot of information locally through informal channels.''[28]

Members also continue to obtain information and candid assessments from relationships that are products of earlier Washington rather than local installation assignments. This is especially true of officers who have worked in a service (LL office) and are then reassigned to duty in operational units around the world. Good relationships are rarely allowed to flounder. Members enjoy tracking an officer's career as he moves up the service ladder and as he is rotated in and out of Washington assignments. One Member who was emphasizing the importance and prudence of flag officer–Member relationships excitedly pulled from his overflowing in-box a four-page personal letter written on personal stationary by a senior flag officer who once worked closely with this Member in LL:

Now that's a relationship! I think of this officer as both a friend and a professional. His military service thinks highly of him. Even though he is half way around the globe, he bothers to write. He provides me valuable insights about how things are where the rubber meets the road. I can tell from his letters that he is keeping up with the major defense issues being debated in Washington. If something is really screwed up out in his unit and the larger issue is being addressed in Washington, he knows that his call into me on the subject is welcome. I also know how to contact him if I need someone to bounce ideas off that I can trust and whose judgment I value.[29]

FINDINGS

It is apparent that the liaison roles involving collaboration and advocacy accepted by both branches place LLs, and especially senior military flag officers, who are the real and most effective message carriers, in sensitive situations that allow them to serve their civilian political superiors in both the executive and legislative branches. As members of the executive branch, they serve in being effective justifiers and sellers of the administration's legislative program. Likewise, they serve as an invaluable informal and occasional formal source of expertise and professional military judgment for Members in those areas where Members are uncomfortable with the DOD position. This informed ''second look'' at executive branch decisions by the legislative branch with the constitutional responsibility for making decisions in defense areas is consistent with American government, and maintains the critical concept of civilian control over the military.

Collaboration and advocacy activities of LL and senior military officers on positions not supported by the administration are clearly of a more complex nature. First, both LL and senior flag officers are obligated to support the President's budget and programs publicly; if they can not do this, they must resign. But support requires only that a senior flag officer is willing to carry out those policies and is willing to accurately explain those positions to the Congress; it does not require the flag officer to passionately sell that position to Members or to lie about their personal opinion or professional judgment on the issue if asked by a Member.

Second, most senior military officers do not visit the Hill to strategically alter or counter administration positions. While that occurs on occasion and more frequently with some services than others according to interviews, it must be understood that most flag officers are placed in that position because of individual interests of a Member. A senior flag officer may be on the Hill addressing and advocating an administration position when he is formally or informally asked his personal position on an issue. In most cases they agree with the administration position or do not feel strongly about the position one way or the other. The problem comes when they do feel strongly that a position is unwise. However, because most flag officers adhere to values of honesty and integrity, they will be inclined to give that Member some signal of their displeasure with an administration position in the form of a personal professional opinion.

Finally, there is a healthy tension that keeps this activity from getting out of control. The inherent risks and professional liability associated with a reputation of being a maverick in the eyes of the senior political leadership in the Pentagon constrain advocacy against administration positions and limit it to select issues viewed as most important by the uniformed military. In addition, from the congressional perspective, a senior military officer's personal assessment, which may differ from those of other officers, is viewed as one piece of information to be considered with many others in making policy.

Senior flag officers who are led by their convictions into this particular field of collaboration and advocacy with Congress must know what they are doing. Because of the potential career ramifications, this requires experience in Washington and the Pentagon, and a firsthand sensitivity to the roles and norms of executive-legislative interaction. If LL and senior flag officers carry out these roles successfully, they enhance the important communication that must take place between the two branches to maintain a strong but affordable defense capability.

Members require information and professional assessments in areas beyond their expertise in order to effectively evaluate the merit of the administration's positions and understand individual service's capability to accomplish the national military strategy. As military experience in the Congress declines, it is especially important for Members to have trusted relationships with senior flag officers who feel comfortable and safe enough to offer candid analysis. While LLs bring greater coherence to the President's legislative program, Congress would never have accepted their executive established roles and allowed them to operate in such a permissive environment if they were not benefitting from them as well. Certain service LLs and certain senior flag officers are more skilled and experienced in meeting the "dual needs" of their executive-legislative clients. They understand the importance to the nation of personal relationships with external audiences that can only develop by embracing effectively the agency liaising roles of policy collaboration and advocacy.

The Constitution expects and promotes this nuanced conflict and tension between the legislative and executive branches. What the Constitution does not safeguard against is service culture that makes certain services less willing to participate in this conflict and less prepared to participate effectively. This is the danger that emanates from an imbalance in advocacy efforts being made by different services on the Hill.

The direct advocacy role by LL and senior military leaders of administration positions is seen as legitimate activity by both sides of the Potomac if conducted congruent to congressional norms and by the proper people. This advocacy role incorporates higher risk, but it still legitimate, when Members of Congress ask senior military liaisers for their personal professional judgement on an administration position that they officially support but on which they personally disagree. The legitimacy of this candid, often not public, exchange of information or advice, which better informs and equips constitutionally empowered civilians in Congress to make decisions, has not been contested formally by the senior political leadership in the executive branch. The experienced senior military officers who succeed in their policy collaboration role and are respected by the congressional audience and others in the Washington community can carry out this difficult and often avoided advocacy role without risking their careers.

NOTES

1. Abraham Holtzman, *Legislative Liaison: Executive Leadership in Congress* (Chicago: Rand McNally, 1970), 18–41.

2. Ibid., 42–76.

3. Ibid., 82–83. Holtzman included policy collaborator and advocate under the same role of "lobbyist," which is appropriate at the DOD legislative affairs (LA) level where his research was focused. Unlike service LLs, DOD LA operation is headed by a civilian political appointee instead of a uniformed flag officer. Working with White House LL, DOD LA is far more likely to mix partisan and policy activities involving grassroots activities and/or interest group coordination that more closely approximates lobbying activity defined earlier.

4. Ibid., 83–84.

5. Holtzman's emphasis on partisan qualities of LLs at the cabinet/departmental level applies accurately to political appointees serving in the Office of Secretary of Defense Legislative Affairs operation.

6. The appropriators have historically been liaised by individuals from the services' financial management (FM) and comptroller sections, rather than the LL offices. A separate flag officer and group of field-grade officers with comptroller background work the appropriations issues. The chiefs of the various LLs have to be extremely careful in their interface with appropriators and their staff. The heads of the LL operation must shepherd and synchronize indirectly and more from a distance the activities and efforts of the comptroller-type liaison personnel in their service who work directly with the appropriators, with parallel efforts being taken by his own LL officers working directly with the authorizers.

7. Holtzman, *Legislative Liaison*, 212.

8. According to interviews, the head of the Marine Corps HLD and the head of its Senate counterpart, both colonels, e-mail and communicate directly with the Commandant of the Marine Corps (a four-star general) without being expected to go through their flag officer who heads Marine Corps', much less Navy's, LL operations.

9. According to interviews, the manner in which certain senior leaderships (civilian and uniformed) informed key Members of Base Realignment and Closure (BRAC) 1995 recommendations produced many "former friends" of that service. The point was not that the service supported a "bad news" decision for that Member, but the fact that the service withheld advance notice of the decision to a "friend," catching that Member off guard and unable to package the bad news with the most effective spin before the news was in the hands of the media or their constituents.

10. Holtzman, *Legislative Liaison*, 190–191.

11. Ibid., 82.

12. *Webster's New International Dictionary*, 2nd ed. (Springfield, MA: C & C Merriam, 1960), 39.

13. Congressional Member, HNSC, #44, interview by author, May 16, 1995, Washington, DC.

14. Congressional MLA, SASC, #50, interview by author, April 18, 1995, Washington, DC.

15. Sam Brick, Director, Legislative Reference Service (LRS), Office of General Counsel, Office of the Secretary of Defense, interview by author, June 14, 1995, Washington, DC. As director, he and his staff are the focal point in the DOD for the control, coordination, and management of the DOD legislative program, executive orders, and related activities. The LRS develops the DOD legislative program for each Congress. It confers and negotiates differences in policy considerations on legislation within the DOD to ensure a coordinated, acceptable conclusion is formulated. The LRS obtains Secretary of Defense decisions when issues cannot be resolved. The LRS provides legal advice on draft legislation and on the legislative comment process within the DOD. The LRS obtains OMB clearance for written comments by DOD officials on matters involving legislation to include reports to Congress on pending legislation and testimony on legislation. In the 103rd Congress, it managed over 3,000 items regarding the above. It also manages congressional comment activities of the military departments and defense agencies.

16. Circular No. A-19, rev., "Legislative Coordination and Clearance" (Washington, DC: Executive Office of the President, Office of Management and Budget, September 1979).

17. Ibid., 10.

18. Ibid., 11.

19. Ibid. "In cases where an agency has not submitted a report (or congressional testimony) for clearance and its views on pending legislation are to be expressed in the form of oral, unwritten testimony, OMB will undertake such coordination and give such advice as the circumstances permit. In presenting oral testimony, the agency should indicate what advice, if any, has been received from OMB. If no advice has been obtained, the agency should so indicate."

20. See U.S. Code 5, Section 3331 for information on the oath of office uniformed military officers must take. In fact, an individual, except the President, elected or appointed to an office of honor or profit in the civil service or uniformed service must take the same oath: "I, ———, do solemnly swear (or affirm) that I will support and defend the Constitution of the United States against all enemies, foreign and domestic; that I will bear true faith and allegiance to the same; that I take this obligation freely, without mental reservation or purpose of evasion; and that I will well and faithfully discharge the duties of the office on which I am about to enter. So help me God."

21. Congressional Member, HNSC, #32, interview by author, September 7, 1995, Washington, DC.

22. Congressional Member, HNSC, #63, interview by author, September 13, 1995, Washington, DC.

23. Congressional Member, HNSC, #59, interview by author, July 12, 1995, Washington, DC.

24. Congressional Member, HNSC, #32, interview by author, September 7, 1995, Washington, DC.

25. Congressional Member, HNSC, #43, interview by author, June 27, 1995, Washington, DC.

26. Congressional Member, HNSC, #63, interview by author, September 13, 1995, Washington, DC.

27. Congressional Member, HNSC, #58, interview by author, September 13, 1995, Washington, DC.

28. Congressional Member, HNSC, #26, interview by author, September 13, 1995, Washington, DC.

29. Congressional Member, HNSC, #32, interview by author, September 7, 1995, Washington, DC.

Chapter 3

Patterns of Army–
Congressional Relations

The stereotype is that the Army is the most inept at playing the Washington game. That is not fair. It is not a question of ineptness, but a reluctance to play the game.[1]

—Professional Staff Member on the
House National Security Committee

Now we turn to delineating patterns of Army LL and leadership behavior distinct from the other services, according to congressional perspective. Based on extensive interviews with three different subgroups of Congress—Members of Congress, PSMs, and MLAs—seven patterns of Army behavior toward Congress can be identified as being distinct from those of the other military services. Four patterns are based largely upon the perceived behavior of Army general officers on the Hill, and three patterns concern the Army's use of its other agency resources to improve its relations and effectiveness with Congress. Some of these patterns were recognized by all subgroups, but many were strongly perceived by a particular subgroup as a result of their responsibilities or the status and attention afforded them by a particular service. Only after acknowledging these perceived patterns can we dig deep, with the cooperative input of senior Army general officers, to find the values and, most importantly, the basic assumptions that undergird these behaviors.[2]

All these patterns are related in one key aspect. They demonstrate that, in the eyes of their supposed target audience on Capitol Hill, the Army is perceived to be more reluctant to proactively participate with Congress in the Washington policymaking process and to understand Congress less than the other services. In earlier chapters, we identified legitimate liaising that seems rational if a public agency is trying to optimize its agency resources or assets to enhance the

Table 3-1
Members of Congress with Military Service

Congress/Years	House	Senate
92nd/1971–1972	316 (72.6%)	73
93rd/1973–1974	317 (72.9%)	73
94th/1975–1976	307 (70.6%)	73
95th/1977–1978	313 (72.0%)	64
96th/1979–1980	242 (55.6%)	58
97th/1981–1982	269 (61.8%)	73
98th/1983–1984	229 (52.6%)	78
99th/1985–1986	215 (49.4%)	76
100th/1987–1988	200 (46.0%)	70
101st/1989–1990	203 (46.6%)	66
102nd/1991–1992	196 (45.1%)	64
103rd/1993–1994	185 (42.5%)	54
104th/1995–1996	144 (33.1%)	49
105th/1997–1998	140 (32.2%)	48
106th/1999–	136 (31.3%)	43

Sources: Data for the 92nd–100th Congresses are cited from Frederick H. Black, ''The Military and Today's Congress,'' *Parameters* (December 1987): 39–40. Data concerning the 101st to 104th are original work, with information compiled from the *Congressional Staff Directory* and the *Congressional Directory* for the relevant years. Additionally, the data relied on information contained in Michael Barone and Grant Ujifusa, *The Almanac of American Politics, 1996, 1998,* and *2000* (Washington, DC: National Journal, 1995, 1997, 1999). Military service is counted as any active, reserve, and/or National Guard duty that a Member of Congress may have served.

agency–congressional relationship. Distinctive patterned behavior that tends to defy this rational approach is fertile ground for cultural underpinnings.

However, before we begin discussing how the Army relates to and communicates with Congress, it is important to examine the composition of Congress, especially in regard to previous military experience. This can be done by highlighting the important and continuing overall trend of decreasing military experience for Members of Congress on the defense committees, and focusing on the service experience of both Members and staff to ascertain the value of that alumni status in the service–Member/staff relationship.

DECLINING MILITARY EXPERIENCE IN CONGRESS

Members of the House of Representatives and Senate now have much less military experience than in the past, a trend evident for many years (Table 3-1) and continuing with the 106th Congress. In the House of Representatives, only 31 percent of Members have any military experience, compared to 46.6 percent in the 101st Congress a decade earlier. This trend is also reflected in the Senate, with only 43 percent possessing some form of military service in the 106th Congress, compared to 66 percent with military experience in 1989. This trend is even more pronounced if just freshmen are considered. Only 25 percent of the freshmen in the 104th Congress had served in the Armed Forces, compared to the 39 percent level of military service in the 103rd Congress.[3] The 105th Congress, however, temporarily reversed this trend, with 35 percent of freshmen arriving with military experience (19 House Members and 7 Senators). However, in 1999 the 106th Congress continued the larger trend, with only 21 percent of the freshmen having served in the U.S. military (10 of 40 House Members and 0 of 8 Senators).

However, declining military experience in Congress is compounded by a significant decrease in military service among Members on the two "cue-giving" Armed Services Committees. Less than 42 percent of the HNSC in the 104th Congress had any prior service. Four years later, only 33 percent of the same Committee has military experience in the 106th Congress. This change in military experience becomes a salient factor if one believes that military veterans in Congress have a different political orientation or attitude toward the military than non-veterans. Declining familiarity with military issues and lack of emotional commitment to supporting the services are two drawbacks most often cited. A *Parameters* article makes these points:

One can speculate that prior service experience may prove most critical when voting on defense issues, where the member's military experience may provide an emotional commitment to the military's position. As such experience becomes less prevalent, the military will no longer enjoy the benefits of a member's personal familiarity with such issues. The result may be a greater reliance on the committees and staffs for behavior cues.[4]

The SASC was able to stop a dramatic decline in Member prior service experience (from 70 percent in 1989 to 50 percent in 1993) by ensuring that two of its three new members to the Committee in the 104th Congress had military experience and then by decreasing the size of the SASC for the 105th Congress. The SASC has been able to retain its Member military experience at 60 percent with the 106th Congress. However, the longer trend of declining military experience is evident and likely to continue, even in the traditionally more conservative SASC.

Echoing this concern, in a speech to the 1986 annual meeting of the Association of the United States Army, the Secretary of the Army stated:

Today in the House of Representatives, more than half of the members have not had military service, and that figure is increasing with every Congress. This is not a criticism; however, it points out that a basic frame of reference that was once shared by a large majority of the legislative body no longer exists. This makes the educational requirement for national security more important.[5]

It is probably safe to say that military experience provides a basic foundation of familiarity with particular defense- or service-related issues and probably produces some degree of emotional proclivity to understand and possibly support the military or service position. Although it will be likely to vary according to the individual experience, we should expect that possessing a life-shaping experience such as military service and especially service in times of war, should somehow color how one initially approaches service and defense issues. A member of the HNSC with no military experience and Army facilities and jobs in his/her district that are threatened to be closed or cut back, admitted that his predecessor who had World War II military experience shared a closer and substantially different relationship than he with the military services:

I see the Army and the other services as just another government agency asking for a handout that I don't have to give. At times, with our deficit situation, I feel as if I am an executor of a bankrupt organization. My predecessor saw the Army, the other services, and the DOD leadership as special. In my eyes, they are no longer special. I see them as I see those advocating housing, highways, or education. These are different times and I'm a different Member from those who served in World War II.[6]

There is probably little debate that former military experience simplifies to a degree the educational efforts that a service might have to undertake. Knowing ahead of time that a Member or staffer had x amount of time in a particular service and when that duty took place is valuable in assessing how and at what level to pitch a brief or discussion.

Does the fact that a Member or staff has military experience with a particular service equate to an inherent advantage that this audience will be more receptive to a "service" message or position? From congressional interviews, it depends on the service affiliation. The emotional support variable is most often observed in Members and staff who served in the Department of the Navy and in the Marine Corps. They often repeat the old adage, "Once a Marine, always a Marine," and their attitude is seen at work on the Hill. The following comments from a Member of Congress with Navy experience who had Army, Air Force, and Marine Corps interests in his district are typical, and they emphasized this phenomenon and how it equated to powerful pressure on Committee members:

I'm not sure how the Marine Corps does it, but their greatest strength lies in their alumni, both Members and constituents. Anytime a Marine Corps program or interest is threatened, these Members and constituent retirees come out of the woodwork. Now I have all kind of retired Army in my district; they do not contact me on behalf of an Army issue or program, only reference specific individual benefits they are concerned about. It is not just Congress that receives this Marine Corps pressure, but DOD as well. Remember how the Marine Corps responded to the decision to cancel the V-22 aircraft program?[7]

Whether it is past service affiliation or other individual factors, it is significant and highly desirable to have Members or staff with an emotional and concerned interest in support of the service's interests and positions on legislation. It appears the Marine Corps benefits greatly from its Member alumni. Their emotional commitment to Marine Corps concerns turns them into willing and most effective lobbyists. Based on their access to other Members, these alumni Members and staff are probably far more effective lobbyists than "outside" Marine Corps LL and flag officers carrying the same message: "If these Members are not sitting on one of the defense committees, they go to other Members who are, to ask for their support."[8]

Whether it is past service affiliation or other individual factors, it is significant and highly desired to have Members or staff with an emotional and concerned interest in support of one's service interests and positions on legislation. This type of emotional alumni support is least apparent in Members and staff with experience in the Army. Rather than the espirit de corps exhibited by Members who had served in the other services, a person on the Hill with Army experience was more likely to comment "I did my time."[9]

On the other hand, many observers argue that the impact of past military experience may be exaggerated and result in lost opportunities. Some of the Army's best friends on Capitol Hill have no military experience at all compared to others who have served in Army green and are of little assistance in garnering support for the Army requirements. If you asked someone in the defense community to name one influential Member who is a strong advocate of Army concerns, you would often hear the name of Rep. Ike Skelton (D-MO)—who has no military experience. As a young polio victim, military service was never an option for him. What undergirds Rep. Skelton's concern for the Army is his study and interest in military history. He sounds the alarm to avoid the past mistakes of a weakened and ignored Army in peacetime that resulted in unnecessary casualties when the nation sent its Army into harm's way. He wants to avoid future Task Force Smiths.[10] Additionally, Rep. Skelton has a young son who is an officer in the Army.

PATTERNS OF ARMY–CONGRESS BEHAVIOR

Pattern 1: The Army Is Seen as the Most Honest, Straightforward, and Credible of the Four Services in Reacting and Responding to Congressional Requests

Congressional staff, especially the PSMs, cite very different experiences with the services on the issue of candor. A common description was the "devious, defiant, and dumb" analogy for how the services operate in Washington. The Air Force is slick and devious; they will lie. The Navy is defiant and will ignore you: damn the torpedoes, full speed ahead. The Army is dumb; they will talk when they should keep their mouths shut. One staffer remembered a similar observation from an OSD official working during the McNamara years at the Pentagon. "The Air Force will try to outsmart you. The Navy will pretend you don't exist. The Army will try to out-cooperate you."[11] The staffer commented how some things never change.

A different SASC staffer gave a similar analogy based on different service reactions to a Tailhook-type affair. "The Army would say, 'Yes there was a party, it was horrible, here are the details, warts and all, and these are the procedures we plan to follow to get to the bottom of this disgusting affair.' The Air Force would say, 'What party? You can't tie the Air Force to that party.' They'd lie. The Navy would say, 'So what about this party?' The outsider is assumed to be incapable of understanding what is involved here."[12]

For Members of Congress, this was one pattern that was difficult for most to acknowledge in interviews. Telltale signs of it were more apparent, however, in Member comments concerning service investigations of accidents or misconduct of its personnel. Both the Navy and the Air Force have shown greater propensity to raise the suspicions of Congress that their service investigations are lacking or that information provided is incomplete or distorted (e.g., shootdown of two Army helicopters, Tailhook, Iowa explosion, etc.).

However, this pattern was most strongly recognized by the PSMs of the HNSC and the SASC. The work of Congress largely takes place within the committee system. It is the professional committee staff that do the lion's share of work that keeps the committee system functioning. They prepare oversight hearings, perform the major effort in framing the authorization marks, and are on the front line in preparing a committee member for an issue or agenda the Member feels is important. In the course of these activities, they are evaluated by the committee and their sponsors on the quality of the hearings, the successes and lack of embarrassments in the mark-up process, and the quality of their staff work in investigating and providing analysis for the committee on an issue. To succeed in these endeavors they require timely, accurate information from the services. A senior Committee staffer on the SASC stated: "The Army tends to be the good soldier, no end runs, straightforward; doesn't overstate its case. The Army is good at reacting and providing information to Members and staff on the Committee. When asked, the Army does that well."[13]

A senior PSM on the HASC addressed this aspect:

Of all the services, I get the sense the Army is most sensitive about the role of its LL operation and how they interface with the committee. We get the straightest answers from the Army. We are less likely to see them up here marketing and advocating their interests. This reputation is not all bad and does benefit the Army at times. It is a double-edged sword. When the Army does deliver information it is not received with the cynicism that other services information is often greeted with. However, the Army is often taken to the cleaners. Whether you are talking intraservice beatings the active Army takes from the more sophisticated Army National Guard or in recent years fight on the transfer of M1A1 tanks to the Marines, the Army usually has a stronger case to present than usually comes through over here.[14]

An MLA with a Navy background now working for a senator on the SASC addressed how differently the services react to bad news:

If the Army screws up, they are the best at dealing with it candidly, and laying out the procedures for rectifying the problem. I am most impressed with the way the Army addresses a sexual harassment complaint we raise. They will tell you right off the bat what the procedures are for dealing with this problem and work with the Congress and constituent complaint to rectify the concern. The Air Force and Navy tend to read it in the paper first, and then are mostly concerned with damage control rather than the problem at the source.[15]

Another senior PSM with Navy background emphasized the importance of a service's operational background and character in understanding its communications and approach to external audiences:

The Army produces leaders for combat on land, and in producing these leaders in this large hierarchical organization they emphasize the values of honesty and straightforwardness. The Army finds comfort in detail and precision in its internal communication. If the Army tells you something, they tell you warts and all. . . . Contrast this with the Air Force. Their operations are more comfort-based with a character that eschews personal hardships. At the same exercise, you'll find Marines in bivouac and the Air Force housed up in a hotel. It is sad to say, but our committee initially accepts anything the Air Force says with a large grain of salt. The Air Force doesn't enjoy a reputation of being honest on the Hill. The Navy as an operational organization tends to be geographically remote from higher headquarters. . . . They prefer bare essentials rather than detail in their internal communication to retain flexibility. Creativity and ingenuity are stressed. Likewise, the Navy is extremely imaginative and effective in coming up with dollars for traditional programs.[16]

One former Navy PSM with over 17 years of experience on the Hill, stated:

The Army is trusted as being "on the reservation" [trustworthy, playing by the rules] by most on the Hill; to give you the truth, warts and all. The Navy and Air Force suffer because people on the Hill don't respect their commitment to truth telling. Bad experiences with the C-17, Tailhook, the Iowa, and so on, create suspicion and erode credibility.

The Marine Corps hasn't really suffered in this area. Every now and then they are seen as being off the reservation—as to what they want and how they go about getting it. But in large part, they are respected up here. The problem for the Army is that their credibility does not outshine the other shortcomings. The Army should combine their credibility with the aggression that the Marines show. You tell the truth but also know when to keep your mouths shut. There is no reason why the Army couldn't incorporate a marketing strategy with their natural constituency and maintain their reputation of being honest and credible.[17]

Pattern 2: The Army Sees Congress More as a Hindrance than a Help; Dealing with Congress Is Seen as a Burden to Bear Rather than as an Opportunity to Engage; and They Don't Understand the Role Congress Plays

This pattern touches directly on the overall perception that the Army senior leadership, more than that of other services, is uncomfortable or wary of congressional involvement in shaping Army and defense policy. The pattern reflects an attitude or institutional body language that conveys unease, caution, and a sense of obligatory burden on the prospect of congressional interest and recommendations on fundamental Army issues. Rather than a help, Congress is viewed more as a hindrance. Rather than an opportunity, a fragmented Congress is seen more as a burden. Rather than a team player, Congress is viewed more as an institutional adversary. The Army approach is wary of Washington conflict, and it fears being drawn into the uncertain legislative forum of competing interests and prefers to stay above the fray, resting upon the principled correctness of its positions.

The Constitution, by design, invites conflict between the two branches in the realm of defense policy. Since World War II, the Congress has increasingly asserted itself by retaking the reigns of its constitutionally invested authority in defense matters. Lacking the greater independence of the Navy at sea and the closer economic ties with Congress that initially colored the Navy–Congress relationship because of shipbuilding and commerce interests, the Army has historically been within easy reach for more effective executive branch control and possessed little economic or constituency interest to the Congress. With a more assertive Congress, the Army now has two powerful masters, rather than one, that are often at odds on policy or budget issues. However, the Army seems particularly uneasy about Congress's role in the process. Rep. Ike Skelton (D-MO), a strong supporter of Army concerns, noted an Army wariness toward Congress he believes is related to an insufficient understanding by Army officers of Congress's constitutional role in defense policymaking:

It goes back to how the services view Congress. There are those in all services who see Congress as an irritant and obstacle. However, it's the degree to which a service hierarchy and its officer corps carry those sentiments that is significant. Unfortunately the Army holds these sentiments to the greatest degree. It is clearly reflected in the actions of today's senior hierarchy and the officer corps who will replace them. I was dismayed on a visit to the Army War College in Carlisle, PA, that only 2 or 3 officers in a group of 70 could tell me what was significant about Article I of the Constitution of the United States. *Those who understand the Constitution and the constitutionally defined role of Congress get along with use.* . . . The Army doesn't especially like us (Congress).[18]

Many on the Hill noted this unproductive, patterned approach by the Army and held little hope that the Army behavior and attitudes would change in the near future. Regarding this book, a senior Member on the HNSC, considered to be a "friend of the Army," stated: "You are wasting your time. No one will read it [this]. Those who read it, won't believe it. Those who believe it, won't do anything about it."[19]

The formulation of defense policy usually involves the integration of good problem solving, a strength of the military, with good politics, a congressional interest. This is not an easy task and is not largely the responsibility of the senior military leadership, which rightfully rests with the civilian decision makers in Congress, the service secretariats, OSD, and higher levels in the administration, according to interviewees. However, senior military leaders should be instrumental players in shaping final decisions. Their professional expertise is valued by the Congress and can serve as a useful rudder to prevent the prevailing political component from overwhelming the problem-solving component in the policy marriage. Likewise, the congressional audience expects to be viewed as legitimate team players by the military in shaping policy proposals being considered in the Pentagon. A form of policy and information collaboration hopefully takes place.

The importance of the "political scrub" to our political system's policymaking process was made by a former Army career officer and SASC PSM, six months after arriving to the committee:

One of the biggest adjustments I had to make, despite the fact that I arrived to the SASC with considerable experience working with Congress as a green suiter (Army LL), was my tendency to propose a solution to an issue that was focused primarily on fixing the problem. The more experienced staff would say "That's fine, but you haven't considered *x, y,* and *z* political considerations that complicate the adoption of your recommendation." The goal of a good SASC staffer is to orchestrate the marriage of good problem solving with good politics in making policy. The latter has always and will continue to be important. Some services understand that better than others.[20]

Defense and military service policymaking, the attempt to collaborate and orchestrate the marriage of good problem solving with good politics is often a difficult and extended, but very critical, process. The outcome of good defense policy could be jeopardized if the Army does not stay persistently engaged with other congressional "team" players at all levels and during all phases of the policy orchestration. There has to be an Army strategy that optimizes a service's agency resources for taking this long-term team-player approach with Congress.

The danger to Army and the nation's interest comes when the Army fails, in a relative sense to the other services, to serve as that collaborative rudder throughout the entire process. From earlier comments, it is easy to see the Army adopting a self-righteous stance of "We gave you the right answer, the 'truth' as we see it, to the problem earlier in the process. If you choose not to accept our professional recommendation, that is your prerogative."

An HNSC PSM with Army experience stated that the Army must be wary of its proclivity to send the sanctimonious signal that "it won't play in this fight," as if this behavior was a badge of honor. "It's very easy to conclude . . . your service positions . . . are based on facts—'Truth with a capital T.' In Washington, no such thing exists. Instead, there are a bunch of little 't's running around. In Congress, we put the 't's together in a way that is a combination of factual, political, and affordable."[21]

A senior PSM on the SASC with a military background stated that all services, except the Marine Corps, can be characterized as suspicious or wary of Congress to varying degrees. The Army could learn a lot studying the Marine Corps' attitude and behavior toward Congress. The Marines are far more adept at using the agency resources available to enhance their relationship with Congress and other external audiences. While Army sends a clear signal that dealing with the Congress is nothing short of a burden, Marines approach the legislators in a way that makes the legislators feel responsible for them. An SASC PSM explained the Marine approach: "[They] present themselves to the Congress as the creation of the Congress, . . . and totally dependent on the Congress to take care of them. 'If the Congress doesn't take care of us nobody else will. We are your Marine Corps. We really belong to the Congress, and you have to take care of us.' [The Marines] . . . really do cater to the Congress in a lot of ways that the other services just don't."[22]

This wariness among the services is partly a function of the orientation of the congressional staff and how they view and approach issues. The military–congressional relationship, according to a senior PSM, juxtaposes an initial makeup of a majority of staffers who possess a large and, they believe, healthy dose of cynicism combined with a strong political orientation, compared to military service elite who are mission-oriented and at least desire to be apolitical. The Army, with its good-soldier, mission-oriented, and non-political focus, occupies a place on the far end and to the right of the other services on this unidimensional spectrum, which is more pronounced because of its relative experience operating in Washington. Therefore, a cultural communication-barrier between staff and the military services exists to varying degrees from the start. Most Members of the Committee and a large percentage, though not majority, of staff are inherently positive toward the services. They possess a predilection to believe and go along with the services' military leadership.

The way the services operate in this communication cultural gap, according to this senior staffer, is influenced by past history and traditions:

The Navy historically was more independent, less concerned if problems surfaced. . . . The Army is more conscientious and concerned when problems surface, but is not as willing as the Navy to communicate to resolve that problem or increase understanding. . . . This disinclination to communicate to external audiences further reduces its ability to represent its interests with Congress.

A former Army PSM on the HNSC stressed the criticality of constant dialogue and mutual understanding in negotiating and collaborating to make good defense policy:

There needs to be ongoing constant dialogue between the services and the Committees that is candid and frank. However, there also has to be a mutual understanding so when there are differences of viewpoint, those differences don't become disruptive to the process. . . . *Most things in Congress are negotiable.* If the Army or other services don't realize that, they do themselves and the Congress a disservice. They will not understand this unless they work the process.[23]

Possessing an anticipatory, positive, and engaged approach with Members of Congress and staff is difficult work, where senior flag officers will be challenged or critiqued on what can appear as small or parochial matters. It is easier to remain in what one staffer referred to as the "splendid isolation" of the Pentagon. In that environment, senior flag officers feel more comfortable and safe, less likely to be challenged, especially by individuals 20 or 25 years their junior. But conflicting viewpoints, working persistently to persuade and educate, making compromises, and participating in shifting coalitions on different issues are fundamentals to the Washington political process. It is not easy work, but it's important for the Army and the nation.

"Taking the moral high ground" by staying above or away from the fray is actually a decision to cede influence over final policies. Senior Army leaders tend to send subordinates to react to events on the Hill that in many instances could have been avoided had those senior leaders viewed Congress and the Washington policymaking process in more positive and proactive terms.[24] By seeing the policy process as a burden rather than an opportunity to serve the nation, the Army remains less skilled and less effective at shaping that policy, according to most interviewed. More importantly, its actions and view of Congress are powerful socializing agents on its younger officers learning these habits. Finally, the Army message and its priorities increasingly get lost in the shuffle of the other services' more astute and positive embrace of the Hill.

Before a new Chief of Staff of the Army (CSA) was selected to replace General Gordon Sullivan, an experienced senior officer on the Army staff with considerable experience on Capitol Hill was asked who would be the best person for the job. He stated that before this question could be answered, three more important questions should be answered before selection. "Which general officer understands where the Army currently is at and has a true vision of where he wants to take the Army? Which general officer understands how to achieve that vision? In other words, which general officer understands the rules of the Washington game, both in the Pentagon and in Congress? Which general officer will not view the Washington game as a burden and something to be avoided?"[25]

One senior SASC MLA with Navy interests in his state made it clear that changing the current Army culture of impeding close and effective service–Hill relationships will not be easy:

I won't feed you a rosy line about Congress. Ninety percent of folks working on the Hill suffer from "rectal cranial inversion," but that is all the more reason for your best and brightest of officers to play in the Washington game and help them see the light. If you don't think they are important—then ask them. And in fact they are. They vote and make our laws.[26]

Pattern 3: Of All the Services, Senior Army General Officers Are the Least Represented and the Least Engaged on Capitol Hill

One of the most distinctive aspects of Army relations with Congress is reflected in this pattern, which is also a prime example of a valuable agency resource—the access and credibility of its senior general officers—being uniquely minimized rather than optimized in enhancing the Army–Congress relationship. The following points emerge:

- Army senior flag officers are viewed as the least visible and engaged with Members and staff.
- As senior flag officers have a unique ability to influence Members and staff because of their rank and experience, failure to use this resource undercuts the effectiveness of their efforts on the Hill vis-à-vis the other services. This relative disengagement diminishes the Army's effectiveness in communicating its more difficult message to the congressional audience.

Less Visible and Engaged Military Army Leadership. There is a congressional perception that insufficient appreciation for the importance of close and effective congressional relations, a sense of discomfort from lack of experience with Congress, and an institutional desire to protect their senior flag officers from Congress result in far less engagement by senior flag officers in the Army on the Hill compared to the other services.

Senior flag officers can have two important types of interactions with congressional leaders: engagement and visibility. Let's discuss the congressional perceptions that the Army lags behind the other services on both of these and explore congressional views on reasons for this.

In the eyes of Congress, Army general officers are least visible and engaged on Capitol Hill. Visibility, unlike engagement, does not necessarily imply working issues on the Hill, but it reflects the frequency of visits and the importance given to developing relationships with Members of Congress and their staffs before a crisis arises. This requires spending time on mutual education to better understand the world of the other person in the relationship. The building of credibility with each other is likely to grow from these meetings.

A seasoned MLA for a Member of the HNSC and Army Caucus who has Navy and Army interests in his district stated: "There isn't the regularity and familiarity of Army visits to our office that you find in dealing with Navy programs. We get senior flag officer aviators, submarines, former directors of

Navy legislative affairs, CNOs all coming around to see us on Navy concerns."[27]

A recurring point that surfaced in interviews is that the congressional audience seems to associate senior Army general officer meetings with an impending problem or crisis to which the Army is reacting. Less frequent is an Army general officer dropping by just to say "hi" and talk with a Member or his staff on a more relaxed and personal basis. Politics is personal. That is often what congressional leaders want and what they value in their associations with senior flag officers. These planned or impromptu "non-issue" gatherings not only promote familiarity, understanding, and trust among the parties, but often lead to more substantive issue discussions.

The importance of this point was emphasized by Rep. Skelton, who at the time chaired the Military Forces and Personnel Subcommittee of the HASC:

The Commandant, even before I became Subcommittee Chairman, would come by to see me just to talk and say hi! He never really asked me for any help on anything until the OSD plan came out that recommended 159,000 endstrength for the Marines. On that occasion, he gave me a personal lay down of the problem and showed me that 174K endstrength made more sense. So I made 174K happen on the House side. . . . When [Admiral] Boorda [then Chief of Naval Operations] was head of Navy personnel, he was always dropping by to see me. He would say, "I don't want anything," but would just sit down and we'd talk.[28]

The following account of a hurriedly arranged "drop-by" meeting initiated by General Hartzog, the new TRADOC Commander and Senator Warner (R-VA), the SASC Subcommittee Chairman for Air and Land Operations, reiterates the importance of getting together without a specific issue, agenda, or crisis as the basis for the collaboration and engagement.[29] The Senator greeted the General with a reminder that they had met once before, "Operation *Just Cause* in Panama was just one day old when Senator Robb and I visited your Operations Center. You were the J-3 [Operations Officer] for Southern Command and were busy running the operation; cool as a cucumber, calm as can be. Good to see you, General, what are you here for?"

General Hartzog replied, "I just dropped by to say hello, Senator." Senator Warner looked shocked and exclaimed, "Just to say Hello?" He looked over immediately to Les Brownlee, an SASC PSM and retired Army colonel working on the subcommittee, "Les, do you believe that? This is great!" The Senator jumped to his feet rubbing his hands together and told the General, "Thanks for giving me some of your time and not just coming to see me when you need something or have bad news." They sat back down and just began to talk informally. However, within ten minutes they were talking substantive issues important to the Army.[30] In most cases where visibility demonstrates the critical willingness to develop a close working relationship, the more valuable "islands of competence'' relationships usually develop from more substantive engagement on issues.

Engagement is usually, but not necessarily, a product of good visibility and relationships. The Army leadership, as reflected in earlier congressional remarks, has problems engaging with a Member, even when it is clearly visible in the Member's world and has a personal relationship. I define engagement as working as team players, rather than as adversaries, in helping to shape policy in a way that, at a minimum, addresses both parties' professional concerns. It entails a willingness of the military leadership to respond creatively in seeking ways to resolve the Member's concerns rather than reflexively focusing on the reasons why it cannot do so. Engagement implies candid discourse between the two parties, a mutual respect for the roles both professionals play in our constitutional policymaking process, and a proactive rather than reactive attitude toward the other. Therefore, being visible and engaged in a proactive manner with members and staff are preconditions if senior flag officers are to exercise their legitimate role of being effective policy collaborators and, hopefully, credible advocates as they liaise on the Hill.

An MLA for one of the Army's strongest supporters on the HNSC stated: ''The Army is clearly the weak sister of the military services when it comes to the approach taken by its general officers in delivering their message to Congress.''[31] Another House MLA for a member on the HNSC reflected that:

What's missing from the Army is a general willingness of your senior generals to get in the middle of a fight during critical debate times; the Army's big guys are less present during these crunch times. Meanwhile, Admiral Boorda may not succeed, but he is out there visibly working the Speaker of the House on behalf of the *Seawolf* submarine during the waning hours of the HNSC mark.

There is a lack of flexibility and risk taking that characterizes Army General Officers on the Hill. This may serve them well on the battlefield, but it fails them in Washington in terms of flexibility.

Army generals have opportunities to be forthright when the Secretary of the Army is not sitting at their side. We're at a point in time that being forthright is important. The Army is seen as being less candid behind closed doors. A member will say, ''General, I understand that position, is there more we can talk about,'' on whatever the issue. Army general officers seem more constrained and you get the sense that their bureaucracy back in the Building is far more involved. They feel uncertain and uncomfortable about discussing what is possible, because to make anything happen is problematic with all the hoops they would have to go through with that deal.[32]

An influential MLA for a senator on the SASC with Marine and Navy interests in his state was upfront in highlighting the importance of visibility and engagement between the senior military leaders and Members of Congress. He uses the word ''responsive'' to imply sincere engagement by the service in trying to resolve a Member conflict or concern.

The Navy and Marine Corps do the best job at getting their senior flag officers over on the Hill; more than the Air Force and the Army put together. The Army, however, is the weakest in this regard. The Navy is obstinate and sticks to what it wants. The Chief of Naval Operations and my senator work closely together. They don't always agree with each other and often go nose-to-nose on an issue, but they are engaged. No one from the Army has been in to see the senator talking policy this year. No one is talking to me about Army tanks. The Army claims sealift is important, but I don't see any coordinated action on their part with Congress.

The Navy will work with you on something other than the President's budget: "no fingerprints." There is a rule that the Army tends to forget: Everything is politics. The Navy and the Marine Corps understand this. Do you know what motivates individual Members? Not just pork and state interests. What is also important is how you deal with Members and staff. When a service appears unresponsive (in working fluid situations with a Member), that motivates the Member and his staff to focus their attention and efforts on the services that are responsive.[33]

Members and staff interviewed explained this less visible and engaged senior Army leadership with three commonly held perceptions. The first was that the Army officer corps had an insufficient appreciation for the importance of congressional relations and discounted the importance of time, efforts, and other resources directed toward these agency or organizational tasks.

As they should, Army general officers and their supporting staff manage and place high value on their time and agenda focus. However, getting the senior Army general preferred by Army LL (and Congress) to agree and find time to go the Hill is a difficult and often time-consuming task. Part of Army LL activity is trying to convince the senior Army general that the time spent on the Hill will not be wasted. It is here that the related aforementioned "hindrance rather than team player" pattern raises its head. Many three- or four-star Army generals view an LL recommendation to go to the Hill as an unnecessary burden, often resolving the problem by designating more junior subordinates to go in their place. This perceived sense of burden to cross the Potomac translates downward throughout the officer hierarchy and Army staff.

An influential MLA and former Army officer who wants to see the Army put its best foot forward displayed his frustration at the relative isolation the Army senior leadership imposes on itself relative to his Member, who has supported the Army in the past:

The Army top military leadership is not externally focused. The CSA believes he can serve the Army well by being internally focused. *Congress looks more to the military leadership than the [Pentagon's] civilian leadership for engagement on issues.* My boss is the Chair of a critical defense subcommittee dealing with land and air power. Neither Secretary of the Army, CSA, or VCSA have met with him since January 1995. We've had folks call to Army LL and the Army staff offline strongly recommending to get the CSA over. It's almost May and it hasn't happened. The Chairman has met with the Secretary of the Navy twice, the CNO twice on separate occasions. They, not my boss, asked for the opportunities to get together.

The USMC and the Navy are best at this outreach. The Commandant will deal with all on the Hill. He made big points with the full committee staff when he gave them the USMC's FY96 budget briefing a few months ago. It's not because he is a poor manager of his time, he truly believes Congress, its staff are the key to the bank. *The Army doesn't know how to get to members.* The Army leadership hasn't been willing to lead the change in turning around this internal focus. The Army used to have better outreach than it does now.[34]

It is not just Army general officers in Washington who are least represented in the halls of Congress, but also those assigned outside Washington. The other services do a better job of getting flag offers assigned in key positions around the globe back to Washington on occasion to meet with Members and share their experiences.

One MLA with Navy and Army interests in his district stated that the Navy values established relationships of senior flag officers with Members and staff and nurtures these relationships regardless of geographical distance:

Admiral Bud Flanigan, Commander of the Atlantic Fleet, at his level, will drop in to shoot the shit with us. . . . Navy admirals around the world drop in or call in to my and other Members. For example, the commanding officer of a ship in the Mediterranean Sea suddenly found his vessel in the middle of a large-scale Soviet exercise. He filmed this extraordinary event with a camcorder right off the deck of his ship. Soon after docking into Norfolk, he was up in the Member's office showing a VHS tape of the exercise to the Member and staff while enjoying drinks together. I think this is encouraged by the CNO rather than frowned upon.

We tell the Navy leadership, get guys with skipper aircraft carrier experience to come up in their "whites" and walk the halls of Congress. The Navy is responsive to these suggestions. You make the same suggestions to the Army and those suggestions disappear somewhere.[35]

A second congressional perception explaining the less visible and less engaged senior Army leadership is a palpable sense of discomfort exhibited by senior flag officers, due largely to their lack of experience in working on the Hill and in Washington. A most senior PSM on the SASC stated bluntly: *"The average Army flag officer would rather go to the dentist than come to the Hill.* I know newly promoted Army brigadier generals are told how important it is to go to the Hill, but they just don't want to come up here."[36]

Comments from the Hill describe senior Army generals as not only being less visible, but because they collaborate less in relation to the other services, they appear to be less comfortable when they do meet to engage with Members. Their demeanor and body language reflect both their discomfort with the crisis at hand and the lack of a close collaborative relationship with that Member:

They convey in their whole demeanor that they do not like being on the Hill. They go out of their way to inject in the conversation that they are warriors or soldiers out of their element. They remind the audience they are uncomfortable and feel disadvantaged or out of place in this political environment. They will say "Good to see you, sir. You know why I'm here." The subliminal message is—I wouldn't be here if it wasn't a crisis. Or they will say "Well, here is the way I see it, of course I can't tell you anything about how this will play on the Hill, that's definitely not my area. I'm not here to lobby." Again the reminder is telegraphed that they are a fish out of water on the Hill.[37]

An SASC PSM contrasted the style and manner in which the various services deal with senators on the Committee:

The Army comes across as being in awe of and/or afraid of senators. They approach all senators as five-star generals. If you hear someone in with a senator say "I hope I didn't track in mud on your carpet" or "I hope I'm not inconveniencing you but," you've dropped in on an Army general officer visit. Compare that with the Air Force. Their general officers come across as if the senators should be in awe of them! When they meet with a senator, you're likely to hear "Here's what we need to do, John," rather than typical Army deference. The Navy and Marine Corps are the best. The Navy shows due deference but not awe. The Marines have the advantage of the Navy to carry their water on big issues, but when they deal with a senator on strictly Marine issues, there is no begging or sniveling. It's "Here is what we need; here is how we plan on doing it." The Marine Corps senior flag officers and their LL come forward as the most professional of all.

Several House Members interviewed noted a patterned Army discomfort, formality, reservation, or fear when describing communications between Member and general officer:

The Army respects Congress as an institution. They understand that the legislative process is important, but they are fearful of Congress due to a lack of understanding of that process. The senior Army general operates from a different paradigm from the politician. The general's paradigm is one of a trustful soldier, where the politician's is more personal in nature. *Politics is personal.* Unless a service has a strategy to get out and get to know people it will be less effective in the Washington political environment. The Army is not that personal; probably the least personal of the services. They need to address that shortcoming.[38]

This sense of discomfort on the Hill is more characteristic of today's Army four-star generals than their counterparts of 15 or 20 years earlier. General Max Thurman, former Vice Chief of Staff of the Army and later regional Commander-in-Chief of Southern Command during Operation *Just Cause* in Panama, did not fit this pattern. General Thurman's understanding of Washington and his willingness and skills, as an Army combat arms officer, to engage Congress (and officials in OSD) for the good of the Army and nation is legendary within Army, Pentagon, and congressional circles. General Thurman stressed in our interview that today's senior Army leadership "must break down the imagery that these folks (Members) are unapproachable.... Building relations is important. It is primarily done on a non-confrontational and non-issue basis.... You want the member to respect the fact that the advice you give him is good."[39]

A respected Member of Congress on the HNSC attributes Army general officer discomfort on the Hill to a greater lack of Washington experience and a more inadequate understanding of Congress and the Constitution than was the case for the most promising of Army officers when he came to Congress. He asked, "Where are the Max Thurmans in today's Army?" In addressing the notion of fearing that which you do not understand, he went on to state, "Max Thurman wasn't afraid of us [Congress], he understood us."[40]

Representative (now Senator) Reed (D-RI), a West Point graduate, made the comment that the "senior Army military leadership mistakenly discount their own importance on the Hill. Members are more impressed with the CNO or the CSA dropping by unannounced for a visit than they realize. Members value the professional skill and bearing of senior flag officers. Army senior general officers tiptoe around us, as if we are so powerful or too busy to want to meet and talk with them. That is not the case."[41]

A third congressional perception explaining the less visible and less engaged senior Army leadership is an institutional desire to protect the more senior Army flag officers from the uncertainties and perceived risks of the Hill.

Rather than agency resources viewed by Congress as effective in shaping the legislature battlefield, the Army seems to view senior flag officers as resources requiring protection from the volatilities and uncertainties of that legislative battlefield. Insulating and safeguarding senior general officers reduces the likelihood of a more broad, timely, and substantive engagement with Members and staff alike. This makes it more difficult for them to become part of the policy-making team and influence or shape legislative outcomes. An SASC PSM recognized this Army penchant for protecting its senior military leadership on the Hill:

Before sending its top senior leaders to the Hill, the Army tends first to send out its scouts. The Army wants to know what the answer is before they send the Chief of Staff over to the Hill. They want to ensure a safe environment for the Chief-of-Staff-of-the-Army. The Commandant and CNO [Chief of Naval Operations] are more willing, and are likely to feel more confident, to go over when answers are not known and the situation is still fluid—a norm for the Hill.[42]

This Army institutional proclivity to shield its senior flag officers from the unexpected, transient, and sometimes confrontational aspects of the legislative battlefield helps explain the Army's reduced presence on the Hill, but it reflects a deficient understanding of Congress and its role in policymaking:

The Chief of Staff of the Army may get badgered by a Senator on a minor issue. Over here, he is just another bureaucratic functionary. Actually, the Chiefs of the services get treated much better than other bureaucratic functionaries. In the Chief-of-Staff-of-the-Army's eyes, a visit to the Hill only exposes him to demeaning, unpleasant, and irrelevant experiences that he would just as soon do without. However, the visit with that Member is important, even if it's a minor home state issue, it's important. I'm afraid there is a degree of sanctimoniousness that can intrude in the attitude of military officers. Many of the Members are serving the nation well in a conscientious fashion. On the other hand, not all of Member actions reflect self-sacrifice. The root of the problem is that *many in the Army*, like the American public at large, *do not understand Congress as an institution.*

An SASC PSM stated that the other services take a different tack with Congress:

Other services have a much more frequent and personal contact with senators and staff who make suggestions. These suggestions are often incorporated into service plans and garner political support in the process. The Army tends to stay in its assembly area with its plans and ideas until the operation begins. The senior army leadership then runs out and expects the external world to embrace those plans and ideas.[43]

A former SASC PSM for an important subcommittee chair stated that an obvious difference in the services' approach is conveyed when the CSA compared with the other chiefs or four-stars:

This year before the budget hearings, the Army Chief of Staff was the only service Chief not to come over to talk with the Senator about his service's budget for FY96. The senator sits on the important SASC subcommittee that all Army programs go through. We, the staff were aware that the other Chiefs had met with the senator and were trying to help the Army from stepping on it. The Army Chief of Legislative Liaison told the staff that the Army was thinking of having the Vice Chief of Staff come in lieu of the Chief. Neither ended up meeting with the senator prior to the budget hearings. The new Chief of Staff, General Reimer, never requested a meeting with the senator before his confirmation. Compare that with General Krulak [Marine Commandant after General Mundy] who called once he was nominated to ask for a preconfirmation meeting. We had to finally call General Reimer to set up his preconfirmation meeting. It's just a difference in sensitivity and political sophistication. You can't help but pick up the feeling that the Army senior leadership would rather be anywhere else but on this side of the river.[44]

Why Are Visibility and Engagement of Senior Flag Officers Important? The presence and engagement of three- or four-star generals in positions of authority in the Army leadership are agency resources valued on the Hill. Because of their rank and experiences, they have a uniquely strong impact on Congress that cannot be matched by executive branch officials or lower ranked military officers. In addition, other services make use of these flag officer resources; the Army's willingness to do so is necessary to balance the other services' representational efforts. Finally, the most senior flag officers' willingness to engage sends a clear message to subordinates that working with Congress is a top, not rhetorical, priority.

Whether the Army feels comfortable with the role or not, the Congress and its defense committees place a heightened value on the presence, professional assessments, and opinions of these military officers. While four-star flag officers cannot be everywhere and do all things, the choices they make in where and how they spend their time have great significance on the congressional audience; they have a muted but institutionalized celebrity that accompanies their rank and position that opens doors and usually minds. Three- and four-star generals possess what one PSM for a senior Member of the HNSC refers to as the "gee whiz" factor:

When General Shali walks into a room to talk about any subject, members and staff on the Hill are far more likely to "sit up and listen" than if the colonel from his legislative-liaison staff comes in to discuss the same topic. This same "gee whiz" factor is at work when Admiral Owens, Admiral Boorda, General Fogelman, General Mundy, and yes, General Sullivan, walk in to speak with a Member or staff on the Hill. The Chief of Staff of the Army over the last 10 years have had that resource in their pocket, but for some reason have decided not to use it as effectively as others on the Hill.[45]

More important, the congressional audience places a great and unique value on the professional assessment and opinions of senior military officers. A senior PSM working for the Democratic side of the Committee stated:

The SASC trusts military officers. They feel that the civilians in the (services and OSD) Pentagon are political appointees and are more likely to fall in line with an administration or OSD position. . . . We expect [flag officers] to tell us [during confirmation that] they will give us their personal opinion when asked. The relationship between the Congress and the military hierarchy should be one of mutual respect.[46]

A senior staffer for a chairman of a powerful SASC subcommittee also confirmed this view: "Congress looks more to the military leadership than the civilian leadership for engagement on issues."[47]

The Army's senior leadership has everything to gain and little to lose from greater visibility and engagement on the Hill. A senior MLA for a senator stated that the Army would have fewer problems in the SASC marks if they were more engaged on the Hill: "When you are approaching an SASC mark-up, senators tend to listen to the senior military guys. Very few times will the committee go against their strong recommendations."[48] An MLA for a senior Democratic senator on the SASC stressed that timeliness, accuracy, and candidness combine to make relationships with the military leaders of greater value than their civilian superiors: "I do practically all my business with the uniformed Army. When the s— hits the fan, I don't call the civilian leadership. It's the uniformed guys who get the job done. They give us straight answers in a timely manner."[49]

Despite the value of this agency resource with the congressional audience, the Army is more likely to allocate it elsewhere or ineffectively to the Hill, a pattern that frustrates Army supporters in Congress. A Republican PSM for the SASC commented that Army general officer underrepresentation on the Hill equates to the Congress being more reliant on the executive branch's view of this one service. This relates to a pattern concerning problems with the Army's message being understood on the Hill, discussed later in the chapter:

We rely on the uniformed senior leaders to speak candidly on issues and not be reluctant to express their personal professional judgments. Our concern is that those personal professional judgments stop over in the Pentagon and don't make it over to Congress. We don't get the information we need and the overall process is hurt. . . . The Army will stand there scraping the ground with its foot, chafing as it defers to the wisdom of its civilian [executive branch] superiors. . . . My concern with the Army, its lessened engagement with Congress and the way it softpedals rather than candidly articulating its needs, is there is a dangerous disconnect in what Congress expects and what the Army senior leadership knows it can deliver. *The Congress is expecting a greater output from the Army and sitting content on the committee believing the necessary inputs have been provided.* For example, when the Army leadership states to Congress that current funding levels for this year are "adequate." Army leaders have an image of what adequate means. . . . "Adequate" to many Members implies a certain level of robustness that won't be there. An increased understanding of Army requirements can only be enhanced with increased and more willing engagement of senior Army generals who, by their position, have natural and automatic access to Members.[50]

An earlier comment by a Senate MLA, "The Army doesn't know how to get to Members,"[51] parallels a comment by a senior member on the HNSC: "Army senior general officers just don't have the touch."[52] Both comments begin to make sense when the perceived pattern of Congress as a hindrance or adversary rather than a team player is combined with the pattern of disengagement of the Army's most senior flag officers. The two patterns combine to ignore a basic tenet of human nature that people have egos and like to feel important. When that tenet is applied to individuals in positions of authority, it can take the form of Members and staff valuing both the attention of the senior military leadership and being treated as contributors and team players to new service proposals, programs, or positions.

This tenet allows the political elite to become involved early in the process, voice any concerns in private, make suggestions while a proposal or program is in the draft stage, be able to claim credit and part ownership of the proposal, and most importantly, assist the service in building support for it. This commonsense aspect of human nature undergirding effective liaising behavior (as discussed in earlier chapters) is captured well by a retired Army officer who now serves as a senior PSM on one of the authorization committees:

Army officers see the Congress as a nuisance; they resent that people over here can get into their knickers and change things that they want to do. And what they really need to do, I believe, is get over here and elicit a cooperative "We're here to work with you," "We'd like to have your views on this," "We need your help," kind of attitude.

Senators are like everybody else. They've got their own feelings and pride. If you make them feel [part of your process], "Senator, . . . We need your help because of your long experience on these matters. Here's what we're fighting and here's what we're trying to accomplish,'' the Senator responds, "Well, okay, I remember back when . . . I heard someone got a deal like this. . . . Why don't you look at something like this?'' The service responds: "Okay, sir, we'll do that.'' The service doesn't have to change their course 180 degrees . . . [but] just incorporate a little bit of something in there. Then they come back and say, "Hey Senator, you were very helpful to us in this and we changed our plan accordingly to incorporate *x, y,* and *z* of your concerns or recommendations.'' And then they have a senator on board, and he's part of it. But the Army senior leaders don't even want to come up here and tell him what their plan is about, much less ask for his input. They only come when they have a crisis or are required to come. And even then, like before the hearings this year, I don't think they even made routine calls on these senators.[53]

This next comment underscores the importance of stroking the ego of a Member by demonstrating a sincere effort at addressing his or her concerns, rather than merely stating why those concerns cannot be resolved. This MLA works for a powerful senator with Marine and Navy interests in his state. Being responsive to this Member's office equates to a willingness to try and work out a satisfactory deal or resolution of the Member's concerns:

The Navy does an outstanding job of pushing their agenda items for budgets. Navy admirals and Marine Corps Generals have bowed up in the past and tend to be more independent vis-à-vis OSD. They are aware that their agenda items are incredibly expensive and accordingly you find a responsive (to Congress) Navy leadership. The Army modernization budget, on the other hand, is severely underfunded. The Army leadership doesn't achieve budgetary success because you call on the Army leadership and they don't respond. . . . They ignore individual Members and ignore the Hill in a more collective sense. . . . The Army's response is too often "Senator, we can't do that. Now we'll be glad to tell you why we can't do that: it's too hard, too expensive, or doesn't fit into our plans.'' The Army doesn't get a second chance of engagement with that Member.[54]

Congressional interviewees repeatedly highlighted the importance of the military services' flag officer presence and engagement on the Hill by contrasting the visibility and engagement of the CSA on the Hill with the great liasing skills and habits of his counterpart in both the Navy and Marine Corps. Those interviewed on the Hill believe the approach adopted by the senior uniformed leader significantly influences the tone, example, and priorities that subordinate flag and field grade officers will adopt toward Congress. Both Admiral Mike Boorda, then CNO, and General Carl E. Mundy, Jr., then Commandant of the Marine Corps, were praised consistently for their visibility and enlightened engagement on the Hill.

General Mundy was praised for his understanding of and attention directed toward the legislative process. He had a reputation for being readily available to both Members and staff. While congressional committee staff found it difficult to get the CSA over to meet with their Member before budget hearings or committee marks, General Mundy consistently made time to do this. However, he also focused attention on influential staff working on defense issues. He was less concerned with protocol and precedent and more focused on timely engagement and effectively taking Marine concerns to the Hill for resolution and protection. He understood that over time MLAs tend to become committee staff (PSMs); committee staff tend to get appointed assistant secretaries of their military service or equivalent positions in OSD. Armed Services Committee staff repeatedly recounted how this four-star general impressed them by taking time to personally brief them (and MLAs of Members on those committees) on subjects ranging from the proposed FY96 Marine Corps budget to the Marine Corps' roles and missions.

General Mundy would drop by frequently to see Members and staff without a problem or issue to discuss. However, when an issue later arose, he was not slow to sit down with a Member and state his case in a most timely manner. General Mundy also understood how to use his LL personnel to enhance his liaising efforts on the Hill. He eliminated bureaucratic roadblocks and allowed his House and Senate LL division chiefs to communicate directly with him. When these lieutenant colonels recommended seeing someone, they did not have to send a memorandum through the Marine Corps staff hierarchy attempting to convince the staff and Commandant that the visit was important. Members and staff were aware of this close relationship and thereby afforded greater access to these particular LL personnel, knowing the message would reach the top Marine Corps leadership. Likewise, this LL person is likely to have just spoken to the Commandant on this issue and understands and can accurately articulate the Commandant's position. To a degree, this allowed some of the Commandant's ''gee whiz'' aura to rub off on the LL personnel. Unlike the CSA in recent years, General Mundy would never think of excluding his LL personnel from Member and staff discussions. General Mundy worked to boost rather than deflate the stature and influence of his LL personnel with Members and staff because he understood they were instrumental in optimizing a valuable agency resource for the Marine Corps on the Hill—the Commandant's time and engagement activities.

Some in the Army claim that it is easier for the Commandant to be so visible and engaged because the Marine Corps is a significantly smaller organization to manage and because the Navy addresses many of its concerns or issues on the Hill, thereby allowing the Commandant to focus on a more narrow agenda. These same individuals were forced to come up with a different set of excuses to explain the great respect and praise directed toward Navy senior uniformed leader on the Hill, Admiral Boorda.

Becoming CNO of a large organization in an environment of declining defense budgets following a series of publicized Navy problems like Tailhook, the Iowa explosion, and Navy performance in the Gulf War, Admiral Boorda used the resources of his position to counter the organization's cultural proclivity to communicate a patterned "we know what is best for the Navy" attitude that had damaged the Navy's relationship with civilian leaders in both the Pentagon and Congress.

Before his untimely death, Admiral Boorda had a reputation for effective liaising and for being everywhere on the Hill. As a new CNO, he visited close to 400 congressional offices in the first four months of 1995. He visited Members and staff regardless of whether they had naval bases or any military installations in their districts. He showed a new openness to engage Congress and address or fix problems that had been resisted by his predecessors; an approach many on the Hill found refreshing. He had experience in Washington, understood the Hill, and seemed to enjoy engaging with Members and staff on Navy and defense issues. He knew whom he needed to engage and was not shy or slow about doing so during busy "pre-mark" periods. He mastered the art of "drop-by" unscheduled visits on the Hill. He would scoff at the notion of some Army generals that drop-by visits were a waste of a four-star flag officer's time and energies. Although similar episodes had been recounted repeatedly in Hill interviews, good fortune allowed the rare opportunity to witness Admiral Boorda as he practiced the "art of liaising" on the Hill. Personal observations enforced the ideas that "politics is personal"; time can be maximized by engaging staff to enhance or nurture relationships; Members are approachable, even for drop-by visits with the military leader; and not surprisingly, the congressional audience appreciates seeing these senior military leaders when they do not need something and are not in the middle of a crisis. During a surprise "drop-by" visit to Rep. Norm Sisisky (D-VA), Admiral Boorda asked if he could leave a personal note for the Member. On a stenographer's pad, he inked a short note expressing his concern and wishing the Member good health (the Member had undergone chemotherapy a few months before). He soon left after expending fewer than four or five minutes in the outer office with everyone in that room assured that the Navy cares about Rep. Sisisky. However, within 45 minutes, the CNO returned to Rep. Sisisky's office, but this time with three junior Navy flag officers in tow, to find the Member back in his office and all were soon meeting together behind closed doors.[55]

Not only were the CNO's efforts to engage Rep. Sisisky successful, but three junior Navy admirals were being socialized and taught by a master the "art of liaising," and seeing the payoffs before their eyes. At least a generation of Army officers have been deprived of such socialization. Many Members and staff pointed out the importance of senior flag officer engagement with Congress by indicating what is being lost by the Army generals' more distant and wary approach: influence and trusted relationships with the men and women constitutionally empowered to approve resources for the Army as an institution: "The Army is underresourced. One of these days, the senior Army generals are going to wake up and learn that they need to come over here and earn those resources—by making their case."[56]

Pattern 4: The Army Is More Reactive and Less Proactive than the Other Services in Representing Its Institutional Interests and Concerns to Congress

Congressional interlocutors repeatedly pointed to the Army's tendency to be "reactive" rather than "proactive" on legislative issues as one its major short-comings. Reactive and proactive behavior both infer timing, but proaction implies a formal or informal strategy involving *initiating* calculated liaising measures to move particular actors in the process to support or oppose a particular position before support for that position has gelled. These calculated steps are intended to shape the legislative battlefield in ways that give your position a decisive advantage. *Reaction* implies the lack of a strategy. It involves executing calculated measures to move particular actors in the process to oppose a position that has materialized and already possesses some degree of political support. The degree of difficulty for the reactor will depend on how early or late in the process the proactor's intentions are discovered and how effectively the proactor initially garnered its targeted political support and shaped the legislative battlefield.

If an agency is seen as being less visible and engaged with Members and staff on the Hill, but also viewed as honest and responsive to requests for accurate information, it should come as little surprise that much of the Army activity is viewed as reactive rather than proactive in nature. Additionally, this pattern is greatly influenced by the Army's unfounded concern that anything proactive (the essence of unsolicited information) to Congress violates or moves too closely toward the grey area dealing with the anti-lobbying statutes:

The Army is more tentative, more respectful of the process and the traditional separation of the military and the government. The Army sees prohibitory regulations when thinking of Congress; more concern with lobbying; and more focused on supporting the President. The other services are more focused on a message, are continually refining that message, and targeting that message. The other services are adept at circumventing the President's budget.[57]

A senior PSM on the HNSC stated that proaction is the only way to succeed in Washington:

Does the Air Force cross the line in advocacy of their programs? You betcha! But they'd be fools not to. Their moves are calculated, they play politics and understand in these high stakes battles, to sit back passively like the Army and just provide information when asked is the worst approach to take. Success equates to being aggressively engaged, building coalitions of support, and then feeding those supporters with credible arguments and accurate information.[58]

The point that proactive strategy in representing Army interests with Congress is viewed with such discomfort within Army circles was reflected by an SASC

staffer commenting on possible implications and opportunities for the Army that
the November 1994 elections had brought. Instead of having an SASC staff
director who was a brigadier general in the U.S. Marine Corps Reserves
(USMCR), the SASC now had a Chairman who had served in the Army and a
retired Army general as staff director. However, he believed that the Army
leadership was uniquely incapable of proactively using this new situation to its
advantage in representing its interest to the Committee and Congress: *"They
consider it almost to be a criminal activity to sit down and theorize and stra-
tegize on how you can get what you want out of the Congress.* They take what
the Congress gives them. . . . [They do not do well] coming over here and lobbying Congress."[59]

An SASC PSM addressed the reactionary character of the Army's interface
with the Congress. Although his comments relate to the next pattern, which
concerns congressional understanding of the Army message, it goes to the heart
of the Army's reactive versus proactive pattern. The Army leadership waits to
react or defend against a materialized threat to an Army interest rather than sell
proactively a preferred position as a part of the larger Army message:

I don't think the Army makes a big effort to market itself to staff on its big picture. The
Army is more reactionary and focused on the issues that are 99 percent of the time
responses to SASC questions or otherwise responding to a pending newspaper article
about to be published. I don't see a coordinated "this is what America's Army stands
for" type of presentation.

The Army is "proactive in the defensive" rather than "proactive in the salesmanship"
mode. The other services are more proactive in the salesmanship mode and more likely
to show what good things are going on in their respective service.[60]

The problem for the Army in conducting effective proactive representation is
that Army leaders have been programmed to be uncomfortable with it, often
equating it to unprofessional lobbying of Congress. Early in this book the point
was made that there were very few prohibitions against unsolicited information
directly communicated between a service and the Congress. If the Army senior
leadership has learned to be wary of providing unsolicited information to sell
its message or a position, or does so only through its LL lieutenant colonels or
CLL, then it will tend to be reactionary to other actors' (to include the other
services') proactive representations:

The Army likes to think they are above the political fray. It's called representing a
group's or organization's interest. That is what pluralism and democracy are all about.
*There is no way Congress can stay abreast of all defense matters. I welcome unsolicited
information. Those who are proactive benefit.* Those who wait for a Member or staff to
initiate the request on a particular subject will lose time and opportunities. The Marine
Corps is the best, followed by the Navy, then Air Force, and finally, the Army.[61]

An SASC MLA stated that effective agency "lobbying" [liaising] required proactive behavior. Providing unsolicited information early on concerning subjects of key interest to a service that is accurate and credible keeps Members and staff from starting something that could cause problems down the road and be difficult as well as embarrassing to stop, once it gains momentum:

If you fail to lobby Members and staff to let them know your concerns, you leave them free to go find a better way to do it. *Always remember: ignorant people are dangerous!* If you are reactive rather than proactive in your senior leadership engagement, don't be surprised if Members and staff come up with creative ways to take money out of your account to put those dollars in an item of their concern.[62]

The Army's pattern of reacting to events on the Hill rather than shaping them ahead of time would be less problematic if it was not for the cumulative effect of other patterns already discussed. It is one thing to react to materialized efforts against one's interests and combat them in a timely, forthright manner. However, it is all important how early and accurate an assessment the reactor receives on that materialized effort. If the Army is perceived by Hill insiders to a greater degree than other services as viewing the Congress as a hindrance rather than a team player, it reduces the likelihood that the Army will get an early and accurate "heads up" of the materialized effort against its interests. Additionally, if the Army's senior flag officers are perceived as less visible and engaged on the Hill, the Army has fewer "working" relationships to give it early warning. All this combines to increase the likelihood that the Army will be "surprised" late in the process. The task of turning back the materialized effort gets exponentially more difficult when it goes unnoticed and suddenly surfaces in a committee mark.

Proactive and collaborative engagement with Members and staff on the Hill, if conducted in an honest and credible manner, lead to relationships of trust and friendship where information and candid assessments are exchanged between these two very different worlds. Rather than being surprised by an action against one's interests and having to work to solicit support to turn that action around, it is best to have people out on the Hill and in the Pentagon with their ears to the ground who will call you when a rumor surfaces. Of the services, most on the Hill believed the Army was far more likely to be surprised by an unfavorable Committee mark. Only friends will provide you those timely, heads-up notifications:

In the game of influencing Congress, it's wise to be friendly enough with, work at establishing relationships over the years with congressional staff and Members to where they will call you on *your* issue. It means you won't have to call them asking for support. Instead, they call you when they first hear of something. Many times this proves to be valuable information that allows the service to counter and respond before things have gone too far along in the process.[63]

The Army appears to have the best reputation of the services for those types of activities that do not require proactive and engaged activity by its higher echelons. Much Army LL work involves responding to questions and concerns submitted by Members and initially written or called in by Members' constituents. The Army treats all these cases as legitimate and top priority. It assigns a caseworker to get a quick and accurate answer back to the Member and does its best to resolve any problem discovered in the course of the investigation. These actions are largely handled by civilian and field-grade officer personnel; rarely are any flag officers involved. A senior MLA in the Senate stated that the various services were effective in different areas:

When you speak about effectiveness of the services in working with Congress you must specify which of two areas you are addressing. One area is the legislative agenda and service budgets. In this area the Marine Corps is first, the Navy second, Air Force third, and Army dead last. However, when it comes to conducting case work for service personnel it is a much different matter. The Army is better than the Navy and Air Force with case work.[64]

An SASC PSM makes the final point that a reactionary approach limits senior Army leadership ability to lay the groundwork effectively for addressing fundamental Army problems three to five years in the future. The reactionary approach does not require a long-term legislative strategy:

The Army wants to fight only the immediate fight rather than fight problems you know will be there in FY97 and beyond. To do the latter requires a long-term legislative strategy. But the Army leadership has mastered the art of constipating themselves. For an organization that prides itself in its flexibility, responsiveness, speed, and maneuverability on the battlefield, the Army senior leaders are frozen in the headlights when it comes to showing those qualities and working effectively in this environment.[65]

Pattern 5: Limited and Less Sophisticated Outreach

Outreach efforts to Congress by Army LL and the Army senior leadership are perceived by the congressional audience to be the less apparent and less sophisticated of the four services. "Outreach" in this instance is defined as "an act of reaching out; an organized effort to *extend* services beyond usual limits, as to particular segments of a community."[66] For purposes of this study, outreach will refer to the organized efforts by a service's LL and its senior leadership to extend their service presence, assistance, and information to a wider segment of the congressional audience. Extension in this capacity means to *initiate* the offer of contact, assistance, and information rather than *react* or respond to congressional requests for the same. Through this initiated effort, relationship building and understanding between service and Hill participants can flourish if the liaising effort is maintained over time.

Army LL outreach is characterized generally in two ways. First, the effort seems less apparent than what takes place by the other services. Army outreach is seen to cast a relatively small net and ignore significant segments of the congressional audience. Second, the outreach that is visible seems less sophisticated and attuned to the interests of the congressional audience that the Army is targeting. Army outreach is more likely to be ill-timed and less likely to be encouraging participation than the other services' efforts in this area.

Now let us examine the Army's use of the LL outreach tools, which fuel the patterned perception of its outreach program as casting a small net and being less attuned to congressional interests, and look at how these tools are used in reaching and connecting with new or neglected segments of Congress:

1. The Army relies too heavily on the same small group of Members for support.
2. Unlike the other services, the Army seems to discount the importance of outreach to MLAs. In particular, the Army does not use its collocation on the Hill as effectively as the other services.
3. The Army does not use its agency "travel" resource as effectively as the other services.
4. "The Army isn't sexy or glamorous like the other services" rationale becomes a self-fulfilling prophesy.
5. The Army doesn't use its social functions agency resource as effectively as it could.

The Army Relies too Heavily on the Same Small Group of Members for Support. My interviews highlighted the congressional view that the Army senior leadership is focused on a relatively small pool of Members and staff for support. The Army tends to go to the same small group of Members if it has a crisis and needs "champions" in Congress on an issue. In doing so, it misses opportunities to cast a wider net and build broader support, magnifies the damage of a champion's departure from the Congress or majority party shifts, and places a heavy burden on a few individuals. It was felt by many on the Hill that the other services do a better job of recognizing, keeping track of, and nurturing the relationships of friends.

A PSM HNSC with over 20 years on the Hill stated that, unlike the Marine Corps and Navy, the Army refuses to outreach widely on the Hill, to include members of Congress:

I haven't seen the Chief of Staff of the Army at anything but his required presence at hearings. It makes me believe the senior Army leadership has not seen a need to engage Congress widely. . . . The Army tends on relying on a narrow base of stalwarts who are active in the Army Caucus who will help them move Army programs in Congress. This strategy works until a program runs into question and is thrown into a wider arena where the Army lacks that base support. I doubt this small pool of Member support in the Army Caucus provides adequate platform for achieving Army interests. . . . The Army just does not sell itself to a broader audience of Members. From the Hill perspective, it appears that the Army has an institutional (cultural) view that Congress is a group we *have to* deal with; therefore, who are the fewest number of Members we *have to* talk with. Therefore, the Army pursues its old legislative strategy of going to their "old reliables." That strategy made more sense when you had a large number of WW II and Korea vets in Congress who would take their cue from this small pool. Those days are long gone.[67]

This theme was equally prevalent in discussing Army outreach in the Senate. A PSM on the SASC observed:

The Army's senior flag officers should try to reach out to more senators and staff. The Army tends to focus on a few horses they know. . . . They should try to reach out to other Members. . . . The Army doesn't work to bring people into their tent. . . . The Army is wary of approaching senators without Army facilities in their states. I think some of the Army's reluctance goes back to this "lobbying is illegal" bull that poisons their water. Lobbying [liaising] goes hand in hand with the senior Army leadership's professional responsibility.[68]

An MLA for an influential senator on the SASC stated that the Army senior leadership has always overlooked his boss because they assume he would not be interested in Army issues because of the lack of Army units or facilities in his state. The other services do not make this false assumption:

My boss is one of the most ardent supporters of a strong defense. Because there is no Army installation in our state you are correct that he is not obliged to support your concerns. But it is folks like my Member, on the SASC, who are often swing votes, because of the lack of military presence in our state, that you would think you would want to work. My senator will be more likely to push for doing the thing that makes the most sense from a national security perspective. . . . The Navy and the Marine Corps, and the Air Force to a lesser degree, work hard at their most senior military leadership levels on reaching out to my boss.[69]

While a Member might lack Army installations in his district or state, there are often many other factors, some personal, that would provide an immediate affinity for a senior Army general officer to nurture and further develop a relationship on the Hill. Commenting on missed opportunities, an MLA for a subcommittee chair, stated:

The Navy and Marine Corps have fans up here. But the Army doesn't count my boss as a friend. He is more familiar with the Army than the other service. He wasn't in the Army, but his Dad was. The senior Army leadership must look at his bio sheet and assume because he wasn't in the Army, he therefore must be neutral. There are many fans of the Army who never served in the Army. The Army doesn't do a good job of saying "These are our friends." The Marines excel at knowing who their friends are and enlisting their help.[70]

The Army senior leadership must not only want to meet with Members from a wider base of the Congress, but must be politically sensitive to the impact of Army positions on these Members whose support they would like to have. Such an approach in 1995 might have been prudent in dealing with Senator Cohen, who became the Secretary of Defense in 1997:

There are some very powerful senators over here that are intelligent and good debaters, and the Army should always want them on their side. Senator Cohen was identified to the Army a year or so ago [for targeted engagement]. They piss him off every year some way with some petty-ass something that doesn't amount to a hill of beans. And Cohen would like to support the Army, but they just have a way of finding something to piss him off about every year over something that's peanuts. They're about to do it again.[71]

The potential long-term benefits of an energized outreach effort to use the access and magnetism of the senior leadership to bring other Members and staff under the Army tent should be obvious. An energized outreach by the senior Army leadership would need to be non-crisis-related. It would entail devoting time and effort to non-pressurized opportunities for both parties to meet and better understand the other's world.

The Army's neglect in building relationships was raised by an SASC PSM who stated that the Army "focuses on Members in shallow ways. Once they make contact, that's it! It's like they check a name off a list as if they completed some required chore."[72] Relationship building takes time and is a long-term but vital institutional investment. It is the responsibility of the senior Army leadership to ensure this outreach is as wide and genuine as possible. This is something the other services and their senior flag officers understand.

If the Army leadership and LL operation decide to widen the net they cast for Members, the senior leadership and LLs should focus not only on frequent engagement with newly targeted Members, but widen their net of effective engagement with the MLAs of these Members as well. As the next section describes, the Army is significantly behind the other services' outreach efforts to MLAs on the various defense committees.

The Army Discounts the Importance of MLAS and Army Collocation Agency Resources. The clearest complaint of the "small net" tendency in Army outreach effort can be heard from MLAs for Members on the authorization committees, especially on the House side. Unlike the Army, the other services tend to target MLAs more as a group with the specific needs and interests of MLAs in mind. This targeting and engagement appear in the eyes of the congressional MLAs to emanate from the other services' liaison offices collocated on Capitol Hill, and take the form of drop-bys to see the MLA; trips designed to orient, educate, and network MLAs; and social functions targeted for networking MLAs.

It is in many of these outreach avenues that the Army experiences problems. As noted earlier, of all the aforementioned outreach techniques, the Army does best in responding to questions and requests for information and briefings in an honest and timely manner. However, MLAs rank the Army lowest in the other areas. The problem seems most evident with House MLAs, especially with those working for Members on the HNSC. This is true as well on the Senate side, but to a lesser degree (as will be explained later).

MLAs of the two defense authorization committees often feel they are discounted or ignored as a group and as individual staffers by the Army in relation to the other services. They believe the Marine Corps does the best, followed closely by the Navy, then the Air Force. The Army finishes last. Many MLAs felt compelled to highlight their role and the shortsightedness of ignoring them: "MLAs are important. As his principal staff on armed services issues, I give him very frank recommendations. Don't kid yourself into thinking that MLAs don't frequently cajole Members into positions."[73]

This perceived problem of outreach is partially a result of a jurisdictional problem between the more issue-specific LL officers who work in the Army's LL Programs Division in the Pentagon and the non-issue specific LL officers, collocated on the Hill, who work in its House Liaison Division (HLD) and its Senate Liaison Division (SLD). As observed in Chapter 1, LL officers in Programs Division, with its Policy and Hardware sections, currently are responsible for the two defense authorization committees, to include Members, PSMs, and MLAs of those Members serving on those committees. The HLD and SLD LL officers are generally focused on everyone else, except for appropriators, and tend to frequently travel worldwide on congressional delegations with members from non-defense committees.

The jurisdictional debates and tension over which division in the Army LL operation has responsibility for MLAs working for Members on the HNSC and SASC are unimportant to the MLA. What is important to MLAs is that services other than the Army, using their HLD or SLD resources, are far better at meeting their informational needs and are more available for outreach and other valued relationship-building activities.

In comparison to both Committee PSMs and Senate MLAs, House MLAs on average tend to be younger and less experienced on the Hill and often lack a detailed understanding of armed services issues. A few might have some military experience, but that is rare. Accordingly, many of these MLAs do not have the status and influence that the PSMs on the committee or many Senate MLAs possess. There are many exceptions to this profile, especially with MLAs who work for more senior Members of the committees. However, maturity, Hill experience, influence with the Member and committee, and understanding of armed services issues possessed by these MLAs still do not earn them the same attention from the Army as the other services.

MLAs have to be jacks of all trades. They need information that covers the entire spectrum of armed services issues. PSMs, on the other hand, have narrower issue-area responsibilities, have been around long enough to know whom to call in a service's LL Programs Division, and have a wealth of contacts in the Pentagon they can contact for information. The MLA, who is usually younger and less experienced in an issue area, has more issues to cover and usually fewer contacts for information. These unique and particularized needs of the MLA color their view of the world. They appreciate the other services' HLD and SLD efforts that address their needs and simplify their tasks. These MLAs, hungry for timely information, naturally are wary of getting passed from one bureaucrat to another in the Pentagon. They appreciate knowing someone who is readily available to answer the easy questions, or at least ensure that they get the right answer in a timely manner. That personal involvement is a relationship builder:

It is important for service LLs to keep wired with the MLAs. This contact doesn't have to be with the CLL or the Army's senior leadership. The Navy and Marines HLD LL folks will drop by unannounced to say "Hey, how are you doing? Any problems?" I'm just talking about a 5-minute deal. Or if they are with a general officer, they might stick their head in and say "we were walking to see Congressman X, we just wanted to see how you are doing." The Army is not getting its bang for the buck out of its HLD office in the Rayburn Building. I know an MLA with a major Army command in his district. He knew no one in the Army HLD shop so he would just call directly to the installation. There seems to be more of a "one stop shopping" philosophy in the other services and more of a connection with the MLAs. MLAs are not likely to call the Army HLD shop because there is no face to the name when they call.[74]

A similar cry for simplicity and for a trusted face to help them navigate through the Army's bureaucratic maze was voiced by a House MLA. Again, the U.S. Marine Corps House Liaison Division seems to be the standard for what MLAs value in carrying out their duties.

If I want to talk Army [LL] personnel (issues), there is one guy in the Pentagon . . . for readiness, still another; for military installation and facilities, another guy is involved. There is no telling if I know these folks; are they available or on vacation? If he or she is on vacation, will I be shuffled off to another faceless bureaucrat? There is no one interface on these matters in Army House Liaison Division. The Hill doesn't operate like the military. Staffers hate running through the bureaucracy of any agency. Colonel Sattler, head of Marine House Liaison, will call the person in the Building to get me an answer. If a more detailed response is needed, he'll have the expert in the Building give me a call. Again it seems like they are more concerned with maximizing the efficiency of staffers' time which is appreciated.[75]

A House MLA with over 17 years of experience echoed a typical complaint with Army outreach in general:

I don't have a clue what the Army HLD office does. They must have a more narrowly defined mission: casework and CODEL [congressional delegation] travel abroad. We never really use them except for case work. . . . Because of the lack of information and relationships with the Army, we have placed our efforts in establishing reliable contacts at the local level. We'll call the Post Commander at the local Army installation when we have questions.[76]

The other services appear more sophisticated in understanding and addressing the needs of the MLA. The following addresses the products that the services know the MLA will be required to produce for the Member wishing to support or comment on a particular issue or program:

You can tell the programs the Navy and Marine Corps really want. They know how Congress operates and understand what it is, the product the MLA will have to produce for the Member. They provide you information formatted and structured so that any new MLA can turn it into a press announcement or release, a ''Dear Colleague'' or other type letter, or floor speech quickly with minimal hassles.[77]

This sophistication saves even an experienced MLA's time and effort and makes that MLA look better to that Member. The service LL gets timely and effective member support. Win-win situations of this nature are the lifeblood of strong relations on the Hill.

The MLA outreach problem appears to be more acute with House MLAs, but it is obvious from Senate MLAs that the other services are more astute at meeting their needs and developing relationships as well.

The Senate is a more formal and closed body than the House when it comes to its Members and even staff. You have to put more of your agency resources into building these relationships over time. Senate MLAs tend to be older, more experienced, and knowledgeable than the average MLA on the House side. Senate MLAs, however, still sit up and take note when a senior flag officer shows them special attention. According to my interlocutors, this special attention is required and is being directed toward Senate MLAs by the other services, especially the Navy and Marine Corps:

The Navy and Marine Corps do the best on the Hill because they understand the [Senate] and the process up here better than the Air Force and the Army. . . . The Navy and Marine Corps understand how to maximize the access of their flag officers. . . . Senior flag officers score points when they drop in to see a Senate MLA. Staffers like the attention. The Navy/USMC LLs know how to optimize that access.[78]

Another senior Senate MLA commented that the Navy and Marine Corps look for special opportunities to engage MLAs:

When Lieutenant General Zinni came to town to brief the Pentagon and administration on the evacuation mission of personnel from Somalia, Colonel Terry Paul, Marine Senate Liaison Chief, initiated the action to get him over to brief Senate MLAs. Zinni attracted a room full of staffers for an hour. The brief and discussion was well received. . . . The Marines and the Navy tend to do more with the staff than the Air Force and the Army. Their LL organizations understand what motivates Senate MLAs and Senate PSMs. Senate staff are always hungry for information. The more information that we have, the better staff we are. Senior general officers who have just completed key operations or senior general officers on the service staffs willing to address staff on important subjects will always draw a crowd. The Marine Corps' senior general officers seem more willing to engage the staff one-on-one or in small groups. It makes a favorable impression and is effective in delivering a message.[79]

Taking advantage of agency resources to create special events that Senate MLAs and PSMs will value and attend is not an Army strong suit. One SASC PSM pointed to the need for more such events and stated that these events could be as simple as informal sessions where a senior Army leader makes himself available for dialogue with the staff as a group:

You want special events that are going to catch attention. I think General Tilelli [the VCSA] is seen over here as open, sincere, and personable, but like most senior Army generals, he doesn't get over here enough. The Army needs to have that level of person who gets closer to these people. *You're not going to get closer to them unless you use your big guns.* The Army should take a guy like Tilelli and have him periodically available to talk with Senate staff and anyone else who happens to drop by. You'd have coffee and doughnuts available. People would stand around and drink coffee for ten or fifteen minutes and then sit down and he'd give a little preamble of things going on. He'd just be there to talk and answer any questions they might have about the Army and its Army programs. This would be a special event that would be noticed and valued on the Senate side.[80]

While the Committee staff will cooperate with MLAs of Members on the Committee, many MLAs want to have their own independent access to information. This allows them to better serve their Member, who is often too junior on the Committee to be able to handpick a PSM (normally his former MLA) to the Committee:

You don't want to rely on strictly committee staff for your information. Not only are they terribly busy and getting a hold of them a possible problem when you have a deadline to meet, but they may be less than forthcoming if my Member is working an issue in a different direction from the subcommittee or committee chairs that hired them. My responsibilities are to my Member.[81]

Understanding the importance of the MLA to a Member on the HNSC or SASC is essential and can contribute to increased support for a service's programs and concerns. The question that the other services seem to do a better job in both asking and answering is, "How can I assist in making you more effective in doing your job for the Member?" To answer this question it is necessary to understand the demands of their job in general and then evaluate where they exist on the continuum of experience and knowledge on the Hill and armed services issues. Once this evaluation is made, a service member can assist in filling gaps MLAs have in information about the service and help them network among their fellow MLAs.

In summary, dropping by to see MLAs and devoting time to get to know them, providing them one-stop shopping for timely information, and providing this information in packaged formats that save MLAs' time and make them look good to their bosses are examples of closer, more effective, and more attuned engagement that pay off for the other services' LL outreach efforts. These are best accomplished by services who optimize their dual-agency resources of col-location on the Hill and issue-specific LL expertise in their Programs Divisions in the Pentagon.

In addition, today's MLAs will be tomorrow's PSMs on the Committee. PSMs from the defense committees are often selected for senior politically appointed positions in the various service secretariats and OSD. Attention and resources directed toward developing trusted relationships with these MLAs early in their legislative careers are wise short- and long-term investments. The other services understand this and are making these investments now as they cast a very wide net.

The Army Does Not Use Its Agency "Travel" Resource as Effectively as the Other Services. House MLAS feel relatively ignored as a group in regard to Army travel and orientation trips.

Congressional staff trips are important. The greatest contacts and relationships are forged on these trips. . . . It is human nature. I have been on a lot of Navy and a few Air Force trips, but only one quasi-Army trip to Huntsville, AL, on a Ballistic Missile Defense issue. I have never been asked by the Army to travel to their National Training Center or Ft. Knox or any other Army facility to help orient me on the Army.[82]

The ability to travel with Members and staff is a great agency resource, but currently it is not being used as effectively by the Army as by the other services, according to my interviews. Travel can be an orientation trip that introduces a Member or staffer to service personnel, their weapon systems, facilities, and operations. It can also be a more narrowly focused trip where a Member and/or staffer seeks a more comprehensive understanding on a particular issue or pro-gram. Both types of trips provide important information that Members and staff require that cannot be acquired from a briefing in Washington.

Additionally, traveling with a Member or staffer enables the service or LL to get them away from the competing distractions that are the norm in Washington. Throughout the trip, the service LL has opportunities to get better acquainted with the congressional person. The service LL escort officer is able to discover similar interests and better understand how this Member or staffer approaches a range of issues. In casual conversations, he discovers what is important in this person's world.

Access is suddenly not an issue, because it is available over a more extended period. This trip is designed to meet and exceed the requirements specified by the congressional person when arrangements were made. The Member and staffer are by circumstance dependent on the service LL officer. Prompt, professional, and flexible execution of LL escort duties is usually appreciated by congressional Members and staff. Relationships are forged and trust is strengthened on these trips if they are planned and carried off properly.

Acquiring congressional participation on these informational trips is more difficult than many senior officers less familiar with Congress might expect. Members are very busy, and most Members feel compelled to spend time when not in Washington in their districts shoring-up local support and with their families. The Members who are most in need of orientation visits are the new Members of Congress. Rep. McHugh (R-NY) who co-chairs the Army Caucus, stated his frustration at getting new folks out to discover the Army:

It is difficult to get new Members of Congress to travel during their first term. They believe it is political suicide to travel to the National Training Center [NTC] as a new Member. They are concerned their challengers in the next election will portray their information-gathering trip as a taxpayer defense boondoggle. The NTC is located at Fort Irwin in the California desert. It is isolated and austere; no place to go to shop. But still they fear the label of traveling on the taxpayer's dole.[83]

Understanding the pressure of Members' schedules and the importance that travel must appear strictly business back home, it is important to get the senior Army leadership involved in the travel outreach effort. A Member is more likely to participate on an Army trip if he knows in advance that he will be accompanying the Secretary of the Army, the Under Secretary of the Army, Chief of Staff of the Army, Vice Chief of Staff of the Army, or even the Deputy Chief of Staff for Operations and Plans to a particular training event or installation. If the senior Army leadership uses its "gee whiz" agency resource of rank and position to meet and talk with these Members before, a follow-up session where the invitation is offered has a good chance of working. Persistence and follow-up invitations must be offered until both schedule and "gee whiz" combine to make the trip occur.

However, consistent with previously discussed patterns, Members of Congress stated they were more likely to be approached directly for service orientation travel by senior flag officers of the other services. An MLA expressed a double-edged frustration that only recently had his boss received his first invitation to visit the Army's National Training Center (NTC): "The Under Secretary of the Army invited my boss a couple of weeks ago to go to NTC. It's the first invite he's had from the Army and he's a subcommittee chair on the HNSC with Army interests in his district. I haven't been invited either."[84]

All service LL organizations, including the Army, understand the relationship-building potential that travel provides, but the Army tends to focus on simply getting Members and PSMs to travel. However, both Senate and House MLAs commented that the Army does not provide many opportunities for MLA travel, missing an important chance to educate, seek support for key programs, and build relationships. As the MLAs often progress to positions of greater influence, the other services consider this a good long-term investment of agency resources. MLAs stress that they take this travel very seriously, wanting full substantive schedules and opportunities to interact with both service and other congressional staff.

An MLA for a Member who chairs a subcommittee on the HNSC noted the different outreach philosophy of the Army when it comes to travel:

I take a question to the other service LLs and they respond with an offer of a trip. *I have never been invited on an Army trip.* The Navy and Marine Corps planned a trip where they had us sleep overnight on a carrier out at sea in which they would have Marine pilots land on a carrier at night for the first time. It was a special event for the Navy and Marine Corps as well as for the staffers witnessing the event. I have deployed for a day on a submarine. The Air Force and Navy combined to take a group of MLAs to Seattle where Boeing makes the B-2 bomber. We then headed to San Diego for three days where we saw every type of surface vessel and submarine. We were briefed on Navy Seal operations and capabilities and then were taken to nearby Camp Pendleton for time with Marines where we all got to shoot M-16 rifles.[85]

An MLA for a member with significant Navy and some Army interests in his district highlighted the importance of travel and how the Navy and Marines do it so well:

The Navy and Marines took me on a trip to Corpus Christi, Texas, and Pensacola, Florida. There I got to look at strategic aircraft, naval aviation, introductory undergraduate training for Navy helicopters, etc. I have been on trips with them to Norfolk where I have visited Aegis destroyers, Marine amphibious ships, surface and subsurface vessels, and have taken helicopter flights to aircraft carriers underway at sea. You come away from these trips far more informed than when you started. They are invaluable![86]

One experienced HNSC MLA compared Army and Navy approaches to outreach via travel for MLAs. In this staffer's view, the Army is losing opportunities to educate key civilians on its essence: its soldiers. This form of outreach enables staffers to come into a service's world, which cannot be replicated in a sterile brief given in Washington:

There are two types of approaches I see in service outreach efforts with Congress. First, you have the very direct Navy/USMC approach . . . [where on] a regular basis they set up trips for MLAs to allow us to see sailors and marines in action out in the field handling the hardware. You are looking at what you are getting briefed on. There is no substitute for hands-on demonstrations that allow you to talk to military personnel who operate and maintain those systems. . . . The other "catch as catch can" approach is more characteristic of . . . the Army. I have never received an invitation to travel to see any Army hardware, like Army tanks, and we have tank interests in our district. The Army is more likely to offer us a briefing instead; one that makes your eyes glaze over. . . . Unlike the

Army, the Navy and USMC really focus on staff and their needs. So many MLAs are young and have no military background. It is especially important for these staffers to experience as much as they can first hand rather than from a brief in Washington. These staffers don't understand why all the cars stop on post at 5 PM and folks get out of their car when the flag is lowered. They don't understand the taboo of sitting in the Captain of the ship's chair. They especially don't understand the soldier in the field with his heavy pack on his back; so young and so enthusiastic. You can't brief that![87]

In the spirit of casting a wide net, other services often engage MLAs and other staff who are relatively junior or who work for Members not on defense committees. The services often see this as a long-term investment in educating and garnering support:

The Navy gave an invitation for an orientation trip to the West Coast to a young staffer who helped work a Member's schedule. They took her out on a prop C-2 onto a carrier. She was thrilled. No other service directed any such attention in her direction. The key thing the Navy LL recognized was how sharp and personable this young staffer appeared. She is now working defense issues for a new Democrat member. The less a Member cares about military issues, the more he relies on the MLA's recommendation. That can be important in getting co-sponsors for legislation, garnering support for "Dear Colleague" letters and how they should vote on an issue. Schedulers often become legislative correspondents who then become legislative assistants. Our secretaries on the Hill often have master's degrees. Marines show no reservation in driving these folks around in tanks.[88]

Proposals by Army LL officers to plan and arrange MLA trips like the ones described above were met immediately with resistance and concerns over availability of military airlift and/or travel budget to make these trips on commercial air within the Army Travel Office in the Pentagon. Accordingly, MLAs were usually included on trips only if the travel request was centered around the Member's or PSM's participation. However, it is not just casting a smaller net in trying to set up trips that hurts the Army, but the lack of sophistication, creativity, and attunement to the needs of the targeted audience evident from the congressional perspective.

For example, the Marines are the best at using their trips to lay the foundation of support for the big issues they plan on pushing on the Hill and in the Pentagon:

The first time I got to see tanks fire was at 29 Palms observing Marine, not Army, tanks in action. When the issue came up last year that the Army was fighting against the legislative proposal to transfer a certain number of tanks to the Marine Corps, my initial sympathies were with the Marines.[89]

I remember I was going on a trip with the Marine Corps to see things on issues that had nothing to do with the V-22 aircraft.[90] There was one leg of our trip that the Marines had us fly by helicopter using the CH-46. This aircraft is the type that the V-22, if funding continues, is scheduled to replace. Now here is where the Marines show their savvy over the Army. The Marines got me airborne in this piece of . . . that looked ragged and was shaking like a bucket of bolts. In my mind, the aircraft was ready to disintegrate at any moment. As I kissed the ground on arrival, I asked the Marine escort officer about the horrid condition of that helicopter. Without missing a beat, he replied that the condition of that helicopter was the reason the Marines were so strongly behind funding the V-22. Funding the V-22 suddenly made more sense to me than it had earlier. It was another example of the Marines' finesse in knowing how to get their primary concerns showcased to the Congress. Now if that had been the Army, they would have ensured we fly in the best maintained and best conditioned of their helicopters rather than one that appeared to be on its last leg. You know the drill, the Army takes VIPs around to their best barracks and goes to great lengths to put their best foot forward.[91]

A House MLA recounted the same attention-getting CH-46 helicopter experience on another trip he had taken with the Marine Corps:

The trips the other services plan and conduct to get MLAs smart pays them tremendous benefits. The Marines flew us in a CH-46 helicopter to show us what a piece of crap it is. It's an effective technique. They know what they're doing. Can you imagine the Army flying staff around in their old OH-58 helicopters to show how beat up they are and to clarify the need for the Comanche helicopter? I sure can't.[92]

The Army Isn't Sexy or Glamorous Like the Other Services. One of the Army's institutional explanations for why it does not do better in outreach efforts to Members and key staff is that it is easier for the other services to get external audiences interested in flying in a jet, visiting an aircraft carrier at sea, or spending time submerged in an attack submarine. As stated in an earlier chapter, the other services have an easier time offering exciting and glamorous trips. However, congressional contacts wonder why the Army does not compensate for this disadvantage by devising more imaginative trips and events that would entice these external audiences. It might take more effort and creativity, but it would be a constructive move to balance the orientation of minds on the Hill.

Those on the Hill who have visited the NTC come away impressed and more knowledgeable about the importance and complexities of land warfare. Excitement and electricity are in the air as VIPs speed through the desert at 40 mph in Army HMMWVs alongside the main advance of a "friendly" Army armored battalion of 48 M1A2 tanks engaged in a force-on-force attack against a trained and ready NTC-stationed opposing armored force. NTC clearly has sex appeal, but few Members and staff have been there. At the time of my interviews, most MLAs also had not been invited to this premier showcase of the Army's essence.[93]

A former PSM on the SASC addressed the sex appeal factor and how the Army, of all the services, fails to capitalize on this with external audiences:

Until NTC, the Army had no sex appeal. However, the Army spent the first six years of NTC's existence trying to keep folks, especially Congress, from visiting there. The Army refused to build hospitality quarters for visitors during the NTC's first four years. If that had been the Navy or Air Force, they would have been coming to Congress for additional funds before the Center began operations to expand the quarters capability for Washington visitors.[94]

Other staffers continually made the point that the Army's "We're not glamorous or sexy" assumption becomes a self-fulfilling prophecy if not addressed directly:

Many in the Army assume that because they don't have ships and jets—the glamorous stuff—that it is harder for them to compete in getting Congressional attention and support. I believe that assumption is erroneous and part of the Army's problem. Many over on the Hill would be interested in what the Army does. Most staffers would love to view through high powered binoculars a force-on-force warfight exercise at the NTC. Imagine the impact on a staffer that is aboard a plane when the 82nd Airborne makes a jump. The Army has a natural constituency out there in Congress and America. There are many who served in the Army, whose dads or uncles served, or who participate in one way or another in an Army reserve component unit in their local area. This constituency is there, but the Army never takes advantage of this opportunity. By virtue of ignoring this natural constituency, the Army leaves the field to every retired Marine.[95]

He went on to describe a group of Army generals he observed who understand the importance of Congress and are skilled at engaging and holding congressional attention: those serving in and commanding Special Operations Forces. But he is quick to add, "They really are not Army, they are Special Operations Command."

The Army should take lessons from some of the Army generals engaging Congress in the Special Operations Command. We've seen special operations exercises. They really know how to market [what they do]. We are flying in this 727 civilian aircraft getting a briefing in-flight by the ranking general officer down there. As he concludes his brief, the back of the plane suddenly opens up and he parachutes out leaving all the staffers with mouths agape. The plane immediately turns to land. As we get off the plane, the Army general is there to greet us and move on to the next event on the itinerary.[96]

It is no accident that Congress is fully behind funding Special Operations Command and their budget has escaped the cuts that have been typical since the end of the Cold War.[97] Another Senate staffer made the same comment that the Army possesses the glamor but no one in a position of authority will make a decision to showcase it in or near Washington: "The Army doesn't do well at showing themselves. . . . The Army ought to drop a battalion out near here someplace. A mass parachute drop should be planned where members and staff can come to the drop zone, see the drop take place and meet the soldiers who made the drop afterwards. That would be exciting and folks would show up!"[98]

Another Senate staffer made the comment that greater creativity and persistence needs to be employed in the Army's outreach to Members and staff. This includes luring Members and staff out of Washington by offering them exciting experiences that are inherently Army. Only by getting them out of Washington and into the Army world will they begin to understand Army capabilities that no other service can provide:

There are a lot of things staffers would like to know but are always too afraid or proud to ask. How does an automatic weapon operate? They'd go nuts firing a .50 caliber machine gun. They have seen tanks only in the movies or on trips with the Marine Corps. They'd love to speed around in an M1A2 tank. Imagine the thrill a staffer would get hanging out the side door of an Army Blackhawk helicopter watching an Army air assault training exercise at Fort Campbell. Staffers would enjoy going down to the Army's Airborne School and jumping out of the tower.

The Army has got a lot of sex appeal, but little effort is made by the Army in exposing it to external audiences. Unless you start using that sex appeal to draw these folks out of Washington, civilians in Washington won't have an appreciation of how difficult and physically demanding are Army missions. They won't understand that what the Army does is hard and takes special skills found in no other service. . . . They will never appreciate what makes an Army unique unless you get them out with soldiers doing soldier things. You can't do that by copping out with the excuse that your service lacks the glamour and appeal of the other services. It's a self-defeating attitude.[99]

Other services are more likely to create special events for, or at least include, congressional audiences in previously scheduled events. It takes creativity, hard work, early coordination, and planning. It can easily be categorized as a training distractor and therefore something to be avoided. It all comes down to whether inclusion of external audiences is viewed as an opportunity or a burden. It is a calculation of potential long-term benefit versus short-term costs. According to congressional sources, the Navy and Marine Corps believe it is worth the effort; the Army does not seem to agree.

The Army has special training or testing events taking place regularly but is less adept at sharing them with external audiences from Washington. A Senate MLA and former SASC PSM stated that if the senior Army leadership genuinely attempted to include Members of Congress and staff in special events that take place on a regular basis in the Army, they would form stronger and closer working relationships with the Senate.

The Army Misses Outreach Opportunities. Informal gatherings, receptions, and social events are important agency resources and opportunities to outreach and promote relationship building. Despite making some recent improvements, the Army is still considered the least effective in using this resource. Hill observers noted that the Army hosts fewer functions, targets a limited group to be invited, and is less likely to include senior Army leadership.

Congressional staff interviewed noted the Army's reputation as an infrequent host, but they also noted a recent positive change. The Army is now hosting larger receptions for Members and PSMs once every three to four months. The Army claims it does not have the budget to hold the more frequent receptions the other services host. However, congressional sources continue to raise the issue of Army senior leadership participation. Congressional sources commented that they were far more likely to see the senior military leadership of the services other than the Army in attendance at congressional receptions and functions. One HNSC PSM highlighted the point that at a recent reception that attracted 15 or 20 Members and numerous staff, no one from the Army senior leadership was present, representing a significant missed opportunity. Another House staffer with nearly two decades of experience on the Hill reiterated this point:

If you attend the popular annual receptions that draw a large audience of Members and staff, you will often see a large contingent of the senior military and civilian leaders of the services other than the Army. This is no new phenomenon. For example, Speaker Wright used to host the Fort Worth barbecue each year down in the cafeteria. You would see the Secretary of the Air Force and 20 to 30 Air Force generals in attendance. In fact, they would fly in component commanders so they could attend this congressional event. For the Army, you would see its Pentagon Public Affairs and Legislative Liaison flag officers in attendance, but rarely its senior brass. Lieutenant General Don Pihl, who was the Army's spokesman on key Army programs at the time, would often attend, but he was the exception. The Army leadership must see these functions as a waste of time or something that their LL and public affairs guys can handle. I believe they miss opportunities on the Hill with that attitude. What's worse, this view of what is important for the Army is passed on to the next generation of Army officers.[100]

One Member stated that the Navy does the best in getting its top military leadership over to these social functions: "Every function that I have (on my schedule), he (the CNO) is there. He makes the time to be over here. It gives me a chance to get to know him better."[101]

While the Army may not be connecting yet as well as others in its overall use of its social functions, it does on occasion come up with new and successful ways of applying this resource: "One thing Major General Harrison [Army Chief of Legislative Liaison] did for PSMs and MLAs that no other service did, was invite me to a party/reception at his home at Ft. Myer. The staff really appreciated the invitation to the general's home. It felt very nice to be included and improved my relationship with MG Harrison and the Army."[102]

The Marine Corps has a weekly Friday night special event and social that the other services lack. Their Friday night parade and reception at the Commandant's home is tradition and complete with "gee whiz" and social opportunities conducive for relationship building. A service's LL effort would be naturally energized with such an event that includes the direct and regular participation of its top four-star flag officer in his own home. Rather than seeing this event as a burden, the Commandant of the Marine Corps sees it for what it is—an opportunity.

House MLAs were quick to note that the Army, unlike the other services, rarely had socials targeted for MLAs as a group. For many of the same reasons that were highlighted in the travel section, MLAs have special needs. They desire to network with other MLAs and value developing relationships with service LL personnel who will help them bypass the service bureaucracy in the Pentagon. Both these needs can be met by hosting end-of-the-day MLA informal gatherings. The ''win-win'' nature of MLA informal socials hosted by a service is stressed by a House MLA. Whether or not service issues are discussed, the goal is to increase the MLAs' comfort level with the service LL personnel:

The Navy/Marine Corps team has determined . . . that it's in everyone's interests to get MLAs together as often as possible. These social gatherings for MLAs are beneficial and help us do our job. It is a chance to exchange professional information and also rumors. The Navy and Marine Corps team understand an ''inside fact of political life'' that MLAs desire to expand their own resources and networks with each other that they can call on in the future. We are not necessarily talking Marine or Navy issues at these functions. We are developing relationships where those type of issues can be more comfortably and effectively discussed in the future. The Air Force has caught on to this a bit more. I'm not aware of any held by the Army.[103]

The Navy and Marine liaisons sponsor a pizza event every six weeks with a blanket invitation to anyone wishing to attend. They also bring younger officers than the other services into their HLD operations, closer to the age of many young staffers on the House side: ''The Navy and Marine Corps are more likely to bring in young LL officers to create rapport with staffers. They do casework and staff travel. They are aggressive in social events.''[104] The Air Force tends to hold more frequent informal socials, preferring Thursday end-of-day gatherings: ''Air Force tends to do more socials and schmooze more than the other services.''[105]

Pattern 6: Least Effective in Communicating Its Priorities and Larger Message: Why an Army and Why This Size?

The perception that the Army is least effective in communicating its priorities and strategy should be of particular concern to the Army leadership. As has been mentioned before, the Army's message is inherently more difficult to communicate. Because the Army message is inherently more difficult to articulate and understand, congressional sources question why the Army leadership appear less willing to proactively engage in the Washington policymaking process. The Army's behavior would be more rational if its message was the most easily articulated and understood rather than the opposite.

Most MLAs for Members on the HNSC and SASC said they were confused or unsure of the Army's message and top priorities. All could give a general rundown of the other services' key programs or concerns. A Senate MLA for an influential Republican on the SASC was blunt: "I couldn't begin to tell you what the Army's top priorities are."[106] A House MLA speaks of a murky Army message that is unclear in its priorities: "I don't know what the Army's priorities are. I've got a feeling they don't like a decreasing endstrength, but I don't have a sense of what are the Army's do or die issues. . . . The Army is good in giving you good answers on specifics, but has problems in articulating the larger picture."[107]

An MLA who works for a subcommittee chair stated,

I'm not sure what the Army's big issue is now, weapon system or force structure wise. A week before mark-up I might know, but that might also be too late. The Chief of Staff of the Army did visit my boss to talk issues, so we know Army priorities for my boss' subcommittee, but I bet other Members on that subcommittee don't. My boss is [also] on the R&D Subcommittee but we have no idea on what R&D Army priorities are.[108]

One can usually identify a service's top priorities by those with the most senior advocates. However, that is not always an indicator for the Army. Not only are Army priorities murky, but the ones that seem to prompt senior Army leadership action on the Hill appear questionable or odd to congressional audiences. There is a sense that the Army's real priorities do not get promoted and that less central ones do.

In 1995, the Army saw three of its active divisions drop from a readiness status of C-2 to a serious C-3 rating; another reduction in the Army's budget, decreased procurement, and a modernization account problem; a proposed budget $4B less than a previous budget described by a CSA as "on the razor's edge"; an OSD decision to push back procurement and possibly jeopardize the Comanche helicopter program—the Army's supposed number-one priority the previous year; and a recent OSD decision to decrease the active Army endstrength from 495,000 to 475,000, even though the CSA had testified that the former was the bare minimum needed to accomplish the National Military Strategy.

Instead of focusing on these fundamental Army issues, the Army amazed Congress by using its agency resources to garner support for a provision to obtain $14M to buy land for an Army museum. Seeing the Army fight on the Hill for a museum (which was being opposed by the National Taxpayers Association) but not for the Comanche helicopter, not for higher endstrength, and not for a higher percentage of the DOD budget confused many in Congress regarding Army priorities.

There were many on the Hill who wanted the Army to fight for the Comanche, for maintaining its endstrength, and for a larger share of the overall defense budget. To many on the Hill, the Army rolled over and caved in to decision makers in DOD. The Secretary of Defense may have canceled the V-22 aircraft, but the U.S. Marine Corps fought to turn the OSD policy around on the Hill. The perception on the Hill is that the OSD knows the Army will capitulate and accept pain more readily than the other services. One former PSM now working in the administration commented on this compliant perception: ''The problem for the Army is you never get the sense of what is core or essential to the Army. You can move them about with relative ease. The Army senior leadership seems too responsive to immediate political pressure.''[109]

An HNSC PSM with Army background addressed this malleability that sends conflicting signals to the congressional audience, diluting the Army message and over time diminishing credibility of the Army's senior military leadership:

If you want to talk about an Army message, look at how the senior Army leadership began the FY96 authorization bill debate. The Secretary [of the Army] and Chief of Staff [of the Army] signed a letter to all general officers in the field stating that the Army had fought a good fight for $61.7B for FY96 in the Building but only got $56B. It stated that all is okay, we did the best we could. Imagine: $56B is okay after you testified seven months earlier that you had to have $61.7B for a ready Army. That is a stupid letter. It is true to the best principle of the Army, in its ideal view of itself. It's like saying we refuse to play in the fight. Formally and informally some ranking Members on the HNSC are mystified at the Army in rejecting their offers to help in the fight. ''Tell me what I can do to help!'' The Chairman is convinced there is a near-term readiness problem in the Army. The Army is afraid to acknowledge these readiness problems for fear dollars will get moved from modernization to readiness accounts. The Army views modernization as key. My point is why hamstring themselves with noble statements to general officers in the field warning them not to spill the beans and speak with one voice. *I sure didn't see any such letters being sent by the CNO, CSAF or the Commandant of the Marine Corps putting the chains on any information that contradicts the OSD line.*[110]

The similarities and differences in the Army and the Marine Corps are instructive on key readiness and modernization issues that come before PSMs on the Committees:

The Marine Corps are famous for speaking with one voice. If they publicly say things are okay, I'll believe it because I know that privately they will tell me if they have problems. The Army in the spirit of one voice states we must be consistent in message. If the CSA says all is okay, all down the line must say the Army is okay as well. The Army suffers accordingly.[111]

In relation to a message coming to Congress, the Army and Marine Corps are most alike. Once the USMC top leadership makes up its mind, they all walk in lockstep, despite the facts. Once the CSA makes up its mind, the Army won't budge. The Air Force is more detached from Congress. Their hearts are always in the bottom line, but not in the congressional effort. The Navy, being more autonomous, are more willing to question. There is a greater willingness to see different perspective, but less concern in giving straight answers. This is especially true if answers differ from corporate policy. But you have a greater willingness to get deviations from that corporate policy which facilitates engagement over here.[112]

A senior SASC PSM stated his concern that the Army's message was overly complicated and not getting through to external audiences. On background he quoted a highly respected retired Army four-star who had the same impressions: "This Army general bemoaned the Army's priorities of 'digitizing the Army' and 'Force 21' by saying 'What is it? What do they mean?' I'm sure he knows what they mean far more than I, but for this Army general to make this point is important. Sloganeering has got to mean something to us, the external audience."[113]

The other services not only have a less complicated message but also package their message to have an emotional effect that connects with their civilian congressional audience:

The U.S. Marine Corps communicates to Congress in a way that makes your eyes water with their plight and circumstances. They will discuss how Marines have missed four or five Christmas holidays away from home in a row. *Rather than watering your eyes up, the Army makes your eyes glaze over with concepts and processes that have no meaning or relevancy to the Congress.* They talk about "digitizing the battlefield" or attempt to explain the importance of their "Louisiana Maneuvers" that aren't really maneuvers at all.[114]

Pattern 7: Army LL Personnel Transitioning out of the Army

The large number of Army LL personnel who retire after an LL assignment undermines the Army in a number of ways. First, it sends a clear signal to Congress that the Army must not be putting its best people in positions that deal directly with the Hill. Otherwise, they would be getting promoted to colonel and flag officer ranks. In relation to the other services, this is not happening. This is perceived as another reinforcing signal that the Army does not view engagement with Congress as important.

Second, the Army is losing much of its LL expertise to retirement. Because the Army does not fill its LL positions with the most competitive files (from a command board perspective), the signal is sent throughout the Army that it is not a career-enhancing assignment for combat arms officers. A self-fulfilling prophesy takes hold in which individuals gravitate to the organization with other than Army agendas. Many officers see it as a valuable transitional final assignment. When individuals leave after two years or less because of opportunities in the Washington job market, the LL organization and the Army lose the understanding of Congress, the experience in working issues, and the trusted relationships with Members and staff that those individuals possessed.

Third, because command opportunities and promotions for combat arms LL officers are few, soldiers and officers at installations around the world are less likely to be exposed to leaders who understand the importance of Congress and the Army's role in educating and working with that audience. Instead, it allows negative stereotypes about the congressional audience that prevail in larger society to go unchecked.

Representative (now Senator) Reed (D-RI), the only West Point graduate in Congress in 1995, highlighted this clear pattern, which he believes hurts Army effectiveness on the Hill:

The Army sends fine officers to work in OCLL, but they appear to Hill Members and staff as folks who are on their way out of the service. Therefore, it's a natural and logical line of reasoning that the Army doesn't appear to be picking its best people to work with Congress.

The USMC LL seems to be the most effective and liked on the Hill. Currently, Colonel Sattler, the head of their HLD, is leaving his position not to work as a lobbyist here in Washington but to command one of the Marine Corps' 8 regiments. Look at the signal that sends to aspiring junior Marines in the field.[115]

The Army's signal is quite different. Working in Army LL is an important job in as much as all Army jobs are important. However, it is an especially good job to snag if you want to settle in DC and begin to transition out of the Army. The signal to aspiring young officers is that it is a retirement posting and not a desired job if you want to soldier in the future. This shapes and reinforces an already pervasive anti-Washington culture for Army combat arms officers.[116]

Representative Ike Skelton (D-MO) commented that the Army "puts wonderful folks into LL and they leave the Army. You have to get [these same types of folks] who are also promotable."[117]

The relative lack of Army upward mobility for its Army LL officers has been noted consistently: "The services who put their best fast trackers over here with us are the Navy (USMC) and the Air Force."[118] An experienced House MLA spoke about the difference in career potential for excelling in LL in the Navy and the Army:

Going into Army LL appears to be a dead end. . . . In the Air Force, Navy and Marine Corps you see folks moving up the ladder. . . . The sad part is that many Army LL folks are clearly as sharp as the others, their performance, however, isn't appreciated or rewarded by their own institution.

The Navy will put a rising star into one of its LL positions and then rotate that person in and out of Washington. Look at Bud Flanigan. He was the field grade officer in charge of the Navy's HLD office in Rayburn Building; now he's a four-star Commander of the Atlantic Naval Fleet. We value maintaining a relationship with a sharp officer like that who has maintained a foot in both the Washington and tactical world.[119]

Another MLA observed that other services, unlike the Army, seem to select their LL officers with the congressional audience and career grooming in mind.

The folks in Army LL tend to be on the older side. Most staff are younger. The other services tend to bring in a number of promising young officers who are closer in age to many MLAs on the Hill. They not only have more in common, but they begin grooming their LL officers at an earlier point and get more mileage out of them. MLAs naturally gravitate to folks with recent troop experience versus someone who appears to be on his last tour and ready to retire. The Army loses out by going with their "end of the line" crew because they are taking their skills and insights about Congress out of the Army where it is clearly needed. Of all the services, the Army could greatly benefit from having these folks take their knowledge back to their units. The Army is losing these institutional messengers back to the commands who could tell soldiers and fellow officers why Congress is important and ways we could do better.[120]

Staffers and Members notice that there are fewer promotions and more retirements coming out of the Army LL operation. A House MLA comments on this perception in rather stark terms: "From our vantage point, the Army House Liaison Division (HLD) is just a place where old elephants go to die." The staffer goes on to emphasize the point that it is human nature to value associations with professionals who are fast movers up their career ladder:

The heads of the other House operations usually get a command and often get a star. They are seen as fast movers. It is fun to see where they go. They seem to be handpicked for certain tasks that reflect the importance of what their service does and what their service thinks of the Congress. These relationships keep growing even when they are out of Washington. They keep in touch. They also have a knack of coming back to Washington at higher ranks and positions of responsibility. It is natural for us to value these type of relationships?[121]

The Army should not be surprised that the lack of upward career mobility for its LL officers would be so apparent to Capitol Hill. Trusted relationships, where each individual perceives the other as an "island of competence," are a valued currency for getting things accomplished in Washington. Political staffers and Members on the Hill are affected by the good or bad fortunes of the people with whom they associate over the years, and it is natural to value relationships with people moving up the career ladder.[122] The congressional audience is not flattered that the Army people who work with them tend to get bypassed for commands or promotions and leave the service. The congressional audience notices this Army pattern because they value continued engagement with these individuals in their subsequent assignments in and out of Washington at increasingly higher and more important levels.[123] The following comment was typical of the upward mobility awareness among staffers working defense issues on the Hill:

Look at the Navy. Off the top of my head you have Admiral Bud Flanigan. He was the House Liaison Division Chief, commanded a destroyer group, served in the Pentagon's Legislative Affairs, and is now Commander of the Atlantic Fleet. Mike Bowman [now a three-star admiral] was the Chief of the Navy's Senate Liaison Division [SLD] and was promoted later to be head of the Navy's Legislative Affairs. The current Navy CLL had previous Hill experience.[124] Rick Kirkland, a Navy Captain and former Chief of their

SLD, was an admiral-select working for Sandy Stewart in the Pentagon [he has since decided to retire]. Cutler Dawson, who just left Navy SLD as its Chief, is now an admiral-select [he is now a two-star]. LTC Jimmy Jones ran the Marine's SLD and he now has two stars.[125] For the Air Force, a recent SLD Chief by the name of Don Cook, just appeared on the two-star list. I have been here over 10 years, and I can recall four of their Chiefs of SLD who went on to make flag rank. In the Army, you have [now retired] Dick Reynard [former majority SASC Staff Director and now a retired one-star general] and a recent Army CLL as examples of LL field grade officers who continued to move up, but they stand out as exceptions.[126]

Many staffers on the House and Senate side highlighted the importance the Marine Corps places in selecting talented officers to work on the Hill, providing them time to master their jobs and develop valued relationships, and still promoting and selecting them for scarce commands. Typical comments stressed:

Colonel Sattler has been here heading the Marine LL operation in Rayburn Building for the four and a half years I have been a MLA on the Hill. However, the Marine Corps don't see him as homesteading or avoiding serving with the troops out in the field. They not only promoted him to colonel, but are giving him one of their few regimental commands.[127]

The Marines know how to send institutional signals both internally and externally. Lieutenant Colonel Terry Paul is a terrific head of their Senate liaison division—he's been here over 6 years. He was passed over on his primary look for [promotion to] Colonel, however, was selected above the zone for colonel on a second look. Not only that, he has been selected for O-6 [Colonel] command. Folks in and outside of the Marine Corps understand the signal: communicating effectively with Congress is important and will be rewarded.[128]

Former Secretary of the Army and former member of Congress Jack Marsh stated that this relative lack of upward mobility for LL personnel in the Army is a more recent phenomenon of the last 10–12 years:

It use to be that getting into congressional relations was the path to the stars. Now it was quite a different thing with Army Public Affairs. Getting into public affairs business was not career enhancing—you'd go nowhere. At the same time I would always hear Army Chiefs frustrated because the Army's message wasn't getting out to the public and the media. You get what you put in. It sounds to me as if the Army would do well to restore incentives where the most competitive officers strive to work with and thereby understand Congress.[129]

According to interviews, the Army needs to correct this patterned behavior to ensure that its most promising future leaders are exposed to and understand Congress and other external audiences earlier and more frequently in their careers. Continuing this pattern with the challenges that lay ahead will work against both Army and national interests. Representative Skelton (D-MO) expressed these sentiments in his closing remarks: "It is more important now with the downsizing of the Army to get future 'General Marshalls' over in Army Legislative Liaison to work with us.''[130]

FINDINGS

Interviews on Capitol Hill highlighted congressional perceptions that the Army, particularly its senior flag officers, are less effective, compared to other services, in promoting its interests to Congress. While Congress views the Army as the most honest and straightforward of the services, the remaining Army-Hill patterns fail to build upon that foundation of honesty and credibility in improving and nurturing congressional relations, when compared with the other services.

From the congressional perspective, a wary Army sees the Congress more as a hindrance than as a help, as a burden rather than an opportunity. This perceived pattern is reflected in Army discomfort toward Congress which is counterproductive to understanding the role and norms of Congress and inhibits long-term relationship building between the two institutions. The Marine Corps clearly leads the other services in its positive team-player approach toward Congress. The Navy is close behind with the Air Force a distant third.

The perception of a less visible Army is rooted in the pattern that senior Army general officers, a valuable agency resource, are the least represented and engaged of the services with Congress. This pattern deprives the Army of its most effective message carriers and relationship builders with Members and staff. Congressional interviewees stressed the great value they place on senior flag officer presence, professional assessments, and personal opinions.[131] The Navy and the Marine Corps set the standard for their allocation of this valuable agency resource on the Hill. The tone and importance of senior flag officer presence and relationship building on the Hill were clearly set at the top by Admiral Boorda, former CNO, and two recent Commandants of the Marine Corps, Generals Mundy and Krulak.

The Army was also viewed as more reactive and less proactive than the other services in representing its interests and concerns to Congress. Congressional interviewees stressed the necessity of proactive engagement by service liaisers in a joint national security framework to carry out Members' legislative and oversight responsibilities. The Army's pattern of reacting to events on the Hill rather than shaping them ahead of time is made more problematic by the cumulative effect of aforementioned patterns. Collectively, they reduce the number of early and accurate ''heads-up'' that the Army receives on developments on the Hill counter to its interests, which makes the task of countering these efforts exponentially more difficult.

The Army's outreach efforts to Congress are viewed as the most limited and least sophisticated of the military services by the congressional audience interviewed. Specifically, senior Army generals rely too heavily on the same small group of Members and appear to discount the importance of congressional staff relative to the other services. These services cast a wider Member and staff net in their outreach efforts. MLAs interviewed stressed that their needs and interests were best understood and proactively met by the other services. The other services tend to follow a long-term strategy of early and continued engagement with Members and staff. Realizing that relationship building takes time, Members and staff tend to remember who engaged (ignored) them in their more junior days, and it is easier and more effective to engage and educate early rather than late in congressional careers.

A particularly disturbing congressional perception is that the Army is the least effective in communicating both its near- and long-term priorities, as well as its larger message: Why an Army and why this size? The congressional audience was often confused about the Army senior military leadership's fundamental priorities and their willingness to fight in the face of political pressure. Overall, the Army message was described as murky, complicated, odd, and suited for internal rather than external audiences. Unlike the Marine Corps approach, the Army message tends to glaze rather than water the eyes of a sympathetic congressional audience.

The seventh Army pattern concerns the congressional observation that Army LL personnel seem to be on their terminal assignment in the Army. This Hill observation reinforces the message that the Army chooses not to put its most competitive combat arms officers in LL positions and does not view their work with Congress as important. Second, the Army's best LL expertise is lost to retirement rather than professionally developed for future contributions at higher levels of responsibility within the institution. Finally, because Army LL officers are rarely selected for command, soldiers and junior officers in the field lack the exposure to combat arms leaders who will stress the importance of understanding and working with Congress. The other services realize that Members and staff are cognizant of the upward mobility of military officers with whom they have worked and developed trusted relationships.[132]

The Army's perceived pattern of honest, straightforward behavior toward Congress is good news and the foundation for good liaising and trusted relationships on the Hill. The bad news for the Army is reflected in the additional six patterns that impede the attainment of both, relative to the other services. These six patterns are similar in that they demonstrate, in the eyes of the congressional audience, that the Army is more reluctant to engage proactively with them in shaping defense policy, discounts by its priorities and the allocation of its more valuable agency resources the importance of that engagement, and understands the Congress and its positive role in defense policymaking the least of all the services. All six patterns are examples where the Army fails to make as effective use of available agency resources as the other services. These resources include the time and attention of the Army's three- and four-star generals devoted to Army–Congress relations, the Army's LL collocation resource in the House and Senate Office Buildings, the Army's travel resource with Members and staff, the Army's social functions resource, the Army's "excitement and appeal'' resource, the Army's ''special events'' resource, and the Army's ''Washington establishment'' expertise resource of LL and other Army staff officers.

The results of interviews indicate that the Navy, and especially the Marine Corps, currently are perceived as the most effective with Congress. This perception is not a result of the Navy and Marines possessing more agency resources; it is because their senior leadership and institutions make the most effective use of their agency resources with Congress. The other services prepare officers to view relationship building as important, provide their most promising officers with the requisite experience and skills to effectively form ties, and instill in these officers the conviction that participating in this activity is a professional responsibility and opportunity, not a burden.

The following chapter will identify and prioritize cultural factors that impede the Army from making more effective use of available agency resources. The thesis of this research is that these cultural impediments, basic assumptions held by senior Army leaders, underlie and partially explain the seven Army–Congress patterns.

NOTES

1. PSM, HNSC, #72, interview by author, April 11, 1995, Washington, DC. The use of the word ''game'' by this staffer comes from political science and analyst jargon (e.g., ''rules of the game,'' etc.) and in no way conveys the sentiment that what Congress does and the importance of liaising effectively with the Hill are not extremely serious activities for the nation. I make this point in deference to a Member of Congress whom I admire, who took offense at the use of the word when applied to the process in carrying out their important constitutional responsibilities.

2. These cultural dimensions were also evident to a few congressional staff who had had careers in the military services.

3. *Congressional Quarterly*, November 12, 1994, 12.

4. Frederick H. Black, ''The Military and Today's Congress,'' *Parameters* (December 1987), 39–40.

5. John O. Marsh, Jr., remarks to the Association of the U.S. Army, Army Public Affairs Update, Speech File service, no. 87–2, Washington, DC, October 13, 1986 (Washington, DC: Department of the Army, Office of the Chief of Public Affairs, November 1, 1987).

6. Member, HNSC, #1, interview by author, June 29, 1995, Washington, DC.

7. Congressional interviewee #44, Member, HNSC, interview by author, May 16, 1995, Washington, DC.

8. Congressional interviewee #44, Member, HNSC, interview by author, May 16, 1995, Washington, DC. See John W. Kingdon, *Congressmen's Voting Decisions* (New York: Harper and Row, 1981), which showed congressmen were more likely to be swayed by fellow congressmen than by other outside lobbyists.

9. Member, HNSC, #19, interview by the author, June 27, 1995, Washington, DC.

10. Task Force Smith, a post–World War II American force based in Japan and dispatched to Korea in June 1950, has come to symbolize the costly price the nation

pays in American casualties and operational ineffectiveness following rapid demobilization and budget reductions in peacetime.

11. PSM, SASC, #69, interview by author, January 25, 1995, Washington, DC.

12. PSM, SASC, #11, interview by author, June 12, 1995, Washington, DC.

13. PSM, SASC, #23, interview by author, April 10, 1995, Washington, DC.

14. PSM, HNSC, #72, interview by author, April 11, 1995, Washington, DC.

15. MLA, SASC, #80, interview by author, May 22, 1995, Washington, DC.

16. PSM, SASC, #2, interview by author, March 20, 1995, Washington, DC.

17. MLA, HNSC, #34, interview by author, April 3, 1005, Washington, DC.

18. Rep. Ike Skelton (D-MO), interviews by author, May 16 and October 23, 1995, Washington, DC.

19. Member, HNSC, #6, interview by author, Washington, DC.

20. PSM, SASC, #69, interview.

21. PSM, HNSC, #2, interview by author, April 11, 1995, Washington, DC.

22. PSM, SASC, #4, interviews by author, April 17 and May 5, 1995, Washington, DC.

23. PSM, HNSC, #2, interview.

24. The attitude of viewing the Hill as a burden manifests itself in a tendency of senior Army general officers finding excuses not to go the Hill and to send subordinates in their place. A retired Army senior general stressed that this ''dread of mission'' is conveyed in the subordinate's presentation to the Member, serving neither the Army nor Member's interests in the process: ''The DCSOPS wants you, the subordinate general officer, to go over to the Hill and sell something. Rather than go to the Hill himself to show its importance and the importance given to the congressional audience, he delegates it to someone below him. This may continue to cascade downward. You, the subordinate, often do not feel it's a good order. How you feel about going over to the Hill is clearly evident to the Members and staff. The Member asks why you are here. The junior general states that my boss wanted me to come over and explain. . . . The Member asks the subordinate how he feels about it and immediately notices the general begin to backtrack and get cautious. It comes across not only in what he says, but in his body language; it creates the appearance of being manufactured and stilted.''

25. Senior military officer, #8, interview by author, June 28, 1995, Washington, DC.

26. MLA, SASC, #79, interview by author, March 29, 1995, Washington, DC.

27. MLA, HNSC, #34, interview.

28. Rep. Ike Skelton (D-MO), interviews.

29. TRADOC is an acronym for the Army's four-star Training and Doctrine Command headquartered at Fort Monroe, VA.

30. This account was presented to me August 18, 1995, at Fort Monroe, VA, by General Hartzog's LL assistant, Mr. Joel Hedstrom, who was a participant in the meeting.

31. MLA, HNSC, #60, interview by author, March 21, 1995, Washington, DC.

32. MLA, HNSC, #66, interview by author, June 5, 1995, Washington, DC.

33. MLA, SASC, #29, interview by author, March 27, 1995, Washington, DC.

34. MLA, SASC, #76, interview by author, April 18, 1995, Washington, DC.

35. MLA, HNSC, #34, interview by author.

36. PSM, SASC, #23, interview.

37. MLA, HNSC, #66, interview.

38. Member, #7, interview by author, May 25, 1995, Washington, DC.

39. General Max Thurman, interview by author, March 17, 1995, Washington, DC. General Thurman is given large credit for saving the "All-Volunteer" Army as Commander of Army Recruiting Command, and Deputy Chief of Staff of Personnel; and largely credited for garnering support and fielding the Army's "Big Five" weapon systems when he was Vice Chief of Staff.

40. Rep. Ike Skelton (D-MO), interviews.

41. Member, #7, interview.

42. PSM, SASC, #65, interview by author, March 20, 1995, Washington, DC.

43. PSM, SASC, #36, interview by author, April 10, 1995, Washington, DC.

44. PSM, SASC, #38, interview by author, May 18, 1995, Washington, DC.

45. PSM, HNS, #54, interviews by author, April 11 and May 5, 1995, Washington, DC.

46. PSM, SASC, #12, interview by author.

47. MLA, SASC, #76, interview by author.

48. PSM, SASC, #38, interview by author.

49. MLA, SASC, #75, interview by author, April 13, 1995, Washington, DC.

50. PSM, SASC, #36, interview by author.

51. MLA, SASC, #76, interview by author.

52. Member, HNSC, #6, interview.

53. PSM, SASC, #4, interviews.

54. MLA, SASC, #29, interview.

55. This event occurred as witnessed by author in Rayburn House Office Building, Rep. Norm Sisisky's office, Room 2371, on February 27, 1996.

56. Member, HNSC, #6, interview.

57. MLA, HNSC, #60, interview.

58. PSM, HNSC, #72, interview.

59. PSM, SASC, #4, interviews.

60. PSM, SASC, #52, interview by author, March 29, 1995, Washington, DC.

61. MLA, SASC, #30, interview by author, June 6, 1995, Washington, DC.

62. MLA, SASC, #29, interview.

63. MLA, HNSC, #34, interview.

64. MLA, SASC, #29, interview.

65. PSM, SASC, #36, interview.

66. Webster's II: *New Riverside University Dictionary* (Boston: Houghton Mifflin, 1984), 835.

67. PSM, HNSC, #54, interviews.

68. PSM, SASC, #36, interview.

69. MLA, SASC, #30, interview.

70. MLA, HNSC, #61, interview by author, March 29, 1995, Washington, DC.

71. PSM, SASC, #4, interviews.

72. PSM, SASC, #36, interview.

73. MLA, HNSC, #17, interview by author, March 30, 1995, Washington, DC.

74. MLA, SASC, #41, interview by author, April 25, 1995, Washington, DC.

75. MLA, HNSC, #61, interview.

76. MLA, HNSC, #34, interview.

77. MLA, HNSC, #17, interview.

78. MLA, SASC, #79, interview.

79. PSM, SASC, #38, interview.

80. PSM, SASC, #4, interviews.

81. MLA, HNSC, #33, interview by author, May 8, 1995, Washington, DC.

82. MLA, HNSC, #74, interview by author, March 27, 1995, Washington, DC.

83. Member, HNSC, #19, interview.

84. MLA, HNSC, #61, interview.

85. Ibid.

86. MLA, HNSC, #34, interview.

87. MLA, HNSC, #64, interview by author, March 30, 1995, Washington, DC.

88. Ibid.

89. Ibid.

90. Secretary of Defense Cheney in 1990 decided to cancel funding for the Marine Corps' V-22 aircraft. This aircraft can operate as both a helicopter and fixed wing aircraft. The Marine Corps, having lost the battle in the Pentagon, turned its sights on the Congress and was able to save the program. It was in this environment that Cheney made the comment to the HASC that "I never realized I knew so many Marines until I cancelled the V-22."

91. MLA, SASC, #75, interview.

92. MLA, HNSC, #49, interview by author, March 21, 1995, Washington, DC.

93. The HMMWV is the Army's High Mobility Multipurpose Wheeled Vehicle, a light, highly mobile, diesel-powered, four-wheel drive tactical vehicle that can be configured with various kit modifications to become a cargo/troop carrier, armament carrier, ambulance carrier, or TOW missile carrier.

94. PSM, SASC, #5, interview by author, March 28, 1995, Washington, DC.

95. MLA, HNSC, #34, interview.

96. Ibid.

97. Special Operation Command's budget has actually grown in the years since the fall of the Berlin Wall, from $2.23 billion in 1988 to $3.04 billion in 1995.

98. PSM, SASC, #4, interviews.

99. PSM, SASC, #36, interview.

100. MLA, HNSC, #34, interview.

101. Member, HNSC, #8, interview by author.

102. MLA, HNSC, #64, interview.

103. MLA, SASC, #41, interview by author.

104. MLA, HNSC, #16, interview by author, March 24, 1995, Washington, DC.

105. Ibid.

106. MLA, SASC, #29, interview by author.

107. MLA, HNSC, #17, interview.

108. MLA, HNSC, #61, interview by author. Later when I interviewed his Member, the reason for the chief's earlier visit became obvious. The CSA came to ask for his help in getting a controversial Army museum provision passed through his subcommittee. Where this priority fit with others was not discussed, only that this was all-important to get through the subcommittee and full Committee.

109. PSM, SASC, #5, interview.

110. HNSC, PSM, #2, interview.

111. Ibid.

112. PSM, SASC, #70, interview by author, March 24, 1995, Washington, DC.

113. PSM, SASC, #12, interview.

114. PSM, SASC, #23, interview. Louisiana Maneuvers explains a new process by which Army four-star generals direct their collective attention at key problems facing the Army that is designed to expedite decisions and focus intellectual attention across the Army Major Commands. Another SASC PSM stated that the Congress doesn't need to know about this process. It is a tool to help the Army leadership make corporate decisions, but of little relevancy to Congress.

115. Colonel Sattler has been promoted to Brigadier General, was an Assistant Division Commander at Camp Legeune, NC, and reassigned back to Washington in 1998 to work on the Joint Staff.

116. Member, #7, interview.

117. Rep. Ike Skelton (D-MO), interviews.

118. MLA, HNSC, #74, interview.

119. MLA, HNSC, #34, interview.

120. MLA, HNSC, #60, interview.

121. MLA, HNSC, #66, interview.

122. Internally, the Army is no different from its congressional counterparts. Army officers, like other services, are attracted to and value relationships with friends or associates who are going places up the professional ladder.

123. See discussion and Member's comment in Chapter 2 on the value placed by Members in continuing LL and other flag officers' relationships when these officers leave Washington to serve in other assignments. The point is made that reciprocal contact is valued and encouraged once these relationships are formed.

124. As of publication submission (1998), this Navy CLL, Admiral Natter, recently left command of the Navy's Seventh Fleet to return to Washington for further duty in the nation's capital.

125. As of publication submission (1998), Jones was awarded his third star and is working as the Military Assistant to Secretary of Defense William Cohen. LTG Jones is a frontrunner to become the next Commandant of the Marine Corps.

126. PSM, SASC, #24, interviews by author, May 5 and December 8, 1995, Washington, DC.

127. MLA, HNSC, #61, interview.

128. PSM, SASC, #69, interviews.

129. The Honorable Jack Marsh, former Secretary of the Army and Member of Congress on the House Appropriations Committee, interview by author, August 17, 1995, Washington, DC.

130. Rep. Ike Skelton (D-MO), interviews.

131. Members also emphasized that they are approachable and that most appreciate senior flag officers making time to engage without an issue or crisis to resolve. Members and staff value relationships with military flag officers they know well and who understand their world and their role in the policymaking process.

132. Army senior officer leadership of earlier years understood better the importance of giving their most competitive combat arms officers significant experience in negotiating both field and Washington terrain.

Chapter 4

Army Cultural Dimensions:
An Inward-Looking Team Player

There is a belief in the Army that the merit of the Army cause speaks for itself. You shouldn't have to involve yourself in politics in selling the greatness and relevancy of the Army. The Army cause by itself tells the story. No lobbying is necessary. Unfortunately, Washington doesn't work that way.

—The Honorable Norman Augustine,
former Under Secretary of the Army

The behavior of Army military leaders in their relations with Congress is profoundly influenced by a complex, reinforcing set of cultural dimensions. Predictably, these values and basic assumptions are a result, in part, of the historical experience and evolution of the U.S. Army, and the individual backgrounds, professional development, and experiences of the Army's senior leaders at a particular point in time.

This chapter examines and assigns priority to the cultural underpinnings of the Army–Hill patterns discussed in Chapter 3, and identifies the cultural dimensions that impede the Army from making greater use of agency resources to improve its relations with Congress today. The seven Army–Hill patterns were presented from the congressional perspective and highlighted a serious Army engagement and communication problem. The congressional observers were not in a position to explain underlying cultural dimensions, but only described the Army's patterned Hill behavior in comparison to the other services.

This chapter relies on candid and experienced insights of active and retired senior Army flag officers to identify and assign priority to the cultural dimensions that underlie the Army's perceived patterned behavior on the Hill.[1] These cultural dimensions contain complex patterns of assumptions held by members of the Army and its uniformed leadership that can often predetermine the organization's behavior and decisions. These assumptions persist, and influence behaviors that repeatedly lead people to make decisions that may have worked in the past. These assumptions are therefore infused into junior members explicitly in training or implicitly by the example of the leadership's behavior.

These assumptions and cultural dimensions recede into the back of people's consciousness with repeated use but continue to influence organizational decisions and behaviors, even when the organization's environment changes. They become fixed and unquestioned, often characterized as "the way we do things here"—even when these ways are no longer appropriate. They are often so basic, pervasive, and totally accepted as "the truth" that no one questions their validity.[2]

There is extensive literature dating to the early 1980s on the importance of organizational culture and its ties to leadership in effecting needed change within organizations.[3] Carl Builder innovatively explored and attempted to map comparatively the distinct "personalities" of the three armed services.[4] His cultural lens was elevated to a macro level, but he highlighted the enduring quality of a service personality that can often lead military service leaders to make decisions that appear to outsiders to make little sense.

Various definitions of culture exist in this literature, but all in one way or another refer to patterned values, beliefs, or attitudes shared and passed to new members of that organization or group. This culture becomes a prescription lens through which problems are seen and addressed by the leadership and collective group desiring to succeed within that organization. Edgar H. Schein defines culture as a

pattern of shared basic assumptions that the group learned as it solved its problems of external adaptation and internal integration, that has worked well enough to be considered valid and, therefore, to be taught to new members as the correct way to perceive, think, and feel in relation to those problems.[5]

Cultural patterns are viewed as "the routine, largely unexamined options deriving from widely shared assumptions, meanings and values of a group or people."[6] These cultural dimensions; shared assumptions, or norms limit the options leaders and other members consciously or unconsciously consider in making decisions and addressing problems.

James Q. Wilson suggests that once a culture is broadly shared by a single group, tasks deemed as central to the mission of the organization are energetically pursued while activities not so defined are often performed poorly or given inadequate resources.[7] Wilson's assertion is particularly relevant to this study. If the Army leadership does not consider effective relations with Congress as central to the Army's mission, it is unlikely that it will provide high-level attention and adequate resources to the relationship.

General Gordon Sullivan, who retired as CSA in June 1995, acknowledged candidly that Army culture underlies many of its problems on the Hill and that its influence is not obvious or easily recognized: "The thesis of your research has merit—culture clearly is at work. However, I didn't spend a lot of time addressing how Army culture might be hurting our effectiveness on the Hill over the last four years."[8]

However, both Schein and Barnes highlight that these cultural dimensions are not fixed and can change over time. They can be "influenced and altered through time by what is going on in other areas of life." More importantly, Schein addresses the critical link of leadership and culture. He stresses the importance of leaders being conscious of the cultural dimensions that shape their organization in order to effect change. In terms of Army–Congress relations, this means senior Army leaders must be more aware of the cultural rationales for their interaction with Congress.

This does not necessarily require leaders to change Army culture in most cases, but simply to recognize aspects of that culture which are counterproductive in particular situations and anticipate in a compensatory manner timely institutional fixes to these dysfunctions. Beyond awareness and subsequent accommodation, specific and targeted cultural change can be engineered by senior Army leaders by using pieces of Army culture that can counter and address dysfunctional aspects of culture on the Hill. (The strategic use of Army cultural values to improve Army–Hill relations is addressed briefly in Chapter 6.)

In priority, the five Army cultural dimensions that underlie the Army–Hill patterns are:

1. The Army's internal fixation at the expense of external focus: the Army values and rewards internal performance and communication to its internal audiences. This inward professional focus is rationalized as enhancing warfighting competence and producing solutions to problems that have merit that should be self-evident to external audiences, but result in insufficient attention to Congress and other external audiences.

2. The Army's value of teamwork and recognition of its own dependency in getting to and winning on the battlefield work against service advocacy on the Hill: [Army officers are less likely to advocate to Members of Congress (who are viewed as relative outsiders) independent service capabilities the Army could provide, because Army officers perceive other services' involvement as an essential contribution to the Army's attainment of decisive victory.

3. The narrow definition or path of career success for Army combat arms officers discourages experience in Washington—particularly with Congress and other external audiences. This lack of experience inhibits Army understanding of Congress and results in both fear and reduced expectations of what can be obtained from the legislative process.

4. The Army's view of itself as the nation's obedient servant works against Army leaders taking institutional interests to Congress that have been ignored in the Pentagon. This dimension is related to the previous one of teamwork and dependency, that in this

case stresses obediently doing one's part as a prerequisite for the success of the larger whole. This makes it more difficult for an Army leader to speak out to the congressional audience against executive branch positions that are viewed by the Army leader as antithetical to Army interests.

5. The Army senior officer corps is more risk averse in peacetime: It is more difficult for the Army than the other services to demonstrate competency in peacetime. As in most large hierarchical organizations, the Army is less tolerant of maverick types; and with a lack of experience in Washington, proactive engagement with Congress and other external audiences appears to be risky for further career advancement.

These five dimensions go a long way in explaining options not taken or examined by the senior Army leadership that would allow it to make greater use of agency resources to improve the Army–Congress relationship. These clearly overlap and reinforce each other in promoting and perpetuating the Army's patterned behavior with Congress, and provide a critical and often missing cultural component to explanations given by Army leaders to the Army's relative problems in representing its interests on the Hill.

These dimensions have their origins in the establishment of the oldest American military service and, later in the development of Army professionalism in the Huntington sense of the word following the Civil War.[9] Before addressing the five cultural dimensions, it is important for the reader to appreciate the organizational culture imposed by early Army leaders who founded the institution.

SUBSERVIENCE TO CIVILIAN CONTROL AND POLITICS AS UNPROFESSIONAL

The scholarly literature on organizational culture highlights the importance of tracing the culture and assumptions of a mature organization back to the values and beliefs of its founders and early leaders.[10] Many of the beliefs, values, and norms that proved to be effective solutions when the Army was first created, and later when it began to evolve into a professional Army following the Civil War, grew into basic assumptions that underlie to varying degrees Army behavior toward Congress and other external audiences to this day.

Subservience to civilian control and subsequent development of Army *professionalism* 100 years later are ingrained and manifest in Army behavior today. These two concepts are a fundamental part of the historical experience and evolution of the U.S. Army. Discussions of the Army's developing professionalism are incomplete and distorted if the reader loses sight of professionalism's bedrock: an ideological devotion by senior Army military leaders of the day to the concept of civilian control of the military.[11] The two concepts pervade all dimensions discussed below that influence the Army's approach to Congress to appear both trusting and obedient, suspicious and uncomfortable.

The principle of subservience to civilian control was tested and upheld by the leadership of General George Washington, Commanding General of the Continental Army. Many Army soldiers and officers lacked confidence in the Continental Congress to satisfy their widespread grievances of not being properly fed, housed, clothed, and paid for their duty during the war.

General Washington effectively put down rebellions, refused offers by a few senior officers to use the Army to seize control of the government, and in a timely meeting in his own headquarters in Newburgh, New York, diffused the Newburgh conspiracy that was calling for "bolder" measures for dealing with a neglectful and weak Congress.[12] The Continental Army and its senior leadership, without an executive branch, chose not to lock up the Continental Congress and make General Washington king.

Foreign and domestic threats, states' rights, and populism combined to promote a reliance on individual state militias (today's National Guard) and inhibit the significant development of professional military institutions prior to the Civil War. Instead, West Pointers focused on technical engineering and nation-building skills rather than warfighting competence. It produced a technical specialization more compatible with civilian interaction.[13]

American military *professionalism* evolved after and as a reaction to the carnage of the Civil War and was largely nurtured by Army officers like General Tecuhmseh Sherman and Major General Emory Upton.[14] They used their positions in military educational institutions and in Army headquarters to inculcate two basic tenets supporting Army professionalism: (1) civilian control was a prerequisite for attaining professionalism, thereby reinforcing 100 years of socialized obedience to civilian supremacy,[15] and (2) military officers should be divorced from and avoid politics, a radical departure from the previous 100 years.[16] The creation of a strong regular professional Army required adherence to these tenets.

Many of the sentiments held by soldiers and officers toward civilian political leaders in the 1780s were still strong in the 1880s, except that expressions of mutiny were replaced with resigned disgruntlement, disdain, and lower expectations by Army officers and soldiers of their political leadership. Sherman and Upton transformed this sentiment as they created an American military profession characterized by the following dictum: you must obey the politicians, but you should not count on them.

The call for officers by Generals Sherman and Upton to avoid politics was valid at the time. Sherman and Upton were concerned about insulating the Army from the civilian corruption that characterized the politics of the day. Stressing obedience to civilian control and attempting to isolate Army officers from the corrupt legislative and executive branch practices commonplace with officials during the Grant administration were viewed together as essential to forming a professional Army.

Huntington makes the point that unlike its European predecessors, American military professionalism "was strictly self-induced" by officers with little ci-

vilian contribution.[17] Therefore, this military profession was largely created independent of American civilian society. It resulted in a separateness from that
society that has at times fueled misunderstanding and hostility of the profession
by society.[18]

A recent essay by Professor Eliot A. Cohen, *Making do with Less, or Coping
with Upton's Ghost,* is both interesting and disturbing in the way the author
interprets the Army's professional development in the period following the Civil
War. The author attempts to tie his interpretation of Army behavior today with
this experience after the Civil War. In his view this reflects not just suspicion
or discomfort with civilian leadership but an unhealthy and dangerous contempt
for it.

Cohen calls this attitude the "Uptonian Hunker," in connection with one of
Army professionalism's architects.[19] This hunker, according to Cohen, reflects
a troubling "distrust of—and disdain for—civilians in general and politically
elected or appointed civilian leaders in particular."[20]

First, Upton believed that the history of American military policy was a *history of the
irresponsibility of legislative authority and of feckless democratic neglect of the armed
forces.* Second, he believed that the basis of civil-military relations in the United States
consisted of irrational anti-military prejudice. Third, he contended that the military rou-
tinely suffered throughout American history from enormous and unnecessary losses because of civilian interference in—we might call it "micromanagement"—of military
operations.[21]

According to Cohen's interpretation, the Uptonian hunker is "an institutional
response to one reading of American history. It is a legacy of turning inward;
cultivating professional skills while expecting the worst from a society that does
not understand the military and quietly nursing a grudge against politicians who
misuse soldiers and then abuse them for failing to deliver as required."[22]

While there is clearly evidence for discomfort or suspicion in the behavior of
professional Army officers toward civilians today, Cohen's limited treatment of
the subject ignores many other profound influences on professional military
behavior. At times, these professional influences produce at least as much, if
not more, trust, obedience, and confidence in civilian leadership by Army military leaders.

Upton believed that the Civil War could have been a short and less bloody
war had the political leadership provided adequate resources for the military in
peace—in other words, a stronger and better-trained regular Army. Uptonian
professionalism is manifest in Army efforts to improve tactical training and
focus, enhance professional military education, and to promote higher force
readiness levels than in the past.[23] These themes of professional readiness are
rooted in the disenchantment of Upton, Sherman, Sheridan, and others with the
corruption of America's post–Civil War government.

However, Cohen fails to take into account the political corruption of Upton's day, and Cohen's interpretation conveniently ignores the larger reverence for military subservience to civilian control that officers like Upton and Sherman held. As the impending crisis of the presidential election of 1876 drew near, General Sherman wrote, in a confidential letter to General Sheridan, that "Personally and officially, we are not charged with the determination of the question as to who is President, but we must sustain the President who is declared to have been elected."[24]

Cohen addresses an inward-looking Army, but he posits a simplistic culprit: Uptonian professionalism of the 1870s rather than the more complex set of cultural beliefs that have a much more profound impact on the narrow Army professional development system in the 1990s.[25] Cohen decided to portray the architect of a stronger professional Army as a potential danger to the concept of civilian control: the foundation upon which Upton's notions of professionalism rest. This allows Cohen to move to his agenda of "civilianizing the military" in order to safeguard "civilian control of the military," as if one guarantees the other or is a prerequisite for national security interests.

Concern shown by Generals Sherman and Upton that professionalism might become diluted or distracted by excessive exposure to political corruption underlies to a significant degree the Army–Hill patterns evident today and how Army officers view their own professional behavior. The Army obsession with integrity that dominated Upton's era continues to find expression in the views and attitudes of today's Army officers. This is one reason the Army is viewed by the congressional audience as the most honest and straightforward of the services. It also accounts for the prominent legal and investigative structure and focus unique to the Army's LL organization.

After the Civil War, a serious institutional devotion to the military craft of winning wars was undertaken with a relatively free hand because the price tag that external audiences had to pay was kept low. The Army senior leadership engaged with what they considered a corrupt Congress only when absolutely necessary, to gain approval for their proposed solutions.

So long as the Army was kept down to 25,000 men, Congress let the West Pointers run it in accordance with their own ideas. So long as the number of officers was kept low, Congress approved changes in promotion and retirement plans. Sherman, for instance, carefully avoided Congress in setting up the School of Application at Leavenworth; he did not wish it to be "the subject of legislation." Subsequently, he repeatedly pointed out that the schools at both Leavenworth and Monroe required no additional funds beyond "ordinary garrison expenses." And Congress, content with this, shrugged its shoulders and let them be.[26]

By keeping their demands for resources to a minimum, Army officers were at that time given the flexibility to direct their meager agency resources, without congressional interference, to develop a small professional Army that eschewed politics and followed civilian, largely executive branch, directives. By demonstrating obedience to civilian control, the Army was given the flexibility to manage its resources as it saw fit.

Today there is relatively little tension between the most important features of military professionalism (integrity, obedience, and competency) and civilian control of the military. When it does occur, it usually involves perceived civilian intrusion into operational matters, especially if that interference results in or risks unnecessary loss of life. On the other hand, there was and continues to be tension between the requirements of military professionalism and efforts to civilianize the military.

The professional sanctity of civilian supremacy over the military and its corresponding tension between military professionalism and politics are still evident in the Army today. In this connection, the beliefs and attitudes of the Army's early leaders that enabled them to solve problems are passed from generation to generation of members as appealing solutions. Officers in today's Army receive similar emphasis on the two tenets during their early professional development years at West Point and ROTC programs. "Subservience to civilian control" and "Don't get involved in politics" are constant themes in Army leadership and ethics classes. The challenge to an organization's leadership is ensuring that the preferred solutions of an earlier time are applicable to the current environment.

DIMENSION 1: THE INTERNAL FIXATION OF THE ARMY

The most important cultural dimension undergirding the Army–Congress patterns is that the Army, more than the other services, prefers internal focus and rewards internal rather than external performance. It is its internal audience on which the Army fixates and toward which it directs its most valuable agency resources. It looks inward to address and resolve the challenges of maintaining or improving its professional warfighting competence. In this context, internal focus relates to the institutional efforts and communications initiated by its top leaders to its own members in activities directly related to warfighting competence, combat readiness, and doctrine. This internal focus is seen by Army military leaders as a characteristic and prerequisite of Army professionalism; they see it as strictly Army business and view it as essential to maintaining and improving its ability to fight and win the nation's wars.

External focus relates to the institutional value placed by its top leaders on the effective relations, communications, and engagement of the Army with the political leadership, the bureaucratic entities external to the Army, and the public at large. According to senior flag officer interviews, communicating effectively with external audiences, to include Congress, appears to be valued less by the senior Army leadership than it is in other services and does not approximate the value placed in engaging effectively with its internal Army audience. External focus and activities are not seen as "professional" in the same sense as internal focus and activities. This emphasis on the internal, at the expense of the external, is a clear example of Wilson's assertion that in a shared culture, missions considered central are enthusiastically pursued; those not so considered are often performed poorly or given inadequate resources.[27]

A former CSA acknowledged this dimension and the difficulty it causes in communicating or representing interests to external audiences:

Except for selected cases, we do focus internally. That is because our core concern is our warfighting competence. As Chief of Staff of the Army, it took a great deal of energy for me to push issues with external audiences. I had no problem with getting the [Army's] internal constituency behind a problem; the problems were with the external constituencies.[28]

Another former Chief mentioned this internal focus and its impact on the ability of rising stars in the Army ranks to discuss clearly and comfortably defense and security issues that transcend Army institutional boundaries:

It has been my observation that Navy and Air Force O-5- and O-6-level officers that are fast tracking are more glib and comfortable with talking about service issues than their Army counterparts. This really is evident by the time they make Brigadier General. These Air Force and Navy flag officers are more glib, natural and expansive than their Army counterparts on interservice and defense issues. The Army fast trackers are more narrowly focused on professional matters within the Army.[29]

An Army field grade officer working with top senior Army leadership described this tendency to look inward as an "institutional self-absorption" that is hurting the Army's effectiveness not only with Congress but also with OSD and the Joint Staff:

The Army is in its own cocoon. In comparison with the other services, it still retains its WWII structure and organization. Times have changed, but the senior Army leadership resists fundamental change in its organization that inhibits effective communication and engagement with other external entities. It's not just Congress that we have problems with, but significant disconnects with OSD and the Joint Staff. *We aren't organized to be effective with these external audiences.*[30]

Manifestations of this proclivity to turn inward while focusing significantly less resources on external audiences are evident in the Army's unique sense of professionalism; "merit of the Army cause speaks for itself" attitude; and discounting of assignments dealing with external audiences.

The Inward-Looking Professional

One cultural explanation for Army behavior on the Hill is related to senior Army officer's view of themselves as professionals in the art and craft of successfully managing land warfare. There is a certain degree of remoteness (some characterize it as arrogance) toward audiences outside the Army institution when addressing warfighting issues. As professionals, senior Army uniformed leaders see themselves as the most knowledgeable about what is necessary for success in military land operations. Likewise, they are wary of civilian outsiders who lack this knowledge but still attempt to micromanage or challenge Army professional positions.

One highly regarded senior combat arms officer on the Army staff explained the relationship between the Army–Hill patterns and Army professionalism:

There is this sense that we shouldn't have to sell or compromise our [Army Staff] plan, proposal or program [to these external audiences], therefore we won't because it is patently obvious what the right answer is. *Arrogance may not be quite the right word, but this insular distancing from external audiences would be built on the idea that we are the military professionals in the Huntington sense of the word.* Senior Army military leaders, as professionals, see themselves as the most knowledgeable people about what it takes to succeed in winning the nation's wars.

Having worked so hard internally within the Army to obtain the consensus of the four-stars, the senior Army military leadership sees that consensual internal Army decisions as the best professional judgement of its military leaders. This is what needs to happen. You should accept it on its obvious merits because it is the Army professional position. If Congress or OSD choose not to accept our recommendation, then there is nothing we can do about it but try to make do with what we are left with.[31]

Earlier, the turning inward and disengagement from Congress and other political civilians of the post–Civil War professional Army was highlighted as an institutional reaction to the corrupt politics of that era. This Uptonian reaction, while not an optimal strategy for increasing influence with Congress, served both to protect the sanctity of the concept of civilian control over the military and insulate the Army's cultivation of professional skills from rampant political corruption. However, today Congress and the executive branch are not the corrupt institutions with which Sherman and Upton had to contend. What is it about being an Army professional in today's environment that reduces Army expectations of what it can gain from civilians in Congress, increases its fear of congressional intervention in Army operational matters, and makes engagement with these external audiences appear inappropriate and unprofessional? How much of this distancing is a part of how Army officers perceive themselves and their professional obligations?

A combat-arms officer serving as a division chief on the Army staff stated that there are remnants of a disdain for civilian involvement in Army operational matters:

You must separate out programmatic [budget, force structure, etc.,] and operational issues. The Army will fight the good fight within the [Pentagon] Building on a programmatic issue, but make do with civilian input and decisions, nonetheless, proclaiming they can succeed with what they get. Less so on operational matters.

There is clear disdain for civilians who try to involve themselves in operational readiness and warfighting issues. Civilians often lack the information they need to make the most informed decision in operational matters. The military shapes the options presented to civilians to prevent civilians from taking precipitous action and screwing things up. . . . It goes back to this strong feeling that civilians have no place interfering or micromanaging operational matters. The military should be able to do its own thing when the war starts. We'll win the war and then hand it back to you [civilians]. *That is why* Desert Shield *and* Desert Storm *were viewed so positively by Army officers because there wasn't this sense of civilian micromanagement.* Even to the end, it was Schwartzkopf who determined that we [the military] had met our objectives on the ground.[32]

The quote—and the feelings that underlie it—reflect the continuity of the beliefs and assumptions that supported Army professionalism immediately after the Civil War.

In seeking to trace all the great mistakes and blunders committed during the [Civil] war, to defects of our military system, it is important to bear in mind the respective duties and responsibilities of soldiers and statesmen. The latter are responsible for the creation and organization of our resources, and, as in the case of the President, may further be responsible for their management or mismanagement. Soldiers, while they should suggest and be consulted on all the details of organization under our system, can alone be held responsible for the control and direction of our armies in the field.[33]

Why would professionalism as manifest in a general wariness or suspicion of external audience involvement in operational matters be more acute in the Army than in the Navy, being that the Navy also experienced an inward-looking drive for professionalism after the Civil War? Three possible explanations surfaced in the course of interviews and research:

• The Army will be the only service blamed for losing a war.
• The Army, because of the nature of battle, is more inherently exposed to the brunt of death and casualties.
• Army senior political civilian leaders, unlike their Navy counterparts, have been less involved in pressuring its senior officers to reach out to external audiences.

One senior Army flag officer commented that this inward-looking tendency is a result of the tremendous professional responsibility the Army and its uniformed senior leaders uniquely bear in winning the nation's wars. While they do not win them alone, the Army's piece of the equation is indispensable. However, the far more important point is that: "If the nation loses a war, the Army [of the four services] gets blamed. *No one will blame the other services for losing our nation's wars.* If the Air Force screws it up, it just means the Army has to finish it."[34]

The professional responsibility of shouldering potential blame for failed wars is not lost on Army senior leaders. These Army leaders of the 1990s were young officers who served during Vietnam, a war the nation lost. They were appalled by the condition of the Army they entered and frustrated with the Army institution that was severely traumatized by the loss of that war. These leaders decided not to abandon the Army and to rebuild it from within. General H. Normal Schwarzkopf's comments reflect the sentiment that if the Army was going to get healthy, it would have to fix itself:

When I received my commission as a second lieutenant, the Army was suffering from the after effects of the Korean War; in many ways it was ethically and morally bankrupt, which led eventually to the debacle in Vietnam. By the end of my second tour in Vietnam, the Army had not only reached its nadir but also lost the confidence of the American people. I agonized over the question of whether to stay in—and decided I would in the hope of someday getting the chance to help fix what I thought was wrong. As I rose in rank over the years, I saw the Army *transform itself* into a force that Americans *could* be proud of. The units I commanded during *Desert Storm* were the product of twenty years of reform, and soldier for soldier, officer for officer, we had the best trained, best equipped army in the world.[35] [emphasis added]

General Schwarzkopf's reference to "transforming itself" reflects an inward focus that the Army used to fix itself in terms familiar to Upton and Sherman's prescriptions. The Army redefined and rehabilitated itself in part by becoming a "doctrinal Army"[36] as part of its "reprofessionalization" following Vietnam.[37] The establishment of the Army Training and Doctrine Command (TRADOC), issuance of scores of training manuals oriented to its internal audience, and "the creation of a training regime" were focused on its internal audience and instrumental in restoring cohesion and morale in the Army. The current senior Army leadership, through its participation and engagement at the troop level, saw positive changes take place with this internal focus on restoring Army professionalism.

The increased likelihood of casualties that are unique to ground combat makes civilian efforts to micromanage operations of these forces potentially more costly, and resented on the part of responsible senior Army military leaders. Naval and air operations in combat situations, while dangerous, are less likely to produce the same magnitude of casualties.[38]

On the other hand, the Marine Corps, who share this potential for larger casualties in ground combat, could also resent the intrusion and unnecessary endangerment to young Marines. However, according to interviews, the Marine Corps feels more confident than the Army in its skills to communicate with external audiences and use trusted relationships with those audiences to mitigate harmful effects of these interventions. In fact, the Marine Corps attempts to find creative ways to turn this civilian intrusion into an opportunity to showcase its capabilities.

Finally, wariness of civilian intervention on operational matters has a stronger hold on Army officers than their naval counterparts because of efforts since World War II by the senior naval civilian leadership to encourage their admirals and sailors to reach out to Congress and the public for support.[39] While this was especially difficult at first for the naval ''flag plot'' to execute, the importance of having their executive branch senior political leadership extolling the need to engage with external audiences naturally worked to lessen the perceived risks and increased the benefits of proactive relations with Congress.[40]

The Merit of the Army Cause Speaks for Itself

One facet of the Army's cultural proclivity to look inward and value internal over external performance is many Army officers' belief that directing increased agency resources toward communicating their message more effectively with external audiences is unnecessary. This results from a naive trust or arrogance that the Army message is or should be understood by Congress and other external audiences.

Specifically, many senior Army leaders interviewed identified a basic belief underlying Army behavior that the merit of the Army cause is self-evident, that Army officers do not need to justify the relevance of the Army, and that presenting an honest ''right'' position is (trust) or should be (arrogance) sufficient to communicate effectively and influence these external audiences, like Congress. Additionally, this naive trust and arrogance, reinforced by Washington inexperience, are manifest in the nature and quality of the communication products and analysis directed toward these audiences.

Former Under Secretary of the Army Augustine has observed this culture at work among senior military Army leaders:

There is a belief in the Army that the merit of the Army cause speaks for itself. You shouldn't have to involve yourself in politics of selling the greatness and relevancy of the Army. The Army cause by itself tells the story. No lobbying is necessary. Unfortunately, Washington doesn't work that way. I wish it did. It would had saved me a lot of time and effort on the Hill.

When I was [first] confirmed as an Assistant Secretary of the Army, I had zero experience in politics and zero experience on the Hill. I hadn't even met my own member in Congress. But I realized that without support on the Hill there would be no ''Big Five'' [weapon systems] and without the Big Five, the U.S. military would pay a far costlier price on future battlefields.[41]

The sentiment that the relevancy of the Army and its concerns are self-evident to external audiences is reflected in a typical comment by a former CSA:

I may tend to exaggerate to make the point, but it is an important point. There has always been an Army. The Army is a product of the people of this country. The Army wins the wars of our nation. We don't have to justify the need or relevancy of an Army. America

requires an Army. The other services have to justify themselves in terms of their platforms or weapon systems. They are likewise vulnerable and can be attacked in terms of
these same systems. Therefore they are in a constant frenzy to justify themselves. Accordingly their focus is putting people on their essence: these systems. The Army's focus
is putting systems on its essence: its people. There will always be an Army. Therefore
Army officers don't have to justify and are therefore less inclined to do so. The sense
of the Army and American people being inextricably linked goes beyond statute, but is
in the militia cause and its citizen-soldier (not sailor, airman or Marine) implications.
The roots of America and the Army go back to [Army] General George Washington.
Why justify? What do you mean explain why an Army?[42]

Both quotes highlight an arrogance or trust that external audiences should or
will recognize the merit of the Army cause with the current information and
communication effort being directed their way. This is conducive to an inward
focus and reduces requirements and expectations of senior Army flag officers
as effective message carriers. If one believes the merit of the Army cause or the
relevancy of the Army as an institution is self-evident, then it relieves senior
Army leaders from having to direct valuable agency resources to justify and
educate external audiences. It allows one to stay focused on the internal audience, to keep external audiences at arms length in examining one's traditional
force structure, and to avoid initiating interservice rivalries that one fears will
result from more effective engagement on the Hill that could undermine one's
institution.[43]

The naive aspect of this institutional arrogance surfaces in comments that
reflect surprise and later disillusionment that despite its obvious merit, the Army
cause or position was ignored or even defeated by congressional audiences. A
senior Army officer stated that:

Wishful [arrogant] thinking that others will support us and a tendency to spend inordinate
time talking to ourselves reinforce the other in magnifying the obvious merit of an Army
position or program in the eyes of the Army Staff and its military leadership. Senior
Army military leaders are actually surprised or later become disillusioned when Congress
fails to embrace the enlightened and obviously best Army Staff position.[44]

Another senior Army officer used a courtroom analogy to show the naiveté
of assuming the Army cause will prevail on its own merits. He stressed that the
goal should be more than convincing individuals not to oppose your position;
it should be getting enough support that your position is being advanced by
other actors or "witnesses" external to the Army:

Nothing should be assumed to be self-evident in Washington. *The policymaking forum
must be viewed as a courtroom.* You cannot assume that if you are innocent and tell the
truth, that the right verdict will result. You better understand that you also need experienced attorneys and supporting legal team to sell your innocence and truth to the jury,

in this case, the civilian decision-makers in Congress. The Army is more likely to rely on the mercy of the court.[45]

Another senior Army officer attempted to explain the Army's less effective approach in communicating its message to Congress as a response to the inconsistent views of trust and suspicion that Army generals tend to hold toward their target audience:

The Army displays a psychological dissonance that diminishes its effectiveness with Congress. On the one hand the Army military leaders act as if Congress and civilians in OSD will recognize the merit of the Army's case—it's so obvious. Here you find a trusting, almost institutional arrogance at work. It explains why Army generals choose to rely more on formal hearings and posture statements to communicate their message than the other services. At the same time, many senior Army generals view many of these civilians on the Hill and their agendas with suspicion. Naive trust and perceived suspicion—both are evident and working at cross-purposes. And the Army leadership can't understand why the Army position doesn't take hold.[46]

This naive, trusting arrogance, along with relative inexperience and understanding of Washington, is also apparent in the nature and quality of the communication products and analysis directed toward these audiences.[47] As military professionals, senior Army leaders view themselves as the most knowledgeable people about what is necessary for success in land combat operations. They develop and communicate this knowledge in their doctrinal field manuals and publications that are used by the Army's internal audience. According to military and congressional sources, only the Army naively and arrogantly assumes communication products and techniques that work with its internal audience will be understood by its external audiences.

However, these same audiences state that the other services focus more on communicating effectively to both internal and external audiences. They do not naively trust or arrogantly assume that external audiences will connect with the same type of materials or presentation as their internal audience, and thus they craft certain materials specifically for external audiences.

Compare the Navy's slick glossy *From the Sea* publication to anything the Army has put out. We don't understand or care that our manuals glaze the eyes of external audiences. There is a bit of naivete and arrogance at work here. We provide these publications to explain "why an Army?" and the "role for the Army in the 21st century." We naively believe a few will grasp on to these manuals, read them at night, and be sold on the brilliance and comprehensiveness of the presentation. If they don't find value in these publications, we arrogantly dismiss them as hopeless.[48]

The belief that the merit of the Army's cause is self-evident and does not require the degree of justification required by the other services affects Army analysis and its approach to justifying positions to external audiences. *This in-*

*ternal focus exaggerates the value Army military leaders place in their profes-
sional expertise and the weight they believe it carries in influencing external
audiences.* This mind-set deprives the senior Army leadership of the necessary
tools and skills that, if combined with their professional expertise, would likely
sway or persuade external audiences to support Army positions. A recently retired Army flag officer elaborated:

The Army doesn't focus its energy in developing solid empirical data useful in an analytic
sense. Instead the Army leadership tends to rely on subjective arguments and presenta-
tions. "My 30 years of experience and subjective opinion says . . ." is the norm for the
Army. . . . We need a more modern Army but we don't present the empirical data to
support the need. It's an issue of being able to articulate the Army's fiscal problems.
The Army is unwilling to accept empirical data as a basis of making decisions.[49]

Former Assistant and Under Secretary of the Army Augustine stressed the
importance of producing analysis and communications products that effectively
convey a message to external audiences:

On the modernization question back in the early '70s, I asked for analysis similar to
what I saw Air Force and Navy use. What happens if no new aircraft (aircraft carrier)
are produced? As the Assistant Secretary of the Army for R&D [Research & Develop-
ment], I got operations people involved rather than my R&D folks. Let us say we have
two U.S. Armies. One U.S. Army is equipped with equipment available 20 years ago
(but you could have more of it because it is cheaper and development costs could be
avoided). The second U.S. Army is equipped with weaponry available today. I told them
to fight the two Armies in a war game and give me results or answers that could be
understood by external audiences.
    The new Army was three and a third divisions better than the older Army. (It would
take 3.3 more divisions of the older army to stalemate the newer one.) The operations
folks did the analysis. I told them not to give my R&D people a break. The results were:
1) modern equipment is important and 2) a measure was provided with which folks
external to the Army could identify.[50]

A team of senior analysts in Washington, many with career Army backgrounds, stated that the Army lost many of its better analytic people in the early
1980s when resources were more plentiful.[51] At that time, reliance on emotional
appeal for justifying an Army program to external audiences was sufficient. Now
that the resources are not automatic, the Army of the 1990s is disengaging with
discomfort at having this non-analytic approach being rejected. This problem is
compounded within the Pentagon by having political appointees in OSD within
the Clinton administration "populated with individuals from the Hill who were
never impressed with Army analysis."
    A senior Army general on active duty in Washington agreed that Army prob-
lems with analysis have worsened since the mid-1980s:

Through General Meyer's watch (1983), Army Chiefs and Vice Chiefs were far more skilled in using analysis to understand problems and gain support with external audiences. After General Meyer left the scene . . . a few Vice Chiefs of Staff . . . were comfortable with analysis: Max Thurman and Bob Riscassi come to mind. You combine that with how the Army has fallen off in growing its bench in the Pentagon and you end up with fewer general officers who think analytically. Army general officers today shy away from it because they lack the background of working in the Pentagon school of hard knocks.[52]

Builder's treatment of Army analysis in his illuminating 1989 work on service personalities peels back the layers of this naive and/or arrogant Army approach to reveal an institutional fear of interservice and intraservice conflicts and their consequences that may explain its communications with external audiences.[53] Builder saw analysis, "an examination of something by its parts and the relationship of those parts to one another" and as a "window into their [services'] institutional minds." According to Builder, the Army is more concerned with calculating and arriving at *numbers or amounts* (of the forces it needs) rather than *characteristics* (of the forces it needs) that typify the more effective Air Force analyses.[54]

The Army's analytic style for quantifying and calculating is a symptomatic result of the belief that the Army's internal rather than external audience is the true client. "The Army seems quite willing to calculate any requirement. Indeed the Army may do more calculations and less analysis than either of its sister services if one assumes that analysis leads to understanding and calculations lead to numbers."[55] Army analysis, according to Builder, is focused on reactively calculating the answers to problems, rather than illuminating and understanding problems.[56] If the focus is internal and the Army professionals know what the answers to the problems are, than analysis becomes the task of calculating numbers to support those right, professional "internal audience" answers. With this focus, the analysis produced is less likely to illuminate problems and less likely to provide the Army with understandable solutions that its senior leadership can honestly advocate without glazing the eyes of external audiences.

Builder provides two reasons to explain the Army's unique and problematic style of analysis that deal more with Army fears than Army arrogance. First, it gives Army senior leaders a way to shield analytic evaluation on the characteristics of forces needed *within the Army*, thereby protecting the need of making (or involving external audiences in the process of making) tradeoffs internally among the combat arms branches in systems and personnel. Second, this type of analysis allows the Army to produce and justify the requirement numbers for force planning within the Pentagon, but do it in a way that avoids crossing institutional boundaries of the other services and initiating interservice strife.[57]

This fear of interservice rivalry relates to the Army's unique acceptance of the interdependency of the various services (and will be discussed in greater detail in the second cultural dimension). Because external scrutiny might also lead to intraservice branch tradeoffs, the Army senior leadership turns inward with a focus on numbers and proven organizational design that has worked in the past. Builder believes that as long as the Army refrains from defining and communicating the tradeoffs needed to be made internally among its branches, and among joint and allied forces that will certainly threaten Air Force and Navy institutional independence, "The Army will continue to lack significant control over its obligations, resources and risks associated with the national commitments to fight."[58]

In summary, the Army's institutional naive arrogance allows it to assume that the merit of the Army's cause is self-evident to external audiences and to minimize the importance of producing communication products tailored to the unique needs and circumstances of these audiences. This subcomponent reduces the effectiveness of Army justifications by relying more on subjective professional judgment rather than supplementing it with simple, understandable analysis characteristic of the other services. While Army communications and analysis may appear on the Hill as naive arrogance, Builder and others attribute this manifestation to Army fear of uncontrollable outcomes that would possibly result from more effective and connected engagement with external audiences.

Army Discounts Assignments Dealing with External Audiences

The Army's internal fixation is also manifest in the discounted institutional value it places in select positions and assignments working directly with external audiences. Two organizations where this cultural proclivity is evident are the Office, Chief of Legislative Liaison (OCLL) and the Public Affairs Organization (PAO).

According to senior flag officers interviewed, both retired and active duty, the Army experiences problems in communicating to external audiences like Congress because: (1) institutionally it fails to assign its most competitive junior and senior officers to those positions; (2) it does not promote or give field command opportunities to those with legislative experience, limiting the positive cross-fertilization benefit of their experiences to the larger institution; and (3) as a service, it fails to appreciate and provide its officer corps with the skills and experience needed to effectively work with Congress and other external audiences.

The Army's top leaders claim that communicating their message more effectively to Congress and the media is critical for the service, but their actions seem to discount the importance of both endeavors. Institutional signals are clear and read closely by aspiring Army officers moving up the career ladder. The senior Army leadership does not place its most promising officers in LL and does not reward those who excel in LL with career advancement. In fact, it has moved closer to the long-standing pattern of a "dead end" assignment in Army Public Affairs.

General Max Thurman, a former VCSA (1983–87) and former CINC during Operation *Just Cause* in Panama,[59] addressed candidly and head-on the problem that the Army has in communicating its interests to Congress:

OCLL [Office Chief of Legislative Liaison] is a half-assed outfit and operation. The Army doesn't put its best officers in the OCLL game like it did in the past. There use to be a time when Chiefs of Legislative Liaison [CLL] like General Bernard W. Rogers or Weyand rose to be Chief of Staff of the Army. Not only do you no longer see CLLs reach the top, but they are damn lucky to make their third star. If you are not going to put your best officers in it, you are not going to get to first base. The Army senior leadership puts the CLL position way down the pecking order of preferred Major General assignments.[60]

Most of the retired and active-duty Army generals interviewed acknowledged the current problem in selecting and nurturing the careers of LL officers, both senior and junior. These officers uniformly believed improvements were essential, although few were optimistic about near-term prospects for such a change. Former CSA General Rogers echoed the need to put the best people, particularly upwardly mobile combat arms officers, into LL:

You have to groom and grow the right people who can work LL. Members and staff like to be around LL folks who are combat arms, are perceived as going places, and understand their legislative world. Someone who has been a war hero or made a name for him or herself out in the field should be considered for this critical job of educating and highlighting Army institutional interests. But you need someone who understands the congressional beast and has a charismatic personality that folks like to be around.[61]

General Carl Vuono, former CSA, echoed the need for a large-scale institutional change in the way future LL officers are identified and their careers managed:

You have to identify a large pool of fast-tracking young officers and closely manage their professional development over the years to facilitate both key Building [Pentagon] and Washington experience assignments and field troop assignments where the officer is rotated in and out of Washington. You have to build up a corps of young military officers—who are equal and on equal terms with the congressional staffers in terms of respect, who know the field of staffers, know who on the Hill you need to work, know those who are not worth working, and know those who are effective and ineffective. We need officers who have respected relationships with these staffers, know the Building, can't be snowed and can tell if the staffer really knows his business. We have not done a good job of building that corps of young officers. Additionally, we haven't helped our LL personnel in garnering the Hill's respect. The Hill views the capabilities of these young officers partly on the basis of success within the Army institution—who gets promoted and who gets selected for commands. The other services do a better job in this regard.[62]

Former CSA General Edward C. "Shy" Meyer made the point that the Army needs its best officers in LL today even more than in years past, to help Congress learn what an Army can do:

Twenty years ago there were far more Members with military experience on the Hill. Today, fewer Members and staff understand the Army. *Therefore its even more important to put the best of the crop in OCLL to help prepare future Army general officers that can serve the role of teacher and educator in a language and way Congress comprehends.* We need to develop more and better relationships. We need to try and coopt them with our ideas and suggestions. Proactively let them be part of the Army's policymaking process. You have to help Congress build up a knowledge of what an Army can do.[63]

Senior officers interviewed placed special emphasis on the need for strong senior leadership in OCLL. The importance and difficulty of the CLL position were highlighted by a flag officer who served the Army both as its CLL and later as its CSA, General Rogers. He highlighted the importance and difficulty of the CLL position:

The CLL's position is a critical one deserving the best and most promising flag officers being placed in that slot. It is one of if not the toughest and most important two star positions on the Army Staff. The CLL must understand Congress as an institution, be at ease on the Hill, be skilled at articulating Army positions in their language, and *be given the opportunity to pick who he wants to serve in OCLL* [italics added]. Thank goodness I had almost 7 years in the Building as a field grade officer equipping me with the invaluable advantage of exposure to the Hill.... My first 3–4 months as the CLL were the only times in my military career where I can recall consistently walking out my front door in the morning wishing I was walking back into the house. Then it became fun, and I actually missed it after I left the position. However, that experience was invaluable in my subsequent assignments.[64]

General Rogers and others interviewed noted that selecting a very strong senior officers for the CLL position had a positive long-term impact in attracting promising junior combat arms officers into LL work and then ensuring that these officers rose within the Army, bringing their legislative insights, experiences, and relationships with them. However, those interviewed noted that the lack of high-level value placed on LL assignments, including the CLL position, results in a general devaluation of the services provided. Rather than seeing Army LL and officers as critical tips of the spear in garnering the essential political and public support needed to sustain the institution's long-term warfighting interests and capabilities, these officers are often viewed by combat arms officers and some in the senior Army leadership with suspicion. A fast-tracking lieutenant colonel on the Army staff addressed this sentiment:

Army LL officers who excel [in LL work] are viewed with suspicion by many Army senior officers. You are not in uniform, but wear a stylish suit. They cannot see your ranger tab or your crossed rifles. Because many senior Army officers lack your experience or understanding of Congress, they question your agenda and your loyalties. Many have a hard time understanding why a real soldier would want to work in LL or PAO, when the real manly infantry assignments are out with the troops. They just don't understand. They see you operating on this terrain they have rarely walked and dealing with individuals they can not relate to or understand.[65]

The Army used to value and reward service in LL. Former Secretary of the Army Jack Marsh stated that "getting into Army congressional relations, unlike public affairs [PAO] assignments, used to be the path to the stars."[66] Based on interviews and observations of upward mobility for the services' LL officers, this is clearly not the case for the Army today.[67] In fact, many believe the institutional fate and incentives for Army combat arms officers assigned to LL duties are increasingly similar to those assigned to Army PAO assignments.

According to interviews with LL officers from other services and congressional sources, the other services are far better at assigning the most promising officers to LL and then advancing their careers. As a result, their activities are more highly valued throughout the service. For example, according to interviews, Marines understand the importance LL and PAO play in representing institutional concerns to external audiences. Their contribution is appreciated more by rank-and-file Marines and their senior leadership than in the Army. A retired senior general in the Marine Corps put it this way:

Marines who demonstrate skills and develop a political acumen in the areas of legislative liaison and public affairs are not viewed skeptically by the senior flag officers in the Corps because many of these same senior officers possess these same skills and have shared these same types of assignments. Marine generals and junior officers alike have witnessed and experienced the benefits of engagement with external audiences and recognize that it is ludicrous to think these external audiences will go away or not have an impact on the interests of the Corps. Our goal is to make it a positive impact.[68]

An excellent example of both the Marine Corps' positive impact with and the Army's relative disregard for dealing with external audiences is captured by John J. Fialka in *Hotel Warriors: Covering the Gulf War*, which contrasts the divergent approaches of the Army and Marine Corps in dealing with journalists in the war.[69] Fialka acknowledges that the press corps unintentionally distorted the coverage of the war in favor of the Marines, despite their smaller supporting role,[70] because of the significantly superior levels of skill and effort invested by Marines in public relations. He addressed the Army's missed opportunity to educate Americans about its unique capabilities:

The Army provided the crucial finale of the war. It was the Army's moment to shine. . . . As line after line of Iraqi troops quickly folded under the shock of the heavy, rapid [mostly Army] assault, the stage was set for one of the best U.S. Army stories ever. The embargo imposed by U.S. commanders on news of the gigantic troop movement had been lifted. The American public, even the Army brass in Washington, tired of hearing about the Marines, were frantic for news about the troops. But where there might have been a flood of news about the Army, only a trickle ever materialized. *The Army had drifted into a black hole of its own making.*[71]

Fialka commented that the ''differences between the two services' skills in handling public affairs were so vast that reporters sometimes wondered whether they represented different countries.''[72] The Marines were proactively engaged with the press corps, attempting to get as many journalists as they could attached to their units from the Joint Information Bureau in Dhahran. Army commanders, however, ''only grudgingly accepted journalists assigned to them and, at times, could not conceal their deep-seated hostility toward the press.''[73] The different approaches had very clear results in what was communicated back home and to Washington:

A detailed examination of the coverage of the ground war as reported in the nation's four largest newspapers and shown on its four television networks reveals that incidents involving Marines were mentioned 293 times by these outlets, as opposed to 271 mentions of the Army's activities. Viewers flipping channels or comparing newspapers would have been further confused over which military branch had the major role in this war. For example, coverage of the Marines dominated *The Washington Post* (75 Marine incidents versus 61 for the Army) and *The Los Angeles Times* (62 Marine incidents versus 41 for the Army). On the tube, ABC tended to focus nearly twice as much on Marine coverage (37 incidents versus 19 for the Army) and CBS reportage tended to follow in the same direction (30 Marine incidents versus 22 for the Army). *The New York Times, The Wall Street Journal*, CNN, and NBC, on the other hand, all had more incidents involving Army units.[74]

A respected senior active-duty Army general officer stressed that the Army senior uniformed leadership only gives periodic ''lip-service'' to its claims of making it a priority to communicate effectively with Congress and the American people. This same Army leadership fails to back this rhetoric with the necessary agency resources and institutional signals to support their claims.

We need to walk the talk. We say that communicating our message to external audiences is important, but look at the people we place in those positions. For example, the Chief, PAO position is seen as a last tour of duty position [as is the Army's CLL position in recent years]. We just got through identifying the new Army PAO. He . . . had already submitted his retirement paperwork but was asked to stay in for this additional [PAO] assignment. Compare that to the importance the U.S. Marine Corps places in their Chief of Public Affairs. The Marines place general officers in this position who are going places. . . . Brigadier General Boomer filled that position and moved up the ladder to [lead Marine Corps forces in the Gulf War and] become the four-star Vice Commandant. When was the last time you saw an Army Chief of Public Affairs become the Vice Chief of Staff of the Army? Don't hold your breath.[75]

DIMENSION 2: DEPENDENCY, TEAMWORK, AND
LEADERSHIP IN LAND WARFARE

The second cultural dimension is manifest in the sociological discomfort the Army experiences in self-promotion that is a function of the interconnectivity of teamwork, dependency, and leadership foremost in the Army officer's mind and past experiences. In a related sense, the Army is in the business of producing "leaders" in ground combat. *To lead successfully as a professional Army officer on the field of land battle requires teamwork and dependency on other members of the team.* This basic assumption underlies much of the Army's reluctance to self-promote before external audiences.

What is different about Army military leadership development that separates Army leaders from other service leaders? Do these different demands and experiences condition senior Army military leaders to be more uncomfortable in advocating Army interests to external audiences? How are teamwork, dependency, and leadership linked in the development and behavior of a senior Army officer?

Just as we recognize the importance of the beliefs and attitudes imposed by the Army's early military leaders on the Army organizational culture of today, it is equally important to understand how beliefs and values become ingrained through the early experiences of military officers and evolve into basic assumptions by the time they are senior general officers. Arthur T. Hadley captured this cultural socialization process that is different for each of the services. He demonstrates the importance of teamwork and recognized dependency in the early leadership development of Army officers:

The new-fledged Army lieutenant soon learns that he can make no movement without coordination. He cannot go right, left, backward, or forward without informing units on his right and left, artillery, tanks, supply trains, his superiors—all in detail. His unit's success, indeed its survival, rests on the efforts not just of himself, but of outsiders. If he advances too aggressively, his own artillery may fall on him, or the enemy can sneak between him and the next unit to his rear. This tends to make the Army officer more conscious of the needs of others, more supportive of teamwork than are officers in the other services.[76]

He goes on to say that the correlation of teamwork and dependency on others to future operational success continues throughout Army career development, and becomes especially pronounced and reinforced during troop command: "He sees that his battalion and regimental commanders, even his division's commanding general, are themselves restricted in certain ways because they are parts of a whole, whose combined functions produce success. . . . So early habits of coordination and *attention to the abilities of those around him are reinforced*" [emphasis added].[77]

These ingrained habits of coordination and attention to the abilities and likely concerns of others involved in the larger mission become a characteristic feature of the good Army leader. As Army officers progress through the ranks of Army leadership development, these habits become second nature. That is why Hadley and others believe that Army officers tend to perform better than others in interservice and joint command assignments. Army leadership behavior that is reinforced and rewarded requires a significant degree of deference to other participants and avoiding self-promotion at their expense.

According to senior Army general interviews, one must look at the Army's business of producing leaders to win in land combat to understand the Army–Hill patterns. Leadership training in the Army accentuates the importance of building teamwork at the expense of self-promotion. The nature of land combat is qualitatively different from warfare on the sea and in the air and places unique leadership demands on Army officers.

Compare the Army officer's socialization experience that promotes teamwork and accepts dependency with the Navy officer's experiences devoted to a tradition that is centered around the officer's independent command at sea:

The young naval lieutenant experiences a completely different psychological environment. He is part of a self-contained unit, his ship, that can and often does go off by itself for long periods of time. . . . While his own functions are rigidly prescribed—he cannot, for example, move his guns farther down the road; they are fastened to the ship—he sees that his superiors have tremendous leeway. The commander of a ship puts the wheel to the right, or commands a starboard turn, and, self-contained within the ship, all the paraphenelia of battle—ammunition, men, food, fuel—turn right also. There is no coordination necessary, no requesting permission, no letting people know . . . the ship . . . remains totally independent in ways no Army unit attains. . . . The young naval officer sees that . . . seniors, far from relishing coordination and assisting the function of larger units, glory in independence.[78]

In the Air Force and the Navy, the increased technical competence required of its officer corps, and the decreased independent role of their enlisted personnel in actual warfighting, changes qualitatively the leadership demands on these officers. The focus in their warfare is on the interests of the service leader: the Air Force pilot or the Navy ship commander. Army officers, on the other hand, must attempt to motivate their young enlisted warriors actually to face the more probable brunt of death on the battlefield by developing a flexible array of leadership skills that promote teamwork and acknowledge the interests of the combat soldiers they lead. The Army leader's self-interests cannot be the primary focus.

A retired senior Army general officer elaborated on these points. While his service bias influences the tone of his remarks, he highlights some important service distinctions in leadership development that may make senior Army officers more uncomfortable in promoting Army interests to the Hill:

The Army's problems on the Hill are tied to its historical and sociological uncomforta-
bleness in self-promotion and the related fact that it is in the business of producing
leaders. A Navy officer has to be all but a good leader. He is master of his ship with
complete authority out at sea. He can be a tyrant in his ship. There is less requirement
for a ship's commander to humor folks. In the Navy it is not leadership, in the true
Army sense of the word, but technical competence, especially in submarine warfare, that
is most important and valued. Technical competence is even more important in the Air
Force, except here the officers are also the lone trigger pullers. The enlisted personnel
are supporting these technically experienced commissioned officer warriors. They move
through the ranks more as trigger pullers than managers and leaders of men and women.

A good platoon leader in combat is a good gang leader. He has to figure out what it
will take to inspire, trick, or intimidate someone to get them to do what he desires.
Whether it is morally one-upping them, out-smarting them, or threatening to beat the
shit out of them, in combat, a platoon leader has to be flexible and be able to persuade,
humor, cajole, and lead. In the end, the leader has to acknowledge the interests of the
led. The leader's self-interests can't be seen as paramount. It must be with those being
led.[79]

As with Hadley, this Army general officer highlighted the the fact that Army
leaders are more likely to rise to leadership positions outside of their particular
service because of their proclivity to sublimate self (service)-interests to the
larger interests beyond the Army. "Why do you think that there has never been
an Admiral or Air Force general elected President of the United States? The
other Services do not produce the George Marshalls that rise to lead and occupy
key top positions of government at critical times. Those services are not in the
leadership development business."[80]

When asked why Marine Corps leaders seem to be more willing to self-
promote to external audiences than Army leaders despite the fact that they share
many of the same leadership development challenges for land combat, many
who were interviewed highlighted Marine Corps fears about institutional relevancy to explain the difference. Again, Army bias is evident in the tone of the
remarks below, but the reader can still appreciate the point that institutional
survival or legitimacy may partially account for the more sophisticated and engaged approach the Marine Corps takes in communicating with external audiences:

Now while Marine leaders have many parallels with Army leaders in combat, they are
driven by their fear of institutional relevancy and going out of existence. You must
remember they were initially formed to conduct the mission and serve the role of bod-
yguards to keep Navy Captains alive from their own crew. Their moral capacity to lead
in a George Marshall sense of duty runs counter to their self-seeking and promoting
frenzy that puts Marine Corps interests before the nation's interests. Their loyalty to the
Corps pervades their every action.[81]

The Army projects the value it places on teamwork onto its relations with
other services. According to most interviews, Army officers genuinely view their

sister services as part of that warfighting team. To promote or advocate one part of the team in a zero-sum fashion to Congress, considered to be relative outsiders, is perceived by many Army leaders to be parochial, unprofessional, and unwise because other services make essential contributions to the Army's attainment of decisive victory with minimal casualties.

General Meyer echoed this comment:

Going it alone, thinking only of your individual interests without considering the impact on the larger whole or warfighting team is institutionally discouraged. *Unlike the other services that believe in and tout their independent service operations and capabilities to external audiences like Congress, the Army questions and sees such self-promotion as a form of going it alone and of advocating individual [institutional] interests that approaches being unprofessional and parochial.*[82]

A senior Army general officer addressed the Army's uniquely dependent status that places the imperative of being a team player disproportionately on Army shoulders:

The Army is the only service that is dependent on the other two services for getting to the battle. Past agreements ensured that the Army would be dependent on the Air Force for its strategic airlift and on the Navy for its strategic sealift. This places the Army in a precarious and even more dependent relationship with its sister services today since the Army is a largely CONUS based power projection strategic force for the nation. . . . It is hard to imagine any of the other services in the position of being as dependent on another in order to accomplish their mission.

However, some senior general officers stressed that while this emphasis on validated teamwork and recognized dependency is effective in battle, it may be a disadvantage in relations with the Hill because the other services do not share the same reticence to promote their own independent service capability positions at the expense of the Army. According to an active-duty senior Army general: "By the time an Army officer reaches general officer rank, he genuinely has developed a trust in that joint warfighting concept and with the fellow flag officers representing the other services. If he hasn't been in Washington before, this same general officer is typically shocked to believe that individual services were looking out for only their service. They just can't believe it. They are naive."[83]

DIMENSION 3: NARROWLY DEFINED CAREER SUCCESS: MUDDY BOOTS CAN DO ALL

This third cultural dimension underlying the seven Army–Hill patterns refers to a basic assumption that career success for combat arms officers is defined narrowly as being outside of Washington and inside the officer's branch or specialty, particularly serving with troops—"muddy boots." This assumption works to reduce the Pentagon experience senior flag officers possess before serving in key positions on the Army staff and discourage aspiring combat arms officers from seeking Pentagon assignments and gaining experience with congressional and other entities. This is important for this study since senior (combat arms) flag officers are viewed by the congressional audience as the most credible and potentially effective service message carriers, and they occupy most senior Army leadership positions.

Most senior general officers interviewed believe this cultural dimension helps to explain why the Army is not as effective as it could be in dealing with Congress. They also believe this dimension is more of a problem today then it was 20 years ago; that it is being aggravated by the large-scale downsizing of the Army over the last 10 years, and that it needs to be addressed to ensure the long-term viability of the organization.

Former CSA General Vuono, who had multiple tours in Washington prior to flag rank, made the following assessment: "Career success for an Army combat arms officer is currently being defined too narrowly on warfighting competence alone. Ironically, this warfighting career path is too narrow to sustain the institution's long-term interests that allow it to do well in warfighting in the future."[84]

An active Army senior general officer described how success is currently being defined for combat arms officers:

We have bred and defined success of our future Army leadership [combat arms officers] in a narrow predictable career pattern. For senior rank in the Army, you must be a battalion commander. To be a Battalion Commander, you must be a battalion S-3, Battalion XO. . . . The incentives are clearly signaled for staying at the division level or below as long as you can. By seeking assignments that increase the opportunities for additional time with troops at the tactical level, there is little time for Pentagon or Washington assignments. More important, the boards are now more likely to comprise officers who have followed–this same narrow tactical path to success. Board members cast a long shadow.

The only way you are going to change this fact of human nature is for the Chief of Staff of the Army to convince the Secretary of the Army that a problem exists, whereby the Secretary provides the promotion and selection boards with specific instructions for specific types of experience that will deviate from this narrow mean.[85]

Another senior Army general highlights this narrow path of success to flag rank for combat arms officers and the Army's institutional resistance to alternative career paths: "The Army professional development system produces officers to command Army divisions. The Army will resist the promotions of individuals who don't follow that path. . . . Winning the nation's wars is most important for the Army. That produces the division commander mentality that is so prevalent in the Army and is so out of place in Washington."[86]

General Meyer raised a concern that the Army is expecting its general officers to accomplish too many missions without sufficient preparation. The Army system, according to the general, must learn to recognize early that "all cannot do all." Currently, he opined, this narrow track of success produces only one of three types of general officers that the Army will need to sustain itself in the future:

First, you will need one group of generals with primarily troop experience: your future CINCs [commander in chiefs] and warriors. Second, you will need your future bureaucrats, the generals with the technical and administrative skills to build coalitions in the Building [Pentagon] and in Washington to man, equip, and train the force. Finally, you need the political/military interface: those like Powell, Shali, and Crowe while having limited time with the troops, they were exactly right for explaining the military to politicians and Congress in particular. At the same time they had enough exposure to troops to understand the problems of commanders in those levels of command. Other Services intentionally work to get that military/bureaucratic/political mix today. The Army needs to do it better.[87]

General Max Thurman, a combat arms officer who never commanded at the division level but still continued to rise to higher positions of responsibility in the late 1970s and early 1980s, reiterated this concern. He said that to make colonel in today's Army a combat arms officer should do all he can to avoid Washington duty for the first 20 years of his career. While noting that this cultural dimension has been in place for a long time, he stated that there are ways the senior Army leadership can send institutional signals to broaden the narrow troop track for officer advancement:

I was the one who lobbied and won approval as the DCSPER [Deputy Chief of Staff for Personnel] for the selection of non-brigade command combat arms Colonels to the Brigadier General promotion list; however, it was a hard sell. I felt it was critical to send the signal throughout the combat arms community that there was more than one avenue to the top in the Army for some who are gifted and doing a line of work that the Army needs. But that goes down hard in the Army.[88]

General Meyer, a former CSA, also highlighted his efforts to compensate for the culture: "Too much is now tracked on battalion command and not selection to the War College for combat arms officers. If you are not selected for battalion command as a combat arms officer, you are not likely to get selected for the resident War College course. Those two hurdles keep that officer from any real chance at making colonel. I established quotas for War College for those talented officers who didn't get battalion command."[89]

Army General Rogers stressed that senior Army leadership must be aware of this cultural dimension and the power of promotion and command selection boards to perpetuate it:

Because of the cultural underpinnings of favoring service with the troops over service in Washington, the Secretary of the Army and the Chief of Staff of the Army have to closely monitor the cultural bias of Boards to ensure they are promoting and selecting the officers with the skills and experience needed for the betterment of the future Army. The concern should never be lost that Boards are made up of individuals who cast a long shadow like themselves. The Army is served well when some of these shadows are different and tailored to the diversified needs of the Army. The senior leadership, through Secretary of the Army instructions given to the Boards, must harp on the Boards about filling those needs with combat arms officers who don't necessarily fit the pure warrior track.[90]

Many of the senior generals interviewed were particularly concerned with the selection of general officers to key positions on the Army staff despite the fact that they had little or no experience in the Pentagon prior to assuming these key duties. At the very time the Army was downsizing, the interviewees stressed that these individuals lacked the experience to most effectively take on the tough issues, and by their selection, sent the unhealthy institutional signal that avoiding Washington as a field-grade officer was a prudent and strategic pathway to the stars.

One former CSA put it bluntly: "I despair when I see general officers being brought to the Building for the first time as DCSOPS [Deputy Chief of Staff of Operations and Plans]."[91] According to another CSA, "One of the problems I'm sure the Army has now is Generals come to Washington who have never served and never accumulated real experience in the Building. That is disaster-ville in most cases."[92]

General Max Thurman, who had multiple Pentagon tours as a field-grade and general officer, stressed the importance of Washington experience for combat arms officers in learning how to engage Members of Congress:

To be truly successful on the Hill you have to earn your spurs before Congress through testimony and by continually hustling the goods or information over there. I was good at testifying because I got started at an early age and rank. Early on I got the flavor for congressional preparation, congressional testimony, and overall congressional ambience and norms. *I quickly learned that these folks can be approached if you and your staff are together.* I began testifying to Congress as a brigadier general and kept at it for my remaining 16 years as a general officer. It should surprise no one that it got progressively easier with experience.

However, you bring in a lieutenant general to Washington and make him the DCSOPS—you can't expect him to do anything but shy away from Congress. You can't BS over there; Congress won't tolerate poor prep. They expect you to know your business. It's not surprising that the new DCSOPS finds himself uncomfortable on the Hill.[93]

Former CSA General Rogers also stressed the importance of early Pentagon experience and provided an interesting example of how junior field-grade experience serves a general officer in understanding the Army staff and its potentially negative dynamics:

I think it is critical for Army general officers to have had significant time in the Pentagon, preferably at the O-4 [major] and especially O-5 [lieutenant colonel] levels. They need to know how that process works. They need to be sensitive and aware of what I call the "O-6 [colonel] Crust" that runs rampant in the Building. This is a phenomenon in the Building that keeps creative new ideas of bright young Majors and Lieutenant Colonels from breaking up into the senior Army leadership spheres. The O-6 crust wants to play it safe. They are afraid they'll be shown up or that the generals will think I'm nuts for letting this [proposal or idea] percolate up. This is just an example of intra-ARSTAFF [Army Staff] dynamics that you fail to appreciate if you arrive to the Building for the first time at the flag level. It doesn't even begin to touch on the lessons to be learned in working effectively with entities external to the Army proper.[94]

A respected Army general officer who commanded at the four-star level, but also had multiple early tours in the Pentagon, believed this recent "muddy boots can do all" pattern goes well beyond impacting issues with Congress, and hurts the Army in its overall dealings in the Pentagon, in Washington, and with the public in general. He addressed what is missing in these less experienced flag officers:

Officers, especially Army officers, should not have their first tour or assignment in Washington and the Pentagon take place as a general officer. Through a Pentagon assignment, one experiences the uniqueness of the DC and Building environment, and especially the inter- and intra-agency way of life that is totally different from what one experiences commanding at Fort Hood, Texas. *The Army and nation lose if a general officer arrives for his first substantive Army assignment in the Pentagon because this flag officer will always be in the learning rather than the visionary mode.* If he is a visionary, he will be less effective in strategically moving others toward that vision. He will be more cautious, passive, and reactionary to other more experienced actors in and out of the Building.[95]

The tables below highlight the concern of these senior Army general officers that the Army is not grooming and providing the Army staff with senior leadership experienced in the ways of Washington and the Pentagon.[96] Table 4.1 demonstrates that the senior Army military leadership ranks last among the services in cumulative time spent serving in the Washington community prior to assuming their key leadership positions. The large disparity in the experience levels of the services' respective officers indicate that in the best case the Army staff leadership in this small but influential sample has to overcome six years of cumulative experience merely to compete with the next lowest service (Marine Corps)[97] and has just over half the combined experience of the Air Force.

As seen in Table 4.2, Army officers spend the least time in Washington serving below flag rank, which is not surprising given their exceedingly low career Washington service. A more telling figure is the percentage of each service's total months spent in Washington before being promoted to general officer/flag rank. The Army leadership sample has the lowest percentage (51%) of Washington time spent below flag rank designation; in other words, the Army

Table 4-1
Flag Officer Pentagon/Washington Experience (number of months) Prior to Assuming Key Service Positions for 1995 Study Leadership Samples

	Chief of Staff	Vice C/S	DCSOPS	CLL	Total
Army	24	62	17	88	191
Air Force	80	124	85	80	369
Navy	123	44	31	84	282
Marine Corps	128	24	58	51	261

Note: The Army DCSOPS' 17-month service as Deputy Director for Operations (DDO), National Military Command Center, Joint Chiefs of Staff, was included in the Army statistics even though this experience appears more similar to senior operational headquarters-staff positions outside of Washington than to the experience gained from more typical one-star flag positions in the Pentagon. As the DDO, this one-star flag officer heads one of several teams that monitor all military operations around the world on a 24-hour basis, reporting updates and unusual activities and events having military significance to the Chairman, JCS, and Secretary of the Defense. For the sake of objectivity and the fact that serving in this position provides the flag officer with a working understanding of how the Joint Staff is structured, I included it for this study. However, most agree that it provides little experience in developing or defending policy issues and opportunities to work with Congress.

Table 4-2
Pentagon/Washington Experience (number of months) Prior to Flag Officer Selection

	Chief of Staff	Vice C/S	DCSOPS	CLL	Total
Army	0	39	0	58	97
Air Force	27	64	59	44	194
Navy	76	44	31	69	220
Marine Corps	64	18	58	42	182

leadership sample had the least amount of time and experience as junior officers in the Washington community to draw upon when they later assumed their key positions.

While the Air Force leadership sample percentage of 53 percent is only slightly higher, it must be noted that their "below flag rank" service total (194 months) exceeds the *total* Army Washington service total of 191 months. Given the Air Force's preponderance of Washington area service, this percentage is not surprising, and only significant in showing that they value Washington experience throughout their leadership's careers.

The Navy leadership sample, on the other hand, spent 78 percent of their impressive 282 total Navy months of Washington service below the level of

Table 4-3
Number of Washington Assignments, by Average Length of Each (months) and Position

	Chief of Staff	Vice C/S	DCSOPS	CLL
Army	2/12.0	5/12.4	1/17.0	6/14.7
Air Force	3/26.7	4/31.0	4/21.3	4/20.0
Navy	5/24.6	3/14.7	1/31.0	6/14.0
Marine Corps	4/32.0	1/24.0	2/29.0	3/17.0

Table 4-4
Average Length of Time Spent at Each Assignment

	Time Spent (Months)	Average Number of Assignments
Marine Corps	26.1	2.50
Air Force	24.6	3.75
Navy	18.8	3.75
Army	13.6	3.50

flag rank. This provides valuable learning experiences for these future leaders when the risks and impacts are lower, and provides them additional time to understand the Washington policymaking process.

In Table 4-2, the Navy's high percentage is largely because of the significant "below flag rank" Washington service time for two of their leaders: Chief of Naval Operations Admiral Mike Boorda and their Chief of Legislative Affairs Admiral Natter.[98] Congressional comments in Chapter 3 lauding Admiral Boorda's proactive and comfortable engagement of the Congress and the Navy LL's reputation as being the most effective departmental service operation suggest that early and significant experience in Washington pays long-term leadership dividends. Admiral Natter, three years later, was serving as the Commander of the U.S. Naval Seventh Fleet.

In the assignment histories of the service leadership samples (Appendix C), it is significant that both the Navy and the Marine Corps assign their future leaders to the offices of the CNO and the Commandant/Assistant Commandant, providing them firsthand experience in the Pentagon and congressional decisionmaking process. These types of assignments are conspicuously absent from the resumes of the Army leaders.[99]

While the Army (see Tables 4-3 and 4-4) appears to be at the norm for number of assignments that its officers serve in the Washington community prior to

Table 4-5
Washington Experience of Flag Officer, by Month, Prior to Assuming Key Service Positions, Compared with 1979–83 Era Leadership Sample

	Chief of Staff	Vice C/S	DCSOPS	CLL
Army (1981)	105	70	50	124
Army (1995)	24	62	17	88
Air Force	80	124	85	80
Navy	123	44	31	84
Marine Corps	128	24	58	51

assumption of their key senior leadership duties on the Army staff, the average length of each Washington duty assignment is significantly less than for their counterparts in the other services. The Army ranks last among the services with just over a year spent, on average, at each position. Given the complex nature of the assignments occupied by these officers, the short tenure leaves less time for an officer to learn the job, let alone master it. The Marine Corps senior officers, while serving on average in fewer positions, spent twice as much time in each, thereby improving their level of professional expertise and knowledge in those positions.

There was general agreement that this "muddy boots can do all" assumption is more a problem today than it was in the Army 15 to 20 years ago. Table 4-5 supports that notion that past DCSOPS, Vice Chiefs of Staff, and CSAs had tours in Washington over a longer period of time, providing them significantly more time and experience upon which to rely. The cumulative Washington experience reflected in General Meyer's leadership team sample[100] more closely approximates those of the other services today. In earlier days, the path for upward mobility within the Army officer ranks consisted of tactical troop and Washington alternating assignments tracks.

Interviewees point to the fact that this important departure from the past experience of ensuring balance in Pentagon and troop assignments for Army fast-trackers occurred at the same time the Army underwent a reduction of a quarter of a million active-duty personnel and the inactivation of an entire corps of active-duty combat units. During this time of understandable uncertainty for junior officers, who were looking for signals about opportunities that would exist for them in the post–Cold War Army, the senior leadership selections signaled to the Army's best and brightest that Washington experience was not necessary at the field-grade level if you wanted to be competitive for flag rank and senior leadership positions in the future.[101]

Most general officers I spoke to believed that the Army's long-term interests require it to make a correction back to a professional development track that ensures its best combat arms officers alternate between troop and Pentagon assignments.[102] Understanding Washington and developing skills in working service and interservice issues in the Pentagon must parallel the preparation for commanding combat units in the field. According to these interviews, ignoring either could undermine preparation for the resource and readiness challenges of the future. The challenge to the senior Army leadership is to make the two, warfighting competency and Washington experience, mutually inclusive for future Army leaders.

One Army four-star stressed the obligation of the senior Army leadership to provide an officer corps for the twenty-first century with a broader outlook and greater experience in key Washington assignments. Integrating Washington experience into the Army "mainstream" assignment path for the best and brightest Army officers is critical for the effective interface with civilian decisionmaking in our democracy:

In this new and challenging era, without changing fundamental Army values, it would be smart for the Army leadership to make a greater institutional effort to place hand-selected individuals with potential for future senior leadership rank in jobs at OSD, White House, Army LL, DARPA [Defense Advanced Research Projects Agency], etc., to develop and produce a much broader base officer corps who will be needed to represent our interests and build coalitions of support in the Building and Washington community into the 21st century. It is the right thing to do and the obligation of the current Army leadership to provide the officer corps with a broader outlook.

There is an obligation of the professional military in a democracy that we must meet. Our country, unlike all others, has professional military people directly interfacing with civilians while under civilian control. Our military institutionally is not sheltered from civilian decisions and, in fact, we work with civilians in helping them arrive at their decisions. This provides a unique and special responsibility to perform that institutional interface well with our civilian leadership in our democracy.[103]

DIMENSION 4: THE ARMY AS THE NATION'S OBEDIENT AND LOYAL SERVANT

This cultural dimension undergirds many of the Army–Hill patterns and has its roots in the doctrine of civilian supremacy and early Army professionalism. It is manifest in Army military leaders seeing themselves as being the nation's "obedient loyal servant" or "obedient handyman."[104] It is related to Army ideals of subservience to civilian, largely executive branch control and loyalty to the formal chain of command. More than in the other services, it entails a dutiful obedience in making "virtue out of necessity," even if these actions are antithetical to Army institutional interests.[105]

Tracing current Army attitudes back to their earliest days, former Secretary of the Army and former Member of Congress Jack Marsh believes the Army's "can-do" attitude toward the executive branch is tied to Army subservience to civilian control:

Deeply ingrained in the Army's ethos is its *subservience to civilian control*; much more so than you find in the Navy, or Marine Corps or more recently the Air Force. The selfless service legacy of George Washington, in our revolutionary Army, and his sensitivity to civilian concerns that went beyond the Army institution's self-interests were ingrained in the Army.

Clearly seen in the Articles of Confederation is a great fear of standing Armies. Standing Armies were to be maintained only during times of war. The creation of an active and militia Army in the Constitution, defense appropriations no longer than two years, and posse comitatus are all based on this early fear of active duty armies. The legacy and sensitivity of Army commanders to these fears and concerns started with Washington and were manifest in General Washington's refusal to assume leadership as King in the Newburg conspiracy. The Army's more overt subservience to civilian leadership, with the "can do" attitude being just one manifestation, impacts on the other services by setting a positive example.[106]

Huntington notes that both Army and Navy professional officers after the Civil War developed a professional allegiance to their executive branch chain of command and often viewed congressional input into military matters as both complications and intrusions.

The new American professional officer had an inbred respect for the integrity of the chain of command stretching from the President as Commander in Chief to the lowest enlisted man. No place existed in this picture for Congress. The legislature could be placed neither above nor below the President; yet it obviously had to be placed somewhere. Congress existed off to the side, an ever present threat to the symmetry and order of the military hierarchy. The officers preferred to simplify matters and stress only their allegiance to the President. . . . Military officers at times wished for some mechanism to represent the military viewpoint as a whole before Congress, but they were strong in their condemnation of individual officers who succumbed to the temptation to resort to legislative influence and push special bills. They were equally vehement in denouncing Congress for intruding into the military realm.[107]

However, the differing Army and Navy experiences led to divergent notions of what military subservience to civilian control actually meant. This manifests itself in the different ways these professionals responded to directed courses of action by their civilian superiors.

After the Civil War, and with the advent of a new military professionalism, the Army was called to participate in a diversity of often "dirty" tasks which included:

Southern reconstruction, Indian fighting, labor disorders, the Spanish War, Cuban occupation, Philippine pacification, construction and operation of the Panama Canal, [and] the Mexican punitive expedition. Accordingly, the Army developed an image of itself as the *government's obedient handyman* [italics added] performing without question or hesitation the jobs assigned to it. . . . It had no particular field of responsibility; instead, it was a vast, organic, human machine, blindly following orders from on high. . . . By following all orders literally the Army attempted to divest itself of political responsibility and political controversy despite the political nature of the tasks it was frequently called upon to perform.[108]

While this obedient machine analogy may have its cultural roots in the varied distasteful and often politically laden tasks the Army was given during the advent of its professionalism, this sense of loyal obedience has been reinforced by the context and conditions in which Army officers are required to accomplish missions. As discussed earlier, the Army places great value on teamwork and recognition of its unique dependency on other parts, internal and external to the Army institution, that enable it to perform successfully as a whole.

Practicing teamwork and following through to successfully accomplish one's part of the task requires Army leaders first to be good followers. Being a loyal team player and following the directives of higher authorities so that one's piece of the whole fits with other directed pieces become ingrained and rewarded Army officer behaviors. They work against behavior that questions the higher directive and instead reinforce behavior of making a directive that one does not like succeed.

The success of an Army officer is based on obediently making the part fit within a directed plan. Army commanding officers and their units are rarely isolated from civilian communities, and drop-in inspections by their military superiors at any level and any time are a norm. Therefore, Army commanding officers are likely to get more guidance than their Navy counterparts at sea. Because of the necessity of coordination among its many parts that emanates at all levels in the Army, the ability of Army officers to deviate from a directed course of action is much more difficult and risky. All these factors combine to produce a leadership environment that makes questioning a directive from higher authority a more visible and unusual occurrence in the Army.[109]

The Navy, on the other hand, with its reverence for tradition and independent command at sea, had a different culture. Unlike their blindly obedient Army counterparts, the more independent Navy admirals were far more likely to question directives they viewed as antithetical to fundamental Navy, and in their view, national interests.

While stressing the subordination of the Navy to the political direction of the government, naval officers also stressed its responsibility for the country's safety. "Let us remember," warned [Admiral Bradley A.] Fiske, "that the naval defense of our country is our profession, not that of Congress." The naval profession must obey its civilian superiors, but it also has the duty to make its professional opinions known. . . . The naval profession must have room to work out its own "rules of strategy, tactics, and discipline," but in the end, these were, of course, subject to the "general control of the civil authority, to which it must render absolute obedience." The Navy view of civilian control thus assigned a more positive and active role to the military profession than did that of the Army.[110]

The Navy's national stature and independence were key aspects of its identity that admirals were willing to attempt to protect if challenged from its superiors. The "Navy, of all America's services, had the clearest sense of its identity and interests. Navymen knew what they wanted and had their priorities in line. If higher authority differed, then higher authority was usually seen as making a direct assault on the Navy's powerful, ingrained sense of self. Forced or unforced resignations had been the result . . . and they would happen again."[111]

The Navy has been more likely to band together in questioning and opposing executive branch directives that they see as threatening to their relevance, as in the "revolt of the Admirals" following Secretary of Defense Louis Johnson's cancellation of the aircraft carrier *United States* in 1949; and to their independence, as in their strong and largely effective objections to President Truman's efforts to unify the military services following World War II.[112]

So fierce had been the Navy's opposition to service unification, that even Truman was intrigued with one exasperated Army unification proposal which suggested that "the only way to overcome the Navy's resistance would be to do away with the War Department, transfer all of its elements to the Navy, and redesignate that organization as the Department of Defense."[113]

The Army "Can-Do" Spirit

Army emphasis on obedience is evident in its "can-do" attitude and the great difficulty it has in saying it cannot do x, y, or z without unacceptable risk to both its executive superiors in OSD and Members of Congress.

A positive can-do attitude is drilled into soldiers and young officers early in their careers as indispensable prerequisites of teamwork, mission accomplishment, and a functioning chain of command. For example, in Army Ranger School, the adage "cooperate and graduate" emphasizes the importance of immediate and positive obedience to making an assigned mission succeed.[114]

The Army can-do attitude has taken on a more pejorative connotation since the end of the Vietnam War, as scholars attempted to understand and explain how the nation came to lose that war. It is often cited in explaining why senior flag officers of all services failed to question or speak out against the lack of military strategy or the limitations being placed on the way the war was being fought by their superiors.[115] In Harry G. Summer's critical analysis of the Vietnam War, he says "Our military leaders evidently assumed that although their strategies were preferable, the United States would prevail regardless of what strategy was adopted."[116]

Analyses by Summers and others of this period highlight the Army leadership's particularly strong adherence to this "can-do" philosophy.[117] The lack of threatened or actual resignations by senior military leaders over these policies underscores this unwillingness to oppose civilian, especially executive branch, leaders.[118]

Because of the cultural durability of the can-do attitude, former CSA General Meyer believes Summers' message needs to be repeated to the next generation of officers:

This difficulty to say we can't do something or can't do this part of the National Military Strategy without *x*, *y*, or *z* or do so without "high or unacceptable risk" is more of that: yes sir, no sir, no excuse sir, mentality of the Army that is a value that is usually rewarded in the field and in hierarchical organizations in general. . . . The Army lost that 'yes sir, no sir, no excuse sir' mentality after Vietnam. Harry Summers stressed that we had to speak out on issues. This point needs to be reiterated again to another generation of officers. *It is your responsibility, especially the senior Army leadership's, to speak out on the wellness of the force.*

General Meyer went on to tie this professional responsibility to speak out on the wellness of the force to an officer's understanding and allegiance to the Constitution of the United States:

The Army and the Services are supposed to be politically non-partisan. Army officers and especially Army general officers must understand the Constitution. Each officer takes an oath of allegiance to the Constitution. The Constitution requires that we give our personal views to the Congress. My testimony to Congress of a "hollow Army" was my Constitutional obligation. I had already told the SECDEF and President first of my position and intentions. I wrote up my resignation, but didn't have to submit it. A clear lesson that I drew from the Vietnam experience is that the senior Service military leadership have a constitutional obligation to give their personal views on important issues. Granted we must ensure that audience is always aware of the administration position and never misrepresent that position, but we should never be a handmaiden of the party in power but to the Constitution instead.[119]

According to general officers interviewed, the unquestioning and blindly obedient nature of the can-do attitude, which is often associated with Army officer behavior toward the executive branch, is especially relevant to this study.[120] This Army tendency to treat the executive branch with deference and sense of teamwork is qualitatively different from its relationship with its congressional superiors, where a detached and reactive deference alone is the perceived norm.

General Rogers related the Army can-do attitude to its unwillingness to make "end-runs" to Congress. An end-run to General Rogers is where a service meets with Members *A* and *B* to advocate position *Y*, which is opposed by the administration and OSD. While opposing the end-run practice, he implicitly suggests that establishing trusted close relations with the Hill obviates the need for end-runs as Congress often asks senior flag officers for their opinions.

Army culture makes it difficult for the Army to say we can't or shouldn't do something. It is not like the Army to make end-runs around OSD after OSD has made a decision the Army doesn't like. We didn't make end-runs to Congress. *Army culture expects Army officers to play with the cards that were dealt rather than go for aces elsewhere.* Some of the other Services do make end-runs that go outside the bounds of propriety. But it is one thing not to actively work an issue on the Hill that is counter to OSD or the administration position. It is quite another thing to evade giving an honest and candid account of your personal views when asked because it varies with the OSD position. It is also important to realize that the more you are engaged on the Hill, the more likely you are going to be asked about issues. Whenever asked, I would give accurately the DOD position, and then would follow with "This is not my position, this is what I personally believe." I couldn't be a Chief of Staff of the Army [(CSA)] under any type of muzzle that pressures me not to give an accurate account of my personal views. *There are some principles worthy of resignation, and being muzzled by OSD would be one of them for me.*

Former CSA Carl Vuono addressed this sense of loyalty to OSD:

We will fight the battle in OSD; once we lose the battle, we will salute and say "OK, that's it, we're going to support the defense position." And as an institution, we will not end-run DOD. *It's in our nature to support our leaders.* Every school the Army has teaches you mission accomplishment and stresses the values of loyalty up and loyalty down. You forcefully lay out your position to your company commander and once your company commander says "OK Vuono, damn it, that's it." You say "Fine sir, I'm going to make it happen." You learn that up the line. That's ingrained in us. We take great pride in that. We feel to do anything less than that even when you are dealing with Congress is damn near violating your oath.[121]

Former Assistant Secretary of the Army Augustine gave an example of how this obedience or loyalty to OSD has hurt the Army with Congress relative to the other services:

During my time in OSD and the administration, there was a belief by military civilians that the uniformed military shouldn't be over on the Hill in force. They were reluctant having folks in uniform spending a lot of time over on the Hill. Unlike other government agencies out of uniform, military leaders in uniform stand out and it wouldn't provide a positive perception of the military lobbying Congress to the public. Therefore OSD did send a subtle but clear signal that they didn't want the services' uniformed leadership over on the Hill in mass. The problem that gets at the heart of your research is that the Army obeyed it faithfully.[122]

When asked why the Army was less sophisticated with Congress on issues where it disagrees with the administration, one senior Army general officer, who had significant experience working Army issues with Congress, stressed a fear of appearing disloyal to the Commander-in-Chief. This perception of disloyalty to the executive branch chain of command disinclines Army officers from speak-

ing out on their genuinely believed professional assessments to Members of
Congress, even when they are asked for their personal opinions in one-on-one
sessions.

The Army ethos is one where an officer is worried about getting too cute on the Hill;
afraid of getting your wrist slapped if you get too good at working the Hill. More
important, Army officers are worried about being disloyal to the commander in chief.
I'm constantly being asked about the personal opinion questions—guys come to me about
that because they are concerned about being disloyal. I'd rather err on that cautionary
side.[123]

   The Army was seen by most of those interviewed on the Hill and in the Army
to be the most likely of the four services to roll over and concede to officials
in DOD on issues and concerns that had been highlighted earlier by its senior
uniformed leadership as critical. The other services are clearly subservient to
civilian control, but there appears to be an impression that the Army prides itself
in being the most subservient and most likely to jettison its earlier position to
adopt an OSD stance in the can-do spirit of making do with what you are given.
   Supporters of a strong Army in Congress complained in interviews that the
Army's refusal to stand its ground on issues of difference with OSD makes
congressional efforts to help the Army more difficult in two ways. First, it
becomes more difficult for the congressional audience to identify the core concerns for the Army, because of a changing bottom line. Second, if the Army is
unwilling to candidly acknowledge differences with OSD positions when Congress asks for personal assessments, then it undercuts Army supporters' efforts
to garner additional support on the Hill that would increase pressure on DOD
officials to support Army issues.
   For example, many congressional interviewees highlighted the apparent willingness of the CSA to subjugate Army budget needs to OSD positions in his
hearing testimonies over a three-year period.

1994–96 Budget Battles

   In defending the President's fiscal year 1994 budget request, the CSA testified
before the SASC about an Army precariously on the "razor's edge" following
a $5.6B reduction from the previous year's budget. "The point is that there are
the dollars in the 1994 budget to maintain the force that I think I will have [as
the Army continues to downsize]. But if I get an acceleration of that [declining
budget] and if I have fences put around it, *then I and the Army are in trouble,
and I am in big trouble because I'm on the razor's edge.*"[124]
   Congress responded by approving a $61.1B Army budget for that year
(FY94). The "razor's edge" analogy had connected with the congressional audience and seemed to have caught the attention of officials at OSD. The FY95
administration budget request for the Army of $61.1B for the first time avoided

the types of cuts the Army had endured in previous years. In defending the FY95 budget request before Congress, the CSA stated that while this $61.1B level was adequate for the FY95 budget, that $61.1B-plus dollars for pay increases and for inflation would be necessary in each of the outyears in order to "do what it is that the country needs us to do." The CSA stated that no more real cuts should be made in the Army budget. However, he abandoned the "razor's edge" analogy.[125]

The CSA's message of a stable funding base at FY95 buying power levels plus pay increases and inflation was not heeded by OSD. Rather than the $61.7B that a stable funding base would provide, OSD intended to fund the Army at only $56B for FY96. The Army received, however, a partial reprieve in the form of an additional $2.7B supplemental directed late in the process toward its readiness accounts when three of its Army divisions dropped from C-2 to an unsatisfactory C-3 readiness status.[126] Even with this external "fix" for readiness purposes, the Army was almost $3B dollars short of what General Sullivan had told Congress he would need. Dollars were shifted out of Army modernization accounts into its readiness accounts to the point where even the Secretary of Defense voiced publicly that too much had been cut.

Rather than articulating the damage done by not getting the stable funding base, the Army leadership sent out a letter, signed by the Secretary and the CSA early in the year, telling senior Army officers that the Army had fought the good fight but must accept the lower Army budget and speak with one voice in support of this administration's budget request. Army supporters on the Hill were frustrated at seeing this type of letter only from the Army.[127]

The Endstrength and Force Structure Battles

Another contemporary example of the Army's unwillingness to challenge decisions made by its DOD superiors was the handling of the endstrength and force structure issues in FY94. On the issue of endstrength and force structure, many Army supporters on the Hill believed that the Army was being reduced too much and too fast to be able to carry out two nearly simultaneous MRCs. Representative Ike Skelton (D-MO) held a special hearing in October 1993 on the Bottom-Up Review (BUR) where he openly confronted OSD on its plans to reduce the active Army. Rep. Skelton's hearing put OSD on the defensive in having to explain how an Army at roughly 500,000 active-duty endstrength and 10 fully structured active divisions would be able to carry out its requirements to conduct two MRCs as called for in the National Military Strategy. He also convened a second panel that included four retired four-star Army general officers to get respected but politically unconstrained professional assessments on the size of the Army necessary to conduct two MRCs.[128]

Rep. Skelton's hearing was significant in focusing on aspects of maintaining a ready and capable Army that are often ignored or viewed as too complex by civilian audiences. The messages that the Army was both too small and under-

funded were clearly sent in that hearing. As a Democratic Chairman of the
House Military Personnel and Forces Subcommittee, his voice was one that
carried weight with the administration. In the five months between that hearing
and the FY95 Army Posture Hearing, many on the Hill believe opportunities
were lost for the Army to have OSD recognize increasing Army requirements
in carrying out the DOD National Military Strategy that would equate to increased resources for the Army in the outyears.

Congressional staff associated with the Chairman believed that the Member
did not receive the senior Army support necessary to pressure OSD to redirect
additional resources the Army claimed it required. Rep. Skelton had been press-
ing for 12 active divisions rather than the 10 called for in the OSD BUR. The
Army believed that the money to maintain 12 divisions would never be forthcoming from the Hill. Following the tense exchange between General Sullivan
and Rep. Skelton at the FY95 Army Posture and Budget hearing, a staffer told
me "Ike is no longer out there on that limb trying to 'save the Army' . . .
opportunity lost!"[129] Such opportunities are rarely lost with the other services
when they possess this degree of strong congressional support. As discussed in
Chapter 2, when either of the two Commandants of the Marine Corps spoke
about the V-22 issue, which was opposed by the Secretaries of the Navy and
Defense, their candid comments gave official support to the administration's
position but also provided richly detailed information on deficiencies that enabled Congress to make what they perceived to be a more informed decision
about the program. The Marine Corps did not leave its V-22 congressional
supporters out on a limb despite the pressure generated by the executive branch.
Many of the senior general officers interviewed commented on the Army's cultural proclivity to conform and abide with OSD preferences. They believe that
in years past there was enough leeway in the Army budget to support the senior
Army leadership's can-do conformity. The danger they uniformly highlight is
that while Army habits of conforming are still alive and well, the margin in the
Army budget to accommodate this can-do behavior has vanished. They believe
this can-do, "we can make it fit" mentality now poses irreparable harm to a
future Army's being both trained and ready and modernized for the twenty-first
century. General Carl Vuono made reference to this can-do attitude and the
danger it poses for the Army in the years ahead:

You don't hear the Army saying we can't do something. The Army salutes and goes
back to the drawing board to find a way to make it work. It's the culture of the "can
do" attitude. It's a hell of a way to describe it, but this culture says fight, fight, fight,
and when they [OSD] say we'll give you only this—you go and make do with that. The
problem is over the years you had a margin, a buffer of flexibility, that no longer exists
. . . *the (Army) top line is now so low that the opportunities to work the margins like we
had before aren't there.*[130]

General Robert Riscassi, former CINC, U.N. Command in Korea, made a similar
observation:

Back when the Army had 780K in endstrength [rather than 500K] and $78B budget [rather than $59B], there really was fungibility that supported the Army culture to salute and make it work with less than requested. An Army leader could look you in the eye and say we're okay without this and nothing will really fall through the crack. This state of affairs is no longer applicable.[131]

In an insightful comment that attempts to explain why the Army has difficulty in admitting what it cannot do, General Riscassi believes the Army's internal focus on how soldiers will react to its statements about increased risks constraints it from candidly elaborating its deficiencies: "I . . . think the Army is concerned about what the soldier in Baumholder, Germany, or in a foxhole in Korea will think. Army senior military leaders are possibly concerned that soldiers will begin to think they do not have the country's or the political leadership's support."[132] Ironically, such reticence actually increases the risks to the soldier. The Army's can-do attitude also reportedly constrains it from making elaborate shows of its deficiencies. Former CSA John Wickham put it this way: "If the Navy is short ammo they will cancel an exercise or keep a ship tied up at dock. If the Army is short ammo, we won't say we can't train. The exercise will go on and we will train the best we can. The Marine Corps is more like the Army in that can-do attitude than the Navy and Air Force. But it is clearly an Army trait."[133]

A candid conversation between an active-duty senior Army general officer and two top OSD officials highlights outcomes if the CSA decided to resist this cultural dimension:

I was on a trip with [these senior OSD officials]. I said "What the Chief needs to do to you guys, since you don't give us [Army] enough money, is to inactivate down to eight [Regular Army] divisions and say, I cannot do two MRCs [Major Regional Conflicts], I can only do one. I cannot replicate *Desert Storm*, but I have an Army today that I have to keep ready. I have got to have one in the future that must be ready, so I'm taking this Army down and there's only so many things that I can do for you. As far as the defense of the nation, the Army cannot do as much anymore. The Army is now less than the 1939 Army. That should put the heat on you guys!" They responded, "If he did that, if he tries to do that, he will have hell to pay." I said, "If he tried to do that he would be a hero. You guys couldn't take the heat number one. Number two, you could fire him, but he'd go out as a hero, then go public on you. There's nothing you could do; you would have no choice but to roll." Neither one of them would answer that. I think, however, they also believed there was little likelihood that this would ever happen.[134]

The Army wants to be the good, obedient, loyal servant to the nation and sees the executive branch as its primary master in serving that purpose. Builder notes a "split personality" in the Army's shared sense of identity between being the nation's historic handyman or the grander visions of winning the nation's wars as in the latter years of World War II and the Gulf War. Regardless of the purpose, most interviewees believe the Army is inclined culturally to take OSD directives more literally than the other services, and less likely to take "lost bureaucratic" battles with its master across the river to Congress. One senior Army officer gave the following tongue-in-cheek view of his trusting, obedient Army operating in peacetime with reduced resources, with its sense of loyalty to the Commander-in-Chief, its memories of winning the nation's wars in World War II and the Persian Gulf, and its ingrained belief that, when called, "We are capable of succeeding at whatever it is that you ask us to do."

> I see the Army as this aging Irish Setter that wants to be scratched behind the ears and will settle for any old bone that will be thrown its way by its master. This big friendly dog wants to be taken out hunting. You can see the Irish Setter dreaming of the hunt as it lays next to the fire, with its legs twitching as it dreams of glorious past hunts. He'll settle for a nice walk, but he dreams of the big hunt. The Irish setter is only waiting to be called. Yes, he does tend to slobber, but he is obedient to a fault.[135]

In sum, almost all the senior Army leadership interviewed acknowledged that the subservient, can-do attitude imbedded in Army culture was an impediment to the Army's success on the Hill. Many of these leaders were particularly frustrated with their obedient Army's lack of effectiveness in representing its interests in OSD and Congress as typified here: "The Army's preferred strategy for working its interests with OSD and Congress is preemptive capitulation."[136] Former Under Secretary of the Army Augustine shook his head and said, "Thank Goodness the Army was better on San Juan Hill than they are on Capitol Hill. You can't help but admire what the Army does out in the field, but that excellence is in no way reflective of their effectiveness in Washington."[137]

Army Officers: Risk Averse in Peacetime

This dimension assumes that Army senior field-grade and especially Army general officers are more risk averse than officers in the other services. While this was the most sensitive of the issues discussed, most general officers— including a few on active duty—agreed that the risk-averse mentality inhibited Army relations with Congress. The Army's risk aversion is indirectly rooted in the Army's unique role in leader development, which can become skewed in a peacetime environment where the evaluation of competency is more difficult. It is nurtured by a peacetime promotion system that is inflated and has little toleration for mavericks or officers who question the institutional status quo, OSD policy preferences, and otherwise rock the institutional boat with ideas synonymous with fundamental change. It is manifest in Army officers' concerns of not getting out in front of their superior officer, and recognition that they are held accountable for only what they do, not for what they do not do. In peacetime, the best commander is the one who makes the fewest mistakes. In wartime, the best commander makes the enemy make the most mistakes. The latter relies upon action and competence, and is proven with the outcome on the battlefield. Because the other services rely on and value technical competency in their officer corps, this focus weeds out their more incompetent officers, even in peacetime. On the other hand, Army officers have the most difficult time of all the services in demonstrating warfighting competencies in peacetime. It raises the concern that the officers advancing through the ranks in a peacetime Army might not do the best in extended combat. One senior Army general was blunt in making this point:

You look at the flag officers in the Army and you see many more incompetents. In the Army, most of the warfighting technical skills can be faked. The other services can't fake their technical skills. If a ship sails in peacetime, its leaders are doing the same thing, taking many of the same risks they will take in wartime other than firing. You can't fake flying a jet. Those pilots landing on aircraft carriers at night are taking those risks whether in peace or war. Army leaders can go out and fake many of their technical skills. The Army is slower at developing a high level of technical competence. However, NTC [National Training Center] and other training improvements have created more challenging opportunities for officers to develop technical skills in peacetime they will need to demonstrate in combat.[138]

An active-duty senior Army general officer believes the Army needs a few mavericks. He believes the narrow definition of what it takes to be a successful Army combat arms officer in a peacetime environment pertains not only to assignment tracks but leadership styles:

The Army is intolerant of deviant behavior from the established mean. There are no Grace Hoppers or Admiral Rickovers who are allowed to rise in the Army's hierarchy. The other services will allow a few of these really bright and talented maverick types to rise. The Army trains and develops leaders, but maybe in the development of our young officers, we might want to consider a need for greater sensitivity to different styles of leadership and behavior. This will prompt different career paths and provide the Army with a broader base of talent to meet our varied and challenging institutional needs in the future to include outreach to external audiences.[139]

A retired senior Army general officer stated that Army senior flag officer are generally far more risk averse in their activities in the Washington community today than their counterparts were in the early and mid-1980s. Senior flag officers now have less experience in Washington than the other services, and in lacking that experience, they are less likely to make decisions that place them out in front of their boss. Being a "doer" increases the likelihood of making mistakes at this high level. According to this general officer, the Army is less tolerant of these kinds of mistakes or the attention the mistakes might draw:

It is a matter of what is in or out at the time in the Army body politic. . . . Being able to deal in a sophisticated environment is out; being able to make deals out of the Building and have the savvy, know-how and relationships to make them stick in the Building too is out. *You never want to get out in front of the train.* The Navy and Air Force view that as behavior to be rewarded. . . . If you expect subordinate leaders to be out in front, smile when you see their attempts, protect them when they fail, you elicit that type of behavior. The Army has more of a zero-defects mentality now, especially for the ambitious at the higher ranks and especially when it comes to issues involving Army external relationships.[140]

Experience and the lessons you draw from that experience seem to determine the degree of risk a senior flag officer is willing to take. General Max Thurman stressed that "most people will behave based on what they have done, rather than on what they can do. It takes a visionary to do something new. It's not surprising. When an officer reaches flag officer rank or a key leadership position, do we expect that person to put those things away that got him to that point? About 95 percent of folks will do the same."[141] The very nature of civilian control over the military implies that engagement and possible missteps with powerful external audiences in the Washington community are risk laden for senior military flag officers and their upward mobility. The fear of failure and of the unknown combine to nurture this risk aversion that is so evident for the Army in the Washington arena. However, the real or perceived risk is reduced significantly by understanding the Washington environment and external audiences like Congress. Establishing respected and trusted relationships on the Hill actually reduces risk and provides an example (for ever-watchful junior officers) of effective representational activity at the highest levels that involves all general officers and is valued by them. The fear of failure is tied to reputational concerns at the flag officer level and this fear of the unknown is fueled by a more disengaged and less experienced understanding of the Hill. This fear of failure manifests itself in Army senior flag officers declining to engage or sending subordinates, mostly majors and lieutenant colonels, to engage Members and staff in their behest. A senior Army general officer acknowledged this tendency: "There is a tendency among senior Army General Officers to order others, generally subordinates to go over to address a particular issue. I call it the John Alden syndrome. 'Speak for yourself, John Alden.' It is the fear of the unknown and a fear of failure that results in the habit of sending an agent to carry the message you could and should more effectively deliver yourself. By sending a subordinate, it is not my failure."[142]

This risk aversion is also apparent in the senior Army leadership's conscious decision to limit and control Army senior flag officers who are assigned outside of Washington or general officers on the Army staff to engage with Members and staff on the Hill. Fearing that the Army will lose control of its message or get the wrong answer from a Member or staffer following a senior flag officer's visit, the Army leadership loses the benefit of a valuable agency resource: this wide array of respected active-duty Army general officers located in and out of Washington. Many of these officers already have established relationships with Members and staff.[143] General Max Thurman believed this is one of the Army's big problems on the Hill:

The hierarchical Army fear of getting an unsatisfactory answer if they allow other . . . general officers to go over to deal with Congress on issues is a big problem for the senior Army leadership. What you hear is "We'll take care of this at Department of Army level." We don't use field commanders from the state of Virginia, Georgia, the FORSCOM CDR, the TRADOC CDR, etc., to work issues on the Hill to the degree that would be effective. The Chief of Staff's fist around the Hill requires that he deal with the same Committee guys at this most senior level when lower level flag officers could handle the issue with more junior Members on the Committee. A lot of things necessary to get a campaign energized are too closely held by the Chief of Staff of the Army and OCLL [Office of the Chief of Legislative Liaison], as opposed to using all of the multiplicative capabilities [agency resources] one has in the size of the Army to get the job done. This problem was especially acute in the Vuono regime, he especially didn't like to have outside [the Department of Army Staff] guys going to the Hill.[144]

Another example of this form of risk aversion is the senior Army military leadership's uncomfortable relationship with industry and Army contractors. While General Sullivan gets widespread credit for making significant strides in improving this relationship, there still appears to be less cooperation and partnership between Army general officers and the contractors of needed Army weapon systems than is evident between the other services and their industrial contractors. General Max Thurman attributed this to an Army risk-aversion problem:

It's a rare Army general that will risk himself in a room with a contractor by himself. We stiff-arm contractors. Once a contractor has won a contract, we should be partners in getting the product into the hands of soldiers. Army general officers are told by government lawyers they have to adhere to certain ethical standards and abide by detailed provisions when dealing with contractors. This causes Army generals to frown. We don't bring up a lot of folks in mainline combat arms to be acquainted with contractors until they are very senior. When you don't work with contractors on a routine basis, it's hard to be synchronized with them when dealing with Congress on behalf of Army products. . . . This causes us to keep them at arm's length. However, it's important for soldiers out in the field whose lives will depend on these weapon systems for Army general officers to break down this cultural barrier. Contractors: you've got to get next to them.[145]

General Thurman believed the other services felt more liberated to work with contractors because of greater interaction throughout their careers:

You fear that which you don't understand. You fear the unknown. They [other service military leaders] are not lacking in experience with contractors. . . . Very few (Army) Battalion or Brigade Commanders have contractors that are organic to their units, except for certain Air Defense and Aviation Commands, but infantry never, or rarely, see contractors. With the Air Force and Navy, contractors are there, everywhere; modifying airplanes, doing depot level maintenance, and even when they go out to sea, they deploy with 40–50 tech representatives from the contractor. Army combat arms general officers don't feel comfortable because they don't work with them. It's not a matter of training, generals just need to go out and start dealing with them. The Chief of Staff and the Vice Chief of Staff should have contractors come by their offices. I bet it would blow [Vice Chief of Staff of the Army, General] Tilelli's mind to see a major contractor on a major program sitting in his office. I told the Chief that he needed to have frequent dinners at his house where he invites a big contractor to talk with other generals working in that field. Get all the Air defenders together for one group, etc. Find out what is cooking. You have to get next to them. It is a cultural problem.[146]

These sentiments were repeated by a retired senior Army general officer who now works for a defense contractor:

The Army doesn't appreciate to the degree the other services do of what it takes from the civilian industrial base to deliver a program. . . . The Army's uneasiness with that notion of partnership and industrial profit causes the Army not to team with industry the way the other services do. The Army's relationship has improved considerably under General Sullivan and is somewhat better from the days of Ill Wind.[147]

In the recent House National Security Committee mark, we at [a private defense contracting company] were surprised that certain plus-ups had not been agreed to by the Committee. One in particular was the upgrades for [Army weapon system]. The Army was suppose to make a call, but the call came too late and at too low a level. We hired [another Washington lobbying firm] to help us get Navy plus-ups turned around in the House by working with Navy LL. We at [the private defense contracting company] spent our time working with Army LL. The Army spent its time trying to decide what, when and how it was going to do. The Navy spent its time to get the Hill decision reversed, going so far as having the Chief of Naval Operations speak with the Speaker of the House. We [defense contracting company] spent a week working against the Army and trying to get their support. My colleagues spent a week working closely with the Navy. The Army finally decided to support the [Army weapon system] upgrade, but the call came too late and the call was made at too low a level. The whole Army action was handled too mechanically. The Navy knew what they wanted and worked with us.[148]

A final manifestation of risk aversion, that was addressed briefly in the teamwork and recognized dependency dimension, seems to be with the Army's larger fear of representing its interests to OSD and Congress with new ideas that would challenge status quo arrangements concerning resources, roles, and missions affecting the other services. According to interviews, the Army is more concerned than other services about not initiating interservice debate on key issues with external audiences: "No one in the senior Army leadership is calling the other services' cards they have and [that the other services] are still playing.

The Army leadership's refusal to take on the other services is a cover for their stupidity. . . . Taking these issues on is too risky for our Army leaders."[149]

Junior Army officers see an increasing tendency of the senior Army leadership to assume key positions on the Army staff with less Pentagon experience than previously was the Army norm, and certainly less than the norm in the other services. These general officers are less likely to take personal risks with Congress. They are still in the learning and cautionary mind-set rather than the engagement mode with the Hill. These general officers are more likely to fear rather than understand Congress. These Army generals are seen playing it safe, unlike their Naval and Marine Corps counterparts, who are not wary of engaging on issues that are sensitive and fast changing on the Hill. Army field-grade officers observe many colonels who are competitive for promotion to brigadier general following the lead of their superiors by "playing it safe." Many of these individuals are "hurricaned" into the Pentagon and placed into administrative positions in the front office of key senior flag officers on the Army staff for six to nine months, thereby giving them a superficial Washington and Pentagon experience. These officers tend not to take chances or have any desire to be associated with individuals who do. Field-grade officers on the Army staff realize their prospects to serve at higher levels within the Army are currently threatened rather than strengthened, as in the past, by service in Washington. Avoiding Washington and staying with troops is a safe, less risky, and more rewarding combat arms career path. This discussion of the risk-aversion cultural dimension will conclude with the following candid remarks by a highly respected senior active-duty Army general officer:

Now we are not talking about taking battlefield risk, I'm talking about taking political risks within an organization. The problem is we don't practice in our daily life taking risk in the Army. . . . The Army is much better at letting you fail and learn from that than it was in the past. But still while you may fail and not be charged for it, you have a reputational problem with failing something in a peacetime Army that you can't get away from. So we tend to do those things that will keep us from failing. You do that by not taking much risk. The price of taking risk and failing is great—especially on the battlefield. . . . Due to the nature of ground warfare where Army officers are more likely to confront and send their people into the brunt of death, Army combat arms officers tend to mitigate on the safe side. So with that in our professional upbringing, we rarely take risks.

Then when Army combat arms officers step for the first time later in their careers into the political realm that exists in Pentagon and Washington assignments, most Army officers lack the inclination to take risks here as well. I have noticed over the years that the only people that you find in the Army who are successful in working with either OSD or the Congress are those few officers that not only operate on the edge of the envelope, but like it that way. That's where they like to live. Those kind of individuals are hard to find in a peacetime Army.

Now, the problem for that kind of person is all or most of his contemporaries are uncomfortable with him, because they are not that way. So it's rare that a person like that gets very far in the Army. It's important to note, however, that this trait tends to operate well in the Washington environment. But with that effectiveness comes risks for Army officers from OSD and within the Army leadership structure itself.[150]

Asked whether this change could occur because the new general officers' environment and future were now more political in nature, the senior general responded:

These new brigadier generals believe they have become more politically aware and astute. But they're not. They are only more conscious of their political surroundings and as a result become unnerved about living in a glass house. This revelation and adjustment to this new world produces two types of Army general officers.[151]

When you are dealing with general officers you must determine if you are dealing with a general who is telling you the truth or if you are dealing with a general who is telling you the administration's line on an issue. The administration line can take the form of anything from your next higher boss's paranoia or risk aversion to the official executive branch chain of command position. So when you're dealing with a general officer in the Army, you got to figure out which side of ledger he's coming from and more times, 95 per cent of the times he's going to come down on the administration's side of the ledger. He doesn't know that, he just does, because it's safer over there.

You also see risk aversion take place at the lieutenant general and general officer ranks. I hate to say it but many three-star general officers who occupy key positions of power in the Army begin making a run for four star [rank]. Many of those who make it to general now are looking at becoming the Chief of Staff of the Army. These very able men begin to look a little more intensely towards their own careers than they do on what they should be doing for the Army.

Tolerance of risk-averse behavior could be set by whom is picked for the CSA position. According to this general officer, a clear pattern exists for not choosing the strongest and toughest CSA since General Abrams occupied that position in the early 1970s. And, this type of CSA tends to have even less tolerance for risk-takers in key advisory Army staff positions:

I truly believe there has been a move in JCS and OSD for a number of years now, to never make the best guy in the Army the Chief of Staff of the Army. Now that's my personal opinion of it. The Army used to take a different road by ensuring the power guy became the Chief of Staff. Look who they were: McArthur, Eisenhower, Bradley, Lightening Joe Collins, I mean, just look at the Hall of Heroes. The disconnect came as a reaction to the strong leadership of General Creighton Abrams. He comes in as the Chief of Staff of the Army at a time just like we're in right now where everybody is hacking away the Army. Abrams bypasses the JCS and everyone else and walks into [Secretary of Defense] Mel Laird's office. He sits down and they cut a deal on the size of the Army and the Secretary of the Defense says okay. He gets the Secretary of Defense to go public on this and nails the Army in concrete. General Abrams became absolutely the dominant player in the Pentagon—more than the Chairman, Joint Chiefs of Staff and more than the other Chiefs. Of the uniformed officers, he ran the Pentagon. The lesson learned, I believe, says don't ever place a dominant Army officer in there again. They will only rock the boat. If you go back and look at it, the pattern is quite clear if you look at the four-stars who did not get selected. The strong, dominant generals are never picked anymore and I think if you sat down with officials in OSD, the Secretary of Defense, and the Chairman, Joint Chiefs of Staff, they'd say offline "I don't need an Army Chief of Staff that strong. I need a Chief down there that's just going to go with the flow." (see note 151)

FINDINGS

Journeying back to the Army's origin and early professionalization to better understand the roots of today's Army culture, the earliest and most enduring tenet comprising Army culture today is the military subservience to civilian control first stressed by Army General George Washington. One hundred years later, the principle of civilian supremacy over the military was viewed by senior Army generals as a prerequisite to developing a more professional Army. However, key architects of this new professionalism, Generals Sherman and Upton, believed their efforts would be undermined by the politics prevalent in the post–Civil War era. The tenet that politics for officers is unprofessional and should be avoided was less a disdain of civilian leadership per se than a desire by senior Army leaders to insulate and protect Army officers from the political corruption of their day. The professional sanctity of civilian supremacy over the military and its corresponding tension between military professionalism and politics are evident in the Army today. This chapter prioritized five cultural dimensions that are relevant and partially explain the Army's patterned approach or style in representing its interests to Congress and other external audiences. These dimensions help explain why the Army chooses to direct its more valuable agency resources away from engaging external audiences like Congress in a more proactive and consistent manner. Being aware of and addressing these dimensions upfront is a prerequisite for any long-term effort to improve Army–Hill relations. In priority of their impact on Army–Hill patterns, the following cultural dimensions were discussed:

- The Army's internal fixation and preference for resolving problems by looking inward for the solutions.
- The Army's value of teamwork and its recognized dependency on others in meeting its unique national "leadership" responsibilities.
- The Army's narrow "tactical rather than strategic" path of professional development of its future leadership.
- The Army's reflexive can-do obedience grounded in its ideological devotion to subservience to civilian, largely executive branch, control.
- The Army's more risk-averse officer corps produced by hierarchical organizational dynamics and the peacetime difficulty of effectively gauging officer competency.

Collectively, they explain the Army's complex behavior, which oscillates between a naive or arrogant trust that Congress understands the merit of its message on what an Army can provide in national security and a suspicion of
congressional interference in operational matters. However, this suspicion again
turns to a more naive trust when the issues move from more operational matters
to resource-oriented issues concerning budget levels and weapon system acquisitions to a degree not apparent in the other services. This oscillation between
naive trust and suspicion is further colored by a devotion to integrity that pervades its communications even when it is antithetical to its institutional interests.

The Army's internal fixation at the expense of external focus that naively
views the merit of Army causes to be self-evident; its recognized dependency
and team player mentality that works against Army self-promotion to Congress;
its "muddy boots can do all" assumption that robs the most competitive Army
combat arms officers of invaluable Washington experience that other services
value in their future leaders; its can-do obedience to the executive branch that
is essential for an Army serving a democracy, but when unrecognized and combined with other dimensions, inhibits general officer candor to Congress about
vital Army requirements; and the peacetime risk-averse characteristic of senior
Army officers that deters mavericks, inhibits candor, and stifles creative thinking
collectively undermine Army effectiveness with Congress. Together these cultural dimensions now make it extremely unlikely that another General Meyer
or Thurman will rise to lead the current or next generation Army.

NOTES

1. Interview sample includes lengthy interviews with 24 Army general officers (13
four-star, 8 three-star, 2 two-star, and 1 one-star generals) that include 5 CSAs going
back to 1976, several regional Commander in Chiefs, former CLLs, and Corps Commanders. One Marine three-star general officer was also interviewed. Additionally, I
interviewed respected combat Army colonels on the Army and Joint Staffs who had
served closely with and observed senior flag officer behavior toward Members and congressional staff. These interviews were reinforced by a few key interviews with Army
senior civilian leadership: one Secretary of the Army, one Under Secretary of the Army,
and one Deputy Assistant Secretary of the Army.

2. See Jay M. Shafritz and J. Steven Ott, *Classics of Organizational Theory*, 3rd
ed. (Pacific Grove, CA: Brooks-Cole, 1991), 482.

3. For the most scholarly and yet practical examples of this research see Edgar H.
Schein, *Organizational Culture and Leadership*, 2nd ed. (San Francisco: Jossey-Bass,
1992); Don Hellriegel and John W. Slocum, Jr., *Organizational Behavior*, 6th ed. (New
York: West Publishing, 1992); Paul Harris and R.T. Morgan, *Managing Cultural Differences* (Houston: Gulf Publishing, 1987); Thomas Peters and R.H. Waterman, *In Search
of Excellence* (New York: Harper & Row, 1982); and Vijay Sathe, *Culture and Related
Corporate Realities* (Homewood, IL: Irwin, 1985).

4. Carl H. Builder, *The Masks of War, American Military Strategy and Analysis*
(Baltimore: The Johns Hopkins University Press, 1989), 7–10.

5. Schein, *Organizational Culture and Leadership*, 12.

6. See Allan Kornberg, *Politics and Culture in Canada* (Ann Arbor, MI: Center for Political Studies Institute for Social Research, 1988), 3. He comments on the unpublished work of Samuel Barnes, *Political Culture and Politics* (Ann Arbor: University of Michigan Press, 1986), preface.

7. James Q. Wilson, *Bureaucracy: What Government Agencies Do and Why They Do It* (New York: Basic Books, 1989), 90–110.

8. General Gordon Sullivan (Ret.), Chief of Staff of the Army (1991–95), interview by author, October 30, 1995, Washington, DC.

9. Samuel P. Huntington, *The Soldier and the State* (Cambridge, MA: Harvard University Press, 1957), 8–18. Military officership incorporates the distinguishing criteria of professionalism: expertise, responsibility, and corporateness. Expertise: ''Now, however, only the person who completely devotes his working hours to this task [skill of managing violence] can hope to develop a reasonable level of professional competence. . . . It is instead an extraordinarily complex intellectual skill requiring comprehensive study and training'' (13). Responsibility: ''His [the officer] responsibility is the military security of his client, society. The discharge of the responsibility requires mastery of the skill [the management of violence]; mastery of the skill entails acceptance of the responsibility. . . . The motivations of the officer are a technical love for his craft and the sense of social obligation to utilize this craft for the benefit of society'' (15). Corporateness: ''Officership is a public bureaucratized profession.'' Membership is limited and controlled; special complex vocational institutions ''mold the officer corps into an autonomous social unit''; ''levels of competency are reflected in a hierarchy of ranks as well as duties'' (16). Note his excellent discussion of military professionalism and the ideal professional type. He notes the undeniable character of officership as a profession and how ''In practice, officership is strongest and most effective when it closely approaches the professional ideal; it is weakest and most defective when it falls short of that ideal'' (11).

10. Schein, *Organizational Culture and Leadership*, 211–227, for a detailed discussion of how leaders create organizational cultures and how, if effective, their beliefs and values manifest themselves in the organization once it is mature.

11. During the Civil War, even the ''rebels'' replicated this sacrosanct civil-military relationship in the South.

12. For a more detailed discussion of General George Washington's role in establishing the doctrine of civilian supremacy, the different methods he employed in putting down Army rebellions in Pennsylvania and New Jersey, his speedy rebuke to Colonel Lewis Nicola in 1782 for Lewis's ''painful'' and abhorrent ideas, and his handling of the Newburgh conspiracy, see Glenn A. Phelps, *George Washington and American Constitutionalism* (Lawrence: University Press of Kansas, 1993), 40–47. The best account of the Newburgh conspiracy can be found in Richard H. Kohn, ''The Inside History of the Newburgh Conspiracy: America and the Coup d'État,'' *William and Mary Quarterly* 27, (1970), 187–220.

13. Huntington, *The Soldier and the State*, 193–221.

14. Ibid., 20. In Huntington's discussion of the rise of Army professionalism, he highlights significant changes following the Civil War in the development of a professional ethic for the new military man and ''the evolution [and strengthening] of five key institutions of the military vocation: (1) the requirements for entry into the officer corps; (2) the means of advancement within the officer corps; (3) the character of the military

education system; and (4) the general *esprit* and competence of the officer corps.'' In all these areas, control and decisionmaking were left in the hands of the senior military leadership.

15. Ibid., 231. Sherman believed the Army should be ''an animated machine, an instrument in the hands of the Executive for enforcing the law, and maintaining the honor and dignity of the nation.'' This laid the cultural foundation for the Army's obedient servant role to executive and congressional dictates discussed later in the chapter.

16. Ibid. Huntington notes that prior to this new Army professionalism, soldier-statesman was the norm. ''Three of the six Commanding Generals before him [Sherman] had become presidential candidates. With him begins the tradition of political neutrality which, with the exception of [General] Leonard Wood, was to be maintained by subsequent Commanding Generals and Chiefs of Staff until after World War II.''

17. Ibid., 233.

18. Ibid. Huntington contrasts this with European military professionalism which ''was normally an outcome of social-political currents at work in society at large.'' The current Army leadership whose early assignments were in Vietnam experienced this hostility of American society firsthand during and following the war. By turning inward and focusing on enhancing professionalism and warfighting competence they corrected the deplorable conditions they witnessed in their Army that fought in Vietnam. Rededication to and focus on professionalism was the proper reaction to Vietnam experience and responsible, in their mind, for producing the outstanding Army that earned the great victory, praise, and confidence of the American people in *Desert Storm*.

19. Eliot A. Cohen, *Making Do with Less, or Coping with Upton's Ghost*, Strategic Studies Institute Sixth Annual Strategy Conference (Carlisle Barracks, PA: U.S. Army War College, April 1995), 7.

20. Ibid., iii. Upton's negative views on democracies' unwillingness to adequately fund armed forces in peacetime and the disastrous consequences to soldiers were published after his death by the Secretary of War (Army) Elihu Root in 1904. See Emory Upton, *The Military Policy of the United States* (1904; reprint New York: Greenwood Press, 1968).

21. Ibid., 8.

22. Ibid., 7.

23. Ibid., 8.

24. Paul Andrew Hutton, *Phil Sheridan and His Army* (Lincoln: University of Nebraska Press, 1985), 278–279. This expression of devotion to civilian control, written December 11, 1876 (Box 39, Sheridan papers), is especially important when you consider that both men were staunch Republicans and viewed a Democrat (Tilden) in the White House as ''a four year struggle for existence'' of the Army, and would place officers they defeated in battle in power over them through politics.

25. Generals Sherman and Upton were anything but inward-looking. In fact, both were educated in civilian institutions and were innovators. Upton was sent to Europe to look for innovative ways to professionalize the Army. Sherman had a law degree. These were men who understood and were exposed to external audiences (e.g., keeping their distance from the political corruption of their day allowed them to stay true to the more basic principle of military subservience to civilians, etc.). They simply reacted to their political environment. Having witnessed the human cost of the Civil War, they were convinced that a more professional standing Army could have prevented its outbreak or ended it more quickly.

26. Huntington, *The Soldier and the State*, 234. In a footnote, same page, he points out that "five of the six other major advanced schools established by the Army between 1914 and 1965 were first set up by departmental order without prior congressional authorization."

27. Wilson, *Bureaucracy*, 91, 101.

28. Senior flag officer, #32, interviews by author, April 12 and October 4, 1995, Washington, DC.

29. Senior flag officer, #31, interview by author, July 17, 1995.

30. Senior military officer #54, interview by author, June 20, 1995, Washington, DC.

31. Senior military officer, #33, interview by author, May 15, 1995, Washington, DC.

32. Senior military officer, #51, interview by author, October 17, 1995, Washington, DC.

33. Upton, *The Military Policy of the United States*, 305. See Cohen, *Making Do with Less*, 18–19, on the same subject where he gives an example of senior military leaders shaping the options and answers "calculated to deter their civilian superiors from the employment of military force" [in Yugoslavia].

34. Senior flag officer, #43, interview by author, July 10, 1995, Washington, DC.

35. General H. Norman Schwarzkopf and Peter Petre, *It Doesn't Take A Hero* (New York: Bantam Books, 1992), x.

36. As an example see Robert H. Scales et al., *Certain Victory: The United States Army in the Gulf War* (Washington, DC: Office of the Chief of Staff, 1993), 12–13.

37. Cohen, *Making Do with Less*, 10.

38. The resentment to civilian intrusion in operational matters by naval officers will be more a function that the concept of independent command at sea is being infringed or rather than an increased risk of combat casualties.

39. This point rests on the logic that the Army is more likely to have troublesome and dangerous instances of civilian intrusion in operational matters when civilian external audiences are largely uninformed of its capabilities, requirements, and basic operations, and are not engaged with Army senior military leaders in close "island of competence" relationships conducive to candid information exchange.

40. See Isenberg, *Shield of the Republic*, 438–442. He gives an interesting account of the efforts Secretary of the Navy Forrestal took in making Navy admirals, flag plot, engage in selling Navy interests as national interests to Congress and the public. Secretary of the Navy Lehman also worked to turn the flag plot into more effective Navy message carriers. The closest Army generals have come to receiving this type of executive branch political pressure to engage externally was Secretary Jack Marsh, a former Member of Congress. But according to interviews, he worked more to promote and orchestrate Army–Hill engagements, which were certainly beneficial, but never really placed the burden to develop relationships and be the message carriers on the shoulders of Army general officers.

41. Norman Augustine, former Assistant and Under Secretary of the Army (1973–77) and current CEO of Lockheed-Martin, interview by author, July 5, 1995, Washington, DC. The "Big Five" he mentions includes: the M1 Abrams tank, the Bradley infantry fighting vehicle, the Apache helicopter, Blackhawk helicopter, and the Multiple Launch Rocket System (MLRS).

42. Senior flag officer, #31, interview.

43. The Army does not have fond memories of past interservice strife where its purpose was called into question. The Army senior military are concerned about initiating a flare-up of interservice rivalry with external audiences engaged because they believe sister services would fuel questions and concerns directed toward Army public vulnerabilities: the nation's isolationist tendencies; the historical roots of the nation's fear of a large standing Army that relied instead, because of the nature and location of its early threats, on [less expensive and politically more powerful] militias and a very small active duty force in being; on the nation's concern for getting entrapped through our Army ground forces into another nation's wars; and the greater association of using ground forces with American casualties.

44. Senior military officer, #33, interview.

45. Senior military officer, #51, interview.

46. Senior military officer, #54, interview by author, June 20, 1995, Washington, DC.

47. The importance of Washington experience and understanding Congress and their needs will be addressed below in the third cultural dimension that examines the Army's narrow definition of career success.

48. Senior military officer, #33, interview.

49. Army flag officer, #41, interview by author, June 30, 1995, Washington, DC.

50. Norman Augustine, interview.

51. Senior military officer, #52 and #53, interview by author, June 5, 1995, Washington, DC.

52. Senior flag officer, #27, interviews by author, May 22 and October 26, 1995, Washington, DC. He also noted the following: "Two things happened to the Army in the mid-1980s. First, our DUSA-OR (Deputy Under Secretary of the Army for Operational Research) was reoriented away from operational research and analysis to testing. Second, we did away with an Army general officer running our Concept Analysis Agency and turned it over to a civilian. Institutionally, that eliminated a requirement for a smart analytic general officer in the promotion system."

53. Builder, *The Masks of War*, 95–114.

54. Ibid., 106.

55. Ibid., footnote 2, 223.

56. Ibid., 110. According to Builder, the Army relies on large detailed simulations to produce and justify the specific requirements numbers needed in formal JCS and PPBS planning systems, rather than relying on more clear parametric models that illuminate particular problems and options for solving those problems characteristic of Air Force analysis.

57. Ibid., 154–167. In his chapter on implications for military planning, Builder makes these points in his discussion on why the Army refuses to price the national commitments to fight. While written prior to the Army's significant reduction in troop levels in Europe, and prior to it becoming a largely continental U.S.-based power projection force, it still reflects Army fears and passivity, according to most interviewed, in taking institutional risks in the cause of better military planning.

58. Ibid., 161.

59. General Thurman was largely responsible for winning support in the Pentagon and on the Hill for improvements in Army recruitment and retention policies and in getting the Army's "Big Five" weapon systems through OSD and Congress in the late 1970s and early 1980s. The "Big Five" includes the following weapon systems used by

Army soldiers in the Gulf War victory: the M1 Abrams tank, the Bradley infantry fighting vehicle, the Apache helicopter, Blackhawk helicopter, and the Multiple Launch Rocket System (MLRS).

60. General Maxwell (Max) Thurman (Ret.), interview by author, May 17, 1995, Washington, DC.

61. General Bernard Rogers, USA (Ret.), CSA (1976–79), interview by author, April 28, 1995, Washington, DC. General Rogers gave an example: "Take [Colonel] Scooter Burke, worked in HLD [Army House Liaison Division] and eventually headed that operation. He was a Congressional Medal of Honor winner who at the same time didn't take himself or that recognition too seriously. He didn't wear his feelings on his sleeve. He was good at explaining the Army to the Hill. He was a great friend of Congressman Eddie Hebert, the Chairman of the House Armed Services Committee."

62. General Carl Vuono, USA (Ret.), CSA, 1987–91, interviews by author, April 12 and October 4, 1995, Washington, DC.

63. General Edward C. Meyer, USA (Ret.), CSA, 1979–83, interviews by author, April 12, and October 4, 1995, Washington, DC. See the data and discussion in Chapter 4, on the decline of military experience in Congress and its implications for representational activity.

64. General Rogers, interview.

65. Senior military interviewee #54, interview by author, October 6, 1995, Washington, DC.

66. Jack Marsh, Secretary of the Army (1981–88), interview by author, August 17, 1995, Washington, DC.

67. I was unable to acquire data from Total Army Personnel Command that tracked Army LL officer activity from 1990 to 1995 that would support the interview data. It is data in which the Army leadership should be interested in for comparative purposes with LL counterparts of the other services. Even without the empirical data, greater upward mobility is clearly evident, even to the congressional audience, of other services' LL personnel. Recommendation: an additional skill identifier should, as a minimum, be assigned to LL officers to increase the Army's ability to track and professionally manage this undervalued agency resource.

68. Senior flag officer, #50, interview by author, September 21, 1995, Washington, DC.

69. John J. Fialka, *Hotel Warriors: Covering the Gulf War* (Washington, DC: The Woodrow Wilson Center Press, 1991). This book should be on all Army combat arms officers' mandatory professional reading list. By comparing Army and Marine ground commanders' different approaches and results in dealing with the press, the question of how to use the media as a combat multiplier can be considered. It shows the two services' distinctively different approaches to external audiences.

70. Ibid., 7, "There were 295,000 Army troops in that effort and only 80,000 Marines. . . . The Marines fought some interesting battles, but their part in this war was never meant to be more than a sideshow."

71. Ibid., 12. Fialka notes on page 7 that being assigned to an Army pool before the ground war began meant "(1) a substantial risk of getting lost, (2) becoming unable to communicate, or (3) being ejected or isolated by Vietnam-addled field commanders who worried that journalists might get too close to their troops. For those of us who covered Army combat units in this war, it was often a combination of all three." Despite carrying 32 reporters into battle when the ground war began, these pre-war problems were only

accentuated: ''But coverage problems had multiplied as the battle moved. There were no satellite phones out in the field for reporters to use. . . . The Army-designed pony express system of couriers and its teams of reporter escorts were hopelessly understaffed, underequipped, and poorly trained and motivated for the job. The upshot: As the battles raged, we (couriers, escorts, journalists) and news copy, film, and videotapes spent a lot of valuable time lost in the desert.''

72. Ibid., 26.

73. Ibid., 27.

74. Ibid., 7–8. ''To facilitate the bean counting here, an 'incident' is defined as the description of a specific event in the ground war, either reported or depicted. The evening news shows of ABC, NBC, and CBS were compared with a 10:00 P.M. EST recap of each day's events run during the war on CNN.''

75. Senior flag officer, #44, interview by author, August 31, 1995, Washington, DC.

76. Arthur T. Hadley, *The Straw Giant: Triumph and Failure: America's Armed Forces* (New York: Random House, 1986), 67–73.

77. Ibid., 67–68.

78. Ibid., 68–69.

79. Senior flag officer, #43, interview. This openly manifested concern for the interests of soldiers whom Army officers are exposing to combat naturally makes leaders want to minimize casualties and minimize their risk in accomplishing the mission. This aspect will be addressed in the final cultural dimension later in the chapter.

80. This general officer elaborated by saying:

The Army and the nation's interests are aligned. Think about the Army's role in establishing democracies around the world. First, the Army established democracy in our republic. Remember that the word democracy never appears once in our Constitution. From 1776 to 1783 the Continental Army fought with no executive branch. Only the Continental Congress existed and the Army refused to lock these folks up. The U.S. Army stayed on to establish democracy in the Philippines, in Germany and Japan, in Grenada and its attempting to do so in Panama and Haiti. It was the Army who overthrew the Vichy government in France.

The Army's tradition of establishing democracies is significant in understanding its nonaristocratic and populist ties. This tradition limits its psyche and capacity to be a self-promoter and advertise to Congress. It is not seen to be in good form. A Navy Captain or Air Force pilot will eat before their men eat. Self-promotion is expected. An Army officer in a leadership position eats last after all his men have eaten. Self-promotion is not expected or rewarded.

81. Senior flag officer, #43, interview.

82. General Meyer, interviews.

83. Senior flag officer, #27, interviews.

84. General Vuono, interviews.

85. Senior flag officer, #44, interview.

86. Senior flag officer, #43, interview.

87. General Meyer, interviews.

88. General Thurman, interview.

89. General Meyer, interviews.

90. General Rogers, interview.

91. Senior flag officer, #6. This study will demonstrate later in this chapter that the Army professional development system 15–20 years earlier appeared to require more Pentagon experience for those selected to its senior leadership positions on the Army staff.

92. General Vuono, interviews. Ironically, General Vuono was the first Chief to bring a three-star general into the critical DCSOPS position who had never served in the Pentagon.

93. General Thurman, interview.

94. General Rogers, interview.

95. Senior flag officer, #29, interview by author, April 4, 1995, Washington, DC.

96. This was a snapshot taken in April 1995. See Appendix C for the specific data. The information was extracted from official individual resumes obtained from the four services. The leadership samples include four key positions that are influential on fundamental service issues with the Congress: the Chief of Staff or equivalent of the service, the Vice Chief of the Service, the Deputy Chief of Staff for Operations or equivalent for a service, and the Chief or Director of LL for a service.

97. In other words, despite the fact the Marine Corps has far fewer issues and has the Navy leadership helping it on Marine Corps issues, its leadership sample still had a significant edge in Pentagon/Washington experience over the Army.

98. This was an April 1995 snapshot. See note 96.

99. This probably says more about the snapshot aspect of this particular leadership sample of the four services. General Gordon Sullivan's successor (June 1995) as CSA, General Dennis J. Reimer, had a similar profile of Washington experience (DCSOPS, Vice Chief of Staff) as his predecessor except for 26 months in Washington as a Major working as the assistant executive and aide to General Creighton Abrams, CSA (1972–74).

100. See Appendix C for supporting data on this leadership sample. General Meyer, CSA (1979–1983), makes up part of my leadership sample for this earlier era. In an interview, he discussed the extent of his field-grade Pentagon experience: ''I came to the Building as a major working for the Chief of Staff of the Army General H. K. Johnson and Vice Chief of Staff of the Army Creighton Abrams. I watched them work with Congress. I wrote a paper on the importance of the National Guard and Reserve getting called up for Vietnam in 1965. The failure to do so caused General Abrams when he was Chief of Staff to develop the Total Army solution. Then I worked as a lieutenant colonel and colonel on the Joint Staff. I had [the benefit of] that exposure and experience.''

101. Agency resources that send clear signals to organization insiders on what is valued and what is not are selections for command, resident military education, and most important, promotions to higher rank. Additionally, aspiring insiders pay close attention to the general officers selected for key positions within the Army and take note of the career paths taken to reach these coveted positions.

102. In regard to the previous comment, many agreed that General Sullivan was a fine Chief of Staff who was successful in maintaining internal stability for the Army during a downsizing and budgetary nightmare. However, they equally stressed that as good as he was, he would have been even more effective, more visionary, and more skilled in moving other external audiences to that vision had he been provided additional Washington time and experience earlier in his Army professional development.

103. Senior flag officer, #28, interview by author, June 1, 1995, Washington, DC.

104. See Builder, *The Masks of War*, 20 and 33–34. ''What is the Army? It is first and foremost, the nation's *obedient and loyal military servant* [italics added].'' See Huntington, *The Soldier and the State*, 261, where he states, ''The Army developed an image of itself as the government's *obedient handyman* [italics added] performing with-

out question or hesitation the jobs assigned to it: 'the country's general servant, well-disciplined, obedient, performing civil functions'.''

105. Former Chief of Staff General Ridgeway coined this phrase in referring to actions he as Chief of Staff took in downsizing the Army following the Korean War. While he believed these civilian-directed measures were a mistake, which he had acknowledged to his superiors in the executive and legislative branches, he believed it was his duty to obediently carry them out.

106. Honorable Jack Marsh, Secretary of the Army, 1980–88, interview by author, August 17, 1995, Washington, DC.

107. Huntington, *The Soldier and the State*, 259.

108. Ibid., 261.

109. Hadley, *The Straw Giant*, 67–68.

110. Huntington, *The Soldier and the State*, 262.

111. Michael T. Isenberg, *Shield of the Republic*, 436.

112. This willingness to oppose the initiatives of their civilian superiors when they perceive their traditional independence of command and control is being threatened is not limited to the executive branch. Although Army senior military leadership at the time had concerns with key aspects of the Goldwater-Nichols reforms of 1986, the most ardent and noticeable opposition came from Navy admirals.

113. David C. Jones, "What's Wrong with Our Defense Establishment," *New York Times Magazine*, 7 (November 1982), 73, quoted by James L. Lacy in *Within Bounds: The Navy in Postwar American Security Policy*, CNA 05 83 1178 (Washington, DC: Center for Naval Analyses, July 28, 1983), and Builder, *The Masks of War*, 32.

114. Sergeants at Ranger School make the point that leadership entails getting all your people behind one course of action and seeing it through to a successful conclusion. The instructor holds up his hand with five outstretched fingers that symbolize five different ways to get from point A to point B on a patrol. The teaching point is not selecting the optimum path but recognizing that any of the five ways will get you to your destination. It is more important for the leader, for those being led, and for successfully getting to point B, to have everyone obediently fall in line behind the course chosen by the leader and do their individual part for the good of the patrol (whole). Indecision and disunity over the various paths works against reaching point B. The Sergeant then asks all Ranger students to compare the weakness and vulnerability when five outstretched fingers strike a hard object compared to the power of a closed fist obediently joined in common purpose.

115. For example, see Harry G. Summers, Jr., *On Strategy: A Critical Analysis of the Vietnam War* (Novato, CA: Presidio Press, 1982), 42–44, 118–120. This retired Army infantry Colonel makes the point that by refusing to speak out against the academics and sterile system analysts dominating strategy in McNamara's Pentagon, the senior Army military leadership bear partial responsibility for the outcome. Summers makes the point that the senior military leadership favored and came up with plans centered on prudent strategic concepts such as calling up the reserves [to engage support from the American people] and having the Army seal off South Vietnam from the North [rather than reinstitute pacification programs more appropriate for the South Vietnamese forces], but that these officers were unwilling to ''fall on their sword'' if these plans and concepts were not adopted.

116. Ibid. See General Westmoreland's quote of Napolean in acknowledging this point, 120.

117. Ibid., 120–121. Summers makes the point that the senior military, especially Army, leadership share some blame for Vietnam with President Johnson.

118. Herbert Y. Schandler, *The Unmaking of a President: Lyndon Johnson and Vietnam* (Princeton, NJ: Princeton University Press, 1977), 59. From studies of that period, it does not appear that military resignations were threatened and only a few were known to be contemplated. Supposedly, General Harold K. Johnson, CSA, 1964–67, went to his grave a broken man for failing to speak out to the President on the way the war was being fought. He was in his sedan en route to the White House when he changed his mind and told his driver to head back to the Pentagon. See Hanson W. Baldwin, *Strategy for Tomorrow* (New York: Harper & Row, 1970), 13–15 on the fact that General Johnson met privately with the President only twice "in the crucial twelve months from June 1965 to June 1966, when large numbers of U.S. ground troops were committed to Vietnam. . . . The value to the nation in Senators and Congressmen having close and trusted personal relationships with uniformed military officers is highlighted by the fact that President Johnson lacked these as senator and Vice President and not surprisingly had a mistrust of the military at the time he needed their most candid assessments."

119. General Meyer, interviews.

120. The Marine Corps exhibits this can-do attitude as well, but the attitude is directed more broadly to the executive and legislative branches. By approaching Congress as a team player and understanding Congress's role in defense policymaking, the Marine Corps is less likely to have its concerns and preferences go unnoticed. The fact that Congress is more likely to have close relationships with Marine general officers and an understanding of Marine concerns makes the can-do attitude of the Marines appear in the more positive team player light and less in the obedient servant (to the executive branch) light.

The Air Force's confidence and experience in negotiating and winning battles in the executive branch reduces instances where the Air Force and OSD positions are out of synchrony. The Navy's cultural value of independence and activism are more likely to prompt its senior military officers to more effectively speak out and question executive branch preferences or decisions.

121. General Vuono, interview. When asked whether the oath to the Constitution, not OSD, should affect this "can-do" attitude, General Vuono responded: "Yes, your oath is to the Constitution—but some would claim you're waffling and trying to have it both ways. That's why Army officers have taken great exception to officers from other Services who have cut corners—like some colleagues [LTC Oliver North and Admiral Poindexter] in the National Security Council in previous years. That's because their values are different than ours."

122. Norman Augustine, interview.

123. Senior flag officer, #14, interview by author, April 25, 1995, Washington, DC.

124. Congress, SCAS, *Hearings on Department of Defense Authorization for Appropriations for Fiscal Year 1994 and the Future Years Defense Plan*, 103d Cong., 1st sess. (Washington, DC: Government Printing Office, 1994), 630–631 and 637.

125. Congress, HCAS, *Hearings on Army Budget Request for FY 1995*, 103d Cong., 2d sess. (Washington, DC: Government Printing Office, 1994), 521.

126. The Republicans had long been sounding the alarm that the administration's defense budget and Armed Forces were coming down too far and fast, detrimentally affecting readiness and modernization. Shortly after the Congress went Republican in

November 1994, President Clinton announced an additional $25B over five years for DOD, with the Army getting an additional $2.5B of it in its FY96 budget request.

127. See Togo D. West, Secretary of the Army, and General Gordon R. Sullivan, CSA, *Speaking with One Voice—Defense of the President's Budget*, memorandum to Principal Officials of Headquarters, Department of the Army, February 7, 1995. This letter was obtained from an HNSC PSM who had received it from a senior Army installation commander outside of Washington.

128. This second panel consisted of General Carl Vuono, former CSA (1987–91), General Vessey, former CJCS, General Max Thurman, former CINC Southern Command and VCSA, and General Merritt, President, Association of the U.S. Army.

129. Congress, HCAS, *Hearings on Army Budget Request for FY 1995*, 103d Cong., 2d sess. (Washington, DC: Government Printing Office, 1994), 497–498. The point of this endstrength and force structure example should not be interpreted as a call for more Army (active and National Guard) divisions as currently structured, but the lost opportunity of using an influential Member to address endstrength and force structure remedies that would strengthen Army ground forces' abilities to win the nation's wars in the next century. I recommend that the reader become familiar with the debate over restructuring Army ground forces into smaller but more numerous mobile and adaptable fighting units that many Army strategists believe would better address future national security needs. I have often heard that one fear regarding abandoning the twentieth-century division structure is Army leadership concerns that an increased number of smaller, alternative fighting units would be more vulnerable to congressional cuts. The argument goes that they, the Hill, understand what a division is; and there is a fear that the Army would be less successful protecting against pressures to reduce the budget for smaller restructured Army fighting/sustaining units than the more familiar division organization. The point of this book is that enhanced understanding of Congress and respected and trusted long-term relationships on the Hill by senior military liaisers would be the preferable solution in addressing these fears. The insecurity of Army senior flag officers' abilities to work with Congress should not undergird or influence the important debates in answering "What kind of Army and what size?" For just one alternative solution to the current status quo, see Colonel Douglas MacGregor, *Breaking the Phalanx: A New Design for Landpower in the 21st Century* (Westport, CT: Praeger, 1997).

130. General Vuono, interviews.

131. General Robert RisCassi, USA (Ret.), former CINC, U.N. Command Military Armistice Commission, interview by author, April 4, 1995, Washington, DC.

132. Ibid.

133. General John A. Wickham, Jr., USA (Ret.), CSA (1983–87), interview by author, July 17, 1995.

134. Senior flag officer, #27, interviews.

135. Senior military officer, #22, interview by author, June 20, 1995, Washington, DC.

136. Ibid.

137. Senior military officer, #21, interview by author, July 5, 1995, Washington, DC.

138. Senior flag officer, #43, interview.

139. Senior flag officer, #44, interview.

140. Senior flag officer, #38, interviews by author, March 14 and June 7, 1995, Washington, DC.

141. General Thurman, interviews.

142. Senior flag officer, #38, interviews.

143. A senior Army general officer working on the Army staff told me that he had several really good relationships with key Members of Congress that had been developed over the years. However, it is his opinion that the senior Army military leadership is not concerned with making use of these associations and would view it as inappropriate or unprofessional for him to be the message carrier to these Members, since they are issues out of his specific duty area responsibilities.

144. General Thurman, interview.

145. General Thurman told me that his first exposure to contractors was as a major general. I asked General Thurman to explain why his late exposure to contractors didn't similarly inhibit him? He gave me this broad and immodest smile and responded ''I had no problem dealing with them because I have a lot of confidence.''

146. General Thurman, interview.

147. Ibid. He went on to explain ''Ill Wind was a 1987 court case involving an industrial consultant and an Assistant Secretary of the Army who were doing some shady deals in the Pentagon parking lot. This court case within the Army became code word for the campaign to fight waste, fraud, and abuse. There was a knee-jerk reaction in the Army to Ill Wind. Jay Scully, Assistant Secretary of the Army for Research, Development and Aquisition, set out to slam-dunk contractors. The results were that no senior people would meet with industry without a lawyer. Buying from open purchase order contracts stopped. This had immediate impact on operations. For a period of time, we stopped burying folks at Arlington, having folks seen at Walter Reed [hospital] and equipping the Old Guard with contact lenses to name just a few examples of the reaction.''

148. Senior flag officer, #38, interviews.

149. Senior flag officer, #43, interview.

150. Senior flag officer, #27, interview with author, May 22, 1995, Washington, DC.

151. Ibid.

Chapter 5

M1A1 Tank Transfer:
Culture Impedes Army
Effectiveness on the Hill

The Army doesn't understand or appreciate the role Congress plays. The Army thinks it can sit back and that the wisdom of Army choices will sell itself. . . . If the other services have something important, they are over here fighting for it. When you are going into a markup, Members tend to listen to military guys. Very few times does the SASC go against the senior flag officers who engage them prior to the markup.

—PSM, SASC

This case study illustrates Army–Hill patterns in which Army culture either directly impeded prudent courses of action that could have resulted in a more favorable outcome on the Hill, or indirectly impeded Army effectiveness because of the patterned and limited allocation of agency resources directed toward Army–Hill relations in general.

For the second straight year, the Army was reacting to legislative initiatives that openly pitted its institutional interests against those of the Marine Corps.[1] During spring and summer 1994, the Army and Marine Corps engaged in a series of battles on Capitol Hill centered around legislation that would congressionally mandate a redistribution of Army M1A1 Main Battle Tanks. The Marine Corps, having canceled its M1A1 acquisition program prior to the Gulf War, began to reassess that decision in light of the heavy operations in the Gulf War and the DOD's decision to preposition Army heavy forces afloat. As the Army downsized in Europe, the Marines saw Army M1A1 tanks returning to the United States as an opportunity to reverse that earlier Marine Corps decision.

The requirement for these tanks had not been budgeted nor officially requested by the Commandant of the Marine Corps or the Secretary of the Navy, nor deemed necessary by the JCS, the Secretary of Defense, or any serving regional CINC. The Marine Corps never submitted this Marine Corps requirement for additional tanks before established Pentagon processes forged out of the 1986 Goldwater-Nichols reforms that evaluate service acquisition requirements for their legitimacy in supporting larger defense strategy and plans.[2] Instead, the Marine Corps was able to use its extensive ties and understanding of Congress to achieve its goal through a legislated transfer of M1A1 tanks.

Although opposed by the administration, the Secretary of Defense, the CJCS and, until the end of conference, the HASC, Congress, in its FY 1995 National Defense Authorization Act, directed the Army to transfer without reimbursement 84 M1A1 tanks to the active Marine Corps.[3] The legislated transfer of tanks was the result of a conference decision that followed Army success in eliminating this transfer from the House bill, but not the Senate bill.[4] The Army lost more than just 84 tanks. When the smoke cleared from the legislative battlefield, Army leaders realized that bridges had been burned, that political chits had been used for this apparent Army priority with nothing to show for them, and that opportunities had been lost to use these chits for more important Army priorities.

Was preventing the Army tank transfer to the Marines tied to achieving a prescribed long-term vision or strategy? If this was a true Army top priority, why did the Army senior leadership not proactively treat it as one and direct its top agency resources toward a successful outcome? Why was the Army in a reactionary mode? Why did it receive no heads-up about the Senate activity? After the battle waged prior to the HASC mark, was a heads-up essential or should the Army leadership have proactively approached SASC Members, since the issue was so important to the Army? The decision to ''circle the wagons'' on this issue and the Army approach used to oppose the Marine Corps initiative on Capitol Hill are examined in light of the Army–Hill patterns and underlying Army culture.

BACKGROUND TO THE TANK BATTLE

The Marine Corps' Decision to Cancel Its Contract for Additional Tanks

The Marine Corps' acquisition objective for M1A1s was set at 560 tanks in 1985, of which they began outyear funding for 475 tanks.[5] The Corps purchased 66 in 1989 and 155 in 1990.[6] After debating funding priorities with an eye toward greater strategic mobility, Commandant of the Marine Corps General Al Gray decided to cancel any further acquisition of the Abrams tanks and to hold the inventory at 221, diverting the remaining dollars tied to outyear funding of 475 tanks to higher Marine Corps priorities.[7] The difference between the original 560 and the 221 tanks in the Marine Corps inventory was addressed by Marines as an unresourced requirement, which meant they were desirable but not a funding priority in their Program Objective Memorandum (POM).[8]

By the start of Operation *Desert Shield*, the Marines had received only 16 of the 221 tanks.[9] The Army responded immediately to General Gray's request for the loan of 36 M1A1 tanks for its training base at 29 Palms, California, and shipped another 60 M1A1s for front-line Marines to use in Saudi Arabia. General Schwartzkopf also assigned the "Tiger Brigade" from the 2nd Armored Division, equipped with 116 M1A1s, to support the Second Marine Division in the Gulf.[10] With these timely support enhancements, the Marines employed 3 battalions of older M60A1 tanks.

Following the Gulf War, there was no sign that the Marine Corps was concerned about a tank shortage. During hearings that year, Major General Robert A. Tiebout, Commander of the USMC Systems Command, praised the M1A1 tank in his prepared remarks, but did not include it in his listing of significant combat vehicle deficiencies to the Committee.[11] More telling, M1A1s were once again absent from the Marine Corps' FY 1993 budget submission. That same year the Marine Corps began to execute its base force drawdown plan. In each of its Maritime Pre-positioning Squadrons, the Corps replaced its complement of 53 older M60A1 tanks with 30 M1A1 tanks. More important, at the same time that the Marines were limiting their acquisition inventory of M1A1 tanks to 221, they implemented a phase-out of more than 700 M60A1 tanks from their inventory, to be completed by 1994.[12]

One can only speculate on the Commandant's view of Marine Corps armor capability in 1992; without a budget for replacement tanks, he believed either that he was taking the Marine Corps to a lighter, more mobile force where fewer tanks would be needed, or that he could get "free" tanks from the Army. While some argue that these decisions were a calculated bureaucratic ploy to reverse the earlier M1A1 cancellation decision, it also can be argued that in the spring of 1992, the Marine Corps leadership still believed that a lighter, more mobile force was needed for strategic mobility reasons.[13] This latter and less cunning rationale for the 1992 decision to phase out their older but still capable tanks in two years was consistent with the National Military Strategy and vision of the JCS that the Marine Corps would fight jointly with heavy tank force augmentation provided by the Army when necessary. The importance of heavy armor and Marine reliance on Army tank support in the Gulf War appeared, at a minimum, to be new variables in the Corps' thinking on its armor requirements.

In anticipation of downsizing, the Army developed a modernization strategy for a smaller but more lethal power projection force. The Army planned to distribute its superior M1A1 "commons" and the new, improved M1A2 Abrams tanks to its "first-to-fight" contingency forces; provide regular M1A1s to pre-positioned sets and forward-deployed forces; modernize the National Guard separate battalions and fifteen Enhanced Readiness Brigades with M1A1s; and field a mix of M1A1s and "plain jane" M1s (with smaller gun) to the remainder of the Reserve components.[14] In 1994, the Army was short 641 M1A1s for its active force and another 492 for the high-priority National Guard Enhanced

Readiness Brigades. The drawdown of the active Army would free up 816 M1A1s that would support the modernization strategy. The Congress, upset with readiness problems in the National Guard combat brigades, directed the Army in 1992 to modernize the Reserve components at the active force rate.[15] The bottom line was that the Army viewed its number of M1A1/A2 tanks, even after the drawdown in Europe, as insufficient to meet its own needs in modernizing its force.

The Challenge to the Army Pre-position Afloat (APA) Program

The seeds of the conflict over transferring tanks to the Marines were sown in a review and report on roles and mission, and with the DOD's (1992) and congressional (1993) decisions to fund additional sealift and pre-position heavy equipment of an Army brigade afloat. These decisions were prompted by congressionally directed strategic mobility studies and the Gulf War experience that showed a U.S. requirement to project heavy armed forces into a crisis quickly.

Congress had directed the DOD in 1990 to conduct a study to ascertain strategic mobility requirements and identify the type of forces that could best use existing and projected mobility assets in the early stages of a regional conflict.[16] In January 1992, the DOD published its first volume of the MRS recommendations that identified the "need to deploy Marine Corps expeditionary brigades and an Army heavy brigade within 2 weeks of the onset of a crisis."[17] The MRS recommendations established both a Pentagon requirement to fund additional strategic sealift and a requirement for pre-positioning an Army heavy combat brigade and the necessary combat support equipment afloat, to open up a new theater of operations to both engage the enemy inland and enhance the flow of follow-on forces.

Concerned about the roles and missions implications of the issue, the Marine Corps feared that putting an Army heavy brigade afloat would intrude on the Marines' self-promoted role as the nation's "911 force." As the Pentagon conducted its MRS study for Congress throughout 1991, the Marine Corps challenged the need for pre-positioning an Army heavy brigade afloat, claiming that it could perform the same mission with just one additional ship and 30 M1A1 tanks for each of its three MPS squadrons (3 ships, 90 tanks).[18] The Joint Staff and the OSD did not agree with the Marine position in 1992 (or 1993), claiming that enhancing the maritime pre-positioning force in lieu of fielding the Army heavy brigade afloat would move the nation's strategic mobility plan from medium to high risk.

According to many interviewed, as a result of the Gulf War and the Pentagon's MRS decision in 1992, the Marines began to reassess their earlier decision to cancel their M1A1 contract and decided that acquiring more M1A1 tanks was essential to maintaining their relevancy in early entry–type missions and not ceding this capability to the Army. The Marines realized that additional

M1A1 tanks would help boost their case for additional ships and thereby eliminate the need for the Army heavy brigade afloat. Unsuccessful in convincing the Pentagon that Marine pre-positioned squadrons could bring as much firepower and sustain themselves inland as well as an Army brigade, the Marine Corps took its battle across the Potomac.

The Marine Corps found a staunch and able ally for its cause of halting the APA Program in Rep. Paul McHale (D-PA), a Marine reservist who had served in the Gulf War. Although just a freshman on the HASC, he was a dynamic and articulate advocate. Marine Corps staff below the Commandant level were active on the Hill, feeding Rep. McHale and other potential supporters information until General Colin Powell, Chairman of the Joint Chiefs of Staff, "gave them a cease-and-desist order."[19] While this limited the Marines' liaising activities considerably, Rep. McHale led the Marine Corps cause and galvanized 19 votes on the HASC in a failed attempt to halt the program in 1993.[20]

Efforts to Redistribute Tanks in 1993

Many on both sides of the tank issue hoped that General Powell's required Roles and Missions Report, approved by the Secretary of Defense in March 1993, would specify the actual number of tanks required for the Marines. Instead, the wording was ambiguous, allowing both sides to read into it what they wanted. At the time the report was published, each Marine Corps pre-positioned squadron had 30 M1A1 tanks. The Chairman called for the Marines to "retain enough tank battalions to support amphibious operations and fill three maritime prepositioning squadrons—and the Army provide any additional armor units as required."[21] The Secretary of Defense directed the Marines to "meet the recommended requirement" and the Army and Navy Secretaries to "establish joint procedures for the use of Army armor units in wartime when required by the Marine Corps."[22] Realizing that its prospects for stopping the APA Program were not good in the Pentagon or on Capitol Hill, the Marine Corps took a different and less confrontational tack with the Army. Having reduced its M1A1 acquisition objective from 560 to 490 in December 1992,[23] the Marine Corps approached the Army in early 1993 with an informal request for 269 M1A1 tanks, 50 of which were urgently needed to round out 2 active-duty tank battalions and to meet combined arms training requirements at the 29 Palms training base.[24] Despite the large quantity of tanks in the request, Army senior generals agreed to work with the Marine Corps.

General J.H. Binford Peay, Vice Chief of Staff of the Army, and General Walter Boomer, Assistant Commandant of the Marine Corps, came to an agreement in June 1993. The Army would, without reimbursement, transfer 50 of its top M1A1 tanks to the Marine Corps, and additional Marine Corps armor support requirements would be filled, consistent with General Powell's Roles and Missions Report, through attachment of Army armor units as needed.[25] General Peay did not require the stipulations of the deal to be in writing since it was between two four-star generals, but he made that deal with an understanding that if the Army expedited the transfer of these 50 urgently needed M1A1 tanks, the Marine Corps would not attempt to acquire more transfers in the future.[26] The 50 tanks were inspected and signed for by the Corps in the November–December 1993 time frame.[27]

The Joint Army-Marine Complementary Operation Brief and the General Accounting Office Report

This agreement and transfer of the 50 tanks by the end of 1993 seemed to move the Army and Marine Corps back into more traditional methods of resolving differences and prompt more serious cooperation between the two within the Pentagon. This included a joint effort to develop a briefing that would educate congressional audiences on Army-Marine complementary capabilities and operations. In late January 1994, General Boomer and General Peay, with Lieutenant General Tilelli (Army Operations and Plans) and Lieutenant General Ehlert (Marine Plans and Operations) present, approved the idea of a joint Army-Marine briefing to be presented to the HASC and the SASC staff that would highlight the complementary aspects of joint Army-Marine operations in early entry crisis scenarios.[28] Army Major General Garner and Marine Major General Zinni would be a two-man briefing team for the Hill presentation. In early March, Major General Zinni told Major General Garner that he was ready and to schedule a date for the Army-Marine brief with both the HASC and SASC staffers.

Army LL, after coordinating with Marine LL, contacted Tommy Glakas, HASC PSM and former Marine, who worked for the Chairman of the Military Forces and Personnel Subcommittee, and Creighton Greene, SASC PSM, who worked on strategic mobility issues for the Committee, to ask for a recommended time for maximum staff participation.[29] Both seemed pleased at the Army and Marine Corps cooperation. By March 21, Tommy Glakas provided a recommended date of March 29, 1994, for the HASC brief. This date was immediately passed to the Marine LL officer who was in close contact with MG Zinni and everything seemed to be on track. The December 1993 Marine Corps decision to reduce its requirements for tanks from 490 to 443 was seen by many as just another positive sign of Army-Marine cooperation. This was soon to change.

While this joint Army-Marine brief was being developed and refined, the GAO came out with a timely report that stated the DOD study should have made greater use of the Marine Corps Maritime Pre-positioning Squadrons (MPS). This March 1994 report recommended that the Army be directed by the Secretary of Defense to transfer at least 84 M1A1 tanks to the Marines Maritime Pre-positioning Squadrons and possibly 80 additional Army tanks to address combat sustainment and Marine reserve requirements.[30] It also supported the requirement for Marine tanks at the same newly adjusted 443 acquisition objective number. In an effort to solicit DOD support for the GAO recommendations, General Boomer wrote a note to the OSD on March 2, 1994, claiming, "It's absolutely untrue that we do not want additional Army tanks. We have a valid requirement that urgently needs to be filled. Your help will be greatly appreciated in this matter."[31]

If the OSD had agreed with most of the GAO recommendations, the legislative battle over Army tanks would never have occurred. However, OSD challenged many of the report's recommendations and assumptions on substantive grounds. OSD noted the 50 M1A1s the Army transferred without reimbursement in 1993 and stated that further transfers would only delay the retirement of the aging M60 tanks from the National Guard beyond the year 2000. It also emphasized that the intention of the 1993 Roles and Mission Report was that Army units augment additional armor requirements the Marines might have in wartime. The Joint Staff and OSD found many of the GAO findings flawed because they were inconsistent with previous directions and assumptions in the MRS and the National Military Strategy.[32]

In mid-March, an HASC PSM phoned Army LL following a meeting with the GAO report's author, Richard Davis, and offered a cautionary assessment:

It seems to me the Marine Corps will take a different approach than last year. Instead of going directly against the Army Pre-positioned Afloat [APA] and offering the EMPF [Enhanced Maritime Prepositioning Force] as an alternative, they will use reports like the GAO's to say yes, we can use these tanks. If they get the tanks, they will need additional ships. Once you give them the additional tanks and show their increased need for ships, they will strike once again at the [APA] mission.[33]

However, the Army had faith that the Marines would join it to brief that same congressional external audience on their joint complementary and unique capabilities in less than two weeks. This brief would symbolically and substantively present a cooperative message on joint warfighting that was the basis of defense policy in the Pentagon. It would emphasize Army-Marine agreement that the Army would provide additional armor support to the Marines whenever needed. Likewise, this message would counter the argument that Marines required more Army tanks so they could operate independently within their single service operational concept.

On March 25, 1994, the short Army-Marine cooperation officially began to dissolve when the Marine Corps asked for a delay to "review the brief," claiming that "the timing was wrong."[34] To obtain cover from any congressional committee criticism that they were being uncooperative, Marine Lieutenant General Ehlert, Marine Corps Plans and Operations, called his Army counterpart LTG Tilelli, Deputy Chief of Staff for Operations and Plans, and asked for Army support in the delay. The Army senior general agreed without conferring with Army LL or his two-star principal Army staff officer scheduled to give the brief. The official Army position that Marine Corps LL communicated legitimately to the Hill was "The Marine Corps *and Army* [emphasis added] are still working the brief." That evening, Army LL called both Glakas and Greene to communicate this embarrassing position.

Within a few days, the Army general realized his mistake, but high-level Army efforts, along with complementary ones by Glakas, were not enough to put the briefing back on track. Ultimately, the Marine Corps' delay, and the increasing saliency of other issues, including the tank transfer, ensured that no such complementary operation briefing was ever given.

THE BATTLE FOR TANKS MOVES ACROSS THE POTOMAC

Many believe the Marine Corps attempted to reverse the impact of its 1989 tank cancellation decision because of its post–Gulf War/Cold War roles and missions concerns and unsuccessful bid to halt the APA Program in the Pentagon in early 1993. The Marines changed tactics to work cooperatively with Army leaders, which resulted in 50 (rather than 269 they requested) top-of-the-line M1A1s that spring and simultaneously engaged with GAO, which validated their service requirement for 443 M1A1 tanks and recommended getting additional tanks from the Army. However, since most of the GAO key findings were later opposed by the civilian and uniformed leadership in the Pentagon, the Marine Corps decided to take its case across the Potomac to Congress where it believed the report would find a more favorable response.

One can conclude that the Marines realized that the legislative avenue for the redress of their grievances and the potential weight of the GAO recommendations would both be undermined if they allowed Armed Services Committee staffers to witness one of their rising two-star generals giving a brief on Army-Marine complementary operations. Lieutenant General Ehlert's comment to the junior Marine Corps LL officer that "the timing of this [brief] was wrong" makes sense when viewing Marine Corps opportunities on the Hill that would be blocked or complicated by the brief. Once the Marines slipped the March 29, 1994 commitment, they were free to educate members and staff on their GAO-validated requirement for additional M1A1 tanks.

Marine Corps Out-Maneuvered in the Initial House Battle

As early as April 19, 1994, the Army was informed by a Hill source that Rep. McHale was going to offer legislation directing the Army to give M1 tanks to the Marine Corps. Two days later, the HASC Readiness Subcommittee, chaired by Rep. Hutto (D-FL), provided the first official public volley fired on the tank issue when Rep. McHale, a subcommittee member, questioned OSD priorities and prudence in providing M1A1s to the Army National Guard ahead of the Marine Corps, considering the Marines' "shortfall of 172 tanks" and "in light of the failure to use the National Guard during Operation *Desert Storm*," and "the clear likelihood of the Marine Corps being used in combat." While the OSD witness, Louis Finch, Deputy Under Secretary of Defense (Readiness), emphasized the definite combat role the Army National Guard plays in the administration's BUR requirement to execute two MRCs, the Army witness was less prepared to challenge Rep. McHale's point on priorities and his contention that the Army had 1,500 "excess" M1A1 tanks. "I was only recently made aware of this issue; I simply don't know enough to answer," was the reply by Bill Clark, the (acting) Assistant Secretary of the Army for Manpower and Reserve Affairs. Testimony also contributed to casting the debate initially as an Army-Marine rather than an Administration/Pentagon-Marine issue. The Joint Staff witness at the hearing, Marine Corps LTG Sheehan, said "the JCS is not involved in this issue; it's between the Army and the Marine Corps."[35]

Rep. McHale's comments in the hearing and rumors of his intent to offer tank transfer legislation prompted Hill supporters on both sides of the issue to ask the Army and Marine Corps for supporting information. Both LLs served as conduits for tailoring and expediting the information campaign between their leadership and the Hill. Additionally, both services sought a champion to lead their cause in the upcoming Committee marks of the FY 1995 Defense Authorization bill.

As he had done the year before, Rep. McHale led the Marines' fight on the HASC. The Marine Corps' message was effectively attuned to the congressional target audience in a rational and persuasive manner. This year it avoided all mention of "enhanced" maritime pre-positioning forces (EMPF) and criticisms of the APA Program, and insisted that its desire for Army tanks was not a roles and mission issue. Instead it delivered a clear and simple message: the Marine Corps is short tanks and the Army has excess tanks from its downsizing in Europe.

Specifically, Marine proponents stressed that: (1) their Maritime Pre-positioning Forces were operating with only 52 percent of their required M1A1s, (2) their acquisition objective of 443 M1A1 tanks had been validated by the GAO (respected by Congress), (3) the transfer would not severely set back Army National Guard fielding of tanks, (4) they are the taxpayers' not the Army's tanks, and (5) the Pentagon and Congress should equip the "first-to-fight" with the best equipment.[36]

The last point was the most effective one because it incorporated a principle the Army has long used for resourcing and equipping its own forces. The Marines highlighted the fact that the first American tanks to arrive in Operation *Desert Shield* were their aging M60A3 tanks. As noted earlier in Rep. McHale's readiness hearing comments, Marine Corps combat reserves served along side their active duty counterparts in the liberation of Kuwait, while Army National Guard units saw duty only at the NTC at Fort Irwin, California.

Rep. Sonny Montgomery (D-MS) agreed to champion the Army's cause on this issue. He was a savvy and respected senior Member on the Committee known for his strong defense of the Army and Air Force National Guard and reserve components in general. Since GAO, Marine Corps LL, and Rep. McHale's references to Army National Guard participation in the Gulf War implied a questioning of Army National Guard capabilities, Rep. Montgomery was willing to lead the fight against Rep. McHale. The Army's primary message was that there were no "excess" M1A1 tanks. Specifically, the Army (Joint Staff and OSD) proponents emphasized that:[37]

- It had 4,460 M1A1 and 62 M1A2 tanks with no new production programmed. It has a projected requirement for 6,800 M1A1/M1A2 tanks. With a program to upgrade 998 older M1 tanks to M1A2s by FY 2003, the Army would have to fill the 1,300 tank shortfall by relying on older M1 tanks.

- Providing M1A1s to the Marines would delay modernization of the Army National Guard by at least two years and extend retirement of its aging M60 tanks into the next century.

- A preemptive congressional mandate to transfer tanks would violate the intent of the Goldwater-Nichols Act and undercut the legitimacy of the JCS Joint Requirements Oversight Council.

- Diverting Army tanks from the National Guard would discount and unhinge the nation's increased reliance on the Guard, since the Gulf War, as "critical force enhancements," as reflected in the National Military Strategy, BUR, and the Mobility MRS.

- OSD and Joint Staff viewed the GAO report as flawed and strongly questioned many of its key assumptions and interpretations as the appropriate basis for such legislation.

- While the tanks had been bought with taxpayer money, the Army had made hard choices between high priority systems in order to buy those tanks, while at the same time the Secretary of the Navy and the Marine Commandant had canceled the Corps' tank contract, diverting its program funds to other acquisitions.

- Marines lack space for these additional tanks on existing Navy ships; it would require offloading equipment Marines currently deem critical that would have to be deployed by other means.

- It was not just a matter of additional tanks; Marines would have to acquire the necessary fuel and ammunition trucks, recovery vehicles, and other support equipment required with the tanks.

- The GAO cited a 1989 Marine "service only" requirement for additional tanks; the Marine Corps has not requested, justified, or had JCS approve (through the Joint Requirements Oversight Council, JROC, process) a Marine requirement for more tanks.

By late April it was known that Rep. McHale intended to legislate the tank transfer,[38] that the Army was not willing to compromise with the Marines for further transfers to avoid the Hill fight,[39] and that the Army and Marine Corps were preparing to advocate openly, at the highest levels, their respective cases to the congressional audience. Chairman Hutto, in preparation for his subcommittee mark, asked the military heads of both services to highlight their tank requirements in light of a possible transfer of Army tanks to the Marines.

General Sullivan, CSA, stressed in his May 2 letter that the Army had no excess M1A1s. Additionally, as the "nation's principal land combat force," the Army had placed a high priority on procurement of modern tanks, and to divert these tanks would disrupt a balanced modernization strategy "to provide the most effective mix of equipment throughout the Total Army." He reiterated Army-Marine joint efforts that had taken place following the JCS Chairman's direction to establish effective procedures to provide heavy brigades to the Marines in the event of crisis. His final point in the letter would have carried greater significance with the congressional audience had the March 29 Army-Marine complementary operations brief taken place on the Hill, "The issue is not the transfer of equipment among the Services. The issue is the *complementary* employment of each Service's unique capabilities."[40]

General Mundy, Commandant of the Marine Corps, provided a similar letter on May 2, 1994, that was strategically significant in its effect on both its target audience, the Armed Services Committee and its opposition, the Army, to include JCS and OSD:

I am aware of the GAO report which suggests a transfer of tanks to the Marine Corps to fill requirements, and if excess tanks were available, they would be a valid requirement filler. *However, I am also aware of the Army's plan to upgrade and modernize its active, guard, and reserve armor formations, and I would be concerned at an initiative which would significantly impact those plans.* . . . Were excess tanks available, they would not be an enhancement of the Maritime Pre-positioning Program [EMPF], but rather, would be a restoral of Marine Corps combat capabilities not achievable by virtue of fiscal constraints. . . . Finally, I would like to make clear that the Marine Corps applauds the mobility enhancement achieved through the prepositioning afloat of a heavy Army armored brigade.[41] [emphasis added]

General Mundy's conciliatory remarks had the effect of portraying the Marine Corps as a reasonable team player to both Hill and senior Pentagon leadership audiences. Tensions among the JCS were reduced, and many of the Army's senior leaders were now less suspicious of the Marine Corps because of its open support of the APA program as well as its concern for not affecting Army modernization plans. It seemed from this letter that General Mundy was not going to allow the Marine Corps to wage a legislative campaign to acquire Army M1A1s.

Did something change to move the Commandant's position from "I'll take Army tanks for my requirements only if they are excess and do not impact on Army modernization of its components" to "I'll take Army tanks ahead of their National Guard units—we'll get to the battlefield first"? There is debate on whether the Commandant changed his mind after sending Hutto the letter, or whether the letter was a part of a more sophisticated campaign to attain a congressionally directed tank transfer by reducing Army suspicions and advocacy on the Hill and avoiding having the Chairman, JCS, or Secretary of Defense reign in open Marine Corps LL advocacy prior to the SASC mark, the Marine Corps' strategic focus.

The former view was voiced in an interview with Rep. Paul McHale, who stated that Marine Corps senior military leadership were reluctant to fight for the Army tanks on the Hill and had to be urged to do so: "I convinced the senior [Marine Corps] leadership that if they want armor, they better get into the fight. . . . When I saw General Mundy's letter, I thought it went too far in the consensual direction."[42]

Before elaborating on this pivotal meeting with the Commandant, Rep. McHale walked over to a large sketch of a ship on which he had served as a second lieutenant, which was hanging prominently on his office wall. The commander of his ship at that time was a Lieutenant Colonel Carl Mundy, whose personalized note on the sketch as Commandant of the Marine Corps reflected the long and proud history these two men had shared over the years:

I told him no one wants a bull in a china shop, but that [Army-Marine] rivalry on this issue is inevitable. Unlike the previous year where he was honor bound to an agreement [to support an Army Brigade afloat if the Army supported its 174,000 endstrength request], he was not honor bound to any agreement this year. Following that meeting, General Mundy made a clear decision to go for the tanks. The Marine Corps would engage [with their requirements and message] and its LL would be let loose.

Others believed General Mundy's letter was more cunning and strategically directed, from the start, to cementing its primary goal: the transfer, and insulating the Marine Corps from criticisms that it was refighting last year's battle or engaged in a roles and missions legislative battle. John Pack's paper made the following point:

In retrospect, the Army failed to see the Commandant's comments for what they really were–an effort to separate the tank transfer from the previous year's fight over pre-positioned assets and shipping. General Mundy had fired the first volley in a different campaign–an effort to win the tanks on the basis that the first-to-fight units ought to have them. Implementing a new strategy, the Marines no longer contested the heavy brigade afloat or challenged the Army on expanding roles and missions.[43]

Regardless, it is safe to say that the Commandant's letter was not perceived by Army or JCS and OSD leadership in the same vein as General Boomer's letter to OSD desiring external assistance in acquiring more Army M1A1 tanks. The Commandant's stated concern over impacting Army modernization plans was quoted by Rep. Montgomery in garnering support to kill Rep. McHale's amendment.[44] Leveraging the Commandant's written concerns, Rep. Montgomery wrote his second letter in less than a week to Chairman Hutto stressing that "the idea [tank transfer] is not in the best interest of our total forces."[45]

Fewer than two weeks after Lieutenant General Sheehan, the JCS witness, at Chairman Hutto's Readiness hearing, stated that JCS was not involved in this

Army-Marine Corps issue, JCS LL wrote a May 2, 1994 memorandum to General Shalikashvili, CJCS, informing him that Hutto was seeking his position on the GAO and McHale tank-transfer recommendations.[46] With the HASC's subcommittee marks scheduled for May 3–4 and the full HASC mark scheduled for May 5–6, many Members were eager to know General Shalikashvili's position.

The Deputy Legislative Assistant to the CJCS provided background and warned the Chairman that Rep. McHale would offer his amendment in either the Readiness subcommittee or full HASC mark-up. She informed him of efforts made by Rep. McHale and the Marine Corps the year before and alerted the Chairman that Marine LL was engaged earlier in the day distributing copies of the GAO report to Member offices. Finally, she reminded the Chairman that Vice Chairman, Joint Chiefs of Staff, Admiral Owens had decided that the transfer of tanks to the Marines should be a Joint Requirements Oversight Council issue later in the year. The JCS LL recommended that a tank transfer in 1994 would be premature and that Congress should forego legislating the transfer while JCS looked at the issue in detail. The CJCS approved both recommendations and made calls on May 3 to key members of the HASC opposing the tank transfer.

Members of the full Committee were being liaised heavily by LLs on both sides of the issue. Rep. Montgomery's influence and experience, General Mundy's May 2 letter to Rep. Hutto, and telephone calls by the CJCS against the transfer were too much for Rep. McHale to overcome. By the day of the HASC mark, an Army and JCS LL nose count showed Rep. Montgomery had sufficient support to defeat Rep. McHale's amendment. It never came down to a recorded vote. Rep. Montgomery offered and Rep. McHale accepted compromise language in return for withdrawal of his amendment. The compromise House amendment relieved Members of the Committee from having to record a difficult vote for or against a particular service's interests and "directed the Chairman of the Joint Chiefs of Staff to conduct a review of M1A1 tank allocations and report the results to the committee not later than December 15, 1994."[47] Rep. McHale seemed pleased with the compromise language and stated in the mark-up and in later interviews that it allowed the issue to be reviewed and decided at the appropriate JCS level, but that the December 1994 deadline for the review gave "me time to take action if I find their report unacceptable."[48]

Ambushed in the Senate: Legislation to Transfer Tanks to the Marines

Believing it has "won" the key battle in the House, the Army lost sight of an old Hill adage: "The fight on an issue is never over." Although the Army still opposed giving tanks to the Marines, Army leaders were comfortable with the compromise language and indicated they were ready to execute whatever recommendations the JCS's Joint Requirements Oversight Council (JROC) issued.

However, the real battle with the Marine Corps for Army tanks was about to begin in the Senate. The Army was surprised and once again placed into a crisis mode of reactive rather than proactive legislative strategy. Unlike the previous year with the APA issue, Army senior flag officers did not meet with or call senators on the SASC to express Army concerns on the tank transfer issue before the initial HASC mark-up nor in the intervening four weeks following the HASC mark before the important SASC mark-up. In addition, by mid-May 1994, Army LL had been approached by a majority SASC staffer gathering information for a prominent SASC Democrat on the issue of transferring Army tanks to the Marines.[49] Even in combination with the intensity of the earlier HASC fight, this *still* did not prompt a proactive series of pre-SASC mark meetings between senior Army flag officers and senators on this issue.

The Army received no clear heads-up, however, that numerous pro–Marine Corps amendments were being considered seriously by the SASC. Only as the Committee completed its closed session mark-ups of the FY 95 Defense Authorization Bill on June 8–10 did the Army get "closehold" word that the battle for tanks was anything but over on Capitol Hill. On June 14, the SASC formally filed the bill it would send to the Senate floor for approval.

The combination of selective Marine Corps engagement on the issue and the general lack of Army engagement with senators on the Committee *prior to the mark-up* surprised the Army with an SASC bill that included not only the transfer of Army tanks to the Marines, but a series of separate pro–Marine Corps amendments that were not consistent with the MRS recommendations upon which the Army, JCS, and OSD had based their moderate-cost, moderate-risk, strategic mobility plan.[50] Experienced LL officers in the Army, JCS, and OSD understood the likely tradeoffs these SASC provisions represented to their strategic mobility plans and the difficulty inherent in removing them through amendments to the SASC bill on the Senate floor.

The Marines' pre-SASC mark-up engagement resulted in two separate provisions in the SASC bill that transferred M1A1 tanks to the Marine Corps. First, Senator Robert Smith (R-NH), a freshman Senator with no known ties to the Marine Corps and few military installations in his district, sponsored Section 1066, which directed the Army to transfer not less than 84 and not more than 124 M1A1 "common" tanks to the Marine Corps. Further, the section prohibited additional migration of M1A1 tanks to the Army National Guard until the Army satisfied the Marine Corps tank requirements.[51] Rather than engage Senators Glenn (D-OH) or Robb (D-VA) or the Committee's Staff Director, Arnold Punaro, all of who were former Marines, to sponsor and or help champion the tank transfer, the Marine Corps prudently engaged a senator on the SASC with no constituent interests in the issue, who could honestly state he was pushing the transfer because it was "the right thing to do."[52]

Senator Smith's provision was packaged by majority staffers with another one that enhanced its acceptability to the full Committee. Senator Carl Levin (D-MI), a Member of the SASC and supporter of the APA Program the year before, learned that the Army intended to cut $300 million from its new M1A2 upgrade program and reduce the schedule of upgrades from 120 to 90 tanks per year; this would impact negatively on the Michigan economy. In section 111, the SASC created a multiyear M1A2 upgrade procurement contract program. More specifically, section 112 authorized $108M to the Army for 24 additional and unrequested M1A2 upgrades each year of the two-year program. The section went on to direct the Army to provide 24 M1A1 "common" tanks to the Marine Corps Reserve as the M1A2 upgrades become available each year.[53] The SASC justified section 112 by claiming it "would leave the active Army with more M1A2s (which they require), the Marine Corps reserve with the needed M1A1s, and the Army National Guard and reserves modernizing at the same rate under the current Army plan."[54] Of the two sections, the Army decided to liaise against Senator Smith's (section 1066) tank transfer provision.[55]

The Army needed to develop a strategy for the more difficult post-mark-up conditions. The Army received some prudent early advice from the Assistant Minority Staff Director Les Brownlee over the impending fight concerning Section 1066. In mid-June, Brownlee questioned the prudence of fighting the transfer and stressed the following points with Army LL: (1) There is bipartisan support for the tank transfer in the Senate; (2) the Army National Guard argument, as presented, will not persuade senators; (3) the JCS or OSD will have to lead the fight—or the Army will be viewed as selfish and petty; (4) the CJCS will have to visit key members—calls and letters will not do; and (5) the Senate will avoid debating this issue on the floor in front of C-Span cameras at all costs.[56]

The Army also received cautionary counsel from Senator Smith's MLA Tom Lankford. He warned Army leaders that a floor fight on this issue would be contentious and that the Army would lose future support from Senator Smith and his supporters on the SASC if the Army fought the Senator on this issue. The Army's most senior flag officers did not incorporate this congressional input and advice into their reactive legislative strategy.

The Army's more complicated message on the tank issue now had to negotiate the hurdle of garnering Senate floor support for an amendment that would delete or weaken the Smith provision prior to Conference. The one mistake SASC staffers had made was to include the "common" version of M1A1 tanks into their language. These staffers were unaware that M1A1 "common" tanks include special equipment and that these tanks were only issued to the Army's elite contingency XVIII Airborne Corps.[57] Few, if any, senators would support taking these tanks from the active Army's elite contingency corps. This oversight ensured that Marine Corps supporters on the SASC and in the Senate would have to compromise and at least modify Section 1066.

The Army adopted a two-phase strategy that included: (1) enlisting "champions" to co-sponsor a "killer" amendment on the Senate floor, and then, if necessary, orchestrate a follow-on fight in conference; (2) two prongs, Army National Guard and Joint Staff, that would take the lead in fighting the transfer thereby allowing the active Army leadership to contribute in only a supporting role; (3) educating the House and Senate appropriators on the issue; and (4) eliminating the requirement for "common" M1A1s as a minimum from any final bill.[58]

The Army's strategy seemed to show cracks early in the process. First, it discounted Brownlee's caution that the Senate would not be persuaded by the Army National Guard argument. Senators' longer terms and broader constituent interests insulate them far more than their House counterparts from the Guard's political clout. Because this was a transfer of equipment rather than a funding for tanks issue, it was difficult to find champions not tied to and pushing National Guard interests. The Army enlisted Senators Ford (D-KY) and Bond (R-MO), co-chairmen of the National Guard Caucus in the Senate, to lead the Army cause in the Senate.

Second the prospects of Members debating and taking a recorded vote on a killer amendment began to fade. Charlie Smith, MLA to Senator Ford, voiced concerns about the killer amendment strategy, preferring to attack the SASC provision with a barrage of compromise amendments instead.[59] In addition, he reiterated Brownlee's assessment that senators would avoid open debate and taking public positions between the Marine Corps and the Army National Guard in their states. Forcing a killer amendment would place members in that uncomfortable position. Compromise seemed increasingly the more likely result.

The Army attempted to get the JCS out in front on the issue. The JCS LL initially informed the Army they were drafting a letter to be signed by the Chairman and Vice Chairman of the JCS and all service chiefs, and a letter to be signed by the Secretary of Defense and each department secretary to urge the deletion of the tank transfer and several SASC sealift provisions.[60] However, within days the Army learned of the JCS decision to drop the tank transfer issue out of these letters.[61]

Les Brownlee had warned that it would require the lead by the Chairman, Lieutenant General Tilelli, involved earlier in the canceled Army-Marine brief and nominated to be the new Vice Chief of Staff of the Army, was supposed to visit Senator Smith and explain the Army position; the meeting never took place. Instead, Major General Jay Garner, Assistant Deputy Chief of Staff for Operations and Plans (Force Development), was tasked with the duty of placing a phone call to Senator Smith in late June. Although the telephone exchange was cordial, it appears it was the wrong message sent by the wrong messenger in the wrong way too late in the game and accordingly resulted in no change of positions.[62]

From the beginning, the Army wanted to avoid the perception of parochialism and having the tank transfer viewed as an Army versus Marines issue. The Army welcomed the June 23 Statement of Administration Policy, Executive Office of the President, that officially opposed the tank transfer, claiming, "This undermines long-standing defense policy regarding the transfer of tanks between the military departments."[63] The OSD followed a week later with a draft appeal to the SASC provision stating: "Neither the combatant commanders nor the Joint Chiefs of Staff have assessed a shortfall in MPF (Maritime Prepositioning Forces) capability to accomplish those missions with the current number of tanks on hand. The GAO study upon which this proposal is based does not address the full range of tradeoffs that must be considered in developing force structure and military strategy."[64]

After the meeting with General Sullivan around June 20, Senator Thurmond made it clear that a letter from the CJCS was needed. While the Chairman had made several phone calls on the issue to select members, expectations of getting a Chairman's letter to the Hill against the tank transfer had existed unfulfilled since late April before the HASC mark.[65] The Army's strategy required the Chairman taking the lead and personally making visits to key members on the SASC and in the Senate. Not only were these visits not taking place, but the difficulty in getting a letter on the subject from the JCS over a four-week period was an unrecognized indicator that the Army's strategy was unraveling and might require reassessment.

The Chairman's July 1 letter on the tank transfer arrived too late to affect a compromise amendment negotiated late on June 30. The Chairman of the SASC, Senator Sam Nunn, finally allowed the issue to come to the floor Friday morning.

The compromise amendment to Section 1066 entailed: (1) limiting the maximum number of tanks transferred to 84 M1A1s, (2) removing the reference to "common" M1A1 tanks in the language, (3) allowing the Army National Guard to modernize at the same rate tanks are provided to the Marines, and (4) charging the Secretary of the Navy with all transportation and refurbishing costs prior to transfer. Army and Marine Corps champions gave floor speeches to their colleagues that while they were not satisfied with the compromise amendment, they believed the remaining problems could be rectified in Conference with the House.[66] Senators on both sides of the issue were insistent about not taking a recorded vote on this amendment but adopting it by a consensual voice vote from the floor.

Senator Smith suggested an absence of quorum for approval of the compromise amendment, supposedly on the notion that a recorded vote would improve its position in Conference. Senator Nunn immediately dissuaded Senator Smith, saying that a roll call vote was not necessary and that adoption by voice vote would be preferable in the interest of time.[67]

Army strategy had precariously relied on Member concern over alienating state Guard interests, buffeted and legitimized by JCS arguments on defense policy, that would result in a vote to resist legislating the transfer. Army supporters believed that if a recorded vote was forced on the floor, the Army and

JCS position would win the day. However, just as Brownlee and Charlie Smith had warned, the Senate avoided that scenario. Watching the proceedings on C-Span, Colonel Jess Franco, Army LL Programs Chief, realized that senators had escaped individual accountability on the issue and that all future proceedings would be resolved behind closed doors. He shook his head and stated, "We just lost 84 tanks, end of discussion."[68] He was right.

After several days of Conference, the House conferees were holding firm in their position against legislating the tank transfer.[69] However, by August 5, they had been worn down by Senate conferees who refused to budge on the issue and held the tank transfer provision as one of the last conference issues to be resolved.[70] According to those interviewed, the Senate conferees and Arnold Punaro knew exactly which Army programs were most important to House conferees and skillfully leveraged those in keeping the tank transfer alive.

Closed-door negotiations and reduced Committee Member involvement in conference make it hard to determine exactly what finally caused the House to recede to the Senate on the tank issue. One source claimed that Rep. Montgomery ultimately relented because critical funding for other Army National Guard programs was threatened. Others claimed that HASC Chairman Ron Dellums, a former Marine and an opponent of the B-2 bomber, was persuaded to relent by Senate conferees' strategic use of bargaining on the B-2 issue. LTC Pack's paper suggests that the Senate questioned the prudence of House desires to plus-up (increase above the administration's budget request) the Army's procurement of additional helicopters. By caving on the transfer issue, the House was able to get the Senate to recede and fund 23 helicopters that the Army had not requested.[71]

The SASC language became law, and the Army was directed to transfer 84 tanks to the Marine Corps. The appropriators adopted similar language. On the day the House receded to the Senate on the tank transfer, the Commandant of the Marine Corps awarded an impact Legion of Merit award to Colonel Terry Paul, the Chief of the Marines Senate Liaison Division, for his outstanding LL work liaising the Senate on this issue.[72]

ARMY–HILL PATTERNS

The Army Is Seen as the Most Honest, Straightforward, and Credible Service on the Hill

This positive Army-Hill pattern was actually undercut by the Army's strategic and prominent reliance on the National Guard argument in combatting the tank transfer on the Senate side.[73] If the National Guard had used its access and influence to advocate the JCS or other arguments rather than its more parochial, complicated, and less credible argument that a Member's state or district would lose tanks, the outcome might have been different.

The Army and Air Force National Guards have a reputation for their political clout with Congress. This influence is especially noted on the House side where National Guard units and armories are prominent features of a Member's district. The Adjutant General (TAG) of each state oversees the many state Guard units and maintains close contact with its legislators in Washington. When TAGs feel their interests are threatened, they are willing to press their Members for support.

In the tank transfer battle, the TAGs pressed too hard. A senior Marine Corps LL officer captured how this backfired on the Army:

I had at least 5 Members come to me saying . . . they were told by the Guard in their state that the transfer would divert M1A1s away from units in their state. . . . Eventually, we were able to help Members see that their TAG [Adjutant General] was being less than honest about the impact on the Guard units in their state. The Guard, using their state TAG, played hardball with Members. We [Marine Corps] played underdog quite effectively. One Member after talking with his TAG told me, ''I hate being strung out by anyone—the Marine Corps has my support on this issue!''[74]

The Army's Outreach Efforts to Congress Are the Least Apparent and Sophisticated

The Marine Corps' success centered on having the SASC lead its cause on the transfer in conference, and most importantly, enlisting a neutral Member on the SASC as its primary champion with no apparent Marine Corps ties or constituent interests in the state. This champion was willing to fight for the Marines' cause and could tell the world he was doing it because it was the right thing to do.

It appears that the Marine Corps accomplished this feat initially by reaching out and developing a serious trusted relationship with Senator Smith's MLA, Tom Lankford. The development and nurturing of this relationship over the previous year by Colonel Terry Paul, the Chief of the Marines Senate Liaison Division, and senior Marine flag officers contrasted significantly with the lack of similar outreach by the Army LL and its senior flag officers with this Senate staffer. The differences in approach were obvious to Lankford:

In my 7 years working as a MLA, I can count on one hand and only a few fingers at that, when the Army has solicited or invited me to anything designed to orient or educate me on the Army and its programs, either through travel, briefings or even socially. I believe it may be in your culture not to reach out to those Members and staff who do not have a substantive presence like Fort Hood (Texas) in your state. You assume that because we don't have a large Army installation in our state, that my Member isn't interested in the Army. My Member is one of the most ardent supporters of a strong defense.[75]

Mr. Lankford had never been to the Army's premier NTC and had never seen Army National Guard units training; the only M1A1s he had ever seen were Marine Corps tanks. However, he had been engaged by the Marine Corps. As a civilian, he had a better understanding of Marine Corps, rather than Army, attributes, capabilities, and concerns:

I'll never forget the trip the Marine Corps approached me on. It was a trip to San Diego to the Marine Corps Recruit Depot to orient us on "the Making of a Marine." All the MLAs left that trip with a basic understanding of how the Marines and Navy conduct joint operations, build their force, and the synergy between air and ground operations. We got to *drive M1A1 tanks*, sit in the back of a LAV (light armored vehicle), and experienced exciting hands-on demonstrations. They were very effective ways to educate us on Marine and Navy capabilities and concerns. The Army will occasionally have a missile launch or simulated warfighting demonstration but nothing to compare to what I just described.[76]

Lankford agreed with points made earlier in this study that the Army does not cast a wide enough net for Members and demonstrates a lack of sophistication in understanding the concerns and potential influence of military MLAs.

The Army also makes a mistake in fixating too much on the Member or the Professional Staff Member on the Committee. They discount the importance of the MLAs and clearly do not work the MLAs as aggressively as the Marine Corps, Navy and to a lesser degree the Air Force. Working the MLAs aggressively is a good strategy and there is nothing improper about it at all. MLAs have the ear of the Senators far more then any General in the Pentagon does. That . . . general officer, if he has established a relationship with the MLA, can have concerns repeatedly brought to the attention of the Senator, timed and packaged in a way that helps or hurts that general's case.[77]

The importance of services directing valuable agency resources consistently over time to improve service–MLA relationships becomes apparent when one understands how the tank transfer became an issue for Senator Smith. Lankford explained how it gained salience:

Each year I go to each Service and ask them, "What is important for you to improve the lot of each soldier, sailor, airman or Marine." One of the deficiencies the Marine Corps identified were these MPF [Maritime Prepositioning Forces] enhancements and the V-22 [tilt-rotor aircraft]. The Army had mentioned the Comanche [helicopter]. *I put together a list of prospective issues that the Senator may or may not want to weigh in on. He read the GAO report which recommended the tank transfer.* He believed GAO had legitimately and analytically conducted a study based on the current force structure levels for the Army (active and NG) and the USMC. It was his determination after deliberation on the issue that it was only a modest transfer of tanks. The transfer would have no immediate impact on the Army National Guard, but would have a crucial and immediate impact for the Marine Corps active forces. Therefore the Senator decided to go forward.

The Marine Corps better understood that by engaging, winning the confidence of, and reinforcing the MLA with input from the GAO report, the Member might be influenced indirectly to advance its interests. Lankford made the point that "He [Senator Smith] didn't talk to anyone in the Army and Marine Corps [before deciding to sponsor the tank transfer provision in the SASC mark-up]."[78] It seems logical to assume that the quality of the messenger and how he or she presents the message will have an impact on whether a senator adopts a position. The Marine Corps understands MLAs are high-quality and influential messengers on the Hill.

The Army Is More Reactive than Other Services in Representing Its Concerns to Congress

A Senate staffer with MLA and PSM experience with the SASC made the point that the Army suffers for its reactive posture with the Committee:

The Army doesn't understand or appreciate the role Congress plays. The Army thinks it can sit back and that the wisdom of Army choices will sell itself–obviously since they don't get over here and participate [in the process]. If the other services have something important, they are over here fighting for it. *When you are going into markup, Members tend to listen to military guys. Very few times does the SASC go against the senior flag officers who engage them prior to the markup.*[79]

This lack of understanding or appreciation for the role Congress plays and the legislative process in particular was highlighted in this case study. Considering the intensity of the conflict that led Rep. McHale to agree to Rep. Montgomery's compromise language during the HASC mark-up, one must assume that turning the tank transfer issue around on the Hill was important to the Army military leadership. However, even with a month between the HASC and SASC marks, the Army did not take the initiative to engage the senators. Instead, they reacted only after being surprised by SASC marks and attempted to delete via the amendment process troubling provisions of the SASC bill on the Senate floor, a much more difficult and "political chit-burning" endeavor. Most SASC Members were surprised by the Army's fierce reaction to an issue that its senior generals appeared so unconcerned about prior to the mark.

What would the Army have gained by proactively engaging Members of the SASC before their mark?[80] First, if the senior Army leadership had met with Senator Smith prior to the SASC mark-up, they would have demonstrated to him and his staff that the Army valued his opinions and support as a Member of the Committee.[81] Second, at a minimum the Army would have learned about Senator Smith's intentions or inclinations on the issue, and possibly would have been able to keep him from offering the language by explaining the Army/JCS/OSD message before the Senator's name was tied to the issue. Third, all SASC Members engaged prior to the mark would be placed in the position of turning down a senior military leader's personal and professional request. By not engaging, it was easier for senators to support Senator Smith's request instead of adopting the HASC compromise position. Finally, senior Army generals would better appreciate the level of SASC support for transferring tanks to the Marines and would be in a more advantageous position to assess the benefit of continuing the fight, know how hard and long to press, and could weigh the value of compromise language or other opportunities the Army could seek in exchange for not fighting this battle to the end.

Army Senior General Officers Are the Least Represented, Engaged, and Effective on the Hill

The pre-SASC assessment discussed above can only come from senior flag officer engagement and cannot be delegated to LL personnel. The two-star Army CLL and his lieutenant colonels do not have and should not be expected on their own to have the access to senators needed to gauge this sentiment. Committee Members expect and want to see a service's senior military leaders with their LL personnel prior to a mark-up, but not the LL personnel alone.

Major General Harrison, the Army's CLL, stated that in regard to the tank transfer issue, "Our [Army LL] biggest failing was not to have known about it [tank transfer language] before it was marked in subcommittee. It was our failing not to have a heads-up."[82]

The problem of Army senior officer engagement on the Hill is encapsulated in his remarks. As stated before, while "heads-ups" are desirable, their absence should not mandate surprise and reactive behavior on the part of a service. Ambushes are effective only if soldiers assume all is well and that enemy activity is not possible within certain terrain. The tank battle that took place in the HASC should have alerted the senior Army leadership that a similar fight might take place in the Senate as well. More troubling, however, the Army CLL's comments take responsibility for the "surprise" but in doing so serve to mask the culpability of the many other two-, three-, and four-star Army generals serving in and out of Washington who are the "liaisers of choice" of the congressional audience. If Army generals valued, developed, and nurtured Hill relationships to a greater degree, they might have elicited a "heads-up" prior to the SASC mark. A senior SASC PSM says Army LL has become a "crutch" and an inadequate replacement for Army general officer engagement on the Hill.[83]

When senior Army generals engage, it tends to be with a small and less risky group of supportive Members. During his four years as Assistant Secretary and Under Secretary of the Army, Norm Augustine not only was atypical as a civilian political appointee in making engagement with Members a priority, but he targeted all three categories of Members for that engagement:

We'd go over to the Hill frequently. I set a goal of six 30-minute visits to the Hill each week for four years. These visits were never to ask for anything but to tell our story and build credibility for when we did need to ask. That is over 300 visits per year, over

1,200 visits during my time on the Army Secretariat. . . . As you would expect, I met with a small group of *traditional supporters* to tell them why we needed their continued support. I would also meet with another small group of Members who had traditionally been *nonsupporters*. They were valuable in exposing me to the counter arguments, I would gain their respect for at least engaging them and, on occasion, I would be surprised to win their support on a program or issue. However, *most of my time was spent with the larger middle half of Members that were more neutral and open on issues*. They probably had no major Army facilities or Army jobs in their district or state, but were still available and had opportunities to engage.[84]

The most senior Army general to meet with the "traditionally non-supportive" Rep. McHale (D-PA) on the tank transfer issue was MG Harrison, the Army CLL. McHale later stated that he would have been "open to the compromise finally worked out by [Rep.] Sonny Montgomery" had anyone from the Army raised it earlier or seriously engaged him in the matter.[85] Instead, this Member takes credit for persuading the Marine Corps' top military leadership (and not the reverse) to openly fight for the tanks on the Hill.[86] It seems Army disengagement has done little to lessen his concerns that the twenty-first-century Army is a threat to future roles for the Marines. "If the Chief of Staff of the Army had told me that the Army wants to work this out and convinced me that these Army [early entry] capabilities were not redundant but complementary [to Marine Corps capabilities], well that would have been helpful. . . . Rather than discussion, this new Army vision came out in bits and pieces until General Sullivan announced it [before the Committee] as a decision and incorporated it into the Army's 100–5 operational doctrinal manual."[87]

Senator Robert Smith (R-NH) represented Mr. Augustine's "neutral" and more open-minded Member category toward which he directed most of his liaising Hill time. The Army not only failed to build a climate of understanding and trust with the Senator and his MLA in the months prior to the tank transfer issue, but never directed its more senior general officers to meet with them and discuss the issue.[88] Such an engagement, even without the preestablished climate of trust, would have demonstrated to Senator Smith the importance of the tank issue to the Army, giving the Army the opportunity to candidly and confidentially highlight the harmful consequences of an active Army leadership decision to acquiesce on this issue in the National Guard's eyes, and providing the top military Army leadership a critical chance to assess the importance of the issue to the senator, and whether going to the mat on this issue was in the Army's long-term interests.

By relying on Army LL as a constant crutch to communicate, rather than to advise and facilitate its senior flag officers in communicating Army interests to Congress, the senior Army leadership loses considerable control over the fate of future service–Member relationships. One casualty appears to be the Army–Senator Smith relationship. According to Tom Lankford, Senator Smith's MLA: "Major General Harrison underestimated our resolve. I told him, 'Don't burn this bridge with Senator Smith. We're going to win. The transfer won't hurt you at all.' MG Harrison said something to the effect that 'the bridge will just have to burn.' As a result, the Senator and I are not comfortable with trusting the Army when making its case.''[89]

Even when Army general officers engaged on the tank transfer issue, they often did so with more junior general officers than the Marine Corps and engaged in a manner that was more awkward and less effective. While discussing the intensity of liaising by both the Army and Marines prior to the HASC mark-up, one MLA offered an interesting contrast of Army versus Marine Corps engagement on the senior flag officer level:

I'll never forget the ugliest day on the Hill: the impending HASC mark on the tank transfer to the Marines. An Army Major called to ask where my boss stood on this issue. I told him that [my boss] had spoken to the Commandant and was going to support the transfer. An Army lieutenant colonel called back and asked, "Could one of our generals change his mind?" I really didn't know how to answer that question: which general officer? how persuasive is the general? what is their relationship? Soon the CAR [Chief of Army Reserve] called; he must have gotten tagged because my boss was once in the Army Reserves. [My boss] asked that I tell the CAR that he was out.[90]

It should have been apparent that unless the Member had a close personal relationship with this two-star general officer, the best hope of engaging and changing the mind of this Member would be the Commandant's counterpart, the Chief or Vice Chief of Staff of the Army. Had the CSA phoned, the Member would have taken the call. The Commandant's engagement demonstrated to the Member the importance of the issue to the Marine Corps.

The Army Is Least Effective in Selecting and Communicating Its Priorities and Message

In discussing the Army's effectiveness in communicating externally, one must evaluate the issues and messages the Army's senior flag officers choose to communicate. Did Army senior military leaders really view defeating the tank transfer legislation as an Army priority critical enough to expend its important political chits and valuable agency resources on the Hill? If it was an Army priority to resist the tank transfer recommendations in the soon-to-be-released GAO report to Congress, why would the Army provide the Marine Corps political cover that enabled it to slip the March 29, 1994, Army-Marine Complementary Operations briefing to HASC staffers? Was this a battle worth fighting on the Hill?

In retrospect and unbeknownst to Army LL at the time, there appear to have been many senior Army general officers who had no real objections to giving the M1A1 tanks to the Marines. A senior Army general officer serving in a key leadership position on the Army staff at the time of these interviews stated he believed, "The Army should not have fought against the tank transfer."[91] An-other active-duty Army general officer stated that "There were many Army senior officers who had no problem with Marines getting these tanks."[92] This sentiment not only questions the priority the issue supposedly held with the Army leadership at the time, but also questions the skill of Army leaders in selecting the battles the Army wages on the Hill that support its long-term legislative strategy and vision.

A senior PSM on the SASC directly addressed the Army's poor sense of picking its priority battles on the Hill:

The Army really did itself some damage by the way it reacted. From the rational per-spective, the question who needs them [M1A1 tanks] more, Marine Corps or Army National Guard, was an easy one. *The tanks were the wrong battle to fight.* The Navy appears best at picking its battles. The Army tends to pick the wrong battles: with the tank transfer of 1994 and the Army museum this year being prime examples.[93]

Senator Smith's MLA could not understand the Army's hard-line stance on the issue: "They (the Army) sure don't pick their fights well. Here you have the biggest pro-defense guy up here on the Senate Armed Services Committee supporting and appreciating the importance and full spectrum of all the services. My boss carries credibility on defense issues. To burn a bridge with this man on that issue showed surprising naïveté."[94]

A senior official serving in Army LL made the same point: "The Army picks the wrong issues to fight and die on. We made it [tank transfer] our number one priority as far as the political chits used. The tank transfer wasn't as big an issue as we made it. It was more an ego issue on both sides. Except we used the chits, lost the legislative battle, burned some bridges, and lost opportunities to get other things we needed more."[95]

Even accepting the merit of the fight against the tank transfer, the Army's message was poorly framed for the Senate. Brownlee, then serving as the SASC Minority Deputy Staff Director, questioned the prudence of fighting against the transfer. He accurately predicted that the Army would not defeat the SASC language unless the CJCS and officials in OSD were in the lead, visiting Mem-bers with the message that the tank transfer legislation undermined the power of the Chairman as well as the larger 1986 Goldwater-Nichols Act that Congress authored and continues to praise.[96]

The Army's primary message needed to be one of "joint" process that would reinforce JCS and OSD officials' arguments that tanks should not be transferred prior to a DOD-level evaluation of the requirement. The Joint Requirements Oversight Council (JROC) was established by the CJCS to "examine the re-quirements of every major Service acquisition program" and thereby more ef-fectively carry out his 1986 congressionally directed responsibilities.[97] The message had to come from the Chairman that he needed the opportunity to do his job that Congress outlined for him in 1986. This "joint" process message communicated personally by the Chairman or Vice Chairman of the JCS never materialized as the tip of the "anti-tank transfer" spear.

Besides getting out in front of the Army early on this issue and following an uncontested Senate-based strategy, the Marine Corps' primary message was ideally framed for the senatorial audience. The Marines crafted simple and, at first glance, commonsense arguments for Army tanks going to the Marine Corps rather than the National Guard. Marine LL and its senior officers played upon Senate suspicions of the National Guard and its grassroots political clout to their advantage.[98] Many hard-pressing state TAGs only served to support and strengthen these suspicions. The Marine Corps stressed with little dispute that it would get to the fight before the Army National Guard. Therefore, the first-to-fight should be resourced with the best equipment.

There were many other problems with the Army message. Presenting the Army case that the Marine Corps shortfall in tanks was due to Marine Corps leadership decisions to cancel their acquisition contract in 1989, and eliminate in 1992 M60 series tanks from their inventory without identified replacements were both complicated and unsatisfactory national security arguments. One might agree that the Marine Corps made some mistakes and still support transferring 84 tanks to it because it was the right thing to do to correct those decisions. Rep. McHale admitted as much, in an interview, that "There was a failure within the Pentagon to address the armor issue in a forthright and direct manner. *The Marine Corps had allowed itself to drop to 50 percent strength* [in the number of tanks it required]."[99]

Another problematic aspect of the Army message was its more complicated task of explaining its strategy for modernizing its total active-duty and reserve Army forces. The Army explanation that it had no excess tanks, while accurate, was complicated and likely to "glaze" the eyes of an open-minded congressional audience. The Marine Corps' message was more likely to "water" the eyes of that same increasingly sympathetic audience. The "poor cousin" and "underdog" of the military services was just asking for 84 tanks from a downsizing Army that had over 4,500 M1A1 or M1A2 tanks in 1994. "It was hard to justify the Army's reaction to the tank transfer to the Marine Corps. The number of tanks to be transferred was a small percentage of those excess to the active Army. It didn't make a lot of sense. Possibly there was some roles and mission posturing. But still the Army had no real basis for circling the wagons on that issue."[100]

An SASC staffer who is a friend of the Army but a supporter of the tank transfer explained that "The Marines were successful in selling the argument that a large number of Army tanks exist and the rationale for transferring a relatively small number of these tanks to early active Marine deployers who would be fighting side by side with active Army early deploying forces made sense.[101] The countervailing message the Army failed to convey effectively was that because Marine and Army early deployers would be fighting side-by-side, it made operational and logistical sense from a joint and taxpayer perspective to have additional heavy armor needs be provided by the Army. Transferring Army tanks to the Marines reduced their dependency on Army heavy armor and accentuates Marine Corps independent rather than joint operational capabilities.

The message that the "Marines do not need additional tanks—the Army will support" could and often did evolve into a counterproductive Army message that Marines do not use tanks as well as the Army, and did not sell well to the congressional audience for several reasons. First, because of the "wide net" approach and long-standing priority of the Marine Corps to reach out and educate the congressional audience, the only M1A1 tanks they had seen were likely to belong to the Marine Corps. Additionally, the Marine Corps was adept at responding to such accusations from the larger services by playing a besieged and often neglected "underdog" role that earned sympathy with an audience with whom it continually engages as team players rather than adversaries.

The Army was cautioned by supporters on the Hill that a National Guard argument would not sell, but there might have been one limited exception. The senior Army leadership might have sold to the Senate the symbolic importance of the active Army maintaining faith with the National Guard, following the unprecedented and delicate negotiated Off-site Agreement to reduce and restructure the Army reserves. The importance and fragility of this agreement, shaped in an innovative and inclusive process in 1992–93 and sold to the Hill in 1994, would have bolstered the Army case for letting the JCS look at the tank transfer issue, would have diminished the importance of the relatively small number of tanks in the transfer language to the Marine argument, and would have more effectively rationalized Army insistence that tanks not be diverted from the National Guard. If the CSA had met with Senator Smith, before or even immediately after the SASC mark to explain informally how Army acquiescence to his tank transfer language would be seen by the Guard as a breech of faith that could unravel this important agreement, the Senator might have been more willing to allow the JROC, headed by Admiral Owens, Vice Chairman of the JCS, to evaluate the Marine Corps requirement before legislating it. At a minimum, both the high-level engagement and the message would have served to explain the Army's uncompromising position and kept an important bridge with a key defense Senator from burning.

Army Legislative Liaison Personnel Seem to Be on Their Final Assignment

In comparing Army and Marine Corps effectiveness in winning Hill support on their tank transfer positions, it is instructive to contrast the casualties, personnel turbulence, and upward mobility of the LL personnel advising and often executing the legislative campaigns for each camp. The Chiefs of the Marines' HLD and SLD operations, both colonels, took the lead in liaising the transfer issue in their respective bodies. A lieutenant colonel working out of Army Programs Division in the Pentagon was responsible for liaising the issue with both

House and Senate audiences. His liaising efforts were often mentored and assisted by his boss, a colonel and Chief of the Army LL Programs Division. The
Army CLL and the Legislative Assistant to the Commandant were the flag
officers with overall responsibility for the competing liaising campaigns.

The Army LL Programs division team working on the issue underwent significant turbulence. Three different Army LL lieutenant colonels were assigned
responsibility for leading the fight against the tank transfer on the Hill in the
critical May–July 1994 period.[102] In addition, the Army LL officers leading the
battle for the tanks rarely, if ever, spoke directly with the Chief or Vice Chief
of Staff of the Army on the issue, but worked instead through the CLL. The
senior Army leadership appear to be more disengaged from their frontline LL
personnel than is the case with the Marine Corps. The turbulence within Programs Division in 1994 only exacerbated this tendency.

Unlike the Army, the Marine Corps LL "tank transfer" team experienced no
such turbulence that summer in 1994. Both Marine colonels had at least four
years of experience working LL issues in their respective legislative bodies and
were able to translate their familiarity, access, and influence with Members and
staff into results on the tank issue. They also were personally engaged with the
top flag officers in the Marine Corps in synchronizing the use of the institution's
agency resources toward achieving success on this issue. The Commandant tried
to adhere to a rule not to speak with Members or staff on issues without one
of these two colonels at his side. By doing so, he strengthened the credibility
and status of the Marine LL officers in the eyes of the Hill audience. In contrast,
the CSA (and other senior generals) will often ask LL officers to wait in an
outer office, preferring to meet with Members alone, a demeaning gesture not
lost on the congressional audience.

The intensity of the conflict between the two services and their LL organizations laid the groundwork for casualties that materialized only in the Army's
LL operation. Prior to the HASC mark-up, Rep. Montgomery asked that the
senior Marine LL officer in the Navy (Marine Corps) HLD be reassigned because of his open lobbying for the tank transfer in spite of the CJCS's letter
against the recommended transfer. The Marine LL officer was able to demonstrate that a Chairman's letter had never been signed and sent to the Hill. In
addition, the Chief of the Army's HLD went to Rep. Montgomery and, in the
Marine officer's defense, explained that unlike the Army's operation in the Rayburn Building, the Air Force and Navy HLDs do legitimately liaise programmatic issues. The Marine Corps LL officer not only survived this close call, but
the incident failed to hurt his upward mobility.

During the last week of May and fewer than two weeks before the SASC
mark-up, the Army reassigned its LL officer (a fast-tracking brigade command
selectee) responsible for the tank transfer issue to other Pentagon duties. New
to Washington and LL duties in particular, this fine but unseasoned LL officer
shared his less-than-objective feelings about the Marine Corps and its legislative
tactics with the Marines; made an implicit reference to the complicity of the

SASC majority staff director, Arnold Punaro, to this activity; and violated a cardinal Washington principle by communicating this all in a fax sent to the Marine Corps SLD.

With the fax in hand, Punaro called the CSA and CLL, saying that this LL officer was no longer welcome liaising his staff on the Committee. His usefulness to Army LL, commensurate with his access to the Hill, was ended. The Army LL officer's major mistake was allowing the issue to become personal. On the Hill, today's opponent is tomorrow's ally. Agency liaisers engaging in personal criticisms damage the agency's reputation and its issue position. Marine LL personnel did not make this mistake.

Finally, on the issue of upward mobility, the Marine Corps LL team working the tank transfer issue are moving upward in their career track within the institution. Colonel Sattler, HLD, and Colonel Terry Paul, SLD, both were selected for command at the colonel level and are now both flag officers.[103] Colonel Sattler commanded one of the Marine Corps' seven combat regimental commands before being promoted to brigadier general and serving as an Assistant Division Commander at Camp Legeune. He is now a brigadier general in Washington. Paul was also promoted to flag rank and now is serving as the Legislative Assistant to the Commandant. The Legislative Assistant to the Commandant, Brigadier General Ryan, received his next star and orders to undertake career-enhancing operational duties overseas.

The Army's LL "tank transfer" team was less fortunate. Of the three LL lieutenant colonels in Army LL Programs Division assigned the tank issue that summer, only Lieutenant Colonel John Pack, who was given the issue temporarily after the reassignment of his predecessor, attended the National War College, was promoted to colonel, and successfully commanded at the brigade level a combat aviation brigade in Korea. A rising LL star with muddy boots, Pack was scheduled to return to Washington and serve as the Chief of Army Programs Division in Army LL. However, in 1998, he was interviewed by the Army's recently acquired civilian Deputy CLL, a former HASC MLA, and turned down for the position.[104] So much for experience. Pack's successor with the tank issue in 1994 retired from the Army in 1995. The Army Chief of Programs, reassigned from LL in July 1994, retired soon after, as did Major General Harrison, the former CLL in 1995.

ARMY CULTURE AT WORK?

This tank transfer case study is useful in demonstrating the impact of the Army-Hill patterns that were raised in interviews with Members and staff working with the two defense authorization committees. Three of five cultural dimensions discussed earlier seem to underlie the patterns in this case study and will be discussed below. The "obedient loyal servant" cultural dimension that is in response to civilian, largely executive branch direction is less relevant in that the Army position was consistent with the administration, OSD, and JCS positions. However, it would be culturally unimaginable to picture Army LL or its senior leadership openly liaising a position, as the Marine Corps did, that was opposed by all levels of its executive branch superiors. The other cultural dimension of risk aversion is not specifically manifest in this case study for reasons just discussed. However, the lack of proactive senior Army general officer engagement with the congressional audience (prior to and after the SASC mark) is to be expected from senior flag officers with little liaising experience— making the journey to the Hill appear to be an endeavor fraught with risk.

The Army's Internal Fixation at the Expense of External Focus

This cultural dimension helps explain why the Army made resisting the tank transfer efforts a priority without directing the requisite agency resources necessary to ensure victory. The Army was listening to its internal audience in a roles and missions environment that warned of Marine Corps desires to become a second land Army and to its National Guard audience whose interests the Army leadership felt compelled to protect. The Army's tendency to reward, practice, and be more skilled with internal rather than external [to Army] performance is reflected in the failure of Army senior flag officers to engage Members of the SASC prior to their mark-up of the FY 1995 Defense Authorization Bill, its inability to persuade JCS officials to be more personally engaged and visible on the issue, and its refusal to engage Rep. McHale or Senator Smith early once aware of their intended positions.

The Army's internal at the expense of external focus was a great disadvantage in developing messages attuned to a congressional audience. The Army message was complex and packaged for a more knowledgeable internal audience. Less effort was directed toward ensuring a message was understood, because of a naive or trusting arrogance that the merit of the Army's cause was self-evident, regardless of its complexity. The Marine Corps excelled at making a simple, straightforward case. Finally, internal focus impeded Army senior generals' ability to gauge accurately how its external message was received and hampered their ability to reassess courses of action attuned to fluid Hill developments.

The Army's Value of Teamwork and Recognition of Its Dependency on Other Services

This cultural dimension helps explain why a key Army senior flag officer would cooperate and oblige his Marine Corps counterpart with an official Army position that allowed the Marines to slip a scheduled commitment to participate in an Army-Marine Complementary Operations brief to HASC staffers. The Army general officer agreed on a Friday afternoon to a request from his Marine Corps peer; by Monday morning, he realized his gesture to the Marine Corps had reduced greatly any chance the joint brief would be given to the congressional audience that year. He was feeling manipulated by a fellow team member, and trust eroded. Not surprisingly, the official Army position against transfering additional tanks to the Marines was issued from that general's office that same Monday.

This sense of teamwork and recognized dependency also helps explain why many Army senior generals did not really oppose fellow professional Marines getting these few M1A1 tanks before the Army National Guard received them. Many active-duty Army officers seem to relate more closely with fellow active-duty Marine officers than they do with their Army Guard counterparts, seen by some as non-professional "weekend warriors."[105]

If the Army leadership had engaged at the highest level with senators by applying this "teamwork and dependency" dimension toward keeping faith with Army reserve components and the fragile Off-Site Agreement that was simultaneously before the HASC and SASC for approval, it might have found a message with resonance. Keeping faith with the Army National Guard was a genuine concern of the senior Army leadership in 1994.

The Army Senior Leaders' Narrow Path of Career Success

As discussed in the chapter on Army culture, experience counts and the current Army professional development of its most promising senior military leaders seems to be deficient in relation to other services in providing Washington experience and liaising skills conducive to building trusted relationships with Members and staff. The CSA and other senior Army general (non-LL) officers making decisions on this issue had far less experience in Washington and with Congress than their Marine Corps counterparts. General Mundy had 128 months of Washington experience before becoming Commandant compared to the 24 months of General Sullivan. The Army LL officers also had less experience and, unlike their Marine counterparts, were not considered the future stars of their service. Marine Corps officers of this case study had more experience and had been mentored by individuals with more experience, which collectively reinforces the logic and professional necessity of proactive engagement with external audiences.

In conclusion, the Army decided to "circle the wagons" on this issue without proactively directing its more valuable agency resources throughout the fight. Having won the first round in the HASC mark, it naively, trustingly, or arrogantly assumed all was well with its message on the tank transfer during the month prior to the SASC mark. The surprised and reactive stance to the SASC mark was a function of the turbulence in Army LL, a disengaged senior Army leadership prior to and after the SASC mark, and the lack of previous engagement and relationship building over time with Senators that put the Army leadership into a significant relationship deficit compared to the Marine Corps.

Finally, the lack of senior Army flag officer engagement was reflected in the leadership's surprise when the Army lost the issue in Conference. After LL reactively devised a legislative strategy following the SASC mark, it became evident to most observers that key components of the strategy were beginning to unravel. A more engaged Army leadership would have realized this firsthand and reassessed the situation to ensure that they were satisfied with: their participation in carrying the message or getting other actors involved, the political chits being expended, the bridges being burned with Members and staff, and opportunities being lost by fighting this issue to the end.

NOTES

1. In late spring 1993, the Army was reacting to a House congressional initiative that would put a key portion, the APA Program, of the JCS and OSD MRS recommendations on hold to consider redirecting mobility resources toward the Marine Corps' EMPF. This congressional effort was defeated in the full HASC mark-up of the FY 1994 Defense Authorization bill in the summer of 1993. See introduction to Chapter 1 for more on this issue.

2. These congressional reforms were designed to shift power from the individual service chiefs to the CJCS and the CINCs.

3. Conference Report S.2182, *The National Defense Authorization Act for Fiscal Year 1995* (Washington, DC: Government Printing Office, 1994), 19.

4. John Pack, *Tank Battles Along the Potomac: Jointness Listed as First Casualty* (paper, National War College, National Defense University, 1994), 2. Pack, an Army LL officer working Army programs, was assigned this issue in late May 1994 following the HASC mark-up. I have drawn extensively on his National War College paper in laying out the background and history of this conflict.

5. Michael O'Neal, "What Grand Theft Armor?" *Armed Forces Journal International* (August 1994), 26.

6. Conference Report H.R. 4481, *The National Defense Authorization Act for Fiscal Year 1989* (Washington, DC: Government Printing Office, 1989), 274. The Marines had proposed a purchase of only 14 M1A1s in the administration's budget request that year.

7. Justice P. White, "Tanks A Lot Army," *Armed Forces Journal International* (August 1994), 20.

8. For a clear discussion of the resource allocation process in the Department of Defense, see *Defense Requirements and Resource Allocation*, ed. William McNaught (Washington, DC: National Defense University Press, 1989), 44–160. Each year the military services and defense agencies prepare and forward program objective memoranda (POMs) on their proposed programs to the Secretary of Defense to conform with the strategy and guidance, both programmatic and fiscal, contained in the DOD Defense Guidance. The POM is a force and resource recommendation from the military service within specific fiscal guidance that includes rationale and risk assessment, and identifying POM major issues that must be resolved during the year of submission and contain required supporting data. These issues are consolidated by OSD and then reviewed and analyzed by teams with representation from JCS, the services, and OSD. Arguments are presented for and against the various alternatives on these issues, many with budgetary implications for a service. The Defense Resources Board, chaired by the Deputy Secretary of Defense, completes its review of programs with decisions on these POM issues and agreed-upon changes. The Deputy Secretary of Defense confirms these decisions by send-

ing out a Program Decision Memoranda (PDM) to the military services, other DOD components and OMB. PDMs are then used as the basis for making budget submissions.

9. White, "Tanks A Lot Army," 20.

10. These points about timely and willing Army support to the Marine Corps were reinforced in a prepared briefing for the Hill by Tim Muchmore, "Tanks in the US Armed Forces," congressional briefing, Washington, DC, June 20, 1994, 20.

11. Congress, HASC, *Hearings on National Defense Authorization Act for Fiscal Year 1993-H.R. 5006*, 102nd Cong., 2nd sess. (Washington, DC: Government Printing Office, 1992), 93–94.

12. High operating and maintenance costs of the older tanks and the inefficiency of maintaining two unlike fleets (M60 and M1) were given by the Commandant as reasons for retiring the M60A1s.

13. For the first perspective, see White, "Tanks A Lot Army," 23. The M1A1 Main Battle Tank is much heavier (67.5 tons) and incorporates a much larger footprint than the M60A1.

14. Pack, *Tank Battles Along the Potomac*, 4. See also Muchmore, "Tanks in the U.S. Armed Forces," 15.

15. General Accounting Office (GAO), *Warfighting Capability: Some Army Tanks Should Be Transferred to the Marine Corps* (Washington, DC: General Accounting Office, 1994), 12.

16. *DOD'S Mobility Requirements: Alternative Assumptions Could Affect Recommended Acquisition Plan* (Washington, DC: General Accounting Office, 1993), 4. The original congressional direction calling for a DOD MRS can be found in section 909 of the Fiscal Year 1991 National Defense Authorization Act.

17. GAO, *Warfighting Capability*, 9.

18. Skip Ash, "Strategy and Requirements on Proposed Tank Transfer to USMC," letter to the Assistant Secretary of Defense, July 5, 1994. Also note how the 90/3 number of tanks/ships that DOD turned down in 1992 and Congress rejected in 1993 compares to the 84 tanks/2 ships that resurfaced on the Senate side in its FY 1995 National Defense bill in 1994.

19. LTC Kathryn G. Carlson, Deputy Legislative Assistant to the CJCS, "Proposed Tank Transfer to USMC," letter to the Chairman of the Joint Chiefs Staff, May 2, 1994, cited in Pack, *Tank Battles Along the Potomac*, 6.

20. In an interview, Rep. McHale claimed to have exercised independent judgement without Marine Corps liaising influence and believed at times that "The Marine Corps senior leadership was not behind the effort [to stop the APA]. Some of the senior Marine Corps had accepted the choice [of APA]. General Carl E. Mundy, Jr., had made a promise and he kept it." The promise, according to Rep. McHale, was to live by an agreement made in the JCS that the Army would support the Marine Corps' attempt to keep its endstrength at 174,000 (rather than 159K in most planning scenarios) and the Marine Corps would support the APA for the Army. Clearly, however, three- and four-star Marine generals below General Mundy's level were seen frequently on the Hill espousing the need for an EMPF that GAO and other Marine proponents on the Hill were recommending as a cheaper alternative to the APA. These visits stopped after General Powell's directive but were evident on a lower scale up until the final HASC mark. A Marine Corps LL officer liaising undecided Members during the HASC mark was witnessed by JCS LL personnel in attendance.

21. GAO, *Warfighting Capability*, 3.

22. The Army saw the Secretary of Defense's guidance validating the concept of Marine reliance on Army heavy armor support that reportedly worked so effectively in the Gulf War. Army proponents also noted that since there was no recommendation for increasing the number of MPS ships, that to take additional M1A1s (not counting the additional fueler trucks, maintenance assets, and ammunition carriers) onto the currently fully loaded MPS ships, critical equipment already on the ships would have to be removed. Bottom line, expanding the number of tanks raises anew the argument for expanding the number of MPS ships from 13 to 16 (a recommendation not adopted by the DOD MRS). The Marine Corps saw the direction to meet the requirement to retain enough tanks "to fill" three maritime pre-positioning squadrons as recognition it was short tanks. (It used to place 53 older M60A3 tanks per squadron, rather than the 30 M1A1 total it chose to load up with in 1992. The higher figure, in the Marines' thinking, comes closer to the requirement for filling an MPS squadron.)

23. O'Neal, "What Grand Theft Armor?", 26.

24. GAO, *Warfighting Capability*, 1–3.

25. Pack, *Tank Battles Along the Potomac*, 6.

26. This understanding was confirmed in a telephone interview with LTC Randy Kolton, special assistant to General Peay, CINC, Central Command, on December 13, 1995. Kolton had served as General Peay's speech writer in 1993 when Peay was the VCSA. A record of General Peay's thinking on this matter in March 1994 is confirmed in an e-mail letter from Colonel Michael O'Brien, Deputy Chief of [Army] Legislative Liaison to MG Jerry C. Harrison, [Army] CLL, copy provided to the author (subject: *Call from the VCSA*, March 28, 1994). In an e-mail letter from LTC Stephen Scroggs to MG Jerry C. Harrison (subject: SASC Observations, August 5, 1994). An SASC PSM made the comment that it would have helped the Army's case if General Peay had gotten the 50-tank deal with Boomer in writing to reign in the active lobby the Marines put on. The staffer was told by the author that it was a sad day for jointees when that became necessary between senior military leaders at the top level.

27. Pack, *Tank Battles Along the Potomac*, 7. He cites a letter by Anthony D. Echols to the Program Executive Officer for Armored Systems Modernization on Transfer of Tanks to USMC, dated December 22, 1993.

28. This information is recounted in an e-mail message from Colonel Michael O'Brien [Deputy CLL] to Colonel Jess Franco [Chief, Army LL Programs Division], "Army-Marine Corps Team Briefing," February 15, 1994, and an e-mail message from LTC Scroggs [Army LL] to MG Harrison [Army CLL], "Army/Marine Brief to Staffers," March 25, 1994. Additionally, see letter from LTC Muchmore, who worked under Colonel Pollard, to Colonel Franco on same subject, February 28, 1994. Additionally, specifics were communicated to me through conversations with Colonel Pollard, MG Garner, and my Marine Corps LL counterpart, Major Steve Hawkins.

29. See e-mail from LTC Scroggs to Colonel O'Brien, "Joint Army/Marine Brief," March 15, 1994.

30. GAO, *Warfighting Capability*, 10.

31. White, "Tanks A Lot Army," 24.

32. GAO, *Warfighting Capability*, 12.

33. E-mail from LTC Scroggs to MG Harrison, "Tanks for the Marines," March 25, 1995. The leadership was informed that Davis was scheduled to testify before the readiness subcommittee hearing in April.

34. Major Hawkins, Marine Corps LL, telephone interview by author, March 25, 1994. E-mail from LTC Scroggs to MG Harrison, "Army/Marine Brief to Staffers," March 25, 1994. Major Hawkins, who was working the issue, also emphasized that "LTG Ehlert did not say the brief would never happen, just that now is not the right time for such a brief." This was not easily explainable because the briefs had only been scheduled after the Marines' principal, MG Zinni, had given the green light. And, LTG Ehlert could not have been caught off guard on the initiative because he had participated in the meeting more than six weeks earlier where General Boomer, Vice Commandant of the Marine Corps, gave his approval for the pitch to the Hill.

35. Congress, HASC, *Readiness Subcommittee Hearings on Armed Services Readiness*, April 21, 1994.

36. GAO, *Warfighting Capability*, 4–5.

37. Lieutenant Colonel Steve Curry, "Strategy to Save Tanks in the HASC," letter to CLL, April 28, 1994, as cited in Pack, *Tank Battles Along the Potomac*, 9; and Army LL point/counterpoint information paper, May 5, 1994, concerning the question: *Should the Congress direct tanks be taken from the Army to the Marine Corps?*, delivered by Army LL to HASC Members, same date.

38. Rep. Montgomery (D-MS), letter to HASC Readiness Subcommittee Chairman Earl Hutto (D-FL), April 27, 1994: "I understand that our colleague, Paul McHale, will ask that such a provision [transfer Army M1A1 tanks to USMC] be included in your subcommittee mark-up. I strongly oppose such a transfer as I have expressed in my call to you."

39. MG Harrison, Army CLL, to Lieutenant General Bob Billings, Army Programs LL officer working the tank issue, April 28, 1994: "Thanks, spoke with [Rep.] McHale. He's going to work the tank issue unless we compromise with USMC on some # of tanks. Number is 0. No compromise."

40. General Gordon Sullivan, CSA, Department of the Army, letter to Chairman of the HASC Readiness Subcommittee Rep. Earl Hutto (D-FL), May 2, 1995.

41. General C.E. Mundy, Commandant of the Marine Corps, Department of the Navy, letter to Chairman of the HASC Readiness Subcommittee Rep. Earl Hutto (D-FL), May 2, 1995.

42. Rep. Paul McHale (D-PA), interview by author, September 7, 1995, Washington, DC.

43. Pack, *Tank Battles Along the Potomac*, 10.

44. Rep. McHale's amendment to H.R. 4301, *Transfer of M1A1 Tanks from the Army to the Marine Corps*, states: "The Secretary of the Army shall during fiscal years 1995 and 1996, transfer 132 M1A1 tanks to the Marine Corps, of which 84 shall be for the active component units and 48 shall be for the Marine Corps Reserve."

45. Honorable Gillespie V [Sonny] Montgomery, letter to Rep. Earl Hutto on Proposed Tank Transfer to USMC, May 3, 1994, as cited in Pack, *Tank Battles Along the Potomac*, 10.

46. Lieutenant Colonel Kathryn G. Carlson, Deputy Legislative Assistant to the Chairman, "Proposed Tank Transfer to USMC," letter to the CJCS, May 2, 1994.

47. Congress, House, Report 103–499, *National Defense Authorization Act for Fiscal Year 1995* (Washington, DC: Government Printing Office, 1994), 192.

48. "House Lawmakers Call or JCS to Study Viability of M1A1 Tank Transfer," *Inside the Army* 6, no. 19 (May 9, 1994), 14.

49. The SASC PSM inquiry was discussed in a May 16, 1994, Army Programs Division meeting. Besides May 17 e-mail traffic between LL officers at the lieutenant colonel and colonel level in Programs Division about the need for immediate engagement, there is no evidence that the SASC professional staff member inquiry was used by Army LL to galvanize Army senior flag officer engagement with SASC Members on the tank transfer issue.

50. Besides the amendment to give Army tanks to the Marines, the SASC mark contained three sealift amendments that did not support the MRS recommendations and appeared collectively to resemble the EMPF proposal the Marines offered as an alternative to the APA Program a year before to include: (1) deferring $600M funding (and thereby eliminating) contract options for the purchase of 2 Large Medium Speed Roll-On/Roll-Off (RO/ROs) ships (2) diverting $43M for Ready Reserve Force RO/ROs to a National Defense Features program and (3) funding two (of three) Marine maritime prepositioning ships not recommended in the MRS.

51. Congress, Senate, Report S.2182, *National Defense Authorization Act for Fiscal Year 1995* (Washington, DC: Government Printing Office, 1994), 247.

52. Pack, *Tank Battles Along the Potomac*, 12. His telephone interview with Senator Smith on June 20, 1994, captured this professed Member motive. It was supported by Tom Lankford, MLA for Senator Smith, interview by author, Washington, DC, June 6, 1995. Senator Smith was former Navy, but this does not appear to have prompted action on this particular issue.

53. Congress, Senate, Report S.2182, 50.

54. Ibid., 50.

55. See Jason Glashow, "Army Officials Accede to M1A1 Shift: Value of Upgraded M1A2s Outweighs Concern Over Giving Tanks to Marines," *Defense News*, August 1–7, 3. The Army recognized that the M1A2 upgrade proposal (section 112), would shore up the Army's tank upgrade program, which had taken a "$300M hit in the Army's POM, the service's six-year budget plan. The POM cut, according to officials at General Dynamics Land Systems Division, Sterling Heights, Michigan, would reduce tank production from 120 units a year to 70, dramatically increase the price and threaten to drive lower-tier subcontractors from the tank business." However, the Army and Pentagon still opposed Sen. Smith's transfer proposal.

56. Pack, *Tank Battles Along the Potomac*, 13.

57. M1A1 "common" tanks include special equipment packages for fording (which the Marines value), the Position Location Reporting System (PLRS), and the Muzzle Reference System not found on other M1A1s. See Pack, *Tank Battles Along the Potomac*, 13–14, where he cites Bob Gahagan, "Proposed Tank Transfer to USMC," letter to VCSA of the Army, June 3, 1994.

58. Pack, *Tank Battles Along the Potomac*, 14. He cites LTC Curry, Army LL Programs Division Team Chief, "Proposed Tank Transfer to USMC," letter to CLL, June 17, 1994.

59. Ibid., 14. He cites Charlie Smith, interview by Pack, June 21, 1994, Washington, DC.

60. Ibid., 14. He cites LTC Kathryn G. Carlson, interview by Pack, June 10, 1994, Washington, DC.

61. Colonel Thomas F. Giaconda, Legislative Assistant to the CJCA, interview by author, June 17, 1994, Washington. The author, serving in Army LL, conferred with the JCS LL on the 24-star letter and the three Secretary letters that expressed concern on

the SASC sealift provisions. General Mundy refused to sign the 24-star letter and presumably convinced the Secretary of the Navy not to support the Secretary letter. The CJCS subsequently signed the letter and sent it to the Hill prior to the floor debate on the sealift provisions.

62. Pack, *Tank Battles Along the Potomac*, 15. Based on comments from Major General Jay Garner, interview by LTC John Pack following the exchange, June 28, 1994, Washington, DC. Also based on interviews by author with Tom Lankford, MLA to Senator Smith and MG Garner.

63. Executive Office of the President, *Statement of Administration Policy*, June 23, 1994, 3.

64. Department of Defense, *Defense Appeal to Fiscal Year 1995 Defense Authorization Bill*, June 30, 1994.

65. A month earlier, the basis of Rep. Montgomery's (D-MS) strong protest of Marine lobbying out of their HLD was his incorrect belief that the CJCS had written a letter against the tank transfer to the Hill.

66. Pack, *Tank Battles Along the Potomac*, 16. He cites C-span video, U.S. Senate, July 1, 1994.

67. Some Army interviewees believed that Senator Smith came close to making a tactical error by asking for a recorded vote because the amendment would be seen as anti-Guard and lose support. They contend Senator Nunn recognized this danger and his quick action was a critical event for the tank transfer effort. Senator Smith's proponents claim Smith knew he had the needed votes and was doing what all Members do to strengthen their position for Conference. They contend Nunn only wanted to avoid additional time and get the bill off the floor.

68. Ibid., 16. Colonel Jess Franco, interview by LTC John Pack, July 1, 1994, Washington, DC. This accounting of events was confirmed by Colonel Jess Franco, interviews by author, September 22 and October 18, 1995, Washington, DC.

69. LTC Scroggs, "Full Conference Session," e-mail to MG Harrison, Army CLL, July 28, 1994. Also Al Bemis, MLA for Rep. Sonny Montgomery (D-MS), interview by author, September 15, 1995, Washington, DC.

70. LTC Scroggs, "Conference and the Tank Issue," e-mail to MG Jerry C. Harrison, August, 2, 1994. This correspondence demonstrates how the Senate conferees were successful in holding the tank transfer issue off to the side rather than resolving it early allowing it to hang in the balance juxtaposed to other issues they believed the House wanted more. "Word from the Hill today seems to point that the House is weakening in its resolve to resist the Senate position on the tank issue. The pressure of time seems to be our [Army] nemesis more than ally it seems. Montgomery's folks are having 'one-time only tank transfer' language drafted that reflects this weakening mood."

71. Pack, *Tank Battles Along the Potomac*, 17.

72. Congressional staff, #4, interview by author, 1995.

73. The Army was advised early in June by Les Brownlee and others that the Senate, being more insulated from Guard pressure, would not be persuaded by the Guard argument. However, the active Army and the Army National Guard refreshingly found themselves allies rather than adversaries on a salient Hill initiative. Additionally, because the SASC provision was a transfer of equipment rather than a procurement or jobs type of issue with the Hill, it was difficult to reactively and quickly find a champion that was not doing so as a representative of Army National Guard interests.

74. Senior military officer, #55, interview by author, June 1, 1995, Washington, DC.

75. Tom Lankford, MLA for Senator Smith (R-NH), interview by author, June 6, 1995, Washington, DC.

76. Ibid.

77. Ibid.

78. Lankford went on to add that "It wouldn't have mattered if the Army–Senator Smith relationship had been better." While this may be true, it would be hard for the MLA to say otherwise in 1995—after explaining the Senator's position was based solely on doing the right thing. The important point is the Army's relative (to the Marine Corps') poor outreach effort and disengaged relationship with the Senator's primary defense issue advisor did not help the Army's case with the Senator on this issue.

79. Congressional staff, #38, interview by author, May 18, 1995, Washington, DC.

80. Although other services come close to having senior flag officers engage all Members prior to the mark, the Army could have targeted select senators from the full Committee and all Members of the subcommittee that addressed the tank transfer language.

81. Although it is best not to begin relationship building when asking for help, ignoring a Member's position on the Committee when a concern arises is not prudent.

82. MG Harrison, interview by author, November 14, 1995, Washington, DC.

83. Congressional staff, #23, interview by author, April 10, 1995, Washington, DC.

84. Norman Augustine, former Under Secretary of the Army and CEO of Lockheed Martin, interview by author, Washington, DC, July 5, 1995.

85. Rep. Paul McHale (D-PA), interview by author, September 7, 1995, Washington, DC.

86. Rep. McHale's pro-defense voting record is juxtaposed with a deep suspicion, as a former Marine, of the Army's post–Cold War institutional vision for the future. He is suspicious of the Army's CONUS (continental United States)-based power projection doctrine that he believes moves the Army "into ground previously occupied by the Marine Corps." He views the Army's CONUS-based power projection, early entry capability as being too similar and threatening to the Marine Corps' enabling force role. There is a possibility that if the Army's top senior leadership had seriously engaged McHale in 1993 and 1994, and stressed Army-Marine Corps complementary operations, the Army-Marine Corps battles on the Hill might have been avoided. The lack of senior Army leadership engagement reinforced his suspicions and did nothing to diffuse the Army-Marine Corps tensions on the Hill.

87. Ibid.

88. The most senior Army flag officer to meet with Senator Smith on the tank transfer issue was MG Harrison.

89. Tom Lankford, Military Legislative Assistant for Senator Smith (R-NH), interview by author, June 6, 1995, Washington, DC.

90. Congressional staff, #82, interview by author, May 8, 1995, Washington, DC.

91. Senior flag officer, #56, interview by author as LL officer, September 1994, Washington, DC.

92. Senior flag officer, #57, interview by author, December 22, 1995, Washington, DC.

93. Congressional PSM SASC, #70, SASC, interview by author, March 24, 1995, Washington, DC.

94. Tom Lankford, interview.

95. Senior military officer, #11, interview by author, November 15, 1995, Washington, DC.

96. See Senate Report 99–280, *Department of Defense Reorganization Act of 1986* (Washington, DC: Government Printing Office, 1986), 52. In this Act, Congress directed that the Chairman would be responsible for: "Advising the Secretary (of Defense) on the extent to which the program recommendations and budget proposal of the military departments and other components of the Department of Defense for a fiscal year conform with the priorities established in strategic plans and with the priority requirements of the unified and specified combatant commands."

97. See House Report, *Hearing Before the Committee on Armed Services* (Washington, DC: Government Printing Office, 1993), II-6. Additionally, the principle of the Army providing heavy armor support to the Marine Corps when needed "rather than the Marine Corps becoming a second and equal land force" was expressed by the CJCS in a congressionally required Roles and Missions report in 1993.

98. For example, it was SASC members who have entertained ideas of creating a commission similar to the BRAC Commission that would remove much of the politics from the necessary task of reducing National Guard force structure. As stated before, the Senate, with its longer terms of service and larger constituencies, is more insulated from direct Guard pressure.

99. Rep. McHale (D-PA), interview.

100. Congressional MLA, SASC, #29, interview by author, March 27, 1995, Washington, DC.

101. LTC Scroggs, "Re: SASC Observations," e-mail to LTC Pack (copy to MG Harrison), August 5, 1994.

102. One lieutenant colonel was reassigned after the HASC mark-up. Another lieutenant colonel working aviation program issues immediately picked up responsibility prior to the SASC mark. In July, before Conference, primary tank issue responsibility had been passed to still another lieutenant colonel who was newly arrived to Army LL Programs Division. Losing the first officer just prior to the SASC mark was a significant setback for the Army LL effort. With a two-phase strategy (Senate floor and Conference) that was only half complete and looking bleak, the Army reassigned the Chief of Army LL Programs Division, approximately 30 days later and just one month prior to Conference. This untimely move did not enhance Army prospects for success in conference deliberations.

103. Both Marine LL officers were promoted to colonel after spending several years in these two lieutenant colonel LL positions. They were doing such an outstanding job for Marine LL they were kept in those positions as colonels.

104. The Army Deputy CLL position use to be an Army brigadier general slot before being down graded to a Colonel authorization slot in the 1980's. Several years ago, former Secretary of the Army Togo West urged that this position be made into a civilian position, a circumstance not found in any of the other service LL's Deputy CLL positions. The Army leadership did not oppose this change nor the recommended HNSC MLA being recommended for the position. It is the author's strong belief that this position should be reverted back to a Brigadier General slot (see Chapter 6 recommendations).

105. This cultural bias and distrust among the Army components were recognized and overcome in negotiating the 1994 off-site agreement and selling it to Congress. This case study of recognized Army culture that was supported on the Hill was addressed in Scrogg's unpublished 1996 Ph.D. dissertation.

Chapter 6

Findings and Recommendations

The unique function of leadership that distinguishes it from management and administration is this concern for culture. Leaders create culture and . . . must manage and sometimes change culture.[1]

—Edgar H. Schein

GENERAL CONCLUSIONS

This research draws four general conclusions.

- Despite the existence of statutory law prohibiting "lobbying" of Congress by public agencies, liaising is viewed by the congressional audience not only as a legitimate activity, but as essential to Members carrying out their constitutional responsibilities.
- Relative to the other services, the Army is viewed as the least effective in conducting this representational activity and supporting it with the service's more valuable agency resources.
- The Army's less-than-rational (in the eyes of the congressional audience) patterned approach with Congress is a function of unmanaged Army culture.
- The impact of culture on the Army leadership's ability and willingness to represent its institutional interests effectively to Congress has troubling implications for the nation's security interests in the uncertain and still dangerous post–Cold War world.

Liaising Is Viewed by Congress as a Legitimate and Crucial Professional Activity Expected of Senior Flag Officers

Research supports earlier studies demonstrating that liaising activity is viewed by Members as legitimate and essential to their ability to carry out their constitutional responsibilities. Congress has limited and, in the process, defined the boundaries of permissible public agency lobbying or liaising through formal and, most importantly, informal means. The *formal* limitations include the Anti-Lobbying Act, related appropriation provisions, and legal interpretations that serve to caution public agency liaisers against promoting grassroots pressures on Members and providing financial support to their campaigns. The more significant *informal* restraints on LL officers and senior flag liaisers are centered around closely guarded congressional norms and needs that include restrictions against overly crude styles of agency liaising, attempts to limit or control congressional ties back to the agencies, and a clear extra-legal prohibition against liaising its appropriators.[2] Together they allow norm-conscious public agency liaisers to liaise Members and staff directly and proactively, but also warn them to avoid any perception of grassroots pressure on Members. These formal and informal limitations send a somewhat ambivalent signal that agency pressure will be monitored by Congress but that agency efforts to proactively provide information to Congress are not only acceptable but essential to our constitutionally based government. Members consistently voiced their desire for military liaisers to collaborate with them in shaping policy and to advocate military service positions in a candid and proactive manner.

Research also showed that the congressional audience values the presence, engagement, and advice of senior flag officers of the military services in this liaising capacity. More than their partisan and usually less technically competent political-appointee superiors, military flag officers are seen as valuable sources of accurate, reliable information and the more professional and long-term stewards of the public institutions they represent. Members also value personal and working relationships with bright, fast-track warrior-type officers that evolve into a trusted channel of frank and informative exchanges on service, defense, and congressional issues. Senior flag officers may not be the best liaisers to respond to a specific or narrow Member inquiry, but they are viewed by both Hill and Army interviewees as the most effective for providing Members with big-picture assessments and personal professional judgments on issues, when asked. With declining military experience in Congress and an increasing post–Cold War focus on domestic concerns, Members on the HNSC stressed that the nation's security interests require more rather than less liaising from the services' flag officers, to help them make a more convincing case to the larger congressional audience for directing sufficient resources toward the defense budget in these uncertain times.

The Army Is the Least Effective of the Services in Conducting and Supporting Liaising

This study showed that the Army is viewed by the congressional audience as the least effective of the four services in representing its interests on the Hill. On the basis of over 80 interviews with Members and their personal and Committee staff associated with the House National Security and SASC, this study identified seven perceived patterns of Army-Congress behavior. Except for the first pattern, where the congressional interviewees judged the Army to be the most honest, straightforward, and credible of the four services in reacting and responding to Congress, congressional interviewees identified the Army as the least effective of the four services in six other important representational and liaising areas.

First, congressional interviewees perceive the Army senior leaders, more than the other services, as uncomfortable or wary of working with Congress in shaping Army and defense policy, and as seeing this activity as a burden to bear rather than an opportunity to engage. Congress is viewed more as an adversary than as part of a team. Congressional sources generally attribute this discomfort to a lack of understanding and appreciation of Congress's constitutional role in defense policymaking. The Marine Corps, followed closely by the Navy (on fiscal year programmatic/policy concerns), is perceived to be the best at making the Congress feel like team players and seeking opportunities to collaborate with the Hill at the highest levels in shaping policy.

Second, congressional interlocutors believed senior Army general officers to be the least of the services represented and engaged on the Hill. Given congressional views, these military leaders have an extraordinary advantage in communicating their message and developing relationships on the Hill because of their perceived ''warrior'' experience, professionalism, and objectivity. Failure to use this resource effectively is viewed as a missed opportunity. The Navy and the Marine Corps once again set the standard for their allocation of this valuable agency resource on the Hill, according to interviews.

Third, congressional interviewees judged the Army to be more reactive and less proactive than the other services in representing its institutional interests to Congress. Stressing the importance of proactive engagement, providing the congressional audience unsolicited information to carry out their responsibilities, and balancing the representational efforts of other services, congressional interlocutors believed this pattern has resulted in damaging surprises for the Army and in the lack of ''islands of competency'' relationships on the Hill to counter adverse situations effectively when they arise. The M1A1 case study dramatized both these problems. Most of the interviewees viewed the Marine Corps and Navy as the best in strategically planning how to get what they want from Congress, with the Air Force placing in a not-too-distant third. On the other hand, in areas that require a service to react or respond to congressional inquiries, such as constituent casework on military personnel, the Army was perceived as the best service.

Fourth, the Army's outreach efforts to Congress were also evaluated by Congress to be the least apparent and sophisticated of the military services. Specifically, according to congressional interviews, this problem was largely the result of senior Army generals who rely too heavily on the same small, established group of Members and appear to discount, relative to the other services, the importance of other Members without direct Army (service) ties, and of congressional staff. The other services, most notably the Marine Corps and the Navy, cast a wide Member and staff net and are more persistent in reaching new contacts, often at the beginning of their careers, and nurturing these relationships over time. These services do not view these efforts as matters just for their LL team.

Fifth, the Army was perceived as the least effective in communicating both its near- and long-term priorities, as well as the broader rationale for its size and its mission capabilities. The congressional audience said they were often confused about the priorities of the Army's senior military leadership and the extent to which they would fight for certain Army programs or positions. The descriptions of the Army message as murky, complicated, odd, and usually suited for internal rather than external Hill audiences place the Army at a distinct disadvantage, relative to the other services, which the congressional interviewees judged to be superior to the Army but relatively equal to one another in their ability to convey service priorities and larger long-term "relevancy."

Sixth, congressional interviewees see the Army personnel policies regarding its LL officers, which do not place the most promising combat arms officers in this area and do not take advantage of the skills of those who do work there by promoting them within the institution, as a clear sign that the Army does not assign the same importance to relations with Congress as other services do. The knowledge, skills, and relationships with Congress are rewarded by the other services because these are seen as crucial elements of a service's effectiveness with Congress, *an advantage the Army has denied itself.*

Collectively, these patterns show that despite the foundation of good liaising that comes with its reputation as most honest and straightforward, the other Army–Hill patterns work against the formation of close and trusted working relationships between the elite of the two institutions, relationships that are more evident in the other services, and the lack of which undercuts the ability of the Army to gain the congressional support necessary for promoting its interests and balancing those of the other services. While these patterns are a snapshot of recent behavior and relevant only in relation to the perceived behavior of the other military services, they are important to those who are interested in the military's long-standing interservice competition for resources, roles, and missions in Washington.

Both congressional and Army interviewees made the point that these problematic Army–Hill patterns are associated with Army officers who, as a service group, have the least appreciation and understanding of the unique role and vital perspective Congress provides in shaping Army and defense policy. This lack of understanding taints the Army leadership's view of the Washington policy-making process, affects how they view congressional interest in shaping Army policy, and increases Army flag officer reluctance to work proactively with Congress in putting the Hill's imprint on Army policy and programs.

The study demonstrates that Army senior officers tend to discount more than the other services the appropriateness and importance of the liaising activity that best serves Members' constitutionally based role in defense policy. This is reflected in the Army's tendency, relative to the other services, to direct its most valuable agency resources away from areas and activities that would enhance its liaising activity with Congress. Examples of valuable agency resource misallocations include: limited general officer time and energies spent on the Hill; disincentives for the most competitive Army combat arms officers to acquire significant experience in Washington and in LL and other external audience assignments; relatively little in officer military education curriculum on understanding the important role of Congress; Army LL offices collocated on the Hill that stay clear of Army programmatic issues with defense committee MLAs; and a lack of orientation travel and social gathering opportunities for MLA outreach.

Frustrated Members and staff on the Hill who want closer relations but are not engaged by senior Army officers as team players made the following points: Participating in the policymaking process and dealing with Congress appear not to be options for the Army. Doing both effectively appear to be options the Army leadership chooses not to pursue. The perception is a more disengaged, less proactive, and less personal Army leadership approach in communicating and informing Members and staff. Congressional observers compare this with other services' aggressive strategies to maximize agency resources in the Washington environment to garner institutional funding and political support. Their conclusion was that they receive information from other services earlier, more frequently, and with greater participation by flag officers.

Interviews with both congressional and Army people indicated consensus that Members and staff are less knowledgeable about Army requirements, capabilities, and the rationale for a power projection Army in the post–Cold War era. What is confusing to Army congressional supporters is that they know, and they know Army leaders are aware, that the congressional audience is less knowledgeable on Army issues; yet, unlike the other services, Army flag officers do not appear to see it as their personal and professional responsibility to ensure this constitutionally empowered civilian audience understands "Why an Army?" and "Why this type." Instead, the Hill audience sees a discounted Army LL team used as a "crutch" and hopelessly attempting to fill that Army flag officer void. Greatly enhanced general officer engagement, with a clear and persuasive message, is seen as essential.

The Army's Less-Effective Liaising Approach Is Shaped by Unrecognized and Uncompensated Army Culture

This study has made the point that despite having a more complicated message and lacking structural advantages conducive to obtaining congressional support possessed by the other services, the Army continues a more disengaged and baseline liaising approach with Congress, compared to the other services. It posits that it is Army culture—largely unrecognized, unmanaged, or unchanged—that primarily impedes today's Army senior military leadership in its efforts to more effectively represent Army interests in Washington. This culture predisposes the way the Army liaises and explains the "routine, largely unexamined options" Army leaders adopt in this important activity that appear odd to congressional and other external audiences. This culture sets boundaries on permissible behavior, labels and often stigmatizes activity that cannot or should not be done, and becomes a prescription lens through which problems are viewed and addressed by the leadership and those more junior who desire to succeed within the organization.

From candid "insider" interviews with some of the most accomplished and respected senior Army general officers, this study identified five cultural dimensions that undergird the Army's less rational and effective approach to Congress relative to the other services, and helps explain why the Army directs its most valuable agency resources away from engaging external audiences like Congress in a more proactive way.[3] These individuals are uniquely qualified and knowledgeable of shared basic assumptions and values that Army officers tend to adopt in order to succeed.

The most important cultural dimension undergirding the Army–Hill patterns is that the Army, more than the other services, focuses on and rewards internal rather than external performance and communications. It looks inward to address and resolve the challenges of maintaining or improving its professional warfighting competence. In this context, inward focus relates to the institutional efforts initiated by its top leaders in activities directly related to warfighting competence, combat readiness, and doctrine. This internal focus is viewed by Army military leaders as a characteristic, a prerequisite, and an identifier of Army professionalism, and also as essential to the ability to fight and win the nation's wars.

The Army and its senior military leaders will likely continue, as professionals, to fixate internally at the expense of more effective relations with external audiences as long as they:

- Are without Secretaries of the Army who will emphasize and inculcate the importance of senior general officers' professional role in carrying the Army message to the Hill and general public.[4]

- View the "merit of the Army cause to be self-evident" rather than a cause or position that must be honestly *and* skillfully advocated to civilian decision makers on the Hill.

- Allow an inflated opinion of their "professional" Army solutions to diminish the importance of collecting and using empirical data and simple analysis to justify positions to external audiences.

- Continue to discount the importance of skills and experience that come from assignments working directly with Congress and other external audiences.

• Continue to evaluate their effectiveness with these external audiences by only comparing their actions and approach with those of other Army generals rather than with their counterparts in the other services.

The second most important cultural dimension is manifest in the discomfort the Army—which places high value on team work and interdependency among the services—experiences in self-promotion of its interests at the possible expense of other services. To lead successfully as a professional Army officer on the field of land battle requires teamwork and dependency on other members of the team, including sister services. To promote or advocate one part of the team in a zero-sum fashion to Congress, who are seen as relative outsiders, is frowned upon by Army leaders as unprofessional and parochial behavior. This contrasts with other services that believe in and advocate their independent service capabilities.

Another strong cultural bias undercutting Army-Hill relations is a widely shared assumption that career success for combat arms officers is defined narrowly as being outside Washington and inside the officer's branch or specialty, an assumption that works to reduce the Pentagon experience senior flag officers possess before serving in key positions on the Army staff and the appeal for aspiring combat arms officers to seek Pentagon assignments at the field-grade officer level.

This study provides supporting statistical data that demonstrate that the Army, relative to the other services, is not grooming its senior leadership with experience in Washington and the Pentagon. Data comparing the "Pentagon experience" across all four services' leadership samples rank the senior Army military leadership a distant last among the services in cumulative time spent serving in the Washington community prior to assuming those key leadership positions. In the best case, the Army staff leadership in this small but influential sample has to overcome six years of cumulative Washington experience merely to match the corresponding experience level of the next lowest service, the Marine Corps, and has just over half the combined experience of their Air Force counterparts (almost 15 years less experience).[5]

Army military leaders' perception of themselves as the nation's "obedient loyal servant"[6] or "obedient handyman," which entails a dutiful can-do obedience in making "virtue out of necessity" (even if these actions are antithetical to Army institutional interests), is another cultural dimension that works against Army policy collaboration with and advocacy of its interests to Congress.

Tracing the different post–Civil War experiences of the Army and Navy with regard to the notion of subservience to civilian, especially executive branch, control, this study suggests that the Army placed a greater premium on the need to perform without question a variety of dirty or "handyman" tasks that the executive branch so directed.[7] The Navy, however, socialized its officers to question executive branch directives they viewed as antithetical to fundamental Navy, and in their view, national interests.[8] In today's environment, this Army cultural norm can inhibit overall service advocacy of its interests and general officer candor about the true requirements and capabilities important to the security needs of the nation. It works against Army uniformed leadership taking battles they have lost with their executive branch superiors across the Potomac River to Congress, a constraint that other services, such as the Marines, do not share to the same degree. The result is a Congress that may have less understanding of Army requirements relative to the other services. One can also argue that this cultural norm, apparent to many on the Hill, makes it more likely that OSD officials may be tempted to make cuts in Army, rather than other service programs or funding, because there is considerably less likelihood of a service-generated backlash from the Hill to this executive branch decision.

Candid interviews by senior Army general officers identified a fifth cultural dimension that undergirds many of the Army–Hill patterns: a risk-averse senior officer corps, the result of a professional development system that has little tolerance for mavericks or officers who question the institutional status quo in peacetime. The nature of civilian control over the military implies that engagement and possible missteps with powerful external audiences like Members of Congress may have an adverse effect on the upward mobility of senior military flag officers. This is particularly true because the lack of actual Washington/congressional experience and an ingrained wariness of Congress (discussed earlier) increase both the real and perceived risk of dealing with Congress. The fear of failure inhibits greater general officer engagement on the Hill.

The Army's internal focus keeps it from addressing the more effective way the other services do business with Congress and other external audiences. Rather than comparing the Washington/Pentagon experience provided Army senior flag officers with that provided their counterparts in the other services, at best the Army compares the Pentagon experience of its senior Pentagon leadership against other less experienced Army generals outside the Beltway. A CSA may compare his performance on frequency of visits to the Hill with that of his predecessors, but not with his sister service counterparts.

Recognizing and addressing upfront the cultural dimensions identified in this study are prerequisites for any long-term remedy in improving Army–Hill relations and enhancing Army effectiveness in the nation's capital. Until this occurs, the Army military leadership is prone to naively (or arrogantly) view the merit of the Army cause to be self-evident rather than a position to be honestly but skillfully advocated by its most experienced liaisers to civilian decision makers on the Hill. Both congressional and Army senior flag interviews stressed that the other services have established "leadership" career paths that are more attuned to developing the liaising competencies needed in their senior officers at these higher levels. Many senior Army generals believe the "muddy boots can do all" dimension has deprived a generation of Army officers and future Army leaders of the necessary socialization in the "art of liaising."

Most generals did not call for a fundamental change in Army culture because they recognize the importance of values of teamwork, obedience, and internal (doctrinal) competence to Army success in battle. However, they believe these dimensions should be recognized and compensated for in relations with Congress to avoid impeding the effective institutional advocacy required of general officers operating within the unique terrain of the nation's capital.

Dangerous Implications of Unrecognized Culture on the Nation's Security Interests

This study provides an example of the problems, highlighted by James Madison, of factional self-interest in a free society. According to Madison, the deleterious ''mischiefs of faction'' are contained by pitting ''ambition'' against ''ambition'' in a continual battle of countervailing selfish interests. Madison therefore favored a setting that allowed for the largest, most effective, and widest variety of factional competition to prevent any one narrow factional interest (military service) from gaining a position of dominance in our government and society. With respect to the U.S. Armed Forces, the assumption is that not only is the playing field on which the various military services approach Congress a level one, but also that each service is equally equipped to, and capable of, liaising its interests. This study has demonstrated, given the Army's cultural proclivities and less effective congressional relationship, that this is an incorrect assumption that has serious consequences in the post–Cold War world.

Many Members and staff made the point that they and their peers do not understand the Army's larger ''relevancy'' message for this new, uncertain era and probably inflate the meaning of ''adequate'' when they hear Army senior leaders use it to describe their resourcing requirements reflected in budget requests to the Hill. Most on the Hill are expecting more from the Army (outputs) than is realistic, considering the inputs the Congress is investing. However, no one from the Army is telling them that they are on or over the razor's edge, or asking Congress to address these problems.

It is too difficult for Army senior flag officers to say they cannot do something and they see it as their professional duty to make a size 10 foot fit in a size 7 shoe. The Army's can-do attitude has worked against the Congress's fully appreciating the Army's stretched but extremely capable potential. Senior Army generals repeatedly made the point that a decade ago a buffer existed in all service budgets that allowed an Army chief to salute and go back to the drawing board to find other bill payers for needed requirements. There is no more buffer, but the reinforcing culture and patterned behavior work against that being communicated to the civilian decision makers on the Hill who have the constitutional authority to do something about it.

This could have serious consequences if one believes many of the Army's institutional interests go hand-in-hand with the nation's security interests. There are compelling rationales for maintaining and even increasing the Army's roles and resources, independently and vis-à-vis the other services, both within the Army and in many academic/think tank communities. It is not the domain of this study to evaluate these arguments, but it does become clear that, if the other services are expending greater and more valuable agency resources to present their perspectives to the congressional audience, the requirements of balanced and well-informed policymaking require the Army to do the same. Army institutional interests are too important for the nation's security not to be presented to the congressional audience in a manner that they can understand and thoughtfully balance with those of the other services.

This study cautions against making the assumption that senior Army generals are prepared and willing to engage the Congress on the same congressional field of play as their counterparts in the other services. Instead, the task of ensuring that the congressional audience understands Army interests is being left either in the Army locker room or to be communicated by its willing but less able and resourced second-string team (the LL staff). This critical representational game upon which the nation depends is naturally being lost.

The Army's Problem Isn't on the Hill but in the Pentagon

One respected senior Army general officer disagreed with this study's thesis. He told me he believed the Army was successful on the Hill and in its relations with Congress, and stated there was much myth in this subject that tends to perpetuate itself. He instead believed the Army's principal failure was tied to resource allocation and lost battles within the DOD:

The most critical resource battle is not the legislative cycle on the Hill. That is worked on the margins. Nothing really provocative happens. A Member adds a small amount here and there based on Member interests, but it is largely tinkering on the margins. The real problem for the Army is its relations with DOD [Department of Defense].

The resource allocation in DOD has been one that has troubled me for my period here because I feel the fiscal guidance and the apportion for the U.S. Army is under funded by a fairly significant margin. I attributed that in the Reagan and Bush years to the strong emphasis on strategic versus conventional systems. I thought after the fall of the Berlin Wall and the USSR, after the revised National Military Strategy and the increased OP-TEMPO [operational tempo] of conventional forces, that I would see a shift from strategic to conventional, not for the parochial point of view, but because the National Military Strategy would implicate a shift. I'll be candid with you, that shift has not occurred nor does it look like it's going to occur. I think that is an error and a fundamental flaw in the fiscal guidance in the DOD.

In spite of the strongest protestations of the Army's senior leadership, we have been unable to change the minds of those in the Office of Secretary of Defense [OSD]. I do not think it is a cultural thing about our ability to do that. I've had the senior leaders with their feet under the table with the SECDEF [Secretary of Defense] and the Dep-SecDef. We haven't solved that problem. I don't know that answer. But there is a huge bureaucracy at OSD that is key to the distribution of resources and is worked harder on a daily basis by the other Services. I'm persuaded of that. That is an area that is worthy of additional focus by the U.S. Army.

Am I organized for success within the Army Secretariat and ARSTAFF [Army Staff] for the Program Objective Memorandum battle?[9] I'm persuaded that I'm not. This problem has tentacles back to how I've been organized in the past and how I culturally go about my business in the Building [Pentagon].

This general's comments reflected a line of reasoning in the senior Army military leadership that infers the Army–Hill and the Army–DOD relationships are distinct and unconnected. However, it became clear while doing this research that the two are closely related, and an inadequate effort with Congress has a damaging impact on the ability of the Army to prevail in interservice contests within the DOD.

A more sophisticated, externally directed examination and agency resourcing of its relations with Congress are required if the Army is serious about improving its relationship and liaising ability within the DOD. Not only would the OSD receive more pressure from a better informed Congress, but in the process of educating Members and staff in Congress, future officials in the DOD would be educated and influenced. It is important to note that three of the last four Secretaries of Defense were sitting Members of Congress when they were appointed and confirmed. In addition, many congressional staff become senior officials in the Pentagon. The current Deputy Secretary of Defense, John Hamre, was earlier appointed and confirmed as DOD Comptroller from his position as a widely respected PSM on the SASC. Norm Augustine, a former Under Secretary of the Army in the Carter administration, made the point that over the years there has been an increasing trend of administrations selecting former congressional professional staff members to fill assistant secretary positions in the Pentagon.

It is a trend I began to notice back when I was serving as the Under Secretary [of the Army] back in the mid 70's, but one that you can see in spades today. I believe over time the attractiveness of serving in government as a whole has gone down. The increased problems of getting through confirmation hearings and the myriad of conflict of interests laws that make you practically unemployable afterwards, has made it a tougher task to get good folks from outside the government. As the Pentagon looked across the Potomac and began to realize where the dollars were, more and more you would see Assistant Secretaries be former staffers. These are folks with good reputations and excellent ties to the Hill.[10]

This long-term trend must not be lost on the Army leadership. Army–Hill and Army–DOD relationships are integrally linked in our constitutional system of shared powers. It appears the other services are more aware of the connection between their respective relations with the Congress and OSD.[11] For the Army, both relationships have significant problems and it is naive to assume one can be fixed without taking into account the other. Although it is beyond the scope of this study, it is possible that many of the cultural factors that impede Army effectiveness with Congress are also at work in impeding Army effectiveness within the Pentagon as well.

RECOMMENDATIONS

This section presents some brief preliminary recommendations that, if adopted, would begin to address the Army's inadequate liaising of its institutional interests to the congressional audience. The study recommendations cover four broad areas and in most cases advocate directing more valued Army resources toward its liaising efforts with the Hill. They suggest that the current Army senior military leadership should

- Dramatically increase its engagement with Congress.
- Begin to prepare future Army generals to serve more effectively in Washington.
- Strengthen the Army's LL operation.
- Provide a compelling rationale for enhanced congressional interaction using aspects of Army culture conducive to such engagement to combat aspects of Army culture which discourage it.

Current Army Senior Military Leaders Should Dramatically Increase Their Engagement with Congress

1. The Army senior military leadership must begin to evaluate their performance on the Hill by comparing Army policies, actions, and approach at all levels with the other military services and specifically their counterparts in the other services, rather than the typical type of internal comparisons made with other general officers Army-wide, or those made with their Army flag officer predecessor who occupied the same position.

2. In the short term, the Chief of Staff, the Vice Chief of Staff, and the primary three-star Deputy Chiefs of Staff of the Army should send a clear "lead by example" signal to other Army general officers by spending significantly more time engaging on the Hill. Otherwise, their urgings for more flag officer presence on the Hill will be seen as merely rhetoric rather than a course correction. The goal is more relationship-building visits throughout the legislative calendar, and more involvement of general officers at higher levels on critical issues during crunch (pre-mark or conference) periods.

- Army general officers should spend *more* time on the Hill in proactively developing relationships with Members and staff than they do in reactively addressing particular Members or Army concerns. They should strive to replicate the Admiral Boorda style of meeting with Members, that is, liaise even when no issue or "crisis" exists and walk the halls for "target of opportunity" drop-ins.
- Army general officers, at the highest possible level, should meet with Members and staff on important "potential crisis" issues prior to impending hearings and mark-ups

of legislation. They should not delay or delegate to Army staff subordinates or LL personnel Army engagement with the Hill on volatile and sensitive issues. Instead, they should use these subordinates for advice and to facilitate successful meetings on these issues between Army general officers and Members and staff.

• Army general officers should spend more time early in the process of developing Army policy in continuous dialogue with Members and staff who might be affected by the policy outcome and whose support for or, as a minimum, understanding of that Army policy solution will be needed. This will help the Hill better understand Army decisions and the currently masked "hard choices" Army leaders are making on primarily budgetary grounds.

3. The Chief and Vice Chief of Staff of the Army cannot carry the liaising ball by themselves. They should encourage and evaluate Army general officers on their ability and willingness to cultivate respected relationships on the Hill and in the Washington community.[12]

4. The Army senior military leadership should actively encourage and seek opportunities to get Army generals outside of Washington to walk the halls of Congress and meet with Members and staff.[13]

Prepare Future Army Generals to Serve More Effectively in Washington

1. The top Army military leadership must change future Army general officer behavior by communicating to the Army's officer corps, and especially within its combat arms officers, a different philosophy toward the Hill that highlights the requirement for a more sophisticated understanding of our Constitution and Congress's legitimate role in the nation's defense policymaking process.[14]

2. The senior Army leadership should use Washington/Pentagon experience as a major criterion in selecting general officers and assigning them to the Pentagon. Experience matters in all endeavors; future Army generals serving in Washington should have significant Washington/Pentagon experience prior to making flag rank.[15] The Pentagon operates differently at the field-grade rank; generals need that lower-level experience and perspective to understand better how to build coalitions of support.

3. Promotion and selection boards should be wary of rewarding fast-tracking combat arms officers with 19 or more years of service who have worked the system to avoid service in the nation's capital. Although they rationalize this track as symbolizing their true concern for soldiers, their lack of preparation for key competencies in the Pentagon that they will need as flag officers will not serve well the interests of those same soldiers.

4. The senior Army leadership should consciously set a better example for a watchful, younger Army officer corps on the importance of Congress's role in defense policymaking and of liaising the Army story with the Hill. This positive example should be evident in both intra-Army discussions about and personal

activities with the congressional audience. Within the Army's long-term legislative strategy campaign plan, it should institutionalize an annual legislative
battle drill (of events and actions to take) in synchrony with the generic legislative calendar that legitimizes the importance of liaising activity in the eyes of
the next generation's officer corps.

5. The link of public and congressional support with the welfare of the soldier
and our future Army capabilities should be made by the senior Army leadership
to its internal audience and serve as a consistently emphasized theme to officers
and soldiers in the field.[16]

6. The importance of communicating effectively to external (to the Army)
audiences should be an additional Officer Evaluation Report (OER) measure by
which all field-grade officers are evaluated, whether assigned to Fort Hood,
Texas, or Washington, DC.[17]

7. The senior Army leadership should consider instituting changes in its officer personnel management system that signify the importance of key liaising
and other "external audience" missions to the institution.

- The Army should consider creating a Washington "external audience" area alternate
  specialty which includes LL, public affairs, key fellowships, and assignments serving
  senior political leaders, in and out of the DOD, in the nation's capital. This alternate
  specialty would help prepare a small but certain percentage of future generals for
  service in key Washington leadership positions a decade from now.

- At a minimum, LL duties and positions should be assigned an "additional skill identifier" that would help Army leaders track and more effectively manage LL officer
  professional development.

- Consider acquiring approval to designate several LL positions as "joint" due to their
  involvement and close interaction with the other services and to provide an incentive
  for the most competitive combat arms officers to seek field-grade exposure to Capitol
  Hill.

8. The Army's institutional training and schooling should incorporate instruc-
tion about Congress, its legitimate role in shaping defense budgets and programs,
the status of the Army–Hill relationship, the importance of recognizing cultural
impediments to that relationship, and Army senior officer roles in informing and
working as team players with civilian decision makers in Congress. The importance of understanding the positive role of Congress in Army policy matters
must start at the Officer Basic Course level and get more specific and sophisticated at each higher level.[18]

Strengthen the Army's Legislative Liaison Operation

1. The Army should upgrade the position of the Deputy Chief of Legislative
Liaison back to its original one-star military grade position. This would send a
clear signal to the internal Army (and congressional) audience about the increas-

ing importance to the Army leadership of external, especially congressional audiences. It would also reduce intra-LL jurisdictional tensions at the division chief (colonel) level by having a flag officer, other than the chief of LL, to resolve "turf" disputes decisively, provide more continuity of LL leadership, and allow one of the two flag positions to be used as a Hill exposure assignment for an officer being groomed as a future chief or vice chief of staff. If this remains a civilian position, it is critical that the individual be clearly non-partisan, that the individual be knowledgeable of the Army, and possess a respected reputation for previous Army LL experience on the Hill, preferably at the Division Chief level or higher.

2. The Army's personnel management system must employ agency resources to transform a certain percentage of LL assignments into lucrative opportunities for upward mobility in the Army. Within the organization, two types of officers should be sought.

- A significant percentage of slots should be filled with officers who have the most competitive Army files, who are combat arms officers, and are likely to command at the brigade level. This will expose a sufficient number of future general officers to this important liaising activity that will serve to groom future CLLs and other more senior flag officer positions on the Army staff. In addition, the presence of combat arms officers, who have great credibility with congressional audiences based on their experiences, will enhance the strength of the Army message.

- The Army leadership should direct formal and informal agency resources to another, probably larger segment of officers, to induce the best and most personable LL-type officers to stay within the LL organization for longer periods of time than the one- or two-year "transition out of the Army" tour commonly observed today. They will be reservoirs of relationships at the LL-officer level and the "old guard" trainers for the fast-trackers who move in and out of the organization. Although they may not command at the battalion or brigade levels, the best should still have opportunities to attend the War College and make colonel.

3. The senior Army leadership should look for opportunities to boost, rather than weaken, the stature of its LL personnel in the eyes of the congressional audience. Promotions, command selections, the practice of always including LL personnel in Army-Hill meetings, and acknowledging their contributions openly would be noted and viewed positively by the congressional audience.[19]

4. The senior Army leadership should find new, efficient ways to streamline and more directly communicate with LL personnel working key issues on the Hill and who occupy key LL positions in the House and Senate operations. Currently, there is little direct communication between these officers and the senior Army leadership; that is not the case for the other services. While the direct Commandant-to-Marine LL operation on the Senate and House sides might need modification in accommodating the Army organization's larger size and complexity, it should serve as the goal by which new communication solutions are evaluated.

5. The senior Army leadership should make clear to all Army general officers that they should assist Army LL efforts to engage and elicit greater Member and staff participation in Army outreach events, whether trips to the NTC at Fort Irwin or a conference on Army technological or doctrinal advancements. An Army flag officer can enhance his relationship with and be the catalyst for Member participation if he makes the request and is willing to accompany the Member to this outreach event or devote significant time to a visiting delegation.

6. The senior Army leadership should devote greater resources to facilities that accommodate and transport congressional and other external audience visits to Army training and operational installations. For example, the small number of quarters to accommodate visitors at the NTC limits too severely the opportunity of the Hill to see Army "essence" and land power training on a large scale.

7. The senior Army leadership should consider implementing its own version of the Air Force Intern Program, which provides a career-enhancing opportunity for select captains (in their sixth or seventh year of commissioned service) to gain exposure to Air/Joint Staff experience. The 15- to 22-month program was designed to develop its most promising Air Force leaders, combining the experience as an intern in JCS/OSD/Air Staff and Secretariat with academic graduate courses in leadership and management. Interns will have the option of completing a Masters of Arts degree from George Washington University."[20] The Army program should include exposure to LL operations on the Hill.[21]

8. The senior Army leadership should be wary of Army officers "self-selecting" themselves into the Army LL organization by the mere fact that they were first accepted into a congressional or White House fellowship program. While these programs provide outstanding opportunities to better understand the legislative and executive branches of our government, respectively, there should be no assumption that participation in such programs makes them the Army's desired LL officers.[22] Army culture is responsible for the attitude that an Army congressional fellow who is subsequently reassigned to a troop or staff assignment outside of Washington, DC, is providing the Army and/or the Congress little or no benefit. Once again, Army senior leadership should look externally at the caliber and process by which the other services' LL officers are selected. They will see a concerted effort to expose a wider and more competitive segment of their officer corps, and thereby their military service, to the Hill that does not just center on fellowship programs.

Use Culture to Remedy Culture

The senior military leadership should conduct a much needed "Army value clarification" to determine how Army culture and ethos, represented in documents like Army document FM 100–1, *The Army*,[23] can be used to justify and encourage greater interaction with Congress. While there are aspects of Army culture discussed in this study which inhibit effective representation to Congress, there are other facets of Army culture, such as notions of duty, integrity, selfless service to the nation, commitment, competence, candor, and courage, that could be used to encourage more effective congressional relations. The senior Army leadership should make a compelling case for improving congressional relations utilizing these shared values that are pervasive, underlying tenets of Army culture and that work well for the Army out in the field environment.

NOTES

1. See Part Four in Edgar H. Schein, *Organizational Culture and Leadership*, 2nd ed. (San Francisco: Jossey Bass, 1992), 209, that addresses "The Role of Leadership in Building Culture."

2. Abraham Holtzman, *Legislative Liaison Executive Leadership in Congress* (Chicago: Rand McNally, 1970), 64–76. Holtzman's discussion of informal limitations imposed on executive lobbying is by far the best and appears, from my interviews and experience in working Army LL, to be accurate 25 years after the publication of his work.

3. My interview sample includes lengthy interviews with 24 active components Army general officers (12 four-star, 8 three-star, 3 two-star, and 1 one-star generals) that include five CSAs going back to 1976, several regional Commander-in-Chiefs, former CLLs, and Corps Commanders. One Marine three-star general officer was also interviewed. Additionally, I interviewed respected combat arms Army colonels on the Army and Joint Staffs who have served closely with and observed senior flag officer behavior toward Members and congressional staff. These interviews were reinforced by a few key interviews with Army senior civilian leadership: one Secretary of the Army, one Under Secretary of the Army, and one Deputy Assistant Secretary of the Army.

4. See Michael T. Isenberg, *Shield of the Republic* (New York: St. Martin's Press, 1993), 438, on the important role played by Secretary of the Navy Forrestal after World War II in turning the inward professional focus of the Navy's "flag plot" (naval flag officers) to one more comfortable with engaging external audiences and selling Navy interest as national interests.

5. See Chapter 4, Tables 4-1 and 4-2, as well as Appendix C. The leadership sample is a snapshot of each service in April 1995 (when most of the congressional and military interviews were conducted) that included four key positions that carry significant credibility on fundamental service issues with the Congress: the Chief of Staff (or equivalent) of the service, the Vice Chief of each service, the Deputy Chief of Staff for Operations and Plans or equivalent for a service, and the Chief or Director of Legislative Liaison (or equivalent) for each service.

6. Builder, *The Masks of War*, 20 and 30–34.

7. Huntington, The Soldier and the State, 261–262.

8. Navy reverence for tradition and independent command at sea, and its grander role of "enforcing the national will in foreign affairs" and serving as "the nation's first line of defense," further gelled Navy identity and how it viewed its interests. See also Isenberg, *Shield of the Republic*, 436, "If higher authority differed, then higher authority was usually seen as making a direct assault on the Navy's powerful, ingrained sense of self. Forced or unforced resignations had been the result . . . and they would happen again."

9. For a clear discussion of the resource allocation process in the Department of Defense, see *Defense Requirements and Resource Allocation*, ed. William McNaught (Washington, DC: National Defense University Press, 1989), 44–160. Each year the military services and defense agencies prepare and forward POMs on their proposed programs to the Secretary of Defense to conform with the strategy and guidance—both programmatic and fiscal—contained in DOD's Defense Guidance. The POM is a force and resource recommendation from the military service within specific fiscal guidance that includes rationale and risk assessment. POMs identify major issues that must be resolved during the year of submission and contain required supporting data. These issues are consolidated by the OSD and then reviewed and analyzed by teams with representation from the JCS, the services, and the OSD. Arguments are presented for and against the various alternatives on these issues, many with budgetary implications for a service. The Defense Resources Board, chaired by the Deputy Secretary of Defense, completes its review of programs with decisions on these POM issues and agreed-upon changes. The Deputy Secretary of Defense confirms these decisions by sending out a PDM to the military services, other DOD components, and the OMB. PDMs are then used as the basis for making budget submissions.

10. Norm Augustine, former Under Secretary of the Army and current CEO of Lockheed-Martin, interview by author, July 5, 1995, Washington, DC.

11. It was congressional pressure that over time wore down and finally turned around OSD and Navy opposition to the Marine Corps' V-22 tilt-rotor aircraft. The OSD and the administration now support this program. A military service that improves its ability to liaise on the Hill over time will improve its ability to liaise in the Pentagon as well.

12. General Max Thurman told me: "you need to have some ranking flag officer who can walk into any Member's office because of their personal relationship. You haven't got it organized like that. When you come to DA [Department of the Army], a general officer should be given a list, 'Your obligation is these ten senators while you are on the Army Staff. Invite them to your home for dinner. Your obligation is to get to know those [folks].' " Interview by author, March 17, 1995, Washington, DC.

13. For a number of reasons to include: maintaining "one voice" on specific issues, falling outside of the information exchange loop on an issue with the Hill, and differences between Department of Army and major command positions on an issue, there is this feeling that the Army staff would view liaising by these "beyond the beltway" Army generals as potentially creating more problems than they solve. Therefore, according to congressional interviews, Army division commanders, TRADOC, and FORSCOM (Army Forces Command) Commanding Generals, and Army CINCs are not used as frequently and strategically as in the other services.

14. As one staffer with Army experience put it, "The Army needs to show the outside world that it's not 'unhooah' [un-infantry] to understand and play the Washington game." Having this understanding must be seen as important and part of that infantryman's professional socialization process.

15. Hurricaning an officer for six month executive officer duty as a colonel outside a senior leader's office, while important, does not check the box by itself in this area of liaising experience.

16. Without that emphasis in the field, outside (congressional) visitors, sometime arriving on short notice, are seen as "unnecessary training distractors" rather than important opportunities to explain and justify the Army. The field Army must understand the

role of Congress and that the merit of the Army cause is not self-evident to external audiences.

17. It is too late to teach a Division Chief of Staff (over 90 percent get selected to brigadier general) or brigadier general selectees at a flag officer ''charm school'' the importance of Congress. In most cases, their mould is already cast and solidified at that point.

18. It should attack the prevailing notion that Congress obstructs and micromanages Army policies and programs as ignorant, unprofessional, and counterproductive to both close relations and the interests of the soldier in the foxhole and under the turret. Instead, it should highlight: Article I, Section 8 of the Constitution of the United States; how Congress, over the last 20 years, has taken back the reigns it once abdicated to the executive branch to play an active and legitimate role in shaping defense policy; that Congress is not an adversary, but an important institution that should be proactively engaged and never avoided; and the fragmented, rather than monolithic nature of the Congress that equates to opportunities rather than obstacles to Army interests.

19. When an Army LL officer who has worked a volatile issue over an extended period with a Member's Committee or personal staff, only to be told (in the Member's outer reception room on the day that the Chief or Vice Chief of Staff of the Army meets with the Member on that issue) that he or she should wait outside, stature for that LL officer is lost, especially in the eyes of the congressional staff who are participants in the meeting.

20. Headquarters, Air Mobility Command, Scott Air Force Base, IL, *Air Force Intern Program*, Air Force message 141300Z, April 95.

21. Currently, only one captain is assigned to Army LL and she has little direct exposure to the Hill. This is a shame, since officers at this point in their career probably have commanded a company level and are about the same age as many MLAs working for Members on the HNSC.

22. While being a Fellow might be a factor in considering an officer for duties in Army LL, the more important factors should be based on candidate interviews with experienced LL Division Chiefs and the officer's potential and likelihood for increasing responsibilities and service within the Army institution. It would be preferable to have the Army professional development system encouraging its most competitive officers to compete for congressional fellowships, rather than avoiding them. A utilization tour for participating in this fellowship should not be limited to Army LL but to other key assignments in and out of Washington.

23. *FM 100–1: The Army* (Ft. Leavenworth, KS: Department of the Army, 1994), v and 5–11. This cornerstone Army document ''defines the broad and enduring purposes for which the Army was established and the qualities, values, and traditions that guide the Army in protecting and serving the Nation. . . . All other Army doctrine flows from the principles and precepts contained in this manual.'' See also *FM 22–103: Strategic Leadership*, 1994, Chapter 4, in its discussion of Army core cultural values.

Epilogue

Although the findings of this study are based on candid interviews with congressional Members and staff and senior Army officers conducted in 1995, they are just as relevant to Army–Hill relations in the latter part of 1998. According to sources on the Hill and within Army circles, while there has been some improvement on the margins, the Army still is viewed by the Hill as the least effective of the four services. There is a perception that any positive changes are rooted more in personality than in the institution taking true compensating measures to deal with this significant problem. Depending on the source, some believe that overall relations have actually worsened. This is less a criticism of the current CSA and the recently confirmed Secretary of the Army than a testament to the powerful stranglehold of organizational culture, which causes leaders to resist making ''compensating'' changes, even when aspects of its culture become dysfunctional in particular settings. This book has highlighted the need for institutional compensating measures to address aspects of Army culture that continue to impede Army–Hill relations, including a socialization of Army combat arms officers to be wary of and to avoid Washington and Congress.

The findings of the 1995 interviews and study were shared with the new incoming CSA in early 1996. Without presuming to draw a direct link, the CSA has made some positive changes. For example, after he reportedly expressed concern that there was no specific course being offered to Army colonels at the U.S. Army War College, a ''Congress and Military Policy'' elective course was created and is on the curriculum (offered one semester a year for 18 students) at this prestigious institution. In addition, he reportedly has encouraged Army general officers outside Washington to visit the Hill and increase their visibility and engagement with Members and staff. He has devised a number of vehicles, including a weekly report that goes out to all Army general officers, to let these flag officers know what he has done, the issues of concern, and the message that he is trying to convey to Members on the Hill.

Additionally, the CSA has attempted to go to the Hill with greater frequency, blocking out two hours in his schedule each Thursday for every week that he is in Washington. While the Army's top leadership has often been accused of focusing its limited attention on a few Members, he has reportedly created a better rapport with various professional Committee staff on the authorization committees.

While these are all significant improvements, the changes are largely personality-driven and will not likely have a lasting impact on Army–Hill relations when the current CSA steps down in 1999. While setting a more positive personal example, he has not established institutionalized incentives to induce more Army flag officers to follow his example of greater engagement on the Hill. Further, despite his encouragement, most Army generals have not responded to his call to establish relationships and increase their understanding of the Hill. Army generals, for the most part, appear on the Hill only when they have a problem or perceived crisis on an issue. Changing this pattern will require instituting incentives that reward those senior field-grade officers and generals who show the willingness and ability to reach out to these external audiences.

Moreover, the CSA's increased personal engagement on the Hill is currently being measured by Army LL and Department of Army staff with an internal focus—against his predecessors rather than with his counterparts in the other services, a more valuable comparison—for example, the CNO or the Commandant of the Marine Corps. These are the senior military leadership against which congressional actors judge the effectiveness of a CSA in engaging Members and staff. Such a comparison would highlight the need for instituting changes, many of which are recommended in Chapter 6.

Although the CSA may be engaging more with Committee staff, he has focused little effort on deepening his ties to MLAs, as other services' senior flag officers do. To his credit, he made an initial attempt but failed to follow through and institutionalize the practice. In response to a request from Army LL in September 1997, the CSA not only met with SASC staffers for breakfast but also directed five or six senior generals on his Army staff to be there with him. This meeting, well-timed to occur during the HNSC-SASC Conference, was reportedly extremely well received by the Hill attendees because of the free-flowing discussion of issues and topics between the Army leadership and these key staffers. It was important not only in communicating information on issues being legislated that year, but also in demonstrating that the Army was, at least for that day, seriously engaging these individuals in a professional manner similar to their treatment by the other services. Despite the success, meetings of this scope with these or other staff, including MLAs, from different committees have not taken place.

A serious problem that indicates to both Army and Hill audiences that little institutional change in improving Army–Hill relations has occurred over the last few years is that the CSA's concern for making these improvements is reportedly not shared by his most senior subordinates on the Army staff. Sources with firsthand knowledge of these individuals report that they remain reluctant to engage with the Hill even on the most critical of issues, and have not made serious efforts at relationship building. These generals, with undeniably remarkable professional accomplishments in more traditional "muddy boots" Army missions, do not view strengthening Army–Hill relations as critical, or are clearly uncomfortable doing so. Adding to the damage is that these comments and actions are openly communicated before subordinate combat arms officers who look up to these generals and strive to follow their lead. This 1999 situation in the Army's E-ring of the Pentagon falls squarely within the 1995 patterns, described by the congressional audience, in this book.

With only superficial support from the top Army leadership, the Army continues to rely too heavily on its LL to get its message across to Members and staff. As noted in the study, no matter how high the quality of LL operations, congressional interlocutors do not see them as effective substitutes for top military leaders. In addition, there continue to be strong concerns that the Army is not providing its LL operations with resources that are even roughly equivalent to those of other service LLs, despite the higher expectations and burden placed on Army LL. For example, both Army and congressional sources cite the continued problem of the Army not assigning its strongest officers to LL and not taking advantage of those who do get LL experience by arranging career-enhancing follow-on assignments. This is reportedly compounded by sentiments within Army LL that seem to discount LL experience and resist staffing key LL division chief positions (colonel-level positions) with officers who have served successfully in LL. The Army LL officers have difficulty matching the efforts of their LL counterparts in the other services who are experienced, motivated, and supported by the active involvement of their senior officers.

In addition, while other departmental services benefit from a second senior military flag officer in their LL operations, the former Secretary of the Army chose to place a civilian with no Army experience in the key position of Deputy Chief of Legislative Liaison. A former MLA with experience on the Hill but little grounding in Army affairs, many questioned her effectiveness, despite good intentions, in representing Army issues, communicating effectively within the Army staff, or building a cohesive, motivated Army LL team. As this individual accompanied Secretary Togo West when he became Secretary of the Department of Veterans Affairs, the position was vacant as of late 1998. The CSA should institute an incentive for stronger Army–Hill relations by re-instating the brigadier general authorized slot for the Deputy Chief LL position. Again, the Army is the only military departmental service to have just one flag officer devoted to congressional liaison.

However, the main theme of this book is not that Army LL, as an organization, is broken, but that its current condition is a symptom of the larger attitudes, relative inexperience, and unwillingness to address existing problems at the senior flag officer level of the Army in general. Most of the recommendations listed in Chapter 6 have yet to be taken seriously and incorporated into the professional development and officer assignment norms of the Army. Just as it took several dynamic Secretaries of the Navy since World War II to make Navy and Marine Corps officers and flag officers see their important role in communicating the institutions' interests to Congress and other external audiences, so it will take the dynamic leadership of several Army Secretaries and CSAs, with the continued and hopefully more directed support of concerned Members of Congress, to transform Army general officers into more positive and externally focused Army advocates on the Hill. It will take years to socialize a future generation of Army officers to view and engage Congress in a more positive vein. Through its past and current institutional incentives, attitudes have been set and career experiences tailored that will handicap the behavior and effectiveness of the next generation of Army combat arms officers with Congress; it is from this next generation that the top leadership positions on the Army staff will be filled. This situation explains why change will be so difficult to achieve and why Army LL will continue to be undersupported in its efforts to represent Army interests on the Hill.

A respected Member of Congress on the HNSC said it was a waste of time to believe this study would have any beneficial effect in improving Army relations with the Hill. He said that no one would believe it (the Army patterns), and that those who believed it would not be in a position of power to do anything about it. Therefore, the challenge of this book is directed toward "closet" mavericks still within the Army ranks who recognize the existing problems, and who under the visionary leadership of dynamic Secretaries of the Army, will support the efforts of constitutionally empowered Members of Congress to initiate short- and long-term change to the status quo Hill approach. Several Army brigadier generals do exist who are aware of the problems with the Hill and who are trying to change things from within; they are quietly setting an example by actively seeking opportunities to build respected relationships with Congress.

Change to improve status quo Army–Hill relations will occur only if Army leaders over the next decade are encouraged from within and outside the institution to focus on enacting the required institutional compensations for Army culture in the Washington setting. In other words, it will be necessary in the short term for influential external audiences in both the legislative and executive branches to urge the top Army leadership to institute professional development and other changes now that will make the future Army leadership look less like them—something that runs contrary to human nature and is resisted naturally by promotion boards and aspects of the organization's overall current culture.

However, the stakes are too high to allow the status quo to continue. In the decades ahead, the Army and the national security of our country will be greatly tested and challenged on a variety of fronts, both by future adversaries and by contentious issues that will require bold, experienced leadership that is comfortable navigating in both field and Washington terrain, as resources continue to shrink, affecting manpower, training, weapon systems, and readiness. It is imperative, both as citizens and policymakers, that we ensure that the decision makers charged with funding and equipping the Army, approving its design and structure, setting its manning levels, and authorizing funds for its combat weapon systems, have the same degree of understanding of the capabilities and concerns of America's Army as they do of the Army's sister services. This book highlights in stark terms that this equivalent understanding of Army issues by Members and staff of the two defense authorization committees does not exist and that correcting this dangerous reality is an Army professional responsibility to rectify.

Because Members of Congress must focus on more than just defense and specifically Army issues, the burden is on the Army leadership and the institution to be and to produce, respectively, equally as effective liaisers as its counterpart services, to ensure comparable understanding of Army issues and capabilities in the next millennium. Achieving this goal would go a long way to restoring the true spirit of what Article I, Section 8, of the Constitution requires of Congress. Therefore, the Constitution, which all officers give an oath to support and defend, requires by inference effective military service liaisers. The Army institution must ensure that the future Army leadership is equivalently prepared with the professional competencies they will need to represent Army interests clearly so that they are understood by this all-important, constitutionally empowered external audience.

Appendix A

Research Interviews (as of 1995)

ARMY GENERAL OFFICERS AND SENIOR ARMY (MILITARY) LEADERSHIP

Honorable John Hamre, former PSM, SASC, DOD Comptroller[1]

Honorable Jack Marsh, former Secretary of the Army

Honorable Norman Augustine, former Under Secretary of the Army

Honorable David Chu, former Assistant Secretary of Defense (Programs, Analysis & Evaluation)

General Bernard W. Rogers, former CSA, 1976–79

General Edward C. Meyer, former CSA, 1979–83

General John A. Wickham, Jr., former CSA, 1983–87

General Carl E. Vuono, former CSA, 1987–91

General Gordon Sullivan, former CSA, 1991–95

General Max Thurman, former VCSA and regional CINC

General Robert Riscassi, former VCSA and regional CINC

General William Tuttle, former Commanding General, Army Material Command

General Jack Merritt, former Director, Joint Staff; Director, Association of the U.S. Army

General Don Keith, former Commanding General, Army Material Command

General Jimmy Ross, former Commanding General, Army Material Command

General Leon E. Saloman, Commanding General, Army Material Command

Lieutenant General Don Pihl, former Deputy to Asst. Sec. of Army (Research & Development & Acquisition)

Lieutenant General Chuck Dominy, former CLL; Director, Army Staff

Lieutenant General Walt Ulmer, former Commanding General (CG) of III Corps, Ft. Hood, Texas

Lieutenant General Ted Stroup, Army Deputy Chief of Staff of Personnel

Lieutenant General Jay Garner, Commanding General, Army Space and Strategic Defense Command[2]

Lieutenant General Dan Christman, Assistant to Chairman, JCS[3]

Lieutenant General Hank Hatch, former Commander, Army Corps of Engineers

Lieutenant General William Odom, former Director, National Security Agency

Lieutenant General Lawrence F. Skibbie, former Deputy Commanding General for Research & Development & Acquisition, Army Material Command

Major General Jerry Harrison, Army CLL

Major General Maury Boyd, Deputy Commander, TRADOC[4]

Major General John C. Thompson, Commanding General, Total Army Personnel Command

Major General Bill Eicher, former Assistant Deputy Chief of Staff for Logistics

Brigadier General William A. West, former Assistant Deputy in Army Budget Office

Colonel Bill Foster, Chief, Army War Plans Division, Army Staff

Colonel Ken Allard, former Special Assistant to CSA, General Vouno

Colonel Jack LeCuyer, Chief Army Initiatives Group, Office Deputy Chief of Staff Operations & Plans

Colonel Jon Dodson, Deputy Director for Reserve Affairs, Office of CSA

Colonel Chuck Feldmayer, Chief, Army Financial Management Budget Liaison Division

Colonel Tom Leney, former Chief, Strategy & Plans Div., Office Deputy Chief of Staff Operations & Plans

Colonel Tom Davis, Division Chief, Programs, Analysis & Evaluation

Colonel Roger A. Brown, Analyst, RAND Corporation

LEGISLATIVE LIAISON OFFICERS/LOBBYISTS

Gordon Merritt, Army LL/Hughes, Inc.

James P. Crumley, Air Force LL/Hughes, Inc.

Jim Rooney, Army LL/Rooney Group International

Fred Moosally, Navy LL/Rockwell International

Denny Sharon, Air Force LL/McDonnel Douglas

Billy Cooper, Air Force LL/Kodak

Dave Matthews, Army LL/E-Systems

Bob Lange, U.S. Marine Corps LL/E-Systems

Win Shaw, Army LL/Gulf Stream Aerospace

Cork Colburn, Army LL/General Dynamics

John Schroeder, Air Force LL/Sikorsky Aircraft

Roy Alcalá, Army Staff in General Vuono's Office/Alcalá Associates

Mike O'Brien, Army LL/Lockheed Martin

Mike Landrum, Army and OSD LL/Molten Metal Technology

Jess Franco, Army LL/Chief, Programs Division

Jay McNulty, Army LL/Chief, Army HLD

Colonel Dan Fleming, Army LL/Chief, Army HLD

Lieutenant Colonel Kim Doughtery, Air Force HLD

Commander Sean P. Sullivan, Navy HLD

Colonel John Sattler, Chief, Marine Corps HLD

Colonel John F. Kelly, Chief, Marine Corps HLD

Sam Brick, Army Investigation & Legislative Division/Office of the Secretary of Defense, Director, Legal Reference Service

Karl F. Schneider, Deputy Chief, Army Investigation and Legislative Division, Army LL

Lieutenant Colonel Steve Curny, Army Programs Division, Army LL

[Not listed: several interviews with active military and civilian personnel currently serving in Army LL]

CONGRESSIONAL INTERVIEWS

Members of Congress, HNSC (former HASC): Rep. H. Martin Lancaster (D-NC); Rep. Ike Skelton (D-MO); Rep. John Spratt (D-SC); Rep. John M. McHugh (R-NY); Rep. Herb Bateman (R-VA); Rep. Glen Browder (D-AL); Rep. Paul McHale (D-PA); Rep. Joel Hefley (R-CO); Rep. Chet Edwards (D-TX); Rep. Sonny Montgomery (D-MS); Rep. Jim Talent (R-MO); Rep. Walter Jones (R-NC); Rep. Floyd Spence (R-SC); Rep. Steve Buyer (R-IN); Rep. Owen Pickett (D-VA); Rep. Tillie Fowler (R-FL); Rep. Lane Evans (D-IL); Rep. Jack Reed (D-RI).

Member of Congress, SASC: Sen. Lauch Faircloth (R-NC).

PSMs, HNSC and SASC: Steve Ansley, John Chapla, Bill Andahazy, Robert Rangel, Jean Reed, Doug Necessary, Bob Brauer, Dr. Arch Barrett, Karen Heath, Kim Wincup, Brigadier General Dick Reynard (Ret.),[5] Arnold Punaro,[6] Romie Les Brownlee,[7] George Lauffer, Don Deline, Rick DeBobes, Charlie Abell, Creighton Greene, Patrick P.T. Henry,[8] Joe Pallone, Steve Saulnier, Ken Johnson, and Judy Ansley.

MILITARY LEGISLATIVE ASSISTANTS (MLAs) FOR MEMBERS ON HOUSE NATIONAL SECURITY COMMITTEE (HNSC)

Perry Floyd—Rep. Norman Sisisky (D-VA); Skip Fischer—Rep. Herb Bateman—(R-VA); Nancy Lifset—Rep. Curt Weldon (R-PA); Ned Michalek—Rep.

Chet Edwards (D-TX); Mike Mclaughlin—Rep. Jim Talent (R-MO); Vickie Plunkett—Rep. Glen Browder (D-AL); Jeff Crank—Rep. Joel Hefley (R-CO); Rob Warner—Rep. John Kasich (R-OH); Christian Zur—Rep. Peter Torkildsen (R-MA); Bill Fallon—Rep. Robert Dornan (R-CA); Jim Lariviere—Rep. Steve Buyer (R-IN); Wade Heck—Rep. Terry Everett (R-AL); Cary Brick—Rep. John McHugh (R-NY); Lisa Morena—Rep. Pat Schroeder (D-CO); Hugh Brady— Rep. John Spratt (D-SC); Tom O'Donnel—Rep. Lane Evans (D-IL); Bill Klein—Rep. Tillie Fowler (R-FL); Vickie Middleton—Rep. Duncan Hunter (R-CA); Al Oetkin—Rep. Owen Pickett (D-VA); Bill Natter—Rep. Ike Skelton (D-MO); John Webb—Rep. Walter Jones (R-NC); Lindsey Neas—Rep. Jim Talent (R-MO).

MILITARY LEGISLATIVE ASSISTANTS (MLAs) FOR MEMBERS ON SENATE ARMED SERVICES COMMITTEE (SASC)

Sam Adcock—Sen. Trent Lott (R-MS); Richard Fieldhouse—Sen. Carl Levin (D-MI); Grayson Winterling—Sen. John Warner (R-VA); Tom Lankford—Sen. Bob Smith (R-NH); Joanne Quilette—Sen. Jeff Bingaman (D-NM); John Lilley—Sen. Joseph Lieberman (D-CT); Steve Wolfe—Sen. Edward Kennedy (D-MA); Rick Schwab—Sen. Daniel Ray Coats (R-IN); Matt Hay—Sen. James Inhofe (R-OK); Dale Gerry—Sen. William Sebastian Cohen (R-ME); Ann Sauer—Sen. John McCain (R-AZ); Dave Davis—Sen. Kay Bailey Hutchison (R-TX); Lisa Tuite—Sen. Robert Byrd (D-WV); Andy Johnson—Sen. J. James Exon (D-NE); Geddings Roche—Sen. Duncan McLauchlin Faircloth (R-NC).

NOTES

The individuals listed in this appendix were formally interviewed by the author for this study. In addition, this study cites comments and views of congressional and senior military individuals who are not on this list, based on their request or on the fact that their comments were made in the presence of the author in the conduct of his earlier LL duties. The depicted status of an interviewee's position is based on his/her status at the time the interviews were conducted.

1. As of publication submission (1999), Dr. Hamre is the Deputy Secretary of Defense.

2. As of publication submission (1999), Lieutenant General Garner is now the Assistant VCSA.

3. As of publication submission (1999), LTG Christman is the Superintendent, U.S. Military Academy, West Point, NY.

4. MG Boyd became the Army CLL in November 1995, re-assigned in 1997, and is now serving as the Deputy Commanding General, III Corps, Ft. Hood, TX.

5. In 1995, Dick Reynard was the Staff Director of the SASC.

6. In 1995, Arnold Punaro was the Minority Staff Director of the SASC.

7. By submission date for publication, Les Brownlee was the Staff Director of the SASC.

8. By submission date for publication, Mr. P.T. Henry is the Assistant Secretary of the Army, Manpower & Reserve Affairs.

Appendix B

Washington Experience Leadership Sample Comparisons for U.S. Military Services in 1995: Data Used in Compilation of Figures Used for Tables 4-1–4-4

Officer/Position	Duty Assignments	No. of Months
ARMY		
Chief of Staff of the Army	Deputy Chief of Staff for Operations & Plans (CSA) (DCSOPS)	12
General Gordon Sullivan	Vice Chief of Staff of the Army	_12_
	Total	24
Vice Chief of Staff	Armor Force Integration Staff Officer, DCSOPS	
of the Army (VCSA)		19
	Assistant Director Army Staff, CSA Office	13
General John H. Tilelli	Chief, Ground Combat Systems Division, DCSRDA	6
	Assistant DCSOPS	7
	DCSOPS	_17_
	Total	62
Deputy Chief of Staff for		
Operations and Plans (DCSOPS)		
Lieutenant General (LTG)		
Paul Blackwell	DDO, NMCC, Office of JCS	_17_
	Total	17
Chief of Legislative Liaison	Staff Officer, Weapons Systems Directorate, DCSRDA	10
(CLL)	Military Assistant to Under Secretary of the Army	12
Major General (MG)	Chief, High Technology and Testing Division,	
Jerry C. Harrison	Requirements Directorate, DCSOPS	17
	Deputy Director, Combat Support Systems, DCSRDA	9
	Deputy Director, Weapon Systems, DCSRDA	10
	Chief of Staff, AMC	_30_
	Total	88
Total Number of Months, Army:		**191**

Officer/Position	Duty Assignments	No. of Months
AIR FORCE		
Chief of Staff of the Air Force (CSAF)	Chief, Tactical Forces Div., Directorate of Programs USAF HQ	27
General Ronald R. Fogleman	Dep. Director, Programs and Evaluation, Office of the Deputy Chief of Staff, Programs and Resources; and Chairman, Programs Review Council, USAF, HQ	23
	Director, Programs and Evaluation; and Chairman, Air Staff Board, USAF HQ	30
	Total	80
Vice Chief of Staff of the Air Force (VCSAF)	Executive, and then Dep. Director of Plans and Programs Office of Space Systems, Office of Sec. AF	49
General Thomas Moorman, Jr.	Deputy Military Assistant to Sec. AF	15
	Director of Space Systems, Office of Sec. AF	31
	Director of Space and SDI programs, Office of Asst. Sec. AF for Aquisitions	29
	Total	124
Deputy Chief of Staff for Plans and Operations (DCSOPs)	Tactical Fighter Requirements Officer, DCSRDA USAF HQ	38
Lieutenant General (LTG) Joseph W. Ralston	Special Asst. for Low Observable Technology, DCSRDA USAF HQ	21
	Director of Tactical Programs, Office, Asst. Sec. AF for Acquisitions	19
	Director of Operational Requirements, Office of DCSOPS, USAF HQ	7
	Total	85
Director of Legislative Liaison (DLL)	Air Staff Training Officer, Pentagon	11
	Deputy Director, Director of Administration, Pentagon	27
Major General (MG) Normand G. Lezy	Director, AF MWR	36
	Director of Service, USAF HQ	6
	Total	80
Total Number of Months, Air Force:		**369**
NAVY		
Chief of Naval Operations (CNO)	Office, Asst. Sec. NAVY, EA and Principal Assistant Manpower, Reserve Affairs and Logistics	42
Admiral Jeremy M. Boorda	Acting Asst. Sec. NAVY Manpower, Reserve Affairs and Logistics	7
	EA, Office of Deputy CNO, Manpower, Personnel and Training	14
	EA to CNO	19
	DCNO (MP & T)	41
	Total	123

Officer/Position	Duty Assignments	No. of Months
Vice Chief of Naval Operations (VCNO) Vice Admiral Joseph W. Prueher	Personal Aide to Chief of Naval Material Surface Guided Weapons Program Coordinator, Office of CNO EA and Naval Aide to Sec. Navy	17 13 14
	Total	44
Deputy Chief of Naval Operations Vice Admiral J. Paul Reason	Naval Aide to the President	31
	Total	31
Chief of Legislative Affairs (CLA) Rear Admiral Robert J. Natter	Asst. Section Head, Command and Control Section Force Level Plans Branch, Office of CNO EA to Director, Naval Warfare, Office of CNO Bureau of Naval Personnel Staff Member to HASC Panel on Military Education EA to Vice Chairman, JCS Bureau of Naval Personnel (ACNP for Distribution)	8 26 3 15 14 18
	Total	84
Total Number of Months, Navy:		**282**
MARINE CORPS		
Commandant of the Marine Corps General Carl E. Mundy, Jr.	Aide de Camp to A/CMDT Plans Officer, USMC HQ Dir. of Personnel Procurement, USMC HQ Dir. of Operations, and DCSOPS, and Marine Corps Operation Deputy to JCS	32 32 20 44
	Total	128
Assistant Commandant of the Marine Corps General Richard D. Hearney	Head, Aviation Systems Requirements Branch	24
	Total	24
Assistant Deputy Chief of Staff for Plans, Policy and Operations Major General (MG) Thomas L. Wilkerson	National Military Strategy Staff Officer, Plans Division, USMC HQ Marine Member, Chairman's Staff Group, CJCS	32 26
	Total	58
Legislative Assistant to the Commandant (LA) Brigadier General (BG) Michael D. Ryan	Office of Assistant Commandant (aide) SA Commandant Head of Aviation Weapons Systems Requirements Branch, USMC HQ	15 13 23
	Total	51
Total Number of Months, Marine Corps:		**261**

Appendix C

Army Washington Experience Leadership Sample Run, 1980–81 Era: Data Used in Compilation of Figures Used for Table 4-5

Officer/Position	Duty Assignments	No. of Months
Chief of Staff of Army (CSA) General Edward Charles "Shy" Meyer (June 1979–June 1983)	Office CSA (Coordination & Analysis Group)	30
	Strategic Division, Army Staff; Member, Objectives, Plans & Programs Division, J-S, JCS	25
	Federal Executive Fellow, Brookings Institute	5
	Assistant, Deputy Chief of Staff for Operations	14
	DCSOPS	_31_
	Total	105
Vice Chief of Staff of Army General John William Vessey, Jr. (July 1979–June 1982)	Personnel Management Officer, XO, Artillery Officers Div., Office of Deputy Chief of Staff for Personnel	39
	Dir. of Operations, Deputy Chief of Staff for Operations and Plans (now ADCSOPS)	18
	DCSOPS	_13_
	Total	70
Deputy Chief of Staff for Plans and Operations General Glen Kay Otis (August 1979–July 1981)	Plans Officer, Office of Personnel Operations	24
	Assistant Chief, Manpower Division, Office of the Assistant Secretary of the Army	12
	Special Assistant for Program Review, Office of the Assistant Secretary of the Army	6
	Chief, Manpower Division, Office of the Secretary of the Army	_8_
	Total	50

Officer/Position	Duty Assignments	No. of Months
Chief of Legislative Liaison (CLL) Lieutenant General Dale Franklin (May 1981–July 1984)	Personnel Management Officer, Artillery Branch Office of Personnel Operations	28
	Chief, Programming Branch Industrial Training Directorate, Office Dep. Chief of Staff for Personnel	23
	Force (Manpower) Analyst, Planning and Programming Analysis Directorate, Office, Asst. Vice Chief of Staff	11
	Deputy Chief, later Chief, Plans and Operations Division, Office Chief of Legislative Liaison	29
	Deputy Chief of Legislative Liaison, Office, Secretary of the Army	33
	Total	124

Total Number of Months, Army, 1980–81 Era: **349**

For Further Reading

Aberbach, J. *Keeping a Watchful Eye: The Politics of Congressional Oversight*. Washington, DC: Brookings Institution, 1991.

Allard, C. Kenneth. *Command, Control, and the Common Defense*. New Haven, CT: Yale University Press, 1990.

Berry, Jeffrey M. *Lobbying for the People: The Political Behavior of Public Interest Groups*. Princeton, NJ: Princeton University Press, 1977.

———. "Subgovernments, Issue Networks and Political Conflict." In *Remaking American Politics*, ed. Richard A. Harris and Sidney M. Milkis. Boulder, CO: Westview Press, 1989.

Builder, Carl H. *The Masks of War: American Military Strategy and Analysis*. Baltimore, MD: Johns Hopkins University Press, 1989.

Cohen, Eliot A. *Making Do with Less, or Coping with Upton's Ghost*. Carlisle Barracks, PA: U.S. Army War College, Strategic Studies Institute, Sixth Annual Strategy Conference, April 1995.

Constitution of the United States of America.

Department of Defense, Department of the Air Force. *Relations with Congress*. Air Force Policy Directive 90–4, July 22, 1993.

Department of Defense, Department of the Army. *Legislative Liaison*. AR 1–20, August 13, 1990.

Department of Defense, Department of the Navy. *Procedures for the Handling of Naval Legislative Affairs and Congressional Relations*. SECNAVINST 5730.5G, August 24, 1981.

Department of Defense, Office of the Secretary of Defense. *Assistant Secretary of Defense Legislative Affairs*. DOD Directive no. 5142.1, July 2, 1982.

Department of Defense, Office of the Secretary of Defense. *Provision of Information to Congress*. DOD Directive no. 5400.4, January 30, 1978.

Executive Office of the President, Office of Management and Budget. *Revision of Circular No. A-19, Revised, Dated July 31, 1972: Legislative Coordination and Clearance*. OMB Cir A-19, revised, September 20, 1979.

Fialka, John J. *Hotel Warriors: Covering the Gulf War.* Washington, DC: The Woodrow Wilson Center Press, 1991.

Fiorina, Morris P. *Congress: Keystone of the Washington Establishment.* 2nd ed. New Haven, CT: Yale University Press, 1989.

Hadley, Arthur T. *The Straw Giant: Triumph and Failure, America's Armed Forces.* New York: Random House, 1986.

Headquarters, Department of the Army. *FM 22–103: Strategic Leadership.* Ft. Leavenworth, KS: Department of the Army, 1994.

———. *FM 100–1: The Army.* Ft. Leavenworth, KS: Department of the Army, 1994.

Holtzman, Abraham. *Legislative Liaison: Executive Leadership in Congress.* Chicago: Rand McNally, 1970.

Hornestay, David. "Cultivating Congress." *Government Executive* (November 1992), 42–47.

Huntington, Samuel P. *The Soldier and the State.* Cambridge, MA: Harvard University Press, 1957.

Isenberg, Michael T. *Shield of the Republic.* New York: St. Martin's Press, 1993.

Mayhew, D. *Congress, the Electoral Connection.* New Haven, CT: Yale University Press, 1974.

Rossiter, Clinton, ed. *The Federalist Papers: Hamilton, Madison, Jay.* New York: Mentor, 1961.

Schein, Edgar H. *Organizational Culture and Leadership.* 2nd ed. San Francisco, CA: Jossey-Bass, 1992, 12.

Shotwell, Colonel John M. "The Fourth Estate as a Force Multiplier." *Marine Corps Gazette*, no. 4, 28.

Tierney, John T. "Organized Interests and the Nation's Capitol." In *The Politics of Interests*, ed. Mark P. Petracca. Boulder, CO: Westview Press, 1992.

Upton, Emory. *The Military Policy of the United States.* 1904. Reprint. New York: Greenwood Press, 1968.

West, Togo D., Secretary of the Army, and General Gordon R. Sullivan, Chief of Staff of the Army. Memorandum to Principal Officials of Headquarters, Department of the Army. *Speaking with One Voice—Defense of the President's Budget.* February 7, 1995.

Wilson, James Q. *Bureaucracy: What Government Agencies Do and Why They Do It.* New York: Basic Books, 1989.

Wolpe, Bruce C. *Lobbying Congress: How the System Works.* Washington, DC: Congressional Quarterly Press, 1990.

Index

About the Author

STEPHEN K. SCROGGS is Director of Investment, State of North Carolina Asia Office, North Carolina Department of Commerce. Dr. Scroggs retired from the Army in 1996 after 20 years of service as a Lieutenant Colonel. During his military career, Colonel Scroggs served in both line and staff positions, including service as a congressional staff officer for the Secretary of the Army Legislative Liaison from 1992 to 1996.

ISBN 0-275-96175-3

90000>

EAN

9 780275 961756

HARDCOVER BAR CODE